LEUVEN MAN[U]
INTERNATIONAL L[AW]
TO PEACE OP[ERATIONS]

C000134923

The Leuven Manual is the authoritative, comprehensive overview of the rules that are to be followed in Peace Operations conducted by the United Nations, the European Union, NATO, the African Union and other organisations, with detailed commentary on best practice in relation to those rules. Topics covered include human rights, humanitarian law, gender aspects, the use of force and detention by peacekeepers, the protection of civilians, and the relevance of the laws of the Host State. The international group of expert authors includes leading academics, together with military officers and policy officials with practical experience in contemporary peace operations, supported by input from experts in an individual capacity working for the UN, the African Union, NATO and the International Committee of the Red Cross. This volume is intended to be of assistance to States and international organisations involved in the planning and conduct of Peace Operations, as well as to practitioners and academics.

TERRY GILL is Professor of Military Law at the University of Amsterdam and the Netherlands Defence Academy, and Director of the Research Program on the Law of Armed Conflict and Peace Operations at the Amsterdam Center for International Law and of the Netherlands Research Forum on the Law of Armed Conflict and Peace Operations (LACPO).

DIETER FLECK has served as legal advisor in various Bundeswehr commands, the German Chancellor's Office, and the German Federal Ministry of Defence. He has published on issues of international law and security.

WILLIAM H. BOOTHBY, Air Commodore, retired from Royal Air Force Legal Services in 2011. He has published on conflict law and armed conflict.

ALFONS VANHEUSDEN is a Senior Legal Advisor (Conseiller général) at the Belgian Ministry of Defence, and the Assistant Secretary-General of the International Society for Military Law and the Law of War.

LEUVEN MANUAL ON THE INTERNATIONAL LAW APPLICABLE TO PEACE OPERATIONS

*Prepared by an international Group of Experts
at the invitation of the International Society
for Military Law and the Law of War*

GENERAL EDITORS

TERRY D. GILL,
DIETER FLECK, WILLIAM H. BOOTHBY
AND ALFONS VANHEUSDEN

ASSISTANT EDITORS

MARCO BENATAR
AND REMY JORRITSMA

CAMBRIDGE
UNIVERSITY PRESS

CAMBRIDGE
UNIVERSITY PRESS

University Printing House, Cambridge CB2 8BS, United Kingdom

One Liberty Plaza, 20th Floor, New York, NY 10006, USA

477 Williamstown Road, Port Melbourne, VIC 3207, Australia

314–321, 3rd Floor, Plot 3, Splendor Forum, Jasola District Centre, New Delhi – 110025, India

79 Anson Road, #06-04/06, Singapore 079906

Cambridge University Press is part of the University of Cambridge.

It furthers the University's mission by disseminating knowledge in the pursuit of education, learning, and research at the highest international levels of excellence.

www.cambridge.org
Information on this title: www.cambridge.org/9781108424981
DOI: 10.1017/9781108610100

© International Society for Military Law and the Law of War 2017

This publication is in copyright. Subject to statutory exception and to the provisions of relevant collective licensing agreements, no reproduction of any part may take place without the written permission of Cambridge University Press.

First published 2017

Printed in the United Kingdom by TJ International Ltd. Padstow Cornwall

A catalogue record for this publication is available from the British Library.

ISBN 978-1-108-42498-1 Hardback

ISBN 978-1-108-44113-1 Paperback

Cambridge University Press has no responsibility for the persistence or accuracy of URLs for external or third-party internet websites referred to in this publication and does not guarantee that any content on such websites is, or will remain, accurate or appropriate.

Contents

APPENDICES

Contributors

COMPOSITION OF THE GROUP OF EXPERTS & OBSERVERS

- Col (ret.) Roy H. Abbot (Australia)
- Jens Andersen (Observer, UN, DPKO)
- Suzanne Appelman (Netherlands Army Legal Service)
- Catherine Baele (Belgian Ministry of Defence)
- Marco Benatar (Max Planck Institute Luxembourg for Procedural Law)
- Tom de Boer (Netherlands)
- Antoaneta Boeva (Observer, NATO)
- Dr Bill Boothby (United Kingdom)
- Cdr (Navy) Gianmatteo Breda (Italian Navy)
- Dr Anne-Marie de Brouwer (Tilburg University)
- Col Cheick Dembele (Observer, AU)
- Dr Petra Ditrichová-Ochmannová (Czech Republic Ministry of Defence, formerly Observer, NATO)
- Dr Tristan Ferraro (Observer, ICRC)
- Dr Dieter Fleck (Germany)
- Professor Terry Gill (University of Amsterdam and Netherlands Defence Academy)
- Professor Wolff Heintschel von Heinegg (Europa Universität Viadrina Frankfurt (Oder))
- Remy Jorritsma (Max Planck Institute Luxembourg for Procedural Law)
- Col Ben Klappe (Netherlands Army Legal Service)
- Bright Mando (Observer, AU)
- Luke Mhlaba (Observer, UN, OLA)
- Associate Professor Kjetil Mujezinovic Larsen (Norwegian Centre for Human Rights)
- Dr Frederik Naert (Council of the EU, Legal Service & Katholieke Universiteit Leuven)

- Col Abdulaye Ngouyamsa (Cameroon, formerly ECCAS)
- Col Floribert Njako (Cameroon)
- Dr Aurel Sari (University of Exeter)
- Professor Harmen van der Wilt (University of Amsterdam)
- Alfons Vanheusden (Assistant Secretary-General of the International Society for Military Law and the Law of War)
- Professor Marjoleine Zieck (University of Amsterdam)
- Dr Marten Zwanenburg (Netherlands Ministry of Foreign Affairs)

COMPOSITION OF THE ADVISORY BOARD

- Professor Fausto Pocar (President of the International Institute of Humanitarian Law, San Remo)
- Lt Gen. (ret.) Abhijit Guha (India, Member of the UN High-Level Independent Panel on Peace Operations)
- Dirk Dubois (Director of the European Security and Defence College)

Foreword

In 2011 the Managing Board and Board of Directors of the International Society for Military Law and the Law of War took the decision to ask a Group of Experts to draft a Manual on the International Law Applicable to Peace Operations. Over the years the project generated academic activities across the globe: we discussed the international law applicable to Peace Operations notably at our events in Cameroon, Canada, China, the Czech Republic, Germany, Italy and Peru.

Two of the most intensive and productive project meetings took place in the medieval Belgian city of Leuven. In its long history the city of Leuven has several times been under siege and occupation. Nevertheless, the city has proudly fostered its reputation as a safe haven and driver for knowledge, especially since 1425 with the foundation of the oldest university in the Low Countries, and despite the horrific destruction of its renowned academic library during World War I.

This history and the current status of Leuven as a peaceful and prosperous venue with a thirst for knowledge inspired the International Society for Military Law and the Law of War to name the Manual the 'Leuven Manual on the International Law Applicable to Peace Operations', to connect the city's name to a Manual which intends to facilitate the lifesaving work of policy makers, peacekeepers and those involved in the training and education of such men and women in support of sustainable peace. May the reference to Leuven give hope to the Peace Operations community that war-torn cities and conflict zones can indeed revive their former glory thanks to peaceful human efforts!

We congratulate the Project Management Team, the Senior Academic Advisors and the Group of Experts on the results of their hard work during the past years, and we thank the project's Observers for their commitment and active and invaluable participation throughout the process. On behalf of the editors, we would finally like to express our sincere thanks to Cambridge University Press, in particular to Finola O'Sullivan, for helping to make the publication of the Leuven Manual possible.

Brigadier General (ret.) Jan Peter Spijk and Ludwig Van Der Veken
*President and Secretary-General of the International Society
for Military Law and the Law of War*

Acknowledgment of Support

The International Society for Military Law and the Law of War has gratefully accepted the support offered by the following sixteen organisations or institutions:

1 German/Netherlands Corps (www.1gnc.org)
Academy of Military Sciences, China (http://english.chinamil.com.cn)
Armed Forces of Chile (www.armada.cl)
Freie Universität Berlin (www.fu-berlin.de/en)
Max Planck Institute Luxembourg for Procedural Law (www.mpi.lu)
Ministry of Defence of Belgium (www.mil.be)
Ministry of Defence of Cameroon (www.spm.gov.cm/en/public-administrations/national-security-defence/defence)
Ministry of Defence of Italy (www.difesa.it/EN)
Ministry of Higher Education of Cameroon (www.minesup.gov.cm)
The Netherlands Defence Academy (www.defensie.nl/nlda)
Norwegian Centre for Human Rights (www.jus.uio.no/smr/english)
Swedish Defence University (www.fhs.se/en)
University of Amsterdam (www.uva.nl)
University of Exeter (www.exeter.ac.uk)
Utrecht University (www.uu.nl/EN)
Vrije Universiteit Brussel (www.vub.ac.be)

Table of Cases

International

Court of Justice of the European Union

European Commission for Democracy through Law (Venice Commission)

European Commission of Human Rights

European Court of Human Rights

International Criminal Court

National

Australia

Re Bolton and Another, Ex parte Beanne, High Court of Australia,
Judgment of 9 April 1987, 162 CLR 514, p. 137

Austria

N.K. v. *Austria*, Superior Provincial Court (Oberlandesgericht)
of Vienna, Austria, Judgment of 26 February 1979, 77 ILR
(1979) 470, p. 279

Belgium

L.M. v. *Secretariat General of the ACP Group of States*, Court of Appeal
(Cour d'appel) of Brussels, Belgium, Judgment of 4 March 2003,
Journal des Tribunaux (2003), 684, p. 308
The Prosecutor v. *C.K. and B.C.*, Military Court of Appeal (Militair
Gerechtshof) of Belgium, Judgment of 17 December 1997, *Journal
des Tribunaux* (1998), 286, p. 96
Siedler v. *Western European Union*, Court of Appeal (Cour d'appel) of
Brussels, Belgium, Judgment of 17 September 2003, ILDC 53
(BE 2003), pp. 308, 309

Germany

Anonymous v. *German Federal Government (Arrest of Pirates Case)*,
Administrative Court (Verwaltungsgericht) of Cologne, Germany,
Judgment of 11 November 2011, ILDC 1808 (DE 2011), p. 283
Anonymous v. *German Federal Government (Kunduz Tankers Case)*,
Administrative Court (Verwaltungsgericht) of Cologne, Germany,
Judgment of 9 February 2012, ILDC 1858 (DE 2012), p. 279
D. v. *Decision of the EPO Disciplinary Board*, Federal Constitutional
Court (Bundesverfassungsgericht) of Germany, Judgment of
28 November 2005, 2 BvR 1751/03, p. 308
Shooting Range Extension Case, Supreme Administrative Court
(Verwaltungsgerichtshof) of Kassel, Germany, Judgment of
26 January 1984, 86 ILR (1984) 533, p. 138

Kosovo

Netherlands

United Kingdom

United States of America

Abbreviations

ACIRC	African Capacity for Immediate Response to Crises
ACO	Allied Command Operations
ACT	Allied Command Transformation
ADCON	administrative control
AMIB	African Mission in Burundi
AMISOM	African Union Mission in Somalia
AMU	Arab Maghreb Union
AOO	area of operations
APF	African Peace Facility
APSA	African Peace and Security Architecture
ARIO	Articles on the Responsibility of International Organizations
ARSIWA	Articles on Responsibility of States for Internationally Wrongful Acts
ASF	African Standby Force
AU	African Union
C2	command and control
CAAC	children and armed conflict
CCs	Component Commanders
CDT	Conduct and Discipline Teams
CDU	Conduct and Discipline Unit
CEN-SAD	Community of Sahel-Saharan States
CFSP	Common Foreign and Security Policy
CivOpCdr	Civilian Operation Commander
CJEU	Court of Justice of the EU
CMC	Cluster Munitions Convention
CMPD	Crisis Management and Planning Directorate
CMTF	Conflict Management Task Force
COMESA	Common Market for Eastern and Southern Africa
CONOPs	Concept of Operations
CONTCO	Contingent Commander

CPCC	Civilian Planning and Conduct Capability
CRC	Convention on the Rights of the Child
CSDP	Common Security and Defence Policy
DDR	disarmament, demobilisation and reintegration
DDRR	disarmament, demobilisation, reintegration and repatriation
DFS	Department of Field Support
DPA	Department of Political Affairs (UN)
DPKO	Department of Peacekeeping Operations
DSACEUR	Deputy Supreme Allied Commander Europe
EAC	East African Community
EASF	East African Standby Force
ECCAS	Economic Community of Central African States
ECommHR	European Commission of Human Rights
ECOWAS	Economic Community of West African States
ECtHR	European Court of Human Rights
EDF	European Development Fund
EEAS	European External Action Service
ESDP	European Security and Defence Policy
EU	European Union
EUMS	EU Military Staff
FC	Force Commander
HOM	Head of Mission
HOMC	Head of Military Component
HQ	headquarters
IA	Implementing Arrangement
IAC	international armed conflict
IACionHR	Inter-American Commission on Human Rights
IACtHR	Inter-American Court of Human Rights
IAP	Policy on Integrated Assessment and Planning
ICC	International Criminal Court
ICJ	International Court of Justice
ICRC	International Committee of the Red Cross
ICTR	International Criminal Tribunal for Rwanda
ICTY	International Criminal Tribunal for the former Yugoslavia
IDP	internally displaced person
IFOR	Implementation Force
IGAD	Intergovernmental Authority on Development
IHL	international humanitarian law
IHRL	international human rights law
ILC	International Law Commission
INTERFET	International Force for East Timor

ISAF	International Security Assistance Force
ISOP	Interim Standard Operating Procedures
ITLOS	International Tribunal for the Law of the Sea
JFC	Joint Force Command
KFOR	Kosovo Force
MC	Military Committee (NATO)
MFO	Multinational Force and Observers
MINUSCA	UN Multidimensional Integrated Stabilization Mission in the Central African Republic
MINUSMA	UN Multidimensional Integrated Stabilization Mission in Mali
MONUSCO	UN Stabilization Mission in the Democratic Republic of the Congo
MOU	Memorandum of Understanding
MPCC	Military Planning and Conduct Capability
MPLAN	Mission Plan
NA5CRO	Non-Article 5 Crisis Response Operation
NAC	North Atlantic Council
NARC	North African Regional Capability
NATO	North Atlantic Treaty Organization
NCMP	NATO Crisis Management Process
NIAC	non-international armed conflict
NNTCCs	non-NATO Troop Contributing Countries
OAS	Organization of American States
OAU	Organisation of African Unity
OCHA	United Nations Office for the Coordination of Humanitarian Affairs
OIOS	Office of Internal Oversight Services
OLA	Office of Legal Affairs
ONUC	UN Operation in the Congo
OpCdr	Operation Commander
OPCOM	operational command
OPCON	operational control
OPLAN	Operational Plan
OSCE	Organization for Security and Co-operation in Europe
PCA	Permanent Court of Arbitration
PCC	Police Contributing Country
PCIJ	Permanent Court of International Justice
PCRS	United Nations Peacekeeping Capability Readiness System
PFP	Partnership for Peace
POC	protection of civilians
PSC AU	Peace and Security Council of the AU

PSC EU	Political and Security Committee of the EU
PSD	Peace and Security Department (AU Commission)
PSOD	Peace Support Operations Division (PSD)
R2P	Responsibility to Protect
REC	Regional Economic Community
ROE	Rules of Engagement
SACEUR	Supreme Allied Commander Europe
SACT	Supreme Allied Commander Transformation
SADC	Southern African Development Community
SCSL	Special Court for Sierra Leone
SEA	sexual exploitation and abuse
SFOR	Stabilisation Force
SHAPE	Supreme Headquarters Allied Powers Europe
SOFA	Status of Forces Agreement
SOMA	Status of Mission Agreement
SRSG	Special Representative of the UN Secretary-General
TA	Technical Arrangement
TACOM	tactical command
TACON	tactical control
TCC	Troop Contributing Country
TOA	Transfer of Authority
UN	United Nations
UNCLOS	UN Convention on the Law of the Sea
UNCT	UN Country Team
UNDP	UN Development Programme
UNEF	UN Emergency Force
UNHCR	United Nations High Commissioner for Refugees
UNICEF	UN Children's Fund
UNIFIL	UN Interim Force in Lebanon
UNMIS	UN Mission in Sudan
UNPROFOR	UN Protection Force
UNSAS	United Nations Standby Arrangements System
UNSC	United Nations Security Council
UNSG	United Nations Secretary-General
USG DPKO	Under-Secretary-General for Peacekeeping Operations
WEU	Western European Union
WFP	World Food Programme
WHO	World Health Organization

Background, Purpose and Approach of the Manual

1. In 2011 the Managing Board and Board of Directors of the International Society for Military Law and the Law of War[1] took the decision to ask a Group of Experts to draft a Manual of the International Law Applicable to Peace Operations as proposed by Mr Arne Willy Dahl, the Society's Honorary President. The project was notably inspired by the 1994 *San Remo Manual* on armed conflicts at sea, the 2010 *HPCR Manual* on air and missile warfare and the 2013 *Tallinn Manual* on the international law applicable to cyber warfare. Just like those manuals, this Manual is also intended to serve both practitioners and academics. It is aimed at senior policy makers at both the national and intergovernmental organisation level, at senior military officers involved with the planning and conduct of such missions, at senior level staff in non-governmental organisations which carry out humanitarian and related activities in areas where Peace Operations are being conducted, and at the academic community involved in research and teaching related to Peace Operations.

2. The project built on the achievements of the *Handbook of the International Law of Military Operations*, edited by Dr Dieter Fleck and Professor Terry Gill (which deals, inter alia, with Peace Operations), in that the *Handbook* was a major source of information and its editors participated in the project as Senior Academic Advisors. While the *Handbook* aimed at providing a comprehensive overview of the different rules and legal regimes governing the deployment of armed forces abroad in a wide variety of missions, ranging from full combat to Peace Operations, this Manual limits itself to in-depth coverage of "consensual" Peace Operations, both of the traditional peacekeeping variety and of multi-dimensional Peace Operations which include aspects of peacekeeping and peacebuilding, and support for the political process of conflict resolution.

---

[1] For more information about the International Society for Military Law and the Law of War, please visit www.ismllw.org. All URLs in the Manual were last accessed on 1 July 2017.

The Manual is therefore a discrete work that comprehensively addresses the application of international law in Peace Operations and that therefore deals with questions which have not been addressed in the *Handbook*. As a specific but comprehensive work, the Manual is positioned on a level that goes beyond the *Handbook* as a work on the international law of military operations in general on the one hand, and the various national guides aimed at mid to low level officers at the tactical level on the other hand. It will be of value and interest to a varied audience drawn from policy makers, practitioners, academics and others with an interest in the topic. Its authority rests in its bringing the relevant law and associated good practices together in a structured and accessible form of rules to which all members of the Group of Experts have subscribed. This output is intended to be of assistance to States and international organisations involved in planning and conducting Peace Operations as well as the traditional mixed audience of the International Society for Military Law and the Law of War as a privileged forum where legal practice and academic research and teaching converge.

3. The Manual devotes attention to the various stages of the planning and conduct of Peace Operations conducted both by the United Nations (UN) and by regional organisations and other arrangements. It attempts to address all relevant issues, ranging from the legal basis of such operations, applicable legal regimes in the conduct of operations, in particular international human rights law (IHRL) and international humanitarian law (IHL), relations with the Host State, Sending State and other interested parties, the use of force in self-defence and in the execution of tasks laid out in the mandate, assistance in the maintenance of a stable environment and the maintenance of law and order, and promotion of human rights and the rule of law. It also includes treatment of such issues as the protection of civilians, the maintenance of discipline and prevention of abuse of the civilian population of the Host State, the immunities and the consequences thereof for mission personnel, and questions of international responsibility and criminal liability for violations of international law.

4. The Manual offers a detailed guide to areas of international law which are specifically relevant to the planning and conduct of Peace Operations with a particular focus on those which required further research and clarification in doctrine, and where useful or necessary it offers policy recommendations, notably where the law is silent or unclear. The Manual is intended to provide an authoritative restatement of the applicable law and where relevant of so-called "best practice" in

the planning and conduct of the types of Peace Operations referred to earlier. The Manual consists of "black letter rules" (145 in total) and an accompanying "commentary".[2] The black letter rules reflecting existing law are phrased so as to reflect legal obligation ('shall', 'must', 'have to' ...). Best practices as reflected in the black letter rules are phrased in conformity with applicable law but are distinguished from positive legal obligations by use of appropriate language such as 'should' rather than 'shall'. The black letter rules reflect a consensus of the participating experts and have been endorsed by the leadership of the International Society for Military Law and the Law of War. The commentary devotes attention to the application and interpretation of the black letter rules and reflects the input of the Group of Experts. Observers from the UN, from the International Committee of the Red Cross (ICRC) and from a number of regional organisations and arrangements participated in the discussions during the drafting of the black letter rules and commentary and were given the opportunity to provide specific comments and input on matters directly related to the policies and practice of their respective organisations, some of which are included as appendices to the Manual.[3]

5. The project took several years to complete. The need to ensure a high quality, authoritative guide to Peace Operations prevailed over the desire to present the publication by a specified date. It was also important that the result be a collective work reflecting the views of all project participants, rather than an edited volume of individual chapters. Therefore, the timeline allowed for a sufficient number of face-to-face meetings in order to achieve and confirm that consensus.

6. A conference on the 'International Law of Peace Operations' hosted in Beijing from 9 to 12 November 2011 and organised by the International Society for Military Law and the Law of War with the assistance of its Chinese Group marked the start of the "definition phase" of the project. The 'General Report' of the seventeenth Congress of the International Society for Military Law and the Law of War served as a source of information to prepare this conference. Also the materials from the 41st Round Table on 'International Humanitarian Law, Human Rights Law and Peace Operations' organised by the International Institute of Humanitarian Law at San Remo, as well as from the ICRC's 12th

---

[2] See Appendix I for a compilation of the black letter rules only, without accompanying commentary. Appendix VIII contains a glossary of terms used for the purpose of this Manual.
[3] See Appendices IV, V, VI and VII for the planning and policy aspects of the UN, the African Union, the European Union and the North Atlantic Treaty Organization.

Bruges Colloquium on 'International Organisations' Involvement in Peace Operations: Applicable Legal Framework and the Issue of Responsibility', have helped to identify additional areas to be covered by the black letter rules. Two topics were prepared by individual experts for presentation at the 19th Congress of the International Society for Military Law and the Law of War ('The Application of Human Rights Law in Peace Operations' and 'Operational Detentions and Independent Oversight in Peace Operations'). The 19th Congress was held in Québec City (Canada) in May 2012. At this Congress the project and two papers were presented and discussed. Such discussion generated support for and ownership of the project within the Society's international membership. During the definition phase, several meetings of the Project Management Team and Senior Academic Advisors were held, mainly in Brussels (Belgium). These included a meeting with the Group of Experts in Münster (Germany) on 8 April 2013, which concluded the definition phase.

7. From the start of the project, the ICRC sent Dr Tristan Ferraro as its Observer to the Group of Experts. He reviewed all IHL related research papers and provided the ICRC's comments. The ICRC also placed the materials from its 12th Bruges Colloquium at the Society's disposal.

8. The North Atlantic Treaty Organization (NATO) also sent an Observer to the Group of Experts (Dr Petra Ditrichová-Ochmannová from the Legal Office at Allied Command Transformation Staff Element Europe until 2014, and Mrs Antoaneta Boeva from the Office of Legal Affairs at NATO Headquarters as of 2015). NATO experts also contributed to specific chapters: Dr Ditrichová-Ochmannová supported by the Ministry of Defence of the Czech Republic, and Mrs Boeva in her personal capacity.

9. The European Union (EU) did not formally designate an Observer to the project, but EU expertise was available thanks to the participation in a personal capacity of Dr Frederik Naert (Legal Service of the Council of the EU, and affiliated senior researcher at the Katholieke Universiteit Leuven). Furthermore, the project could count on the participation of the Director of the European Security and Defence College, Mr Dirk Dubois, a member of the Manual's Advisory Board.

10. At the beginning of the "drafting phase" the focus remained on producing first drafts. A face-to-face meeting of the Group of Experts took place in Brussels from 24 to 26 February 2014. Another face-to-face meeting of the Group of Experts & Observers was held in Brussels from 26 to 28 November 2014. The involvement of the UN's Office of

Legal Affairs (OLA), Department of Peacekeeping Operations (DPKO) and Department of Field Support in the project was agreed upon in New York on 19 March 2014. Mr Luke Mhlaba (OLA) and Mr Jens Andersen (DPKO) were designated as the UN's Observers to the Group of Experts. Throughout the project the UN Observers gave invaluable comments and inputs from UN experts in their personal capacity for specific chapters. Other UN experts who gave comments included Mr Charles Briefel, Mr Henk-Jan Brinkman, Mr Dirk Druet, Dr Laurent Dutordoir, Mrs Ann Makome, Mrs Laura Perez and Mr Jonathan Robinson.

11. From 28 June to 1 July 2015 several authorities in Cameroon hosted an expert meeting in Yaoundé with special regional and thematic focus (conference approach). African perspectives, as well as the issue of protection of civilians, were on the agenda. The meeting report was prepared in the form of additional draft chapters and sub-chapters for the Manual. The involvement of the African Union (AU) in the project was secured, and Mr Bright Mando (Office of the Legal Counsel) and Col Cheick F. Mady Dembele (Peace and Security Department) were designated as the AU Observers to the project and presented various AU perspectives at the Yaoundé conference.

12. From 26 to 28 October 2015 another face-to-face meeting of the Group of Experts & Observers was held in Leuven (Belgium). This meeting allowed the experts to finalise a full set of chapters and sub-chapters in draft form, with a view to an independent review by the Advisory Board to the project. The Advisory Board meeting took place in Leuven on 19 and 20 September 2016, and a last face-to-face meeting of the Group of Experts & Observers was held on 21 September 2016 to incorporate the Advisory Board's advice and provide a final review of the content of the black letter rules.

13. After the last Leuven meeting, the "editing phase" was launched, and an Editing Committee composed of the Senior Academic Advisors and certain members of the Project Management Team prepared the texts for publication. The Leuven Manual of the International Law Applicable to Peace Operations was endorsed by the Managing Board and the Board of Directors of the International Society for Military Law and the Law of War on the occasion of their spring 2017 meetings in Stockholm.[4]

14. The project was managed by a Project Management Team, headed by the Society's Assistant Secretary-General Mr Alfons Vanheusden. As the

---

[4] See Appendices II and III for the composition of the Boards of the International Society for Military Law and the Law of War.

Managing Editor of the Manual, he oversaw and co-ordinated all project activities, set deadlines in close co-ordination with the Senior Academic Advisors, and was charged with maintaining regular contact with the members of the Group of Experts & Observers. He was assisted by two Assistant Editors (Mr Marco Benatar and Mr Remy Jorritsma, both from the Max Planck Institute Luxembourg for Procedural Law) and by two Project Management Team Advisors (Capt. Suzanne Appelman from the Dutch Military Legal Service and Dr Aurel Sari from Exeter University). All five of them also participated in the drafting of rules and commentary. The Project Management Team was supported by Mr Luc De Coninck, Member of the General Secretariat of the International Society for Military Law and the Law of War and Editorial Assistant for the Manual. The Project Management Team was also supported by interns on an occasional basis.

15. The project's Senior Academic Advisors were Dr Dieter Fleck, former Director for International Agreements & Policy of the German Ministry of Defence, and Honorary President of the International Society for Military Law and the Law of War; Professor Terry Gill, Professor of Military Law at the University of Amsterdam and the Netherlands Defence Academy; and Air Commodore (ret.) Dr Bill Boothby from the United Kingdom. They advised and where necessary assisted in the recruiting of suitable and qualified members of the Group of Experts specialised in the law and practice of Peace Operations. They also acted in the capacity of General Editors of the Manual, along with Alfons Vanheusden, who also participated in that task. The Senior Academic Advisors ensured the overall quality and cohesion of the Manual, provided input concerning the structure of the Manual and participated in the drafting of rules and commentary.

16. The Project Management Team and Senior Academic Advisors requested selected experts to form the project's Group of Experts. These experts could ask colleagues to assist them in preparing their contributions, but were the single point of contact for the Project Management Team and the Senior Academic Advisors. These contributors were responsible for submitting pieces of publishable quality within the agreed time limits and framework set by the project plan.

17. The Group of Experts was supplemented by the Advisory Board. This Advisory Board provided viewpoints and offered its advice on best practices. They did not have a vote in relation to the content of black letter rules or commentary, although their views were given all due consideration.

18. Support was provided by the respective governments and institutions by covering the costs of their participating experts or hosting project-related meetings. Their support is acknowledged in this Manual.[5] This support was essential, and the Society's annual budgets covered the necessary additional funding for the project. In 2017 the project entered into its "dissemination phase". A continuing focus will be laid on further dissemination and translation of the Manual, including for use in peace-keeping training centres worldwide. The Manual is published in English but in order to reach the widest possible readership translation of the Manual into other UN languages is envisaged.

19. All revenues derived from the publication of the Manual will be used in furtherance of the objectives of the International Society for Military Law and the Law of War, with priority to project-related activities.

20. The Manual is made up of twenty-one chapters. None of these chapters is the result of the exclusive work of one contributor as the Group of Experts jointly worked on all chapters. The Manual including its commentary is a product of the International Society for Military Law and the Law of War, and given the informal process through which this publication was produced, the participation of experts in an individual capacity, and the agreed status of the Observers to the project, the views expressed in the Manual do not necessarily represent those of any institution, organisation or government with which the members of the Group of Experts & Observers[6] are or were affiliated. The final text of the Manual was submitted to the publisher in mid 2017.

---

[5] See Acknowledgment of Support.
[6] For the composition of the Group of Experts & Observers, see List of Contributors.

PART I

Introduction

Scope of the Manual

1.1 Peace Operations are based on three principles: consent of the parties, impartiality and limited use of force.

1. United Nations (UN) peacekeeping has traditionally been based on three basic principles: consent of the parties, impartiality and the non-use of force except in self-defence and defence of the mandate.[1] The same applies to Peace Operations carried out by other organisations, such as the African Union (AU), European Union (EU) and the North Atlantic Treaty Organization (NATO).

2. This Manual covers consensual Peace Operations, including both traditional peacekeeping operations and multi-dimensional Peace Operations which go beyond the traditional tasks of maintaining the post-conflict status quo and monitoring ceasefire and redeployment agreements between warring parties, and include peacebuilding and post-conflict resolution. Such operations rely on consent of the Host State and at the outset also on the consent, or at least acquiescence, of all major parties to the former conflict. A Peace Force operating in the circum-stances contemplated by this Manual may be called upon to use force in situations of temporary breakdown and instability or violence directed against civilians, but will not be expected to become party to an armed conflict and will maintain impartiality and use force only as a last resort in self-defence and in defence of the mandate against so-called "spoilers". All "blue helmet" operations are covered by the Manual, even those oper-ations in which as a result of a temporary breakdown in stability the UN force becomes involved in hostilities with opposing factions. The Manual also covers consensual Peace Operations conducted along the lines of

---

[1] UN, United Nations Peacekeeping Operations: Principles and Guidelines (2008), pp. 31–34, www.un.org/en/peacekeeping/documents/capstone_eng.pdf.

blue helmet Peace Operations which are carried out by regional organisations and arrangements.

3. The Manual does not, however, cover "enforcement operations" directed against a State, or "peace enforcement operations" where the peace is enforced through participation as a party to an armed conflict on the side of a government against an opposing armed group. Similarly, it does not deal with the imposition of a political solution through force of arms upon warring parties. Counter-terrorism, counter-insurgency, counter-narcotics and counter-piracy are also not covered. Situations such as those which involved the International Security Assistance Force (ISAF) in Afghanistan will therefore be excluded. Normal peacetime military activities, such as military training and exercises, will also not be addressed in the Manual.

4. Both traditional peacekeeping operations and contemporary multi-dimensional Peace Operations are premised upon the consent of the Host State. They are bound by the fundamental principles of impartiality and of limited use of force, alongside both consent of the Host State and at the outset consent, or at least acquiescence, on the part of all other major parties involved. Many contemporary Peace Operations are conducted in unstable environments and can include the use of force in the performance of the mandate. Such operations differ from enforcement operations in which armed force is applied against a State, and from peace enforcement operations in which the mission is tasked with providing armed support to a government which is engaged in an ongoing (non-international) armed conflict. They also differ from the imposition of a political solution upon warring parties by force of arms in situations where governmental authority has broken down. While many contemporary multi-dimensional Peace Operations operate under a Chapter VII mandate from the UN Security Council and may contain certain elements of peace enforcement, they nevertheless rely upon the consent of the Host State and at the outset consent, or at least acquiescence, of all major parties to the former conflict.

5. In terms of the applicability of international humanitarian law (IHL), traditional peacekeeping does not envisage participation of peacekeeping forces as parties to either an international (IAC) or a non-international armed conflict (NIAC), and these forces do not generally involve themselves in military operations that cause them to become such parties. Likewise, multi-dimensional Peace Operations are also premised upon the principles of consent of the parties, impartiality and limited use of force, which do not bring about the de jure applicability of IHL.

However, since situations may arise in which Peace Forces are called upon to use force in self-defence and in defence of the mandate, they may apply at least the principles of IHL as a matter of policy, and where the factual and legal conditions for participation as a party to a NIAC have been met, they will be bound to apply IHL as a matter of law for as long as these conditions continue to be met. The Manual thus explores the questions if and when a Peace Force could become a party to the conflict and what the consequences would be if the question were answered in the affirmative.[2] It also identifies gaps in the applicable law and offers suggestions as to doctrine or policy with a view to filling such identified gaps. The substantive content of IHL is, however, adequately addressed in many other publications and does not require specific coverage in this Manual.

6. Considering that international human rights law (IHRL) is, in principle, applicable at all times, in peacetime as well as during armed conflict, the Manual also addresses the obligation of States and international organisations to comply with relevant norms binding upon them in Peace Operations, and to respect human rights obligations of the Host State.[3] It emphasises that applicable human rights obligations cannot be circumvented by reference to the fact that other actors in the same operation have different obligations. It also explains that in case of collision between a norm of IHL and a norm of IHRL, the more specific norm applies in principle.

7. Peace Operations can help bridge the gap between the cessation of hostilities and a durable peace, but only if the parties to a conflict have the political will needed to reach the goal and are in control of armed groups. Initially developed as a means of dealing with inter-State conflict, Peace Operations have increasingly been used in intra-State conflicts, which are often characterised by multiple armed factions with differing political objectives and fractured lines of command. In this context the traditional key peacekeeping principles have evolved along with the evolution of complex multi-dimensional mandates and increasingly volatile operating environments.

---

[2] See Chapter 6.
[3] See Chapter 5.

Short History of the Law of Peace Operations

1. Peace Operations, which were first undertaken in the early 1920s, became more frequent soon after World War II. Yet still today many of them have to be 'invented through trial and error under the stress of urgent circumstances'.[1] A wealth of relevant literature has developed over time.[2] While principles and guidelines for UN peacekeeping operations have been developed in close consultation with field missions, Member States and many other stakeholders,[3] the topic still lacks formal legal regulation. This is not surprising, as a variety of conflict situations, operational requirements and capabilities must be reconciled, and principles and rules stemming from many different branches of international law and the national law of Host States and Sending States are affected.[4]

2. This chapter focuses largely on the history of Peace Operations of the UN. The final paragraphs of this chapter give a short overview of the most important historical and institutional developments with regard

---

[1] M. J. Matheson, *Council Unbound: The Growth of UN Decision Making on Conflict and Postconflict Issues After the Cold War* (United States Institute of Peace Press, 2006), p. 99.

[2] See M. Bothe, 'Peacekeeping Forces', in R. Wolfrum (ed.), *Max Planck Encyclopedia of Public International Law* (Oxford University Press, 2016), www.mpepil.com. For an authoritative look into legal issues which have since taken on historic significance, see A. Cassese (ed.), *United Nations Peace-Keeping: Legal Essays* (Sijthoff and Noordhoff, 1978). For more information, see United Nations Dag Hammarskjöld Library, 'Peace-Keeping Operations: A Bibliography', http://research.un.org/en/docs/peacekeeping.

[3] See UN, United Nations Peacekeeping Operations: Principles and Guidelines (2008), www.un.org/en/peacekeeping/documents/capstone_eng.pdf (Capstone Doctrine). See also thematic Security Council resolutions and Presidential Statements on maintenance of international peace and security – security sector reform, e.g. UNSC Res. 2151 (2014); maintenance of international peace and security – conflict prevention, e.g. UNSC Res. 2171 (2014); threats to international peace and security caused by terrorist acts, e.g. UNSC Res. 2133 (2014); UN peacekeeping operations, e.g. UNSC Res. 2167 (2014); protection of civilians in armed conflict, e.g. UNSC Res. 2175 (2014) and UN Doc. S/PRST/2014/3 (2014); and children in armed conflict, e.g. UNSC Res. 2143 (2014).

[4] D. Fleck, 'The Law Applicable to Peace Operations', in A. Clapham and P. Gaeta (eds.), *The Oxford Handbook of International Law in Armed Conflict* (Oxford University Press, 2014), pp. 228–240.

to Peace Operations undertaken by the AU (see paragraphs 17–21), EU (paragraphs 22–24) and NATO (paragraphs 25–30).

3. Peace Operations of the UN have developed in three phases:[5] (1) During the Cold War period from the late 1940s to the mid 1980s "traditional" or "classical" peacekeeping emerged as a new development, described by Dag Hammarskjöld as falling under "Chapter VI and a half" of the UN Charter, i.e. between peaceful settlement and enforcement measures.[6] (2) During a transitional period from 1987 until late 1991, the Security Council sought and partly succeeded in making more active use of UN peacekeeping to facilitate the settlement of long-standing regional conflicts.[7] (3) An explosion in the number of Peace Operations followed this period with even more robust missions, to include neutralisation of armed elements and increasing efforts to protect civilians.[8] However, there were also major setbacks and failures.[9] Regional

[5] See M. Berdal, 'The Security Council and Peacekeeping', in V. Lowe, A. Roberts, J. Welsh and D. Zaum (eds.), *The United Nations Security Council and War. The Evolution of Thought and Practice Since 1945* (Oxford University Press, 2008), pp. 177–198.

[6] B. Urquhart, *A Life in Peace and War* (Harper & Row, 1987), p. 125. See e.g. UN Military Observer Group in India and Pakistan (UNMOGIP), UNSC Res. 47 (1948); UN Troop Supervision Operation in the Middle East (UNTSO), UNSC Res. 50 (1948) and UNSC Res. 73 (1949); UN Emergency Force in the Suez (UNEF I), UNGA Res. 997 (ES-I, 1956) and UNGA Res. 1000 (ES-I, 1956); UN Operation in the Congo (ONUC), UNSC Res. 143 (1960), UNSC Res. 146 (1960), UNSC Res. 157 (1960), UNGA Res. 1474 (ES-IV, 1960), UNSC Res. 161 (1961) and UNSC Res. 169 (1961); UN Yemen Observation Mission (UNYOM), UNSC Res. 179 (1963); Second UN Emergency Force (UNEF II), UNSC Res. 340 (1973).

[7] See e.g. UN Iran–Iraq Military Observer Group (UNIIMOG), UNSC Res. 619 (1988); UN Good Offices Mission in Afghanistan and Pakistan (UNGOMAP), UNSC Res. 622 (1988); Angola Verification Mission (UNAVEM I and II), UNSC Res. 626 (1988) and UNSC Res. 696 (1991); UN Observer Group (ONUCA) in Central America, UNSC Res. 644 (1989) and UNSC Res. 653 (1990); UN Transition Assistance Group (UNTAG) in Namibia, UNSC Res. 632 (1989).

[8] See the enlargement of UNPROFOR's mandate to protect the distribution of humanitarian assistance in the former Yugoslavia, UNSC Res. 769 (1992); Unified Task Force (UNITAF) in Somalia, UNSC Res. 794 (1992); UN Operations in Somalia (UNOSOM II), UNSC Res. 814 (1993); International Force for East Timor (INTERFET), UNSC Res. 1264 (1999); International Security Assistance Force (ISAF) in Afghanistan, UNSC Res. 1386 (2001) and UNSC Res. 1510 (2003) which soon turned into a non-international armed conflict with coalition forces participating on the side of the Afghan government; UN Organization Mission in the Democratic Republic of the Congo (MONUC), UNSC Res. 1258 (1999) and UNSC Res. 1291 (1999); UN Operation in Côte d'Ivoire (UNOCI), UNSC Res. 1528 (2004); AU/UN Hybrid Mission in Darfur (UNAMID), UNSC Res. 1769 (2007); UN Stabilization Mission in the Democratic Republic of the Congo (MONUSCO), UNSC Res. 1925 (2010), UNSC Res. 2053 (2012), UNSC Res. 2076 (2012) and UNSC Res. 2098 (2013).

[9] See T. Findlay (ed.), *Challenges for the New Peacekeepers* (Oxford University Press, 1996); J. Sloan, *The Militarisation of Peacekeeping in the Twenty-First Century* (Hart, 2001); T. Benner, S. Mergenthaler and Ph. Rotmann, *The New World of Peace Operations: Learning to Build Peace?* (Oxford University Press, 2011); A. J. Bellamy and P. D. Williams (eds.), *Providing Peacekeepers: The Politics, Challenges, and Future of United Nations Peacekeeping Contributions* (Oxford University Press, 2013).

organisations (and arrangements) are now more and more involved in Peace Operations, and post-conflict peacebuilding has become a challenge for civilians and the military, for States and civil society.

4. The term "Peace Operation" is of comparably recent coinage.[10] It goes beyond traditional peacekeeping and is used in current UN terminology to describe 'field operations deployed to prevent, manage, and/or resolve violent conflicts or reduce the risk of their recurrence'.[11] Broader than peacekeeping, this term entails 'three principal activities: conflict prevention and peacemaking; peacekeeping; and peacebuilding'.[12] Widely understood and used as an informal means of effectively containing warring States, international peacekeeping was and is thus used and supported by States for wider purposes: '[W]hile peacekeeping forces were themselves directly engaged in the mitigation of local violence, their deployment also served as a great power instrument for managing relations and preventing war of a far more catastrophic kind.'[13]

5. Clear legal distinctions continue to apply between operations based on and executed with full consent of the Host State and enforcement operations under Chapter VII of the UN Charter. Yet peacekeeping and peace enforcement tasks may be present in one and the same operation. Even those operations in which the element of coercion is not the dominating feature may differ considerably in mandate, size and duration.[14] While all UN Peace Operations are executed within the general framework of the UN Charter (Chapters VI, VII and VIII), the reality is that military forces were often sent to operate on foreign territory without an explicit legal basis, without special agreements in accordance with article 43 of the UN Charter, and without involving the Military Staff Committee under article 47.

---

[10] See N. White, 'Peace Operations', in V. Chetail (ed.), *Post-Conflict Peacebuilding: A Lexicon* (Oxford University Press, 2009), pp. 213–227. For a list of terms as used in the Manual, see Appendix VIII.

[11] See Capstone Doctrine (n. 3), p. 99.

[12] Report of the Panel on United Nations Peace Operations, UN Doc. A/55/305-S/2000/809 (2000), para. 10 (Brahimi Report). See Glossary of UN Peacekeeping Terms, www.un.org/en/peacekeeping/sites/glossary.

[13] Berdal (n. 5), p. 176.

[14] For general information, see the UN website for Peacekeeping Operations: www.un.org/en/peacekeeping/operations. A historical overview and legal assessment of the practice of peacekeeping operations are provided by M. Bothe, 'Peacekeeping', in B. Simma, D. E. Khan, G. Nolte and A. Paulus (eds.), *The Charter of the United Nations: A Commentary*, 3rd edn, 2 vols. (Oxford University Press, 2012), vol. I, pp. 1171–1199.

6. In its 1962 Advisory Opinion on *Certain Expenses of the United Nations*,[15] the International Court of Justice confirmed, despite several dissenting opinions, that in establishing UN Emergency Force (UNEF) I and UN Operation in the Congo (ONUC)[16] neither the General Assembly nor the Security Council had acted ultra vires, as UNEF I was not an enforcement action under Chapter VII but rather a measure recommended under article 14 of the Charter, and in the case of ONUC it was in conformity with the Charter that the Council had authorised the UN Secretary-General to select and invite Member States willing to assist; hence the expenditures for both operations constituted 'expenses of the Organization' within the meaning of article 17(2) of the Charter. In more than fifty years of practice, fundamental elements of Peace Operations (i.e. consent of the Host State, impartiality of peacekeepers and limited use of force) have repeatedly been confirmed both in the Secretary-General's reports on the issue[17] and in the reactions of Member States. Recent developments, especially in Africa, have caused concern as to whether Host State consent is still a key principle of contemporary Peace Operations.[18] The principle of limited use of force has come under strain in several Peace Operations.[19] Yet Sending States and Host States alike continue to underline the importance of all three principles. Consent of the Host State, impartiality of peacekeepers and limited use of force are widely considered today as customary international law requirements in all Peace Operations, whether conducted by the UN or by regional organisations and arrangements.

7. The Agenda for Peace,[20] commissioned by the Security Council at its first meeting at the level of Heads of State and Government[21] and later endorsed by the General Assembly,[22] identified four separate components of the maintenance of international peace and security, i.e. peacemaking

---

[15] *Certain Expenses of the United Nations (Article 17, paragraph 2, of the Charter)*, Advisory Opinion, ICJ Reports 1962, 151.

[16] For both operations, see n. 6.

[17] The first of such reports was submitted by Secretary-General Dag Hammarskjöld after UNEF I: Summary Study from the Experience Derived from the Establishment and Operation of the Force: Report of the Secretary-General, UN Doc. A/3943 (1958).

[18] See D. M. Tull, 'When They Overstay Their Welcome: UN Peacekeepers in Africa', 17 *Journal of International Peacekeeping* (2013), pp. 179–200, arguing that UN mandates were not fully met with the consent of the Host State and that peacekeepers have repeatedly become actors in the domestic power game, as a result of their ever longer and intrusive presence.

[19] See Chapter 12.

[20] An Agenda for Peace – Report of the Secretary-General, UN Doc. A/47/277-S/24111 (1992).

[21] UN Doc. S/23500 (1992).

[22] UNGA Res. 47/120 (1992).

including preventive diplomacy, peacekeeping and post-conflict peace-building. Advocating for an early warning system to identify potential conflicts, and a 'reinvigorated and restructured Economic and Social Council', the Agenda for Peace tried to establish a system of preventive deployment in situations of national crisis, to discourage hostilities in inter-State disputes, and to serve to deter conflict in situations of external threats.[23] Three years later, UN Secretary-General Boutros Boutros-Ghali's Supplement to the Agenda for Peace[24] reiterated the need for hard decisions in view of a dramatic increase in relevant UN activities, as the end of the Cold War enabled the Security Council to begin using its authority under the Charter more extensively.

8. The Brahimi Report,[25] initiated by Secretary-General Kofi A. Annan, conspicuously avoided the traditional distinction between peacekeeping and peace enforcement and addressed doctrinal issues of peacemaking, peacekeeping and peacebuilding in context. The Report is an important contribution towards adapting the three principles of peacekeeping – i.e. consent of local parties, impartiality and limited use of force – to the more complex circumstances of internal conflicts in which consent of the host parties may be unreliable, in which Charter principles are often neglected at least by one of the parties and in which peacekeepers have to operate in a rather volatile safety and security environment. The Report developed practical recommendations, in particular for 'clear, credible and achievable mandates', to be formulated by the Security Council.[26] Accordingly, Rules of Engagement (ROE) (if necessary robust ones) were called for, and adopted with relevant specifications for each mission.[27]

---

[23] See Agenda for Peace (n. 20), paras. 26–32.

[24] Supplement to An Agenda for Peace, UN Doc. A/50/60-S/1995/1 (1995).

[25] See n. 12. See N. White, 'Commentary on the Report of the Panel on United Nations Peace Operations', 6 *Journal of Conflict and Security Law* (2001), pp. 127–146; C. Gray, 'Peacekeeping After the Brahimi Report', 6 *Journal of Conflict and Security Law* (2001), pp. 267–288; D. Bratt and E. Giornet, 'Evaluating the Brahimi Report', 96 *Strategic Datalink* (2001), pp. 1–4; B. Jones, R. Gowan and J. Sherman, *Building on Brahimi: Peacekeeping in an Era of Strategic Uncertainty* (NYU Center on International Cooperation, 2009).

[26] The Security Council has endorsed these proposals in UNSC Res. 1327 (2000), adopting detailed decisions and recommendations resulting from the Brahimi Report, and decided to review their implementation periodically. For a critical assessment, see W. J. Durch, V. K. Holt, C. R. Earle and M. K. Shanahan, *The Brahimi Report and the Future of UN Peace Operations* (Henry L. Stimson Center, 2003).

[27] T. Gill, J. A. M. Léveillée and D. Fleck, 'The Rule of Law in Peace Operations: General Report', 17 *Recueils de la Societé Internationale de Droit Militaire et de Droit de la Guerre* (2006), pp. 109–157.

9. The doctrine of Responsibility to Protect (R2P),[28] developed to articulate the responsibility of States to intervene in extreme situations,[29] was presented by its authors as 'a new international security and human rights norm to address the international community's failure to prevent and stop genocides, war crimes, ethnic cleansing and crimes against humanity'.[30] Yet clear limitations must be considered in this context. At the 2005 World Summit, the assembled Heads of State and Government, accommodating concerns that an unqualified reference to R2P might result in 'an obligation to intervene under international law',[31] gave a cautious response to more progressive approaches by invoking three pillars on which this responsibility rests: (1) the responsibility of the State through appropriate and necessary means to protect its population from genocide, war crimes, ethnic cleansing and crimes against humanity including their incitement; (2) the commitment of the international community through the UN and in accordance with Chapters VI and VIII of the Charter to assist States in meeting these obligations; and (3) the responsibility of States 'to take collective action, in a timely and decisive manner, through the Security Council, in accordance with the Charter, including Chapter VII, on a case-by-case basis and in cooperation with relevant regional organisations as appropriate, should peaceful means be inadequate and national authorities manifestly fail to protect their populations from genocide, war crimes, ethnic cleansing and crimes against humanity'.[32] The doctrine of R2P, later referred to as the responsibility to prevent, the responsibility to react and the responsibility to rebuild,[33] is not so much new law as a different way of presenting some existing legal obligations and sound policy objectives in a new form.

---

[28] International Commission on Intervention and State Sovereignty, *The Responsibility to Protect* (International Development Research Centre, 2001), http://responsibilitytoprotect.org/ICISS%20 Report.pdf; G. J. Evans and M. Sahnoun, 'The Responsibility to Protect', 81 *Foreign Affairs* (2002), pp. 99–110.

[29] International Commission on Intervention and State Sovereignty (n. 28), xi: 'State sovereignty implies responsibility, and the primary responsibility for the protection of its people lies with the state itself ... Where a population is suffering serious harm, as a result of internal war, insurgency, repression or state failure, and the state in question is unwilling or unable to halt or avert it, the principle of non-intervention yields to the international responsibility to protect.'

[30] *Ibid.*, Introduction.

[31] See e.g. US Ambassador John Bolton, 'Letter dated 30 August 2005', www.humanrightsvoices.org/ assets/attachments/documents/bolton_responsibility_to_protect.pdf.

[32] 2005 World Summit Outcome, UNGA Res. 60/1 (2005), paras. 138–140. See E. C. Luck, *The United Nations and the Responsibility to Protect* (Stanley Foundation, 2008), www.stanleyfoundation.org/ publications/pab/luckpab808.pdf.

[33] S. C. Breau, 'The Impact of the Responsibility to Protect on Peacekeeping', 11 *Journal of Conflict and Security Law* (2006), p. 431.

This is equally important for doctrine and practice and clearly has a bearing on current Peace Operations.[34] While subsequent State practice confirmed a continuing reluctance to intervene militarily,[35] the most innovative effect of R2P is not on prevention and military response, acts that are clearly regulated by Chapter VII of the Charter, but on post-conflict peacebuilding.[36]

10. The past decades have seen dramatic changes for international Peace Operations. The Security Council took firm action to reverse the aggression in Kuwait in 1990.[37] It was not as successful in imposing peace in Bosnia and Herzegovina and in Croatia (1992–1995), and it again arrived at an impasse when considering humanitarian intervention in Kosovo (1999) and weapons of mass destruction in Iraq (2003).[38] The Secretary-General had to face particular problems where the Security Council did not act on warning signs, and Belgium withdrew its contingent after peacekeepers were killed. A systematic slaughter of approximately 800,000 men, women and children in Rwanda between April and July 1994 was neither prevented nor stopped, and it took years before an independent inquiry into the failure of the UN was conducted.[39] In July 1995, after Srebrenica fell to besieging Serbian forces, around 8,000 people, overwhelmingly from the Bosnian Muslim community, were killed in and around safe areas. Years later the Secretary-General, tasked to submit a report on this case and the role of the UN Protection Force (UNPROFOR) therein,[40] explained that, due to disagreements between Member States, safe havens were established in Bosnia and Herzegovina without the corresponding resources to implement them, a situation for which the 'international community as a whole must accept its share of responsibility for allowing this tragic course of events

---

[34] See *Ibid.*; V. K. Holt and J. G. Smith, *Halting Widespread or Systematic Attacks on Civilians: Military Strategies and Operations Concepts* (Henry L. Stimson Center, 2008); J. H. S. Lie, *Protection of Civilians, the Responsibility to Protect and Peace Operations* (NUPI, 2008).

[35] See e.g. J. M. Prescott, 'The North Atlantic Treaty Organization', in G. Zyberi (ed.), *An Institutional Approach to the Responsibility to Protect* (Cambridge University Press, 2013), pp. 338–361.

[36] See D. Fleck, 'The Responsibility to Rebuild and Its Potential for Law-Creation: Good Governance, Accountability and Judicial Control', 16 *Journal of International Peacekeeping* (2012), pp. 84–98.

[37] See UN, *The United Nations and the Iraq–Kuwait Conflict 1990–1996* (1996).

[38] For a well-informed assessment of events, see R. Zacklin, *The United Nations Secretariat and the Use of Force in a Unipolar World* (Cambridge University Press, 2010).

[39] Report of the Independent Inquiry into the Actions of the United Nations During the 1994 Genocide in Rwanda, UN Doc. S/1999/1257 (1999).

[40] Report of the Secretary-General pursuant to General Assembly Resolution 53/35, The Fall of Srebrenica, UN Doc. A/54/549 (1999).

by its prolonged refusal to use force in the early stages of the war'.[41] No remedy for the victims was, however, proposed and still after another decade the division of responsibilities between States and the UN in this case remained unclear.[42] In Syria, after years of internal armed conflict that is still ongoing, a six-point peace plan called in vain for an end to violence, for access for humanitarian agencies to provide relief to those in need, for the release of detainees and for the start of inclusive political dialogue.[43] The total number of refugees soon exceeded 4 million, with more than 7.6 million displaced inside Syria,[44] a country estimated to have had roughly 23 million permanent inhabitants. While this tragedy continues to develop dramatically, the international community still appears unable to put an end to it.[45] Peace Operations worldwide are severely challenged today by war crimes and crimes against humanity. Criminal prosecutions are frequently insufficient, at both the national and the international level. Robust measures to protect civilians, especially women and children, have had to be inserted in mandates of Peace Operations.[46] Clear responsibilities of Host States, which are essential for the success of any peace process, are often ignored.

11. In recent years, UN Peace Operations have exploded with an eightfold growth in the personnel deployed.[47] The permanent members

---

[41] *Ibid.*, para. 501.

[42] In *The Netherlands* v. *Hasan Nuhanović*, Supreme Court (Hoge Raad) of the Netherlands, Judgment of 6 September 2013, 53 ILM (2014) 516, the Dutch Supreme Court concluded that the Netherlands was responsible for the death of three Muslim men from Srebrenica, stating that pertinent conduct of Dutchbat, as part of a UN Peace Force, could be attributed to the Netherlands because public international law allows the attribution of conduct in this specific case to the Sending State and not the UN in so far as the State had effective control over the disputed conduct. Other claims by the association Mothers of Srebrenica were dismissed by the Court.

[43] 'UN-Backed Action Group Agrees on Measures for Peaceful Transition in Syria', *UN News Centre*, 30 June 2012, www.un.org/apps/news/story.asp?NewsID=42367#.WWENIMaB31I.

[44] 'UNHCR: Total Number of Syrian Refugees Exceeds Four Million for First Time', 9 July 2015, www.unhcr.org/559d67d46.html.

[45] The UN Supervision Mission in Syria (UNSMIS), mandated by UNSC Res. 2043 (2012) to monitor a cessation of armed violence and support implementation of former Secretary-General Kofi A. Annan's six-point peace plan for Syria, had to be curtailed after a few months on 19 August 2012.

[46] See H. Willmot, R. Mamiya, S. Sheeran and M. Weller (eds.), *Protection of Civilians* (Oxford University Press, 2016).

[47] Approximately 112,000 personnel are serving on sixteen Peace Operations led by the UN Department of Peacekeeping Operations on four continents. The budget has risen to more than USD 7.8 billion a year. More than 81,000 of those serving are troops and military observers, and over 12,000 are police personnel, coming from 128 States; there are also more than 5,000 international civilian personnel, more than 10,000 local civilian staff and some 1,500 UN Volunteers. In addition, the Department of Field Support, established in 2007 to provide support and expertise in the areas of personnel, finance and budget, communications, information technology and

of the Security Council, hitherto reluctant to provide military contingents themselves, have relaxed that policy to meet greater demands, to demonstrate the serious intent of the UN and to prevent the adverse consequences of resistance to its Peace Operations.[48] As the Secretary-General stated in his 2009 Annual Report: 'United Nations peacekeeping is at a crossroads. The Organization needs a renewed global partnership with Member States and its partners within and outside the United Nations system.'[49] The 2015 Report of the High-Level Independent Panel on Peace Operations submitted substantive policy recommendations, urging that

> [P]olitics must drive the design and implementation of peace operations ... [T]he full spectrum of UN peace operations must be used more flexibly to respond to changing needs on the ground ... [A] stronger, more inclusive peace and security partnership is needed for the future ... [T]he UN Secretariat must become more field-focused and UN peace operations must be more people-centered.[50]

The Secretary-General, highlighting this 'renewed focus on prevention and mediation; stronger regional–global partnerships; and new ways of planning and conducting United Nations peace operations to make them faster, more responsive and more accountable to the needs of countries and people in conflict', convincingly called for 'a system-wide effort and the active engagement and support of the entire membership' without which the challenges of Peace Operations in a progressively developing global security environment could hardly be met.[51]

---

logistics, supports another fifteen special political and/or peacebuilding field missions managed by the Department of Political Affairs, as well as a number of other UN peace offices requiring administrative and logistical assistance from UN Headquarters. Since 1948 there have been 3,592 fatalities among those participating in UN Peace Operations and political and peacebuilding missions. See UN, 'Fact Sheet United Nations Peacekeeping Operations', 31 May 2017, www.un.org/en/peacekeeping/documents/bnote0517.pdf.

[48] Cf. Matheson (n. 1), p. 125. British troops participated in the UN Angola Verification Mission III (UNAVEM III) and the UN Assistance Mission for Rwanda (UNAMIR); French and US troops in the UN Operation in Somalia II (UNOSOM II); British, Chinese, French, Russian and US troops in the UN Transitional Authority in Cambodia (UNTAC); British, French, Russian and US troops in the UN Protection Force (UNPROFOR) in the former Yugoslavia.

[49] Cf. UN Secretary-General, Report on the Work of the Organization, UN Doc. A/64/1 (2009), para. 57.

[50] Report of the High-Level Independent Panel on Peace Operations, Uniting Our Strengths for Peace: Politics, Partnership and People, UN Doc. A/70/95-S/2015/446 (2015), viii.

[51] Report of the Secretary-General, UN Doc. A/70/357-S/2015/683 (2015), paras. 2, 8, 132. See I. D. Renn, 'Déjà Vu All Over Again and Peacekeeping Reform? The HIPPO Report and Barriers to Implementation', 19 *Journal of International Peacekeeping* (2015), pp. 211–226; S. von Einsiedel and R. Chandran, 'The High-Level Panel and the Prospects for Reform of UN Peace Operations',

12. The UN Standby Arrangements System (UNSAS), initiated in 1994 and strongly supported in the Brahimi Report,[52] undertakes to bridge the existing "commitment–capacity gap" and to increase operational readiness for deployment. At the *first* level, it provides the UN with an understanding of the forces and other capabilities a Member State will have available at an agreed state of readiness. The *second* level requires detailed technical information to facilitate planning, training and preparation for both the participating Member States and the UN. At the *third* level, UNSAS provides the UN not only with foreknowledge of the available range of national assets and equipment, but also with a conditional commitment to participate on request, following governmental approval in any given case. Based on a Memorandum of Understanding (MOU), UN planners now have the option of developing contingency and "fall-back" strategies when they anticipate delays or when one or more members refrain from participating in an operation. No specific binding commitment ("level 4 agreement") has been concluded so far. Recommendations have been made to earmark capacities for deployment in military operations other than enforcement operations (i.e. for advisory services, preventive action and protection of civilians, peacekeeping, policing, peacebuilding and humanitarian assistance).[53] They include encouragement of all Member States to participate in the UNSAS, to which a *fifth level* (specification of personnel and resources that governments are willing to commit to more demanding Chapter VII operations) and also a *sixth level* (a renewed commitment to article 43 of the Charter and the use of UNSAS as an important transitional measure facilitating that goal) could be added. In order to put these procedures into practice there has been discussion of a phased development of a UN Emergency Service as a rapid reaction capability composed of military, police and civilian volunteers and supplemented by Member States.[54] A proposal by the United States called for a UN Rapid Deployment Police and Security Force of at least 6,000 volunteers recruited globally and directly employed by the UN as a standing force, to address the *time gap*, the *training gap* and the *political will gap* with well-trained,

---

United Nations University – Center for Policy Research, July 2015, http://cpr.unu.edu/the-high-level-panel-and-the-prospects-for-reform-of-un-peace-operations.htm.

[52] See n. 12, paras. 102–145.

[53] See H. P. Langille, *Bridging the Commitment–Capacity Gap: A Review of Existing Arrangements and Options for Enhancing UN Rapid Deployment* (Center for UN Reform Education, 2002), www.pugwashgroup.ca/publications/Langille%20Exec%20Sum%20Small.pdf.

[54] *Ibid.*, pp. 12–13.

professional military and police units that would be able to respond to a crisis within fifteen days of a Security Council resolution.[55] Similar challenges were faced at regional level: in the AU – after several delays – a 2015 deadline was set for the five regions (east, west, central, north and southern Africa) to develop their own standby brigades with military, police and civilian components, but only the first two have complied as of October 2016. In July 2015 the UN Peacekeeping Capability Readiness System (PCRS) replaced the old UNSAS. The PCRS aims to establish a more predictable and dynamic process of interaction between UN Headquarters and the Member States for ensuring readiness and timely deployment of high quality peacekeeping capabilities. It aims to improve efficiency in the management of commitments, to achieve a greater degree of readiness and predictability through a more sustained and collaborative approach between UN Headquarters and the Member States and, in the longer term, to provide a single window for the selection of a Troop Contributing Country (TCC) for deployment. The new system, by adopting clearly defined criteria and related steps, will reflect the actual commitments of Member States.[56] The PCRS is an integral part of Strategic Force Generation and serves as the first step for any new force generation efforts and a gateway for the UN to collaborate with Member States, helping them to build required knowledge and capacity for participation in peacekeeping operations.

13. Personnel recruitment, equipment and funding are increasingly posing problems. For many Peace Operations the Security Council has to

---

[55] United States, United Nations Rapid Deployment Act of 2001, HR 938, www.govtrack.us/congress/bill.xpd?bill=h107-938 (a proposed bill that has not been passed).

[56] The levels of commitment and related steps are described as follows: *Level 1*: TCC makes a formal pledge to provide a unit along with (a) a table depicting the unit's organisation; (b) a list of major and self-sustainment equipment that it will supply with the unit; and (c) certification of completion of basic training and human rights screening. Member States are encouraged to include the time period of the unit's availability and the duration of deployment for each pledged capability including their preferences and limitations if any. Member States can include police and any non-military government-provided capabilities. Emerging and aspiring TCCs that do not yet meet these basic requirements will not be registered in Level 1 but will be engaged as part of a preparatory process managed by the Strategic Force Generation and Capability Planning Cell. *Level 2*: Based on the UN operational requirements, selective pledges at Level 1 will be elevated to this level through the conduct of a successful Assessment and Advisory Visit (AAV) by a UN Headquarters Team comprising members of the Departments of Peacekeeping Operations and of Field Support. *Level 3*: Following a satisfactory AAV, only those units which have achieved a reasonable degree of preparedness will be upgraded to Level 3. Discussion of a draft MOU will be initiated, and TCCs will provide a load list as required by the Department of Field Support. *Rapid Deployment Level (RDL)*: Having reached Level 3, the TCC may pledge to deploy within 30/60/90 days of a request made by UN Headquarters. Elevation to this level will determine eligibility for rapid deployment.

rely on groups of States, regional organisations and arrangements exercising command and control of their forces.[57] The UN works extensively in partnership with other international and regional organisations, such as the AU,[58] EU[59] and NATO.[60] Multi-national operations have become a key feature of Peace Operations. While this has added to the acceptance of Peace Operations and contributed to their effectiveness, it has also posed interoperability problems, the solution of which requires continuous attention and joint activities.

14. A good understanding of the relationship between Peace Operations and peacebuilding remains a challenge for international organisations, Sending States and Host States alike. The UN Peacebuilding Commission, established as an intergovernmental advisory board under concurrent resolutions by the General Assembly[61] and the Security Council,[62] after some promising beginnings, is still in a developing phase.[63] As the success of sustainable peacebuilding depends upon supportive efforts of multiple agencies, appropriate strategies must involve very different actors in fruitful co-operation. Armed forces and

---

[57] See e.g. Implementation Force/Stabilisation Force (IFOR/SFOR), UNSC Res. 318 (1995); Kosovo Force (KFOR), UNSC Res. 1244 (1999); International Security Assistance Force (ISAF), UNSC Res. 1386 (2001) and UNSC Res. 1510 (2003); UN Mission in Sudan (UNMIS), UNSC Res. 1590 (2005); UN Mission in South Sudan (UNMISS), UNSC Res. 1996 (2011) and UNSC Res. 2155 (2014); the Italian-led Operation Alba in Albania, UNSC Res. 1101 (1997); Mission Interafricaine de Surveillance des Accords de Bangui (MISAB) in the Central African Republic, UNSC Res. 1125 (1997); African Mission in Burundi (AMIB), UNSC Res. 1545 (2004); UN Mission in Darfur (UNAMID), UNSC Res. 1769 (2007); ECOWAS Mission in Liberia (ECOMIL), UNSC Res. 1509 (2003); ECOWAS Monitoring Group (ECOMOG) in Sierra Leone, Guinea-Bissau and Ivory Coast 1997–2002; International Force for East Timor (INTERFET), UNSC Res. 1267 (1999); the Australian-led Peace Monitoring Group in Bougainville, Papua New Guinea (BELISI) 1998–2003; the European Missions, e.g. Operation Concordia in FYROM 2003 (UNSC Res. 1371 (2001)), Operation Artemis in the Democratic Republic of Congo (UNSC Res. 1484 (2003)), EUFOR in the Democratic Republic of Congo (UNSC Res. 1671 (2006)), EUFOR Chad/Central African Republic (UNSC Res. 1778 (2007)), EU Naval Coordination Cell (NAVCO) and EU Naval Force (EUNAVFOR) Atalanta (UNSC Res. 1772 (2007), UNSC Res. 1801 (2008) and UNSC Res. 1814 (2008)).

[58] Art. 4(h) Constitutive Act of the African Union (11 July 2000, in force 26 May 2001, 2158 UNTS 3) asserts 'the right of the Union to intervene in a Member State pursuant to a decision of the Assembly in respect of grave circumstances, namely: war crimes, genocide, and crimes against humanity'. See further Chapter 4.3.

[59] See Treaty on European Union (Consolidated Version), OJ 2016 No. C202, 7 June 2016, p. 13, Title V, Chapter 2, Specific Provisions on the Common Foreign and Security Policy. See further Chapter 4.4.

[60] See NATO, Peace Support Operations, AJP-3.4.1 (2001), https://info.publicintelligence.net/NATO-PeaceSupport.pdf. See further Chapter 4.5.

[61] UNGA Res. 60/180 (2005).

[62] UNSC Res. 1645 (2005).

[63] See UNGA Res. 70/262 (2016); UNSC Res. 2282 (2016).

the police, governmental diplomacy and informal activities, economic incentives, and political pressure are realistic means of influencing States and non-State actors in support of peacebuilding. Yet these means cannot be seen as a substitute for a process of reconciliation through direct negotiations. What will be required for sustainable peace are the readiness and ability to co-operate and include former adversaries in common objectives.[64] Aligning mandates and resources to address issues such as disarmament, demobilisation and reintegration (DDR), and on military aspects of security sector reform to core government functions, social services and jobs, is particularly important.[65] This will require greater awareness of the need to strengthen civilian actors in their efforts to establish the rule of law, ensure good governance and promote economic and social recovery, gender equality and inclusion of all parts of civil society in the peace process. Pertinent proposals aiming at a more comprehensive approach to generating resources and to creating incentives for the achievement of practical results in the field still need to be implemented.

15. This role in support of Peace Operations is still less than clearly defined. As Host States are notoriously lacking in resources and in effective political control in post-conflict environments, their rights and obligations vis-à-vis peacekeepers are subject to volatile developments. It may be stated, however, that without Host State support no Peace Operation could be brought to success, and without a considerable measure of international solidarity no Host State could effectively establish a stable peaceful environment. This latter aspect calls for increasing support of the international community and for better burden sharing by Host States, Sending States, Transit States and other States.

16. This short overview of UN Peace Operations illustrates a field of international co-operation that is not fully regulated (and often escapes regulation), but is clearly influenced by various branches of international law. A closer look into these different legal branches and their interplay is desirable in order to better understand existing possibilities for and limitations confronting international Peace Operations:

a.   Peace Operations have become well-accepted international instruments guided by specific bedrock principles (i.e. consent of the Host State, impartiality of peacekeepers and limited use of force). Peace Operations conducted by regional organisations (and arrangements) are governed

---

[64] See D. Fleck, '*Jus Post Bellum* as a Partly Independent Legal Framework', in C. Stahn (ed.), *Jus Post Bellum* (Oxford University Press, 2014), pp. 43–57.

[65] See *Implementing United Nations Multidimensional and Integrated Peace Operations* (Norwegian Ministry of Foreign Affairs, 2008), www.regjeringen.no/upload/UD/Vedlegg/FN/final_operations .pdf. See also United Nations Peacebuilding Commission, www.un.org/en/peacebuilding/.

by the same principles. These principles may be considered as being rooted in customary international law today;

b. More specific forms of conduct may depend on internal regulation by the UN or regional organisations and arrangements, and are thus not subject to direct influence by States;

c. Best practices remain subject to ever changing requirements;

d. The rights and obligations of Host States require specific attention;

e. Principles and rules for burden sharing between Sending States, Host States, Transit States and other States need to be further developed;

f. While various modes of implementation of pertinent principles and rules have developed over time, a comprehensive legal regulation of Peace Operations is still not available. All parties involved are called upon to implement existing principles and rules and to co-operate on their further development even if full regulation may not be desirable.

17. *AU.* Before the turn of the millennium the leading organisation on the African continent was the Organisation of African Unity (OAU). The OAU was established on 25 May 1963 in Addis Ababa, Ethiopia. During its existence, the organisation achieved little success in materialising its belief that on the African continent 'conditions for peace and security must be established and maintained'.[66] Despite the widespread prevalence of African inter-State and intra-State conflicts, the OAU was generally not able to influence national policies and prevent international and internal conflicts and related human rights abuses. The OAU's firm treaty-based commitment to the principle of non-intervention[67] contributed to an attitude of indifference and a reality of impunity.

18. At the Cairo Summit (1993), the OAU decided to create a mechanism for Conflict Prevention, Management and Resolution. The Cairo Declaration recognized that '[n]o single internal factor has contributed more to the present socio-economic problems in the Continent than the scourge of conflicts in and among our countries', but also that in this respect the OAU had achieved 'limited success at finding lasting solutions'.[68] The mechanism had three goals: (1) to anticipate and prevent situations of potential conflict from developing into full-blown wars; (2) to undertake peacemaking and peacebuilding efforts when

---

[66] Charter of the Organization of African Unity (25 May 1963, in force 13 September 1983), 479 UNTS 39, preamble.

[67] *Ibid.*, art. III(2).

[68] Declaration of the Assembly of Heads of State and Government on the establishment within the OAU of a Mechanism for Conflict Prevention, Management and Resolution, OAU Doc. AHG/DECL.3 (XXIX) (1993), para. 9.

facing full-blown wars; and (3) to carry out post-conflict peacemaking and peacebuilding. Despite this newly created institutional backing, however, the OAU largely failed to manage the many conflicts in the second half of the 1990s (e.g. in Angola, the Democratic Republic of the Congo, Liberia, Rwanda, Sierra Leone, Somalia and Sudan). Effective decision-making was often hampered by the requirement of consensus voting among the Heads of State and Government and the idea that outside powers should not meddle in intra-State conflicts which were regarded to be exclusively of concern to the government involved.

19. When the OAU Heads of State and Government met at the Summit in Sirte (1999), it was decided to establish a new organisation, the AU, as the successor pan-African organisation. The Constitutive Act of the African Union was adopted in Lomé, Togo, on 11 July 2000.[69] The first Summit of the Heads of State and Government took place in Durban, South Africa, two years later. The creation of the AU has been marked as a "paradigm shift", changing the organisation's predisposition from non-intervention to non-indifference.[70] By the end of 2003 the AU had created the Peace and Security Council of the African Union (PSC AU) as the new mechanism to deal more effectively with issues of peace and security, including the initiation of Peace Operations.[71]

20. The African Mission in Burundi (AMIB, 2003) presented the first wholly planned and executed AU Peace Operation. AMIB had a deployment strength of 3,000 troops coming from three TCCs: South Africa, Ethiopia and Mozambique. After one year, AMIB was transformed into a UN-led Peace Operation (abbreviated as ONUB) pursuant to UN Security Council Resolution 1545 (2004).[72]

21. Subsequent Peace Operations deployed by the AU include the missions in Sudan (AMIS I and AMIS II, 2004–2007), Comoros (AMISEC, 2006; MAES, 2007–2008), Mali (AFISMA, 2013; later transformed into the UN Multidimensional Integrated Stabilization Mission in Mali, MINUSMA) and the Central African Republic (MISCA, 2013–2014; later transformed into the UN Multidimensional Integrated

---

[69] Constitutive Act of the African Union (11 July 2000, in force 26 May 2001), 2158 UNTS 3.

[70] See e.g. B. Kioko, 'The Right of Intervention Under the African Union's Constitutive Act: From Non-Interference to Non-Intervention', 85 *International Review of the Red Cross* (2003), pp. 807–825.

[71] The PSC AU was set up pursuant to art. 5(2) AU Constitutive Act (n. 69), and the Protocol relating to the establishment of the Peace and Security Council of the African Union (9 July 2002, in force 26 December 2003), www.peaceau.org/uploads/psc-protocol-en.pdf.

[72] ONUB successfully completed its mandate on 31 December 2006. It was succeeded by the UN Integrated Office in Burundi (BINUB), established by UNSC Res. 1719 (2006).

Stabilization Mission in the Central African Republic, MINUSCA). At present the AU has two Peace Operations in place: one in Somalia since 2007 (AMISOM), and one in Sudan, also since 2007 (UNAMID). The latter is a joint AU–UN mission mounted in response to the ongoing violence in Sudan's Darfur region. It was jointly established by the PSC AU and the UN Security Council.[73]

22. *EU.* The EU became active in security and defence matters in the 1990s, and its role in this field has gradually expanded since then. The foundations for the EU's activities in this field were laid by the Maastricht Treaty on European Union, which entered into force on 1 November 1993.[74] This treaty established the EU, which was founded on the European Communities (established in the 1950s), supplemented by the Common Foreign and Security Policy (CFSP) and provisions on Justice and Home Affairs. The CFSP included all foreign policy and security issues but, when it came to decisions and actions of the EU having defence implications, it had to ask the Western European Union (WEU), which became an integral part of the development of the EU, to elaborate and implement these decisions.[75] In its 19 June 1992 Bonn Ministerial 'Petersberg Declaration', the WEU for its part had adopted the so-called "Petersberg tasks": 'military units of WEU Member States, acting under the authority of WEU, could be employed for: - humanitarian and rescue tasks; - peacekeeping tasks; - tasks of combat forces in crisis management, including peacemaking'. Under these provisions and EU–WEU arrangements adopted pursuant thereto, the EU administered the Bosnian city of Mostar,[76] and at the EU's request the WEU conducted a police operation in support of this administration.[77] The WEU also conducted three further operations at the request of the

---

[73] An overview of Peace Operations deployed by the AU can be found in *African Union Handbook 2016*, 3rd edn (AU, 2016), pp. 60–64.

[74] Signed on 7 February 1992, OJ 1992 No. C224, 31 August 1992, p. 1.

[75] One crisis management operation had already been undertaken before the Maastricht Treaty: the European Community Monitoring Mission (ECMM) in the former Yugoslavia, which was established by a Memorandum of Understanding signed on 13 July 1991. It would later evolve into the EU Monitoring Mission (see Council Joint Action 2000/811/CFSP of 22 December 2000 on the European Union Monitoring Mission, OJ 2000 No. L328, 23 December 2000, p. 53) and was terminated on 31 December 2007.

[76] See inter alia Council Decision 94/790/CFSP of 12 December 1994 concerning the Joint Action, adopted by the Council on the basis of Article J.3 of the Treaty on European Union, on Continued Support for European Union Administration of the Town of Mostar, OJ 1994 No. L326, 17 December 1994, p. 2.

[77] See WEU, 'History of WEU: Operational Role', www.weu.int/History.htm#4A.

EU: a "security surveillance mission" in Kosovo,[78] a demining mission in Croatia[79] and a Multinational Advisory Police Element in Albania.[80]

23. Subsequently, the Treaty of Amsterdam, which entered into force on 1 May 1999,[81] strengthened the CFSP, including as regards security and defence. In particular, it enabled the EU to conduct crisis management operations itself, without recourse to the WEU. Article 17(2) of the Treaty on European Union as amended provided that '[q]uestions referred to in this Article shall include humanitarian and rescue tasks, peacekeeping tasks and tasks of combat forces in crisis management, including peacemaking', thus incorporating the WEU "Petersberg tasks". On this basis, the European Council in 1999 (in Cologne in June and in Helsinki in December) launched the European Security and Defence Policy (ESDP). Once the necessary institutional and other arrangements were put in place to support this policy, which included the transfer of some WEU structures and arrangements with NATO,[82] the EU started to conduct military and civilian crisis management operations in 2003. These developments were consolidated and affirmed in the Treaty of Nice, which entered into force on 1 February 2003.[83]

24. The ESDP was renamed Common Security and Defence Policy (CSDP) by the Treaty of Lisbon, which entered into force on 1 December 2009[84] and significantly reinforced this policy. The EU

---

[78] See WEU, 'History of WEU: Crisis Management Operations (1997–2001)', www.weu.int/ History.htm#5; Council Decision 98/646/CFSP of 13 November 1998 adopted on the basis of Article J.4(2) of the Treaty on European Union, on the Monitoring of the Situation in Kosovo, OJ 1998 No. L308, 18 November 1998, p. 1.

[79] See WEU (n. 78) and inter alia Council Decision 98/627/CFSP of 9 November 1998 adopted on the basis of Article J.3 of the Treaty on European Union concerning a Specific Action of the Union in the field of Assistance for Mine Clearance, OJ 1998 No. L300, 11 November 1998, p. 1.

[80] See WEU (n. 78) and inter alia Council Decision 1999/190/CFSP of 9 March 1999 adopted on the basis of Article J.4(2) of the Treaty on European Union on the implementation of the Joint Action concerning a Contribution by the European Union to the Re-establishment of a Viable Police Force in Albania, OJ 1999 No. L63, 12 March 1999, p. 3.

[81] Treaty of Amsterdam amending the Treaty on European Union, the Treaties establishing the European Communities and Certain Related Acts, 2 October 1997, OJ 1997 No. C340, 10 November 1997, p. 1.

[82] On EU–NATO relations, see e.g. F. Naert, 'EU Crisis Management Operations and Their Relations with NATO Operations', in S. L. Bumgardner, Z. Hegedüs and D. Palmer-DeGreve (eds.), NATO Legal Deskbook, 2nd edn (NATO, 2010), pp. 281–300.

[83] Treaty of Nice amending the Treaty on European Union, the Treaties establishing the European Communities and Certain Related Acts, 26 February 2001, OJ 2001 No. C80, 10 March 2001, p. 1.

[84] Treaty of Lisbon amending the Treaty on European Union and the Treaty establishing the European Community, 13 December 2007, OJ 2007 No. C306, 17 December 2007, p. 1. For the latest consolidated version of the Treaty on European Union and the Treaty on the Functioning of the European Union, see OJ 2016 No. C202, 7 June 2016, respectively p. 13 and p. 47.

has continued to conduct military and civilian crisis management operations under the CSDP: since 2003, it has conducted some thirty such operations.[85]

25. *NATO* is an active contributor to peace and security on the international stage. With the end of the Cold War in the early 1990s came great changes to the international security environment. The Alliance witnessed the emergence of new threats, and with these changing conditions came new responsibilities. From being an exclusively defensive alliance for nearly half a century, NATO began to assume an increasingly proactive role within the international community.

26. NATO conducted its first major crisis response operation in Bosnia and Herzegovina. With the break-up of Yugoslavia, violent conflict started in Bosnia and Herzegovina in April 1992. The Alliance responded as early as summer 1992 when it enforced the UN arms embargo on weapons in the Adriatic Sea and enforced a no-fly zone declared by the UN Security Council. With the signing of the Dayton Peace Accord in December 1995, NATO immediately deployed a UN-mandated Implementation Force (IFOR) comprising some 60,000 troops to implement the military aspects of the Dayton Peace Agreement. This operation (Operation Joint Endeavour) was followed in December 1996 by the deployment of a 32,000-strong Stabilisation Force (SFOR) which helped to maintain a secure environment and facilitate the country's reconstruction in the wake of the 1992–1995 war. In light of the improved security situation, NATO brought its peace-support operation to a conclusion in December 2004, and the EU deployed a new force called Operation Althea.

27. NATO has been leading a peace-support operation in Kosovo since June 1999 in support of wider international efforts to build peace and stability in the area. KFOR was established when NATO's 78-day air campaign against the regime of Slobodan Milošević, aimed at putting an end to violence in Kosovo, was over. The operation derives its mandate from United Nations Security Council Resolution 1244 (1999) and the

---

[85] The number depends to some extent on how one counts, including whether successor operations are counted as distinct ones and whether or not supporting and co-ordinating actions, such as EU NAVCO and EUCO Haiti, are included. See e.g. F. Naert, 'ESDP in Practice: Increasingly Varied and Ambitious EU Security and Defence Operations', in M. Trybus and N. White (eds.), *European Security Law* (Oxford University Press, 2007), pp. 61–101; F. Naert, *International Law Aspects of the EU's Security and Defence Policy, with a Particular Focus on the Law of Armed Conflict and Human Rights* (Intersentia, 2010), pp. 97–191. For an overview of current EU operations, see European Union External Action Service, https://eeas.europa.eu/headquarters/headquarters-homepage/area/security-and-defence_en.

Military-Technical Agreement between NATO, the Federal Republic of Yugoslavia and Serbia. KFOR's original objectives were to deter renewed hostilities, establish a secure environment and ensure public safety and order, demilitarise the Kosovo Liberation Army, support the international humanitarian effort and co-ordinate with the international civil presence.

28. In fact, following the operations in the Balkans, in April 1999 during a summit of the Heads of State and Government of the NATO Nations in Washington, DC, an updated Strategic Concept was approved. This committed the Alliance not only to the defence of its members but also to peace and stability in its region and periphery. It thus broadly defined two types of NATO military operations: Article 5 Collective Defence Operations and Non-Article 5 Crisis Response Operations (NA5CROs). Peace Operations are continually developing within the context of NA5CROs. Such operations are designed to tackle the complex emergencies and robust challenges posed by collapsed or collapsing States in an uncertain and evolving strategic environment. Peace Operations are conducted impartially, normally in support of an internationally recognised organisation, such as the UN.

29. Following Kosovo's declaration of independence in February 2008, NATO agreed that it would continue to maintain its presence on the basis of UN Security Council Resolution 1244. It has since helped to create a professional and multi-ethnic Kosovo Security Force, which is a lightly armed force responsible for security tasks that are not appropriate for the police. Today, KFOR continues to contribute towards maintaining a safe and secure environment in Kosovo and freedom of movement for all. Approximately 4,500 Allied and partner troops operate in Kosovo as part of NATO's Kosovo Force (KFOR).

30. Well beyond the Euro-Atlantic region, the Alliance also supports the AU in its peacekeeping missions on the African continent. Since June 2007, NATO has assisted the AU Mission in Somalia (AMISOM) by providing airlift support for AU peacekeepers.

PART II

Applicable Legal Framework for Conducting Peace Operations and How the Regimes Relate to Each Other

3

The Mandate

3.1 **Every Peace Operation requires a mandate to provide a legal basis for the operation and set out the objectives and legal and operational parameters which govern the operation. A mandate can be issued by a competent international organisation or by a Host State government inviting or consenting to a Peace Operation conducted by a competent international organisation on its territory, and in most cases will be a combination of both.**

1. Peace Operations for the purposes of this Manual[1] which are conducted by the UN always operate on the basis of a mandate issued by the Security Council in addition to consent by the Host State. Most Peace Operations as defined in this Manual which are conducted by regional organisations or arrangements will also operate on the basis of a Security Council mandate in combination with Host State consent. However, in some cases, notably when an operation does not involve the proposed use of force beyond personal self-defence, a mandate will not be sought from the Security Council, and the consent of the Host State and related agreement(s) between the Host State and the regional organisation or arrangement conducting the Peace Operation will serve as the mandate. Since this Manual is focused upon operations which are based upon consent of the Host State, this signifies that the mandate issued by the Security Council will, barring exceptional circumstances, be based on this consent and the two will complement each other.

2. Any mandate for the conducting of Peace Operations will have two main functions: first, to provide a legal basis in the absence of continued consent or to complement Host State consent when it has been granted as an additional legal basis for the operation; and second to set out mission objectives and tasks, which will explicitly or implicitly include

---

[1] See Chapter 1.

the parameters for the use of force within the context of the mission. There are no set rules for the formulation of a Security Council mandate, but they tend to follow a general pattern which normally starts with a summary of the reasons for undertaking the mission and which recalls any previous resolutions or other relevant decisions which could serve as a motivation and justification in political terms for the mission. Thereafter the mandate will generally state whether the mission is undertaken in co-operation with and with the consent of the Host State, determining whether all or certain tasks and objectives are to be undertaken on the basis of an authorisation under Chapter VII of the Charter to use 'all necessary means' (or similar wording) to carry out those tasks so enumerated and what the objectives and related tasks and authorisations entrusted to the mission comprise. To the extent a mandate is issued on the basis of Chapter VII, it will include a determination that the situation in question constitutes a threat to international peace and security.

3. Mandates authorising the use of force beyond self-defence will normally be authorised by the Security Council in order to provide an unequivocal legal basis for such force, notwithstanding the fact that a Host State is entitled under international law to consent to the use of force on its territory as long as such force is employed in accordance with international law. An additional reason for this is more political and practical than legal in nature in that many States will not participate in a mission involving the use of force beyond personal self-defence in the absence of a Security Council authorisation to do so. As stated earlier, all UN Peace Operations are conducted on the basis of a mandate issued by the Security Council irrespective of whether force beyond self-defence is authorised or anticipated. However, in some civilian and training missions conducted by regional organisations and arrangements, there will be little likelihood of force beyond self-defence being used, and these operations are consequently not necessarily dependent upon or conducted on the basis of a mandate issued by the Security Council, but will instead be based on the terms of agreement reached with the Host State.

4. A mandate by a regional organisation will, in addition to reflecting the agreement reached with the Host State to deploy civilian or military personnel on that State's territory to carry out agreed tasks, also have to be carried out in conformity with the regional organisation's internal rules and procedures and will have to be authorised by the competent authority of that organisation.[2]

---

[2] See Chapter 4.

3.2 In addition to consent by the Host State, a mandate issued by the Security Council will complement and provide an additional legal basis alongside such consent for conducting a Peace Operation. If the mandate was adopted under Chapter VII of the UN Charter, it will prevail over any terms set by the Host State in consenting to the operation.

1. Host State consent precludes any wrongfulness attached to the deployment of troops and other personnel onto its territory and can include authorisation to conduct operations, including operations involving the use of force independently of, or in co-operation with, the Host State's authorities. Such consent must conform to the requirements under international law for the issuing of valid consent. These include the requirement that any consent must be freely given without any form of coercion or threat of force, the requirement that the consent is granted by an organ of the State authorised under national and international law to grant such consent and the requirement that consent may not be presumed. Moreover, any consent granted may be subject to conditions and may be withdrawn.[3]

2. Whenever such consent has been lawfully granted, the Security Council part of the mandate will serve as an additional legal basis and normally will correspond to and complement such consent. In the event a mandate has been adopted under Chapter VII of the Charter, it will prevail over any conflicting conditions applied by the Host State and may set out objectives and authorisation for the use of force which are not covered by the consent. This flows from the powers vested in the Security Council under the UN Charter and the primacy of the Security Council in the maintenance and restoration of international peace and security. It will additionally prevail over any other obligations arising from international treaties that conflict with the UN Charter.[4] The limitations upon the Security Council are those set out in article 24 of the UN Charter, which require it to act in conformity with the purposes and principles of the Charter; these include peremptory rules of international law.[5]

---

[3] Art. 20 Articles on State Responsibility, with Commentaries, in ILC, 'Report of the International Law Commission on the Work of Its 53rd Session', II (2) *Yearbook of the International Law Commission* (2001), pp. 72–74.

[4] Arts. 24 and 103 UN Charter.

[5] See e.g. E. de Wet, *The Chapter VII Powers of the United Nations Security Council* (Hart, 2004), pp. 187–191; T. D. Gill, 'Legal and Some Political Limitations on the Power of the UN Security Council to Exercise Its Enforcement Powers Under Chapter VII of the Charter', 26 *Netherlands Yearbook of International Law* (1995), pp. 72 *et seq.*

Additionally, before action can be undertaken by the Security Council it must be adopted by the requisite majority of its members in accordance with article 27 of the Charter. This can impose practical limitations upon the Security Council's ability to take action, particularly in the absence of consent on the part of the Host State.

3.3   In the absence of consent by the Host State, a mandate issued by the Security Council under Chapter VII of the UN Charter is a strict legal requirement for the deployment of troops and other personnel onto a State's territory to conduct a Peace Operation. This applies irrespective of whether the operation is conducted by the UN directly, by a regional organisation or arrangement or by individual States operating independently of the UN or any other organisation, but with the authorisation of the Security Council.

1. This Rule is axiomatic and flows from both the UN Charter and from customary international law prohibiting the use of force in international relations, prohibiting armed intervention by any State on the territory of any other State, regulating the use of enforcement measures under the UN Charter and safeguarding the territorial integrity and political independence of all States. It has the status of a jus cogens rule of both a conventional and a customary nature. It applies to any non-consensual deployment as well as any non-consensual use of force for any purpose, aside from the lawful exercise of self-defence. It is abundantly supported by UN and State practice and is well established in legal doctrine and judicial decisions.[6]

2. Article 53 of the Charter predicates the exercise of any enforcement measures by a regional organisation or arrangement upon the authorisation of such action by the Security Council. This is complemented by article 24 of the Charter which attributes primary responsibility for the maintenance and restoration of international peace and security to the Security Council. Article 53 does not specifically state that authorisation must precede any exercise of enforcement measures by a regional

---

[6] Art. 2(4) UN Charter provides: 'All Members shall refrain in their international relations from the threat or use of force against the territorial integrity or political independence of any State, or in any other manner inconsistent with the Purposes of the United Nations.' The peremptory nature of the prohibition has been affirmed by the International Law Commission; see II *Yearbook of the International Law Commission* (1966), p. 247. Cf. *Military and Paramilitary Activities in and against Nicaragua (Nicaragua* v. *United States of America)*, Merits, ICJ Reports 1986, 14, para. 190.

organisation or arrangement, but it implies that this is required, or at the least would be the normal course of action which should be followed in the absence of exceptional circumstances. If the Security Council were subsequently to endorse a Peace Operation which included elements of peace enforcement and which had been initiated by a regional organisation or arrangement, as has occurred on certain occasions, this would arguably erase or at the least mitigate any unlawfulness pertaining to the initial deployment and would in any event qualify as an authorisation for future action within the context of article 53 of the Charter.[7]

3. If no such endorsement were to be forthcoming, any non-consensual deployment and/or use of force by a regional organisation or arrangement, or by one or more States acting on their own volition, would be ipso facto illegal and would constitute a breach of the aforementioned prohibitions of the use of force and of intervention, unless it could be justified as a lawful measure of self-defence.

3.4 Peace Operations are, in addition to the terms and conditions imposed by the mandate, always required to act in conformity with all relevant and applicable rules of international law and to respect Host State law in so far as it is compatible with international law and with the mandate. In addition, Troop Contributing Countries will require their forces to comply with relevant portions of their national law.

1. While a Security Council resolution provides, or complements consent as, the legal basis of an operation and sets out mission objectives, often emphasising the requirement to conduct the operation in conformity with specific areas of international law, this duty exists independently of any mandate and will apply in any situation where a specific body of international law is relevant and applicable to a particular organisation or State on the basis of the legal and factual conditions relating to its applicability. International law will apply to any State or other subject

---

[7] Art. 53 UN Charter is generally seen as requiring prior authorisation for the taking of any enforcement measures by a regional organisation or arrangement. See e.g. C. Walter, 'Article 53', in B. Simma, D. E. Khan, G. Nolte and A. Paulus (eds.), *The Charter of the United Nations: A Commentary*, 3rd edn, 2 vols. (Oxford University Press, 2012), vol. II, pp. 1500–1505; E. P. J. Myjer and N. D. White, 'Peace Operations Conducted by Regional Organizations and Arrangements', in T. D. Gill and D. Fleck (eds.), *The Handbook of the International Law of Military Operations*, 2nd edn (Oxford University Press, 2015), p. 206. Examples include the subsequent authorisation of intervention by the Economic Community of West African States (ECOWAS) in Sierra Leone and Liberia in the period between 1990 and 1998 and again in 2003 in Sierra Leone.

of international law conducting a peace enforcement or Peace Operation whenever a number of preconditions are met. First, the rule must be binding upon and thus applicable to that particular State or organisation. Second, the body of law in question must be applicable to a particular situation or activity in the context of the mission. While conventional rules will apply only to the parties to that treaty, customary law will, in principle, bind all subjects of international law to which it can be applied. For example, the UN is not party to any international human rights law (IHRL) or international humanitarian law (IHL) treaties as an organisation, but as a subject of international law is bound by customary international law.[8] States participating in a particular mission will be bound by those IHRL and IHL treaties to which they are party and which are applicable in factual and legal terms to a particular situation or activity undertaken within the context of the operation, alongside any applicable rules of customary law. For example, IHL, both conventional and customary, will become applicable if the threshold conditions relating to its applicability, namely the existence of an armed conflict to which the mission is party, should arise.[9] Likewise, IHRL of either a conventional and/or customary nature will, in principle, apply to situations in which effective control or jurisdiction is exercised over either persons or territory.[10]

2. There is a general duty to respect Host State law in so far as it is compatible with international law and with the terms of any mandate issued under Chapter VII of the Charter, notwithstanding any privileges and immunities enjoyed by the mission and its personnel under relevant agreements with the Host State or under customary international law. This would include IHRL obligations to which the Host State is subject.[11]

3. Finally, States will require their armed forces to comply with the relevant national law of the Sending State, including its (military) criminal, legal and disciplinary rules and procedures.[12] The UN as an organisation accepting troops for Peace Operations as well as the Host State require from their side that the Troop Contributing Countries

---

[8] The legal subjectivity of the United Nations was affirmed in *Reparation for Injuries Suffered in the Service of the United Nations*, Advisory Opinion, ICJ Reports 1949, 174. The legal position of international organisations was reaffirmed in *Interpretation of the Agreement of 25 March 1951 between the WHO and Egypt*, Advisory Opinion, ICJ Reports 1980, 73, para. 37. See also Chapter 4.

[9] See Chapter 6.

[10] See Chapter 5

[11] See Chapter 9.

[12] See Chapter 10.

(TCCs) be able to enforce disciplinary and criminal laws on their personnel. The UN does so through the Memorandums of Understanding
(MOUs) concluded with TCCs,[13] and the Host State will generally try to
secure this through the Status of Forces (SOFA) and Status of Mission
(SOMA) Agreements.[14]

---

[13] See Chapter 11.
[14] See Chapter 8.

4

Organisation-Specific Legal Framework and Procedures

4.1 INTRODUCTION

1. The applicable legal framework for an international or regional organisation or arrangement to conduct a Peace Operation consists of the legal basis on the one hand and legal regimes on the other. Part of the legal basis and legal regimes can be analysed in an organisation-specific manner as explained in this chapter. This introductory sub-chapter outlines the requirement for Peace Operations to be grounded in, and act in accordance with, international law and the internal laws of the organisation or arrangement wishing to undertake Peace Operations. Sub-chapter 4.2 describes how authority and control over personnel and assets are divided between the UN or regional organisations or arrangements on one hand, and Troop Contributing Countries (TCCs) on the other. The remaining sub-chapters address the internal decision-making process and legal bases for Peace Operations undertaken by the AU (sub-chapter 4.3), EU (4.4), NATO (4.5) and selected sub-regional organisations (4.6).

4.1.1 Every Peace Operation conducted by an organisation or arrangement must have a legal basis in international law and in the internal law of the organisation.

1. As Peace Operations constitute a (physical) intervention in the Host State, they require a legal basis in international law. This is the case for international and regional organisations or arrangements as well as for States.

2. Furthermore, as international and regional organisations or arrangements do not have all of the powers that States have but only

those powers that are allocated to them by their Member States, Peace Operations must also have a legal basis in their internal law.[1]

4.1.2   The competent organ of an organisation or arrangement shall determine the mandate of a Peace Operation conducted by that organisation or arrangement.

1. While each organisation or arrangement is different, they all have in common that the conduct by it of a Peace Operation requires a mandate from that organisation, which must be adopted by its competent organ. This "internal" mandate must respect the "external" mandate under international law, which will normally be a UN Security Council resolution and/or Host State consent.[2]

2. As explained in Chapter 3, Peace Operations undertaken by the UN are always based on a Security Council resolution in addition to consent by the Host State.[3] For such Peace Operations the Security Council resolution provides at the same time the "internal" as well as the "external" mandate. However, Peace Operations undertaken by regional organisations or arrangements require a separate (internal) mandate. The latter is provided by the competent organ of such an organisation or arrangement. As far as the AU, EU, NATO and selected sub-regional organisations are concerned, sub-chapters 4.3 to 4.6 set out which organ that is.

4.1.3   The UN as well as regional organisations or arrangements shall set up and conduct their Peace Operations in accordance with the UN Charter, their internal rules and procedures, and other rules of international law applicable to them.

1. The UN Charter includes a Chapter VIII entitled 'Regional Arrangements', which recognises a role for regional arrangements or agencies. The key principle laid down in article 52(1) of the UN Charter is that '[n]othing in the present Charter precludes the existence of regional arrangements or agencies for dealing with such matters relating to the maintenance of international peace and security as are appropriate

---

[1] For the purposes of this chapter, internal law includes that of regional arrangements that do not have international legal personality. In such cases it includes the international agreement(s) on which that arrangement is based and any other legal instruments applicable to it.

[2] See Chapter 3.

[3] See Rule 3.1.

for regional action, provided that such arrangements or agencies and their activities are consistent with the Purposes and Principles of the United Nations'.

2. For a considerable period of time, the notion of 'regional arrangements or agencies' under article 52(1) of the Charter (as well as articles 53 and 54) was given a restrictive meaning, and only a handful of regional organisations were regarded as falling within its scope or claimed that status themselves.

3. However, since the 1990s this has been overtaken by a very pragmatic approach by the UN towards the role which regional organisations may play in the field of peace and security. In particular, the Security Council has authorised, welcomed or otherwise positively referred to the role and actions of a very wide range of regional organisations, and even other international organisations that do not have a regional scope. Moreover, it has usually done so without mentioning Chapter VIII of the UN Charter.[4]

4. For example, article 53(1) of the UN Charter provides that '[t]he Security Council shall, where appropriate, utilise such regional arrangements or agencies for enforcement action under its authority. But no enforcement action shall be taken under regional arrangements or by regional agencies without the authorisation of the Security Council'. Yet such authorisations can just as well be given under Chapter VII, which has in fact been the Chapter under which the Security Council has authorised action by regional organisations and arrangements.[5]

5. The part of the Rule stating that organisations and arrangements may conduct Peace Operations in accordance with the UN Charter and with the rules of international law that apply to them reflects that there must be a basis under international law for each operation (see also Rule 4.1.1 and 4.1.2). Furthermore, it also covers any international law applicable to the conduct of a Peace Operation. The details as to the law applicable to Peace Operations, and the interaction between these legal regimes, are addressed in other chapters. However, the underlying principle requires some general consideration here. International law was and still is mainly made by and applies to States. Indeed, while provisions

---

[4] M. Bothe, 'Peacekeeping', in B. Simma, D. E. Khan, G. Nolte and A. Paulus (eds.), *The Charter of the United Nations: A Commentary*, 3rd edn, 2 vols. (Oxford University Press, 2012), vol. I, p. 1192; C. Walter, 'Introduction to Chapter VIII', *Ibid.*, vol. II, pp. 1443–1444.

[5] For example, UNSC Res. 2134 (2014), paras. 29 *juncto* 43 and following (mandating the EU to deploy an operation in the Central African Republic).

of their constitutive acts (e.g. on respect for the UN Charter and/or for human rights) and in mission-specific agreements (such as Status of Forces Agreements (SOFAs) or agreements with TCCs) may require international or regional organisations to respect certain rules of international law, they are rarely party to international agreements governing substantive areas of international law,[6] such as international human rights law (IHRL) or international humanitarian law (IHL) (by way of exception, the EU is a party to some such agreements).[7] However, it is widely accepted that international organisations, including regional organisations or arrangements,[8] are bound by rules of customary international law that are relevant to their activities, at least to the extent that they are capable of being applied to or by them.[9] While there may be discussion over the consequences of this in relation to some rules, there can be no doubt that the customary law rules of the legal bases and legal regimes for Peace Operations under international law are among those that apply to international organisations.

6. Each international or regional organisation can furthermore act only within the scope of its competences and in accordance with its internal rules. The sub-chapters that follow address this in relation to the AU, EU and NATO, as well as selected sub-regional organisations. These organisations are, however, not the only ones which may conduct Peace Operations, and for other organisations or arrangements their internal rules will have to be consulted.

7. Each organisation has put in place specific rules and procedures to organise the planning, initiating and conduct of Peace Operations. A summary of these rules and procedures for the UN, AU, EU and NATO was made available to the Group of Experts who prepared this Manual and can be found in Appendices IV to VII to this Manual. Mandating a regional organisation involves planning, start-up and decision-making by the organisation. These must take place alongside work at the level of the Security Council and/or Host State. Hybrid operations and

---

[6] Moreover, regional arrangements without legal personality simply cannot become parties thereto.

[7] See e.g. Chapter 5.

[8] Provided that they have their own international legal personality; otherwise they amount to collective action by the States that are parties to such an arrangement.

[9] See *Interpretation of the Agreement of 25 March 1951 between the WHO and Egypt*, Advisory Opinion, ICJ Reports 1980, 73, para. 37: 'International organizations are subjects of international law and, as such, are bound by any obligations incumbent upon them under general rules of international law, under their constitutions or under international agreements to which they are parties.'

scenarios of close co-operation between two Peace Operations require specific arrangements to co-ordinate efforts.

4.1.4   Regional organisations or arrangements within the meaning of Chapter VIII of the UN Charter shall report to the Security Council on their Peace Operations. All regional organisations or arrangements shall report to the Security Council on their Peace Operations if so required by the Security Council or by their own internal rules. Mandates issued by the Security Council for Peace Operations conducted by regional organisations or arrangements should contain clear reporting duties to the Security Council. In other cases they should report to the Security Council on their Peace Operations as appropriate.

1. The obligation to report Peace Operations to the Security Council follows from article 54 of the UN Charter, which provides that '[t]he Security Council shall at all times be kept fully informed of activities undertaken or in contemplation under regional arrangements or by regional agencies for the maintenance of international peace and security'.[10] While this obligation is addressed to UN Member States, it is reasonable to assume that it is, at least indirectly, also of concern to international organisations falling within the meaning of Chapter VIII of the UN Charter.[11] The obligation to report pertains to the decision to undertake a Peace Operation and its follow-up, but also the contemplation of such activities, i.e. information concerning the motives and plans in advance of the commencement of the operation.[12] The regional organisation or arrangement can undertake the reporting obligation through the submission of the texts of important resolutions or of summary records of meetings, or by the presentation of oral reports in the Security Council.[13]

2. Apart from, and without prejudice to, the UN Charter, the obligation to report to the Security Council may also result from the binding character of Security Council resolutions; where they require reporting, this has to be respected. In case a Security Council resolution merely

---

[10] Art. 54 UN Charter.
[11] C. Walter, 'Article 54', in Simma, Khan, Nolte and Paulus (n. 4), p. 1528.
[12] *Ibid.*, p. 1527.
[13] The annual consultative meetings between the UN Security Council and the AU Peace and Security Council (see Report of the UN Secretary-General on United Nations–African Union Cooperation in Peace and Security, UN Doc. S/2011/805 (2011), para. 6) may provide an appropriate platform to report on matters for the purposes of art. 54 UN Charter.

calls for reporting, this should also be followed. Furthermore, the obligation to report to the Security Council may also follow from the regional organisation's or arrangement's own internal rules. In these circumstances it must be borne in mind that reporting obligations flowing from the UN Charter and Security Council resolutions prevail over any conflicting reporting duties imposed by the regional organisation's or arrangement's own rules.[14]

3. The practice of the UN Security Council shows some variation in the area of reporting by regional arrangements. For example, while Security Council Resolution 2033 (2012) stresses the need for the AU and African sub-regional organisations to keep the Council fully informed 'at all times' of their efforts to settle efforts on the African conflict in accordance with article 54 of the UN Charter,[15] the reporting requirements in resolutions concerning specific regional Peace Operations have used other formulae, some time-specific and others open-ended, such as 'regularly', 'every 60 days' and 'quarterly reports'.[16] Other modalities of reporting, such as the form of delivery and topics covered, should be stipulated in the mandate. Therefore, mandates issued by the Security Council for Peace Operations conducted by regional organisations or arrangements should contain clear reporting duties to the Security Council. This will allow the Security Council, which has the 'primary responsibility for the maintenance of international peace and security',[17] to better fulfil its intended supervisory role. Nevertheless, prior practice shows that the reporting obligation is not always strictly complied with, especially for measures in contemplation, and that the Security Council may to some extent be said to have acquiesced in this regard.[18]

4. The final part of this Rule reflects that in all other cases the organisation or arrangement conducting a Peace Operation can decide at its own discretion whether it wishes to report to the Security Council on that operation.[19] It should do so where appropriate.[20]

---

[14] Arts. 103 *juncto* 25 and 54 UN Charter.

[15] UNSC Res. 2033 (2012), preambular para. 8.

[16] Repertoire of the Practice of the Security Council, Regional Arrangements (Chapter VIII), D (Regional Peacekeeping Operations), www.un.org/en/sc/repertoire/regional_arrangements.shtml.

[17] Art. 24(1) UN Charter.

[18] Walter (n. 11), p. 1533.

[19] E.g. the EU does not report to the Security Council on Peace Operations based on Host State consent that are not based on a UN Security Council mandate.

[20] For any use of force by armed forces outside their territory, the UN Security Council may have an interest, even if it occurs in the framework of a purely consent-based Peace Operation.

4.1.5 Peace Operations conducted by regional organisations and arrangements remain distinct from the UN. When distinct Peace Operations conducted by a regional organisation or arrangement and the UN work alongside one another, co-operation arrangements should be put in place.

1. A regional organisation or arrangement is a distinct entity from the UN. The fact that a Peace Operation conducted by such an organisation or arrangement may be authorised by the Security Council and/or that such an organisation or arrangement may be under an obligation to report to the Security Council does not in any way diminish this. Therefore, in principle,[21] the actions of such an organisation or arrangement are legally attributable to it (and/or participating States) and not to the UN. Consequently, a Peace Operation conducted by a (sub-)regional organisation remains distinct from the UN despite formal links such as authorisation and reporting duties. This has legal ramifications in several areas, such as international accountability and responsibility[22] and the handling of claims.[23]

2. When distinct Peace Operations conducted by a regional organisation or arrangement and the UN work alongside one another, co-operation arrangements should be concluded. This would generally be addressed between the UN Force Commander and his/her counterpart.[24]

---

[21] The situation is more complicated in the case of a hybrid Peace Operation conducted jointly by the UN and a regional organisation or arrangement.

[22] See Chapter 19.

[23] See Chapter 20.

[24] E. P. J. Myjer and N. D. White, 'Peace Operations Conducted by Regional Organizations and Arrangements', in T. D. Gill and D. Fleck (eds.), *The Handbook of the International Law of Military Operations*, 2nd edn (Oxford University Press, 2015), p. 178.

4.2   COMMAND AND CONTROL

4.2.1   The command arrangements which are employed in a Peace Operation are provided for by the organisation which has undertaken to perform the Peace Operation. Peace Operations involve the partial transfer of authority and/or control from a Troop Contributing Country to the UN or to the regional organisation or arrangement which is undertaking the Peace Operation. Generally, operational command or operational control will be transferred, while full command (national command) and administrative control are retained by the Troop Contributing Country. The partial transfer of authority may include certain caveats or restrictions upon the use of the Troop Contributing Country's personnel or assets for the execution of particular tasks within the Peace Operation.

1. While there is no single encompassing definition of command and control (C2 in military parlance), in C2 doctrine, to which NATO is the main contributor,[25] it relates to the authority vested in certain individuals (or bodies) to direct the actions and exercise authority over (elements of) assigned resources, such as members of and materiel owned by the armed forces.[26] An identifiable C2 structure is imperative for the efficient conduct of any Peace Operation. The command arrangements which are employed in a Peace Operation are provided for by the organisation which is undertaking the Peace Operation. While the C2 structure does not differ in general terms among the different organisations, the specific meaning and scope attached to the different levels of command and control can vary.

2. Generally, a multi-layered C2 structure is set in place by the organisation conducting the Peace Operation, meaning a level of "full or national command", a level of "operational command and control" (OPCOM and OPCON), a level of "tactical command and control" (TACOM and TACON) and a level of "administrative control" (ADCON).

Full or national command relates to the authority of the Troop Contributing Country (TCC) and any person duly designated by the appropriate national authority as possessing full command over part or all of that State's armed forces to exercise authority over the armed forces.

---

[25] See NATO, Glossary of Terms and Definitions, AAP-06 (2016).

[26] *Ibid.*, 2-C-8 and 2-C-13; EU Concept for Military Command and Control, EU Council Doc. 5008/15 (2015), p. 28; Draft Guidelines for Command and Control Structure for EU Civilian Operations in Crisis Management, EU Council Doc. 9919/07 EXT 2 (2008), p. 3.

Exercising full command includes the ability to decide whether forces will be allocated for a particular mission, to determine if such allocation will be discontinued and the mission terminated, and to issue orders and instructions to subordinates.[27] Full command encompasses all aspects of military operations and administration and includes plenary authority over the armed forces.[28] Full command exists only at the national level and cannot be delegated to an organisation as it is based on an organic link between the State and its armed forces.

OPCOM is the authority granted to a commander to assign missions or tasks to subordinate commanders, to deploy units, to reassign forces and to retain or delegate such OPCON and/or TACON as the commander deems necessary.[29] It does not include administrative or disciplinary authority over the troops under operational command. *OPCON* involves the authority delegated to a commander to direct forces assigned so that the commander may accomplish specific missions or tasks which are usually limited by function, time or location; to deploy units concerned; and to retain or assign tactical control of those units.[30]

TACOM relates to the authority of a designated tactical level commander to exercise authority over individuals, teams and units or a combination of the former under his/her command to achieve specific tasks or missions assigned by a higher authority. *TACON* is the detailed direction and control of movements and manoeuvres at the local level in order to carry out specific tasks assigned by a higher authority.[31]

ADCON is the direction or exercise of authority over subordinate or other organisations in respect of administrative matters, including disciplinary and jurisdictional authority.[32]

3. *Strategic level of authority.* Within the organisation that has undertaken the Peace Operation, there exists a strategic level of authority which directs and controls the operation and provides political and military strategic guidance as to the mission's objectives.

UN. The Security Council has the ultimate strategic authority over all UN Peace Operations. Through the terms of the mandate, the Security

---

[27] T. D. Gill, 'Legal Aspects of the Transfer of Authority in UN Peace Operations', 42 *Netherlands Yearbook of International Law* (2011), pp. 37–68.

[28] NATO (n. 25), 2-F-7; EU Concept (n. 26), p. 28; EU Draft Guidelines (n. 26), pp. 4 and 7.

[29] NATO (n. 25), 2-O-3; EU Concept (n. 26), p. 28; EU Draft Guidelines (n. 26), pp. 4 and 5; AU, African Standby Force: Command and Control, Final Draft (2006), p. 2.

[30] See n. 29.

[31] NATO (n. 25), 2-T-2; EU Concept (n. 26), p. 28; EU Draft Guidelines (n. 26), p. 5; Draft AU Policy (n. 29), p. 2.

[32] NATO (n. 25), 2-A-3.

Council determines the overall objectives of the Peace Operation. Regarding UN-led Peace Operations, the UN Secretary-General is responsible for the administration and provision of its executive direction. The Secretary-General has delegated this responsibility to the Under-Secretary-General for Peacekeeping Operations (USG DPKO). The USG DPKO formulates policies and develops operational guidelines based on Security Council resolutions. Furthermore, the USG DPKO prepares reports of the Secretary-General to the Security Council on each Peace Operation with observations and recommendations, and advises the Secretary-General on all matters relating to the planning, establishment and conduct of UN Peace Operations.[33]

AU. The AU's Peace and Security Council (PSC AU) is the decision-making authority regarding AU Peace Operations. The PSC AU authorises the mandates of Peace Operations undertaken by the AU and is responsible for setting the overall political direction. The Military Staff Committee composed of senior military officers of the Members of the PSC AU serves as an advisory body to assist the PSC on military and security issues. On behalf of the PSC AU, the executive political direction and control of Peace Operations are exercised by the Chairperson of the AU Commission. The Chairperson has delegated this responsibility to the Commissioner for Peace and Security. The Commissioner and his/her staff of the Peace Support Operations Division formulate policies and operational guidelines based on PSC AU mandates and advise the Chairperson on matters related to the planning, conduct and sustainment of AU Peace Operations.[34]

EU. In EU Peace Operations, the Council has the overall responsibility for military and civilian crisis management operations, and it adopts the decisions to establish and launch these operations.[35] The Political and Security Committee (PSC EU), under the authority of the Council and of the High Representative of the Union for Foreign and Security Policy (High Representative), exercises the political control and strategic direction of EU-led military operations,[36] taking into account the advice of the EU Military Committee, the Committee for Civilian aspects of

---

[33] UN DPKO/DFS, Policy on Authority, Command and Control in United Nations Peacekeeping Operations, Ref. 2008.4, p. 6. See also P. C. Cammaert and B. F. Klappe, 'Authority, Command, and Control in United Nations-Led Peace Operations', in Gill and Fleck (n. 24), pp. 181–184.

[34] Draft AU Policy (n. 29), pp. 9–10 and Annexure C.

[35] See arts. 42 and 43 Treaty on European Union (Consolidated Version), OJ 2016 No. C202, 7 June 2016, p. 13.

[36] See *Ibid.*, art. 38.

Crisis Management and/or the Political Military Group.[37] The chain of command below this political level, as described later, is set out in EU policy documents and is laid down in the Council (legal) acts setting up each operation. So far, the EU does not have a standing military command structure. The EU will establish the chain of command for EU-led military Peace Operations on a case-by-case basis.[38] It has two basic options: autonomous EU-led military operations or EU-led military operations with recourse to NATO assets.[39] Irrespective of the option chosen, the commander at the strategic level will be the EU Operation Commander (OpCdr)[40] who is appointed and authorised by the Council or the PSC EU to conduct the operational planning at the military strategic level. This includes, inter alia, the development of the Concept of Operation, the Operational Plan (OPLAN) and Rules of Engagement (ROE).[41] The OpCdr will be given sufficient appropriate authority (e.g. OPCON and possibly OPCOM) over the national contingents.[42] The OpCdr is supported by the Operational Headquarters which is a static headquarters located outside the area of operations (AOO). If recourse is sought to NATO assets, Deputy Supreme Allied Commander Europe (DSACEUR) in a dual-hatted capacity is designated as OpCdr and the Operational Headquarters will be established at the premises of the Supreme Headquarters Allied Powers Europe (SHAPE).[43] However, it operates under EU political and military strategic control. Moreover, at the end of 2016 the High Representative was requested by the Council and the European Council to present proposals for a 'permanent operational planning and conduct capability at the strategic level for non-executive military missions' within the European External Action

---

[37] For military operations, see EU Concept (n. 26), p. 7. Political control is the setting of political and strategic objectives, while strategic direction concerns the translation of those objectives into guidance, enabling the military operation to be planned and conducted.

[38] EU Concept (n. 26), p. 10.

[39] This C2 option with recourse to NATO capabilities for C2 applies for an entire EU operation; the only caveat is that in such operations, under the Berlin plus arrangements, EU Member States that are not NATO Member States and not Partnership for Peace participants (and therefore have no security agreement with NATO) cannot participate in the implementation of such operations (currently only Cyprus falls into this category).

[40] Sometimes named Mission Commander, combining OpCdr and Force Commander functions.

[41] In a standard planning process, both a Concept of Operation and the Operation Plan are developed and approved. In case of a fast track planning process, it is possible that no Concept of Operation is developed. See Appendix VI.

[42] EU Concept (n. 26), pp. 8, 18 and 19.

[43] Ibid., p. 15.

Service (EEAS).[44] On 6 March 2017, the Council approved concrete measures proposed by the High Representative, in particular the setting up of a Military Planning and Conduct Capability (MPCC) within the EU Military Staff, which will be responsible at the strategic level for the operational planning and conduct of non-executive military missions. The Director General of the EU Military Staff will be the Director of the MPCC and will assume in that capacity (once the MPCC is fully operational) the functions of mission commander for the non-executive (i.e. training and/or advisory) military missions.[45] With regard to EU civilian crisis management missions, the commander at the strategic level is the Civilian Operation Commander (CivOpCdr). He/she acts under the political control and strategic direction of the PSC EU[46] and under the overall authority of the Council and the High Representative. The CivOpCdr is assisted by the Civilian Planning and Conduct Capability, which is part of the EEAS.

NATO. Within NATO, the North Atlantic Council (NAC) is the political decision-making body, which receives advice on military matters from the Military Committee and on the political aspects of military operations from the Operational Policy Committee. NATO has two strategic commands: Allied Command Operations (ACO) commanded by the Supreme Allied Commander Europe (SACEUR), and Allied Command Transformation (ACT) commanded by Supreme Allied Commander Transformation (SACT). Both commands report to the NAC through the Military Committee. When the NAC has decided to undertake a military mission, this formal decision will contain the designation of a NATO Commander. This will be SACEUR, who in turn through a Joint Force Command will direct the Theatre Commander. Member States of NATO participating in such a military operation follow a Transfer of Authority (TOA) process as outlined earlier.

---

[44] Council Conclusions on implementing the EU Global Strategy in the area of Security and Defence, EU Council Doc. 14149/16 (2016), para. 16(a), endorsed by European Council, Doc. EUCO 34/16 (2016), para. 11.

[45] Council Conclusions on progress in implementing the EU Global Strategy in the area of Security and Defence, EU Council Doc. 6875/17 (2017), para. 5; Concept Note: Operational Planning and Conduct Capabilities for CSDP Missions and Operations, EU Council Doc. 6881/17 (2017). Some further steps are required before these new command and control arrangements will be applied, including a revision of the terms of reference of the EU Military Staff and a Council Decision reflecting these new arrangements and amending the Council Decisions on the three existing non-executive missions on this point (the EU Training Missions in Somalia, Mali and the Central African Republic).

[46] EU Draft Guidelines (n. 26), p. 6.

4. The UN, AU, EU and NATO do not have military, police and/ or civilian contingents of their own, as such. It must be noted, though, that their international staff can be deployed in operations. As organisations, they are dependent upon the voluntary contribution of such forces by Member States of the organisation via the process of force generation or an equivalent manning process, as set out in Appendices IV to VII. As a result, TCCs transfer some authority (usually OPCOM/OPCON) to the UN or the organisation or arrangement undertaking the Peace Operation. Full command, meaning national command of a State over its armed forces which reflects its plenary authority over those armed forces, is always retained by the TCCs.[47] In addition, the force generation process may be complemented by the recruitment of (international consultant and/or local) contracted staff and contracting services.

5. In a Peace Operation, the level of C2 transferred to the organisation undertaking it is generally and in any case, at the most, that of OPCOM or OPCON. OPCOM or OPCON involves command over a specific (Peace) Operation within its area of deployment and the authority to assign tasks or missions to subordinate commanders. The transfer of OPCOM or OPCON is done through a formal instrument, e.g. a TOA message, or through a Memorandum of Understanding (MOU). It should be noted, however, that rules concerning general terms and conditions have not yet been formally adopted in the UN.[48] The TCCs may indicate certain caveats or restrictions upon the use of their personnel or assets for the execution of particular tasks within the mission.[49] Restrictions usually refer to the geographical limits of a national contingent or certain limits on the use of force. While restrictions or caveats cannot be avoided, since TCCs are ultimately responsible for their national contingents, they should not be allowed to fundamentally affect the operational effectiveness of a TCC's contribution. A Contingent Commander (CONTCO) must not be given or accept instructions from his/her own national authorities that are contrary to the mandate of the operation.[50]

---

[47] UN DPKO (n. 33), p. 7.
[48] See D. Fleck and T. D. Gill, 'International Law for Military Operations: Conclusions and Perspectives', in Gill and Fleck (n. 24), p. 617.
[49] Gill (n. 27), p. 48.
[50] EU Concept (n. 26), pp. 11, 29; Draft AU Policy (n. 29), p. 12. The importance of a dialogue between the capitals of TCCs and their respective contingent should be acknowledged. The TCC has an interest, but this does not mean that the capital could intervene in the Peace Operation by issuing its own (and possibly divergent) instructions.

UN. In UN-led Peace Operations, operational authority involves the authority to issue operational directives within the limits of the UN mandate, within an agreed period of time and within a specific geographic area. The field-based management of a Peace Operation at Mission Headquarters in the AOO is considered to be the operational level. The main actors holding authority, command and control responsibilities at the operational level are a civilian Head of Mission (HOM), often designated as the Special Representative of the Secretary-General (SRSG), a Head of Military Component (HOMC) or Force Commander (FC), and a Head of Police Component. The HOM reports to the Secretary-General via the USG DPKO. The HOMC reports to the HOM. The HOMC/FC is vested with delegated operational control over the military contingents of the TCCs. The Head of Police, who also reports to the HOM, exercises operational control over all members of the police component of the mission.[51]

AU. Similar to UN Peace Operations, operational authority regarding Peace Operations undertaken by the AU is exercised and co-ordinated by a HOM, who in large and complex operations will be the AU Special Representative, designated by the Chairperson of the AU Commission. The HOM establishes the relationship between the military, police and political elements of the Peace Operation, assigns areas of responsibility and establishes mechanisms to integrate the activities of all involved parties. Next to a HOM, the Chairperson also appoints a FC, a Police Commissioner and the Heads of other civilian components involved in the operation. In Peace Operations where there is a strictly military mandate, the FC may also be the designated HOM. The FC exercises OPCON over all military personnel and is responsible to the HOM for the implementation of the tasks assigned to the military component. The Police Commissioner exercises OPCON over all civilian police personnel and is responsible for the implementation of the tasks assigned to the police component (e.g. the rule of law). The FC (if not serving as the HOM), the Police Commissioner and other Heads report to the HOM. On behalf of the HOM, a Joint Mission Headquarters monitors and manages all AU Peace Operations within the AOO.[52] The TOA by an AU Member State to the AU is, while the AU has its own procedures, not significantly different from the aforementioned procedure when a UN Member State transfers authority to the UN.

---

[51] UN DPKO (n. 33), pp. 7–9.
[52] Draft AU Policy (n. 29), pp. 10–13 and Annexure C.

EU. The commander at the operational level for EU-led military operations is the EU Force Commander (FC), who, acting under the authority of the OpCdr, is authorised to command assigned forces within a designated AOO. The Force Headquarters is the headquarters of an EU-led military force deployed in the AOO, ashore or afloat.[53] For the conduct of a Peace Operation the OpCdr, as not being present in the AOO, normally delegates OPCON to the FC, who is present in the AOO.[54] Instead of nominating both an OPCdr (strategic level) and a FC (operational level), the Council of the European Union can decide to nominate an EU Mission Commander (MCdr) who will exercise the functions of both OpCdr and FC. The MCdr is supported by the EU Mission Headquarters in planning, conducting and exercising C2 over the forces deployed in the AOO.[55] This has been done for a number of non-executive EU military missions, i.e. missions providing training and/or advice. In EU civilian missions, the Council or PSC EU appoints a HOM who will, under the supervision of the CivOpCdr, exercise command and control at the operational level. In addition to the day-to-day conduct of the mission, his/her main responsibilities are, inter alia, developing an OPLAN which must be approved by the Council and representing the respective civilian operation in the operation area.[56]

NATO. NATO's operational level consists of two standing Joint Force Commands (JFCs), which fall under the responsibility of the ACO. Both JFCs can conduct operations from their static locations or provide a land-based Combined Joint Task Force. When NATO is undertaking an NAC-mandated operation, a NATO Combined Joint Task Force Commander is generally delegated OPCON and OPCOM over the assigned Member States' forces.[57] The TOA by a NATO Member State takes the form of a TOA message to SACEUR by the relevant military authorities of the State concerned. This message is sent through the NATO (classified) systems. It sets out, inter alia, the forces concerned, the level of command and control transferred, the duration of the transfer and national caveats to the ROE, where applicable. In the case of non-NATO Member States (partners) contributing forces, participation and detailed financial arrangements will be concluded between NATO

---

[53] EU Concept (n. 26), pp. 7, 8, 20.
[54] *Ibid.*, p. 20.
[55] *Ibid.*, pp. 9, 20.
[56] EU Draft Guidelines (n. 26), pp. 6 and 10.
[57] B. Cathcart, 'Command and Control in Military Operations', in Gill and Fleck (n. 24), p. 266.

and the partner concerned, and if required a technical MOU.[58] Once non-NATO forces designated by the contributing States are deployed to the operational area and are declared operationally ready, the authority over those forces will be transferred to the JFC.[59]

6. TACOM and TACON involve the authority of a subordinate commander to issue detailed instructions to units and subunits within the mission to complete specific tasks assigned within the overall mission. In Peace Operations, TACOM and TACON are normally retained by the TCCs, which will designate a level of authority appropriate at a tactical level, although tactical C2 must be exercised in conformity with operational C2.[60]

UN. Regarding UN-led Peace Operations, the management of military, police and civilian operations below the level of Mission Headquarters is considered to be at the tactical level. For the military components, the tactical level includes all subordinate levels established within the military chain of command (e.g. Brigade, Regional, Sector Commanders). Tactical level commanders report directly to their operational commanders.[61] The military and police components shall co-ordinate military, police or joint operations with the civilian Head of Office, who represents the HOM in the region or sector. The normal practice is for the TCC to appoint a CONTCO who will exercise TACON and TACOM over the national contingent.[62]

AU. The tactical level for AU Peace Operations is similar to the previously described tactical level employed in UN Peace Operations. In operations undertaken by the AU, CONTCOs are appointed as well to exercise TACON and TACOM over their respective contingents. However, the HOM and FC ensure that CONTCOs are also involved in operational planning and decision-making, especially where their respective contingents are concerned.[63]

EU. Regarding the tactical level in EU-led military operations, Component Commanders (CCs), who are designated by the FC or a higher authority, are deployed to the AOO and given the authority

---

[58] NATO Ministers of Foreign Affairs, Political Military Framework for Partner Involvement in NATO-led Operations (2011), paras. 4, 6, www.nato.int/nato_static/assets/pdf/pdf_2011_04/20110415_110415-PMF.pdf.

[59] NATO, Peace Support Operations, AJP-3.4.1 (2001), para. 0616.

[60] Gill (n. 27), p. 49.

[61] UN DPKO (n. 33), p. 10.

[62] Gill (n. 27), p. 49.

[63] Draft AU Policy (n. 29), p. 12 and Annexure C.

necessary to accomplish tasks assigned by the FC. The CCs are supported by CC Headquarters. If no CCs are established (which is often the case), the FC/Force Headquarters will assume responsibility for the tasks at the tactical level. In EU-led civilian operations, TACOM/TACON are not used.

NATO. The tactical level within NATO consists of six Joint Force Component Commands, which provide service-specific land, maritime or air capabilities and support to the operational level. The Joint Force Component Commands are subordinated to one of the JFCs.[64]

7. ADCON, the authority to exercise administrative, disciplinary and criminal authority over national contingents, is also retained by TCCs.[65] Administrative and disciplinary control is exercised by a senior national official of a contributed national contingent. Even though ADCON remains a national responsibility, the organisation undertaking the Peace Operation may take administrative steps in relation to misconduct, such as requesting the TCC to repatriate a member of its contingent.[66] The organisation does, however, exercise ADCON over staff contracted by it.

8. The partial transfer of authority over contingents participating in a Peace Operation to an international or regional organisation and the implemented command structure has implications for the issue of legal responsibility for the parties involved.[67]

4.2.2 Personnel participating in Peace Operations shall observe the authority of the Force Commander and of the international or regional organisation or arrangement involved. While this authority is based on the internal law of the organisation or arrangement, it has to be assigned by Troop Contributing Countries. Command and control arrangements are set out in an agreement between the Troop Contributing Country and the international or regional organisation or arrangement, or in internal arrangements of the organisation involved.

1. Issues concerning C2 are part of agreements between the international organisation and TCCs[68] or form part of the organisation's internal

---

[64] Cathcart (n. 57), p. 265.

[65] UN DPKO (n. 33), p. 11; Draft AU Policy (n. 29), pp. 6, 12.

[66] Cammaert and Klappe (n. 33), p. 161. The power to order and effect a repatriation of an individual or a whole contingent forms part of ADCON.

[67] See Chapter 19.

[68] See Chapter 11.

arrangements, e.g. policy documents.[69] These agreements or policy documents generally provide that TCCs will comply with international standards of conduct and ensure the maintenance of order and discipline by their contingents.[70]

2. The High-Level Independent Panel on United Nations Peace Operations has made three recommendations for reinforcing command and control:

1. The selection of forces for deployment in peacekeeping missions should explicitly take into account any national caveats in determining whether or not to proceed with deploying a contingent;
2. Any additional caveats beyond those accepted by the UN Secretariat at the outset should not be tolerated, and missions must communicate these to the Secretariat; and
3. Force commanders and police commissioners should record instances of failure to follow orders and report these to headquarters.[71]

This recommendation should apply mutatis mutandis to all other types of Peace Operation covered by this Manual.

---

[69] EU Concept (n. 26) (including definitions in Annex A).
[70] See arts. 7–7ter Model Memorandum of Understanding between the United Nations and [participating State] contributing resources to [the United Nations Peacekeeping Operation], UNGA Res. 61/267 (2007) and UN Doc. A/C.5/69/18 (2014), Chapter 9.
[71] Report of the High-Level Independent Panel on United Nations Peace Operations, Uniting Our Strengths for Peace: Politics, Partnership and People, UN Doc. A/70/95-S/2015/446 (2015), paras. 205–209 (HIPPO Report).

4.3   AFRICAN UNION

4.3.1   Peace Operations deployed by the AU require a legal basis under international law and a decision pursuant to the Constitutive Act of the AU. Peace Operations by the AU shall be conducted in accordance with international law (including the UN Charter), and the internal laws and policies of the AU. Peace Operations deployed by the AU shall also comply with mission-specific agreements.

1. The replacement of the former Organisation of African Unity (OAU) by the AU, effectuated in 2002, marked a radical paradigm shift from non-interference to non-indifference.[72] According to its Constitutive Act, the AU has the right 'to intervene in a Member State pursuant to a decision of the Assembly in respect of … war crimes, genocide and crimes against humanity', and its Member States have the right 'to request intervention from the Union in order to restore peace and security'.[73] The AU does not restrict itself to military operations where there is a peace to be restored in the strict sense. Support to peace is equally important. The Common African Defence and Security Policy lists the deployment and sustainment of peacekeeping missions as one of its objectives and goals.[74] This goal can be seen as giving expression to one of the AU's core objectives, namely the promotion of peace, security and stability on the continent.[75]

2. Since its launch in Durban, South Africa, in 2002, and in particular after the entry into force in December 2003 of the Protocol relating to the Establishment of the Peace and Security Council of the African Union,[76] the AU has actively engaged in the efforts of conflict management and settlement on the African continent. The Protocol elaborates

---

[72] See e.g. B. Kioko, 'The Right of Intervention Under the African Union's Constitutive Act: From Non-Interference to Non-Intervention', 85 *International Review of the Red Cross* (2003), p. 819.

[73] Art. 4(h) and (j) Constitutive Act of the African Union (11 July 2000, in force 26 May 2001), 2158 UNTS 3. If the Maputo Protocol enters into force, art. 4(h) AU Constitutive Act will also give the AU the right to intervene, upon recommendation of the Peace and Security Council of the AU, when there is 'a serious threat to legitimate order to restore peace and stability to the Member State of the Union'; see Protocol on Amendments to the Constitutive Act of the African Union (11 July 2003, not in force).

[74] AU, Solemn Declaration on a Common African Defence and Security Policy, 28 February 2004, para. 13(j).

[75] Art. 3(f) AU Constitutive Act (n. 73).

[76] Protocol relating to the Establishment of the Peace and Security Council of the African Union (9 July 2002, in force 26 December 2003), www.peaceau.org/uploads/psc-protocol-en.pdf (PSC AU Protocol).

the new African Peace and Security Architecture,[77] which is the umbrella term for the structure to operationalise and implement decisions in the area of conflict prevention, peacemaking, peace support operations and intervention, as well as peacebuilding and post-conflict reconstruction, in accordance with the AU Constitutive Act.[78] It offers the AU instruments with respect to many facets of conflicts and crises, giving expression to the ever more affirmed willingness of African leaders to play a central role in the promotion of peace on the continent in the name of the principle of ownership and African leadership.

3. Central to the implementation of African Peace and Security Architecture is the Peace and Security Council of the AU (PSC AU), which acts as the successor to the former OAU's Central Organ of the Mechanism for Conflict Prevention, Management and Resolution. The PSC AU is a body consisting of representatives from fifteen Member States, elected by the AU Executive Council[79] based on equitable regional distribution. It meets at the level of permanent representatives, ministers or Heads of State and Government. The PSC AU is the organisation's standing decision-making organ for the prevention, management and resolution of conflicts,[80] and has been given a broad mandate to take the initiative or assist in providing humanitarian action and disaster management, early warning, peacemaking, Peace Operations, intervention, peacebuilding and post-conflict reconstruction (including restoring the rule of law, establishing democratic institutions, election supervision, peace consolidation, and disarmament, demobilisation and reintegration).[81]

4. The PSC AU has the competence to authorise the mounting and deployment of Peace Operations, to determine their mandate and to lay down mission conduct guidelines.[82] Interventions pursuant to article 4(h) of the AU Constitutive Act can, however, be authorized only by the AU Assembly; the PSC AU may issue a recommendation to such effect. Apart from humanitarian action and disaster management, AU doctrine

---

[77] See African Peace and Security Architecture: APSA Roadmap 2016–2020 (African Union Commission, 2015).

[78] PSC AU Protocol (n. 76), preambular para. 16.

[79] As from 2006 the AU Assembly has delegated its power for the election of PSC AU members to the AU Executive Council; see Assembly/AU/Dec.106 (VI) (2006).

[80] Art. 2 PSC AU Protocol (n. 76).

[81] *Ibid.*, arts. 3 and 6.

[82] *Ibid.*, art. 7(c) and (d). See further *Ibid.*, arts. 14 and 15, dealing specifically with the PSC AU's mandates in the area of peacebuilding and humanitarian action.

distinguishes six conflict and mission scenarios in which the organisation may play a role:

1. AU or regional military advice to a political mission;
2. AU or regional observer mission co-deployed with a UN mission;
3. Stand-alone AU or regional observer mission;
4. AU or regional Peace Force for Chapter VI and preventive deployment missions;
5. AU Peace Force for a complex multi-dimensional mission with low level spoilers; and
6. AU intervention.[83]

5. A decision to deploy a Peace Operation is put on the agenda by the PSC AU Chairperson on the basis of a proposal submitted by the AU Chairperson, the AU Commission Chairperson or any of the Member States.[84] Such a proposal may be prompted by information collected through the Continental Early Warning System, which is an observation and monitoring system tasked with collecting and analysing data, and issuing warnings.[85] Formally, a decision by the PSC AU to deploy (or terminate) a Peace Operation is taken by consensus among its fifteen members or, if that is not possible, by a two-thirds majority of those present and voting. In practice, the PSC AU issues communiqués and press releases instead of adopting formal resolutions and decisions.[86]

6. When carrying out its functions, the PSC AU acts on behalf of the AU Member States. According to article 7(3) of the PSC AU Protocol all Member States 'agree to implement the decisions [of the PSC AU], in accordance with the Constitutive Act'. Legally speaking, it is debatable whether decisions of the PSC AU are binding on the few AU Member States which have not become party to the PSC AU

---

[83] AU, Policy Framework for the Establishment of the African Standby Force and the Military Staff Committee (Part I), EXP/ASF-MSC/2(I) (2003), p. 3. As a matter of policy, 'it is to be expected that ... the AU will seek UN Security Council authorization of its enforcements actions': *Ibid.*, p. 4.

[84] See further AU, *African Union Handbook*, 3rd edn (African Union Commission/New Zealand Ministry of Foreign Affairs and Trade, 2016), pp. 49–65; S. A. Dersso, 'The African Union's Mandating Authority and Processes for Deploying an ASF Mission', 19 *African Security Review* (2010), pp. 73–86.

[85] Art. 12 PSC AU Protocol (n. 76). The Continental Early Warning System comprises a "Situation Room" within the AU Commission which is linked with the early warning systems of the African Regional Economic Communities and/or regional co-ordination mechanisms. See further *African Union Continental Warning System: The CEWS Handbook*, 7th draft (AU, 2008).

[86] K. D. Magliveras and G. J. Naldi, *The African Union (AU)* (Wolters Kluwer, 2013), p. 155.

Protocol.[87] In practice, though, this does not appear to have given rise to any difficulties.

7. Prior to or during a Peace Operation the AU may call upon the assistance of the Panel of the Wise.[88] This panel of five eminent persons serves to support the work of the PSC AU and the AU Commission Chairperson, for example by carrying out fact-finding, good offices, mediation or conciliation. The panel may also take such action on its own initiative. Accordingly, it has the competence to offer its advice to the PSC AU and the AU Commission Chairperson on all issues pertaining to the promotion and maintenance of peace, security and stability.

8. Upon authorisation by the PSC AU, Peace Operations are carried out by the African Standby Force (ASF) consisting of standby multi-disciplinary contingents with civilian and military components, ready for rapid deployment at appropriate notice.[89] The ASF comprises five multi-national brigades, each hosted by one of five African regions through their respective Regional Economic Communities (RECs) – i.e. the Economic Community of Central African States (ECCAS), the South African Development Community (SADC) and the Economic Community of West African States (ECOWAS) – or through regional co-ordination mechanisms specifically set up for this purpose – i.e. the North African Regional Capability (NARC) and the Eastern Africa Standby Force (EASF).[90] Each of the five African regions is expected to contribute a capability, consisting of military, police and civilian elements of about 5,000 personnel.

9. The PSC AU promotes close harmonisation, co-ordination, co-operation and exchange of information between the relevant RECs, the regional mechanisms and the AU in order for the PSC AU to effectively carry out its duties under the PSC AU Protocol. The details of this relationship are laid down in article 16 of the PSC AU Protocol, complemented by a (legally binding) Memorandum of Understanding (MOU) which is based on the principles of subsidiarity, complementarity and

---

[87] *Ibid.*, p. 155. As of 1 July 2017, the AU has fifty-five Member States (Morocco withdrew from the OAU in 1984 and rejoined the AU in January 2017), four of which – i.e. Cape Verde, Democratic Republic of the Congo, Morocco and South Sudan – are not party to the PSC AU Protocol.

[88] Art. 11 PSC AU Protocol (n. 76). During the 2010 AU Summit in Kampala, the Assembly enhanced the Panel's capacity by providing for a group of up to ten "Friends" of the Panel of the Wise; see Assembly/AU/Dec.310 (XV) (2010).

[89] Art. 13 PSC AU Protocol (n. 76).

[90] See further Chapter 4.6.

comparative advantage.[91] It has been submitted that in practice the interaction between the PSC AU and the RECs/regional mechanisms is still far from optimal, mainly due to duplication of effort, problems in co-ordination and the lack of institutional and financial means.[92]

10. In terms of operational planning and implementation, the decisions of the PSC AU are supported and carried out by the Chairperson and the Peace and Security Department of the AU Commission. Furthermore, there is a Military Staff Committee, consisting of Chiefs of Defence Staff or senior military officers, tasked with advising the PSC AU on military and security matters.[93] On the planning process for AU Peace Operations, see further Appendix V.

11. In May 2013, pending the ASF becoming fully operational, the AU Assembly created the African Capacity for Immediate Response to Crises (ACIRC) as an interim mechanism for immediate response to crises.[94] As is the case with Peace Operations undertaken by the ASF, the ACIRC is supported by the AU Commission and requires authorisation by the PSC AU.

12. One of the AU's objectives is to promote and protect human rights in accordance with international human rights law (IHRL) instruments, including the African Charter on Human and Peoples' Rights.[95] Within the context of Peace Operations, the PSC AU Protocol translates this objective into the obligation that in the fulfilment of its duties the PSC AU 'shall be guided' by the principles enshrined in the AU Constitutive Act, the UN Charter and the Universal Declaration of Human Rights, and in particular by respect for the rule of law, IHRL and international humanitarian law (IHL).[96] To this end the Protocol prescribes that national ASF contingents must receive training on

---

[91] See art. 4(iv) Memorandum of Understanding on Cooperation in the Area of Peace and Security between the African Union, the Regional Economic Communities and the Coordinating Mechanisms of the Regional Standby Brigades of Eastern Africa and Northern Africa (2008), www.peaceau.org/uploads/mou-au-rec-eng.pdf.

[92] A. S. Bah, E. Choge-Nyangoro, S. Dersso, B. Mofya and T. Murith, *The African Peace and Security Architecture: A Handbook* (Friedrich-Erbert Stiftung, 2014), pp. 42–45, 49, 54, 64–65, 69–74; A. A. Yusuf and F. Ouguergouz, *The African Union: Legal and Institutional Framework* (Martinus Nijhoff, 2012).

[93] Art. 13(8)–(12) PSC AU Protocol (n. 76).

[94] See Assembly/AU/Dec.489 (XXI) (2013). For ACIRC's operationalisation on a transitional basis, see Assembly/AU/Dec.515 (XXII) (2014).

[95] African Charter on Human and Peoples Rights (27 June 1981, in force 21 October 1986), 1520 UNTS 217.

[96] Art. 4(c) PSC AU Protocol (n. 76).

IHRL and IHL, with particular emphasis on the rights of women and children.[97]

13. According to the High-Level Independent Panel on United Nations Peace Operations, any AU Peace Operation receiving UN-assessed contributions should provide regular reports to the Security Council, as well as appropriate financial reporting to the UN, and comply fully with UN standards, such as the Human Rights Due Diligence Policy, and UN conduct and discipline frameworks.[98]

14. In May 2017, UN Secretary-General António Guterres submitted a report[99] pursuant to Security Council Resolution 2320 (2016) of 18 November 2016 in which the Council, inter alia, requested the Secretary-General to continue working closely with the AU to refine options for further co-operation on the relevant AU proposals, including on financing, accountability, joint planning and the process for mandating AU peace support operations, subject to authorisation by the Security Council. The report recalls the findings of an earlier joint review, which found that the AU's willingness to deploy and support Peace Operations has been undermined by the lack of capacity in key areas, particularly financing, staffing, logistics and some key military capabilities. The report mentions that significant steps towards furthering the partnership have been made since the joint review. In particular, on 19 April 2017, the new Chairperson of the African Union Commission, Moussa Faki Mahamat, and the UN Secretary-General convened the first UN–AU Annual Conference at UN Headquarters, where they co-signed the Joint UN–AU Framework for an Enhanced Partnership in Peace and Security.[100] This Framework provides for a strategic approach of the two organisations to address challenges to peace and security across the full spectrum of the conflict cycle.

---

[97] *Ibid.*, art. 13(13).

[98] HIPPO Report (n. 71), paras. 223–232. On reporting to the Security Council, see further Rule 4.1.4.

[99] Report of the Secretary-General on options for authorization and support for African Union peace support operations, UN Doc. S/2017/454 (2017). This report builds on the findings of the joint AU–UN review of available mechanisms to finance and support African Union peace operations authorized by the Security Council, UN Doc. A/71/410-S/2016/809 (2016).

[100] Joint United Nations–African Union Framework for an Enhanced Partnership in Peace and Security (2017), https://unoau.unmissions.org/sites/default/files/signed_joint_framework.pdf.

4.4 EUROPEAN UNION

4.4.1 An EU Peace Operation requires a legal basis under international law. Its required legal basis under EU law is a Council decision adopted on the basis of the Treaty on European Union, following a proposal by a Member State or by the High Representative of the Union for Foreign Affairs and Security Policy. Such Council decisions set up and govern EU Peace Operations.

1. The requirement for an international legal basis is already addressed in Chapters 3 and 4.1 from the point of view of international law.

2. Furthermore, as a matter of EU law, EU operations have to be conducted in accordance with international law, because of the EU law requirement that the EU respect international law. Article 3(5) of the EU Treaty states that, in its relations with the wider world, the Union shall contribute to 'the strict observance and the development of international law, including respect for the principles of the United Nations Charter'. In addition, pursuant to article 21 of the EU Treaty:

> 1. The Union's action on the international scene shall be guided by the principles which have inspired its own creation, development and enlargement, and which it seeks to advance in the wider world: democracy, the rule of law, the universality and indivisibility of human rights and fundamental freedoms, respect for human dignity, the principles of equality and solidarity, and respect for the principles of the United Nations Charter and international law ...
>
> 2. The Union shall define and pursue common policies and actions, and shall work for a high degree of cooperation in all fields of international relations, in order to:
>
> ...
>
> (b) consolidate and support democracy, the rule of law, human rights and the principles of international law;
>
> (c) preserve peace, prevent conflicts and strengthen international security, in accordance with the purposes and principles of the United Nations Charter, with the principles of the Helsinki Final Act and with the aims of the Charter of Paris, including those relating to external borders.

Moreover, in Declaration No. 13 concerning the common foreign and security policy, adopted with the Treaty of Lisbon, the Intergovernmental

Conference[101] 'stresse[d] that the European Union and its Member States will remain bound by the provisions of the Charter of the United Nations and, in particular, by the primary responsibility of the Security Council and of its Members for the maintenance of international peace and security'. Furthermore, the EU Court of Justice has ruled that the EU must respect customary international law.[102]

3. In practice, EU Peace Operations can have different bases in international law. The most common ones are a UN Security Council resolution,[103] consent from the Host State government (which is usually the case in civilian EU missions) and/or a peace agreement. In some cases several of these bases are combined.[104]

4. The requirement of a legal basis under EU law is similar to that of a legal basis in the internal order of other regional organisations, and even of the UN, and results from the functional and limited nature of the competences of each international organisation.

5. The precise treaty provisions on the basis of which the EU undertakes Peace Operations have been amended several times as a result of changes to the EU Treaties. Yet in all cases an act of the Council adopted pursuant to those provisions has been required. EU Peace Operations are conducted under the EU's Common Security and Defence Policy, which in turn is part of the broader EU external action. The more detailed commentary to follow reflects the EU Treaties as last amended by the Lisbon Treaty.[105]

6. Under article 42(1) of the EU Treaty: 'The common security and defence policy ... shall provide the Union with an operational capacity drawing on civil and military assets. The Union may use them on missions outside the Union for peace-keeping, conflict prevention and

---

[101] I.e. the EU Member States, meeting in the framework in which the Treaty of Lisbon was negotiated and signed.

[102] See e.g. Case C-366/10, *Air Transport Association of America*, Judgment of the Court (Grand Chamber) of 21 December 2011, ECR-I13755, para. 101 (when the Union adopts an act, 'it is bound to observe international law in its entirety, including customary international law, which is binding upon the institutions of the European Union').

[103] Such resolutions may specifically refer to the EU, they may refer to regional or international organisations generically, or they may refer to UN Member States.

[104] However, there may be other bases in international law. For instance, in Operation Atalanta, the counter-piracy operation off the coast of Somalia, the UN Convention on the Law of the Sea is also part of the legal basis.

[105] For the latest consolidated version of the Treaty on European Union (EU Treaty) and the Treaty on the Functioning of the European Union, see OJ 2016 No. C202, 7 June 2016, respectively p. 13 and p. 47.

strengthening international security in accordance with the principles of the United Nations Charter.' These missions are further defined in article 43 of the EU Treaty: they 'shall include joint disarmament operations, humanitarian and rescue tasks, military advice and assistance tasks, conflict prevention and peace-keeping tasks, tasks of combat forces in crisis management, including peace-making and post-conflict stabilisation' and may all 'contribute to the fight against terrorism, including by supporting third countries in combating terrorism in their territories'. Although the contrary is often thought, 'tasks of combat forces in crisis management, including peacemaking', cover peace enforcement and hence potentially high intensity operations involving combat. Furthermore, the enumeration in article 43 of the EU Treaty is not exhaustive, and EU operations may vary greatly, ranging from consensual rule of law, police, security sector reform, border assistance or monitoring missions, to peacekeeping and potentially even peace enforcement.

7. The basic legal instrument governing each EU operation, whether it is a military or a civilian one, is a Council decision, adopted on the basis of article 43, in conjunction with article 31, of the EU Treaty.[106] This legal instrument is the successor to the Joint Actions that were adopted pursuant to article 14 of the pre-Lisbon EU Treaty (and in relation to some operations such Joint Actions are still in force). The formal right to propose an EU Peace Operation belongs to any EU Member State or the High Representative of the Union for Foreign Affairs and Security Policy (High Representative).[107]

8. Such decisions of the Council (which is composed of representatives at ministerial level of all its Member States)[108] are acts of the Union and, in principle, are adopted unanimously.[109]

9. Council decisions on EU Peace Operations generally, inter alia, set out the mission and mandate, political and military or civilian control and direction, designate the commanders and headquarters or Head of Mission (HOM) and mission structure, specify the command and control (C2) relations and contain provisions on the status of forces/mission, financial arrangements, participation of third States (i.e. non-EU Member States), relations with other actors, handling of EU

---

[106] These decisions have always been published in the EU's Official Journal.
[107] Art. 30(1) EU Treaty (n. 105).
[108] As of 1 July 2017, the EU has twenty-eight Member States.
[109] See arts. 42(4) and 31 EU Treaty (n. 105).

privileged and classified information and the launching and termination or duration of the operation.

10. In all military operations launched so far, a first Council act setting up the operation was adopted before the planning process was completed, and the Council adopted a separate decision launching the operation together with, or subsequent to, the approval of the Operational Plan and Rules of Engagement (ROE). The Council may at any time amend the initial Council decision, e.g. to change the duration of an operation or to change its mandate.

11. Furthermore, once an operation has been established, a number of decisions can be taken by the Political and Security Committee of the EU (PSC EU), which is a preparatory body of the Council composed of ambassadors from all Member States (as well as a chair appointed by the High Representative). This is based on article 38 of the EU Treaty and the delegation given in each Council decision setting up an EU Peace Operation. Such decisions may, inter alia, relate to amendment of the planning documents, including the Operational Plan, the Chain of Command and the ROE or Rules on the Use of Force (the latter is used for civilian missions), to the appointment of the EU Operation, Mission or Force Commanders and to the acceptance of third State contributions. However, the powers of decision with respect to the objectives and termination of the operation remain vested in the Council.

12. Moreover, the PSC EU exercises, under the responsibility of the Council and of the High Representative, political control and strategic direction of EU Peace Operations.[110]

13. As a final point, it may be noted that articles 42(5) and 44 of the EU Treaty provide for the possibility for the Council to entrust the execution of a task, within the Union framework, to a group of Member States which are willing and have the necessary capability for such a task. Those Member States, in association with the High Representative, shall agree among themselves on the management of the task but, should the completion of the task entail major consequences or require amendment of the objective, scope and conditions determined for the task, the Council shall adopt the necessary decisions.[111] This mechanism has not yet been used.

---

[110] Art. 38 EU Treaty (n. 105).

[111] For a legal analysis, see e.g. Legal Service contribution on the conditions and modalities of recourse to Article 44 TEU – entrusting the implementation of a CSDP task to a group of Member States, EU Council Doc. 5225/15 (2015).

4.4.2 Additional legal acts which may be adopted in relation to EU Peace Operations include Council decisions launching an operation, Council decisions laying down funding arrangements, Status of Forces Agreements or Status of Mission Agreements, agreements on the participation of third States, and Political and Security Committee decisions accepting the participation of third States or appointing Force Commanders or Heads of Missions.

1. This Rule covers the legal acts that are usually adopted in relation to an EU Peace Operation, as well as some related provisions in the EU Treaties. For the adoption of legal acts, the EU Treaties lay down clear rules. By contrast, for planning documents, considerable flexibility exists as long as the prerogatives of the different EU actors are respected. The same applies to various concepts that guide the planning and conduct of EU Peace Operations. The distinction between planning documents and legal acts is therefore important. On planning documents, the sequence between the legal acts and planning documents and process, and relevant EU concepts, see Appendix VI.[112] For decisions launching an operation, see paragraph 10 of the Commentary to Rule 4.4.1.

2. As regards funding, a distinction must be made between military and civilian EU Peace Operations.[113] For civilian operations, most costs are borne by the EU budget,[114] unless the Council unanimously decides otherwise. Financial regulations of the EU apply to all costs covered by the EU budget, and the Council adopts a financial reference amount (for a determined period) in the decision setting up the operation and/or in subsequent decisions. These rules allow for rapid funding for preparatory measures if necessary. By contrast, operating expenditure arising from EU operations having military or defence implications is not charged to the budget of the EU but is charged to the Member States.[115] As a rule, such costs lie where they fall – i.e. every participating State pays for its forces and assets contributed to an EU military operation. However, a number

---

[112] It is, however, worth mentioning two key documents: European Union Concept for EU-Led Military Operations and Missions, EU Council Doc. 17107/14 (2014); Suggestions for crisis management procedures for CSDP crisis management operations, EU Council Doc. 7660/2/13 (2013).

[113] See art. 41 EU Treaty (n. 105).

[114] However, as many staff in such missions are seconded by Member States, who continue to pay their salaries, a significant part of the costs is paid by those Member States. In this context, it should be noted that art. 42(1) EU Treaty (n. 105), provides that the performance of EU missions 'shall be undertaken using capabilities provided by the Member States'.

[115] See art. 41(2) EU Treaty (n. 105).

of costs are common and administered by a mechanism called Athena.[116] These include a number of costs for the preparatory phase of military operations.

3. Article 41(3) of the EU Treaty provides for the creation of a start-up fund made up of Member States' contributions to fund preparatory activities for EU operations which are not charged to the Union budget, as well as for the adoption of 'specific procedures for guaranteeing rapid access to appropriations in the Union budget for urgent financing of initiatives in the framework of the common foreign and security policy, and in particular for preparatory activities' for the tasks referred to in articles 42(1) and 43, i.e. EU security and defence missions and operations. This provision has not yet been implemented.

4. For EU Peace Operations, Status of Forces Agreements (SOFAs) or Status of Mission Agreements (SOMAs) based on model texts are normally concluded with the Host State and Sending States, with the exception of third States participating in an EU operation. These third States are involved through the Council, which adopts the negotiating mandate for such agreements and the decisions on their signature and conclusion.[117]

5. The EU often invites a number of third States to participate in its Peace Operations. Decisions to accept such participation are taken by the PSC EU, on the basis of article 38 of the EU Treaty and a provision in the Council decision establishing the operation. When a third State participates in EU Peace Operations, the necessary arrangements are concluded with the EU, in the form of a participation agreement. Such agreements may be concluded on an ad hoc basis for a given operation (on the basis of a model agreement) or may take the form of framework agreements covering the participation in EU operations generally.[118] In participation agreements, the participating State normally associates itself with the Council decision establishing an operation, commits itself to providing a contribution and bears the costs thereof; it may be exempted from a share in the common costs or budget of the operation.

---

[116] See Council Decision (CFSP) 2015/528 of 27 March 2015 establishing a mechanism to administer the financing of the common costs of European Union operations having military or defence implications (Athena) and repealing Decision 2011/871/CFSP, OJ 2015 No. L84, 28 March 2015, p. 39.

[117] For the EU Model SOFA and SOMA, see on the one hand EU Council Docs. 12616/07 (2007), 11894/07 (2007) and 11894/07 COR 1 (2007), and on the other hand EU Council Doc. 17141/08 (2008). These may be adapted to the specific case as necessary.

[118] Such framework participation agreements have been concluded with an increasing number of third States.

Generally, such agreements also provide that the personnel of the third State participating in the operation are covered by any SOFA or SOMA concluded by the EU and contain provisions on C2, jurisdiction and claims. The EU's decision-making autonomy is safeguarded but usually all participating States have the same rights and obligations in terms of day-to-day management of the operation as participating EU Member States, and the EU will consult with participating third States when ending the mission. A Committee of Contributors in which the third State participates may be established by the PSC EU to provide a forum for the exercise of these rights. Participation agreements also contain provisions on classified information.

4.4.3 Peace Operations of the EU shall be conducted in accordance with applicable EU law and international law.

1. On the requirement for the EU to respect international law, see paragraph 2 of the Commentary to Rule 4.4.1. This applies not only to the legal basis but also to the conduct. It is, furthermore, obvious that applicable EU law must be complied with. This includes, but is not limited to, EU fundamental rights,[119] institutional rules, financial rules[120] and any applicable EU law on staff rules. In addition, contingents and personnel deployed in EU Peace Operations shall comply with any applicable provisions of their Sending State law.[121]

[119] See Chapter 5.
[120] See Rule 4.4.2, Commentary, para. 2.
[121] See Chapter 10.

4.5   NORTH ATLANTIC TREATY ORGANIZATION

4.5.1   Each Peace Operation of NATO authorised by the UN Security Council requires a legal basis under international law and must be based on a decision by the North Atlantic Council. Peace Operations shall be conducted in accordance with international law, the Organization's applicable policies and doctrines, and the national laws of each Troop Contributing Country.

1. NATO is a political–military alliance promoting freedom and security of its Members. Due to its capacities, NATO is one of the United Nations' important partners for the conduct of UN-mandated Peace Operations. The Organization was established based on strong links between the UN Charter and the North Atlantic Treaty[122] but, because in its first fifty years of existence it did not conduct Peace Operations, the practical link between the two organisations was very limited.[123] This approach started to change in the 1990s as realities on the international scene after the end of the Cold War brought NATO and the UN into closer co-operation.[124]

2. Since being established in 1949,[125] NATO has focused solely on the security of its Member States[126] and on promoting solidarity in case of an armed attack against one or more of them (collective defence or so-called "article 5 operations").[127] In 1992 NATO decided to support

---

[122] See Preamble explicitly referencing the UN Charter and further arts. 1, 5 and 7 North Atlantic Treaty (4 April 1949, in force 24 August 1949), 34 UNTS 243 (NATO Treaty).

[123] On the development of the relationship, see M. Zwanenburg, 'NATO, Its Member States and the Security Council', in N. Blokker and N. Schrijver (eds.), *The Security Council and the Use of Force: Theory and Reality – A Need for Change?* (Martinus Nijhoff, 2005), p. 189.

[124] See e.g. NATO, 'Relations with the United Nations', www.nato.int/cps/en/natolive/topics_50321.htm.

[125] The NATO Treaty (n. 122), also known as the Washington Treaty, established the Alliance. The permanent structures were institutionalised only afterwards in 1951 when the NATO Allies signed the Ottawa Agreement (20 September 1951, in force 18 May 1954), 200 UNTS 3, for the establishment of political structures and in 1952 when they signed the Paris Protocol (28 August 1952, in force 10 April 1954), 200 UNTS 340, pursuant to the NATO SOFA for the establishment of military structures.

[126] For consistency reasons this Manual uses the word "State" (except when it makes use of the concept of "Troop Contributing Country" or "Police Contributing Country"). Please note, however, that NATO uses the term "Nation" in its documents when referring to its Members. As of 1 July 2017, NATO consists of twenty-nine Member States, including Montenegro which was the latest to join NATO on 5 June 2017.

[127] Art. 5 NATO Treaty (n. 122), reads: 'The Parties agree that an armed attack against one or more of them in Europe or North America shall be considered an attack against them all and consequently they agree that, if such an armed attack occurs, each of them, in exercise of the right of individual or collective self-defence recognized by Article 51 of the Charter of the

UN operations within the Euro-Atlantic region on a case-by-case basis and through the new concept of Crisis Management Operations further to contribute to peace and security in its region and periphery.[128] Such support culminated in 1995 when NATO conducted its first peacekeeping operation in co-operation with the UN, the Implementation Force (IFOR).[129]

3. Since the 1990s NATO has conducted in total forty-one operations, and only two of them have fallen under the collective defence scheme.[130] The remaining thirty-nine have all been within the concept of Non-Article 5 Crisis Response Operations (NA5CROs).[131]

4. NATO and UN enhanced co-operation in support of Peace Operations brought up a theoretical concern as to whether NATO is or can be considered as a "regional arrangement or agency" as envisaged by article 52 of the UN Charter (Chapter VIII).[132] Because NATO always considered itself primarily as a collective defence organisation, it explicitly dismissed any arguments raised in favour of being considered as a regional organisation[133] unlike some other international organisations which explicitly consider themselves as regional organisations under Chapter VIII, such as the Organization for Security and Co-operation in Europe (OSCE) or the Organization of American States (OAS). Despite the fact that NATO does not consider itself as a regional arrangement as envisaged in article 52 of the UN Charter, and there is some support in legal doctrine for this view,[134] in practice this does not mean that NATO would be excluded from undertaking UN-mandated

---

United Nations, will assist the Party or Parties so attacked by taking forthwith, individually and in concert with the other Parties, such action as it deems necessary, including the use of armed force, to restore and maintain the security of the North Atlantic area.'

[128] Ministerial Meeting of the North Atlantic Council, Final Communiqué, 4 June 1992, www.nato.int/docu/comm/49-95/c920604a.htm.

[129] NATO (n. 124).

[130] Operation Eagle Assist (2001–2002) and Operation Active Endeavour (2001–present).

[131] NA5CRO is defined in AJP-3.4 as 'multifunctional operations, falling outside the scope of Article 5, contributing to conflict prevention and resolution, and crisis management in the pursuit of declared Alliance objectives': NATO, Allied Joint Doctrine for Non-Article 5 Crisis Response Operations, AJP-3.4(A) (2010), LEX-3.

[132] It is interesting to note that while B. Simma's UN Charter Commentary attempts to define regional arrangements or agencies and provides examples of some international organisations (e.g. OAS, AU, League of Arab States) falling under Chapter VIII, the Commentary is silent on the nature of NATO. See C. Walter, 'Article 52', in Simma, Khan, Nolte and Paulus (n. 4), vol. II, pp. 1459–1468.

[133] R. F. Simmons, Deputy Assistant Secretary General for Political Affairs of NATO, speech during UN Security Council 5007th meeting, UN Doc. S/PV.5007 (2004), pp. 24–25.

[134] See e.g. R. Higgins, Themes and Theories: Selected Essays, Speeches and Writings in International Law (Oxford University Press, 2009), vol. I, p. 254.

Peace Operations. The UN's general practice is not to directly authorise a specific regional organisation or arrangement to undertake a Peace Operation;[135] however, in some cases, it is generally understood whenever a specific call to undertake a Peace Operation is only for NATO, as only NATO has relevant military capabilities.[136] Such an approach is further supported by the UN as the UN emphasises that it 'include[ed] … NATO in the scope of its decisions or pronouncements'[137] when referring to 'regional and other international organisations'.[138] The co-operation between the two organisations has proved especially useful in the past two decades when NATO undertook UN Security Council-mandated operations such as the International Security Assistance Force (ISAF) in Afghanistan or Operation Unified Protector in Libya or provided logistical or humanitarian support to a number of UN humanitarian operations (Pakistan, Somalia, Sudan etc.). Based on these realities and to strengthen mutual co-operation, NATO and the UN concluded a Joint Declaration in 2008.[139]

5. The UN mandate for NATO and its Member States to conduct Peace Operations is critical for shaping the purpose and scope of the mission. Any NATO involvement in a Peace Operation, in general NATO terms a NA5CRO, can be effectuated only under the political and strategic direction of the North Atlantic Council (NAC). With regard to NATO we can identify three interrelated layers of "mandate", meaning authorisation, i.e.: (1) an international mandate; (2) NATO's decision on the operation (mandate); and (3) a national mandate.

6. In principle, the legal basis at the international level for NATO to conduct NA5CROs is either a Security Council resolution authorising it to undertake actions (e.g. ISAF in Afghanistan or Unified

---

[135] In its resolutions, the Security Council usually uses general wording: 'authorize Member States acting nationally or through regional organizations or arrangements'. This approach has not changed over time; see UNSC Res. 836 (1993) or UNSC Res. 1973 (2011). The only exception to this approach is UNSC Res. 1031 (1995) establishing IFOR, as it indirectly contains references to NATO ('Member States acting through or in cooperation with the organization referred to in Annex 1-A of the Peace Agreement to establish a multinational implementation force (IFOR) under unified command and control', para. 14).

[136] G. Ress and J. Bröhmer, 'Article 53', in B. Simma, H. Mosler, A. Randelzhofer, C. Tomuschat and R. Wolfrum (eds.), *The Charter of the United Nations: A Commentary*, 2nd edn, 2 vols. (Oxford University Press, 2002), vol. I, p. 862.

[137] S. Mathias, 'UN Efforts in Crisis and Conflict Management: Common Threads, Lessons Learned, and Future Applications', 32 *NATO Legal Gazette* (2013), p. 34.

[138] *Ibid.*

[139] Joint Declaration on UN/NATO Secretariat Cooperation, 23 September 2008, para. 5, www .natolibguides.info/nato-un/documents: 'taking into account each Organization's specific mandate, expertise, procedures and capabilities'.

Protector in Libya), or the request of a State for NATO support (e.g. the request from Greece in 2004 for AWACS coverage during the Athens Olympic Games or Pakistan's request to NATO for disaster relief following the 2005 earthquake and the 2010 flooding). In practice, as the Alliance normally operates under a Security Council mandate for its NA5CRO, only the first option would be relevant in case of NATO Peace Operations. At the internal NATO level, a decision whether NATO undertakes an operation or not will happen only when NATO Member States reach consensus about initiating such an operation in NATO's highest political body, the NAC.[140]

7. The entire decision-making process within NATO is based on consensus and consultations. Before consensus is reached, NATO Member States – actively and on a regular basis – consult with each other. Consultations take place at every level of the decision-making process within NATO, and they are essential for a decision to launch NA5CRO.[141] The cornerstone practice that all the decisions within NATO will be taken by consensus had been applied in NATO since its creation in 1949 despite not being formally recognised in any of its founding documents. As Peter Olson, former Legal Adviser to the NATO Secretary General, points out 'all important (and many unimportant) NATO decisions are taken directly by the Allies at weekly meetings of the NAC'.[142] All the NATO Member States have an equal right to express their views and all their views are taken into account during the consultation process before the decision is reached. Consensus is considered as a collective will of all the sovereign Member States.[143] The consensus principle means that agreements are accepted by each NATO Member. Because of the nature of the consensus rule, the allies do not manifestly vote. Rather, NATO applies a specific procedure called the "silence procedure". It means that a decision can be channelled through a document which will be approved only if no Member State raises an objection within the given period of time. However, if the silence procedure is broken, then further consultations are held on the matter until consensus is

---

[140] The NAC consists of permanent representatives of all Member States. It is the only body directly established in the NATO Treaty (n. 122) (art. 9).

[141] *NATO Handbook* (NATO Office of Information and Press, 2001), p. 155.

[142] P. Olson, 'Immunities of International Organizations: A NATO View', 10 *International Organizations Law Review* (2013), p. 420.

[143] S. L. Bumgardner, Z. Hegedüs and D. Palmer-DeGreve (eds.), *NATO Legal Deskbook*, 2nd edn (NATO, 2010), p. 47.

reached, although it may happen that consensus cannot be reached on a politically sensitive issue even after extensive consultations.

8. When the NAC is considering undertaking a Peace Operation, it first tasks the Military Committee (the senior military authority in NATO, consisting of Chiefs of Defence or their representatives) to provide military advice on this proposal. The Military Committee, supported by the International Military Staff, then turns this proposal into a military direction and tasks Allied Command Operations[144] to produce a report on how to organise and conduct the given operation, including financial and personnel requirements. The report then returns to the Military Committee and finally to the NAC for Member States to reach consensus on the proposal. The whole process by which NATO addresses its aims to manage the crises both internally (through prudent preparatory planning by Supreme Allied Commander Europe (SACEUR)) and externally as it facilitates the political decision-making of NATO Member States is called the NATO Crisis Management Process (NCMP).[145]

9. Because NATO does not have its own military forces (i.e. all forces participating in NATO operations come from individual Member States and, possibly, from NATO partner States), it is NATO's constituent nature that Member States (via their representatives in the NAC) make the decision to initiate and terminate every operation.[146] As a result, all of the NCMP process is subject to decision by the NAC.

10. The central role of NATO Member States is confirmed in the NA5CRO doctrine as it explicitly mentions 'there is no formal obligation for NATO nations to take part in a NA5CRO'.[147] Every operation has different purposes and goals and requires different assets; thus the level of a NATO Member State's participation in NA5CRO may differ from operation to operation, and a State may decide, 'on a case-by-case basis, whether it will commit forces and/or capabilities to the operation or not and what level of forces it may commit'.[148] Therefore, all NATO Member States have to reach a consensus in the NAC with respect to initiating NATO support to a Peace Operation or commitment to conduct an operation, but not all of them are required to participate in such an operation.

---

[144] After the transformation of NATO started in 2003, ACO is NATO's only strategic command tasked with conducting military operations.

[145] See further Appendix VII.

[146] NATO ACO, Comprehensive Operations Planning Directive, COPD Interim V2.0 (2013), pp. 1–2.

[147] AJP-3.4(A) (n. 131), LEX-3, para. 0104.

[148] Ibid., LEX-3, para. 0204.

For instance, not all NATO Member States participated in Operation Unified Protector in Libya and, of those that decided to participate, some contributed with more assets while others with more personnel.[149]

11. To initiate operations planning, the NAC issues an Initiating Directive once NATO Member States reach consensus over acting in a given UN Peace Operation. This directive, taking into account overall NATO needs, has to be further approved at the national level of each NATO Member State and, if appropriate, other Troop Contributing Countries (TCCs) (partners). Such a process represents an indispensable and constituent part of the process for NATO Member States as they keep their full sovereign authority to bind themselves to obligations made through their acts and decisions.[150] Therefore, their collective decision in the NAC needs to be accompanied by the decision of the respective national parliament assemblies or other authorised legislative or governmental bodies. For every NATO Member State, only this decision taken at national level represents the valid constitutional ground for actual deployment of troops and employment of national assets in the name of a NATO operation.

12. In addition to the regular consultations that take place to move ongoing activities forward, at any given time, the NATO Treaty, in article 4, gives each ally the right to bring issues to the table for consultation and discussion with other fellow members: 'The Parties will consult together whenever, in the opinion of any of them, the territorial integrity, political independence or security of any of the Parties is threatened.'[151] Article 4 is critical to NATO's crisis management process, since consultation is the basis of collective action.

---

[149] For instance, only fourteen NATO Member States from a total of (at that time) twenty-eight Member States actually engaged in this NATO-led coalition. For example, France, UK, Italy, Norway and others provided full support. The Czech Republic did not support the operation with personnel or military assets, but permitted its personnel assigned to various NATO commands to continue their work, e.g. pilots flying under the AWACS program. Germany did not join the coalition and even prohibited its pilots from flying AWACS when assigned to a mission related to Operation Unified Protector.

[150] *NATO Handbook* (n. 141), p. 157.

[151] Art. 4 NATO Treaty (n. 122).

4.6   SUB-REGIONAL ORGANISATIONS

4.6.1   Peace Operations deployed by a sub-regional organisation require a legal basis under international law and a decision pursuant to the organisation's constituent instrument. Peace Operations shall be conducted in accordance with international law including the UN Charter, and the internal laws and policies of the particular sub-regional organisation. Peace Operations deployed by a sub-regional organisation shall also comply with mission-specific agreements.

1. Sub-regional organisations[152] play a central role in preventing, managing and resolving conflicts. Especially in conflicts within their own geographic area, sub-regional organisations bring legitimacy and familiarity with local conditions, and are expected to have a greater incentive to bring the operation to a successful completion.[153]

2. In particular on the African continent, sub-regional organisations play an active role in the deployment of Peace Operations. As Regional Economic Communities (RECs), these organisations were originally set up to achieve economic integration. However, over the years they have come to formulate peacekeeping policies and have shown the ability or at least the willingness to act, often when continental or global peacekeeping efforts remain absent. Six out of eight African RECs[154] have formally identified peace and security as their objective, guiding principle or area of inter-State co-operation: the Economic Community of Central African States (ECCAS),[155] the Economic Community of West African States (ECOWAS),[156] the Southern African Development

---

[152] Chapter VIII of the UN Charter uses the term 'Regional Arrangements', but in this sub-chapter 'sub-regional organisation(s)' is used in a generic sense. The present sub-chapter concentrates on the sub-regional organisations (and more informal) arrangements on the African continent primarily because of the more dense practice that they have in the area of peace and security. This is without prejudice to the possibility of other (sub-)regional organisations or arrangements (e.g. the Commonwealth of Independent States, the Organization for Security and Co-operation in Europe, and the International Conference on the Great Lakes Region) playing a role in the deployment of Peace Operations.

[153] J. Cockayine and D. Malone, 'United Nations Peace Operations: Then and Now', 9 *International Peacekeeping: Yearbook of International Peace Operations* (2005), p. 11.

[154] In the two remaining RECs – the Arab Maghreb Union (AMU) and the Community of Sahel-Saharan States (CEN-SAD) – competences and capabilities in the field of Peace Operations are largely undeveloped or altogether non-existent.

[155] Art. 4(1) Treaty establishing the Economic Community of Central African States (18 October 1983, in force 18 December 1984), 23 ILM (1984) 945.

[156] Arts. 4(e) and 58 Revised Treaty of the Economic Community of West African States (24 July 1993, in force 23 August 1995), 35 ILM (1996) 660.

Community (SADC),[157] the Common Market for Eastern and Southern Africa (COMESA),[158] the East African Community (EAC)[159] and the Intergovernmental Authority on Development (IGAD).[160]

3. Most of these sub-regional organisations have a dedicated organ, body or mechanism which deals with peace and security issues, similar to the Peace and Security Council of the African Union (PSC AU).[161] Mirroring the continental design, sub-regional organisations have a body with decision-making power as to the deployment of standby forces to conduct a Peace Operation or an intervention. Generally, this body is assisted by a council of ministers, an early warning system, a council of elders and a defence and security committee with chiefs of staff of national armies and police commanders-in-chief. The ultimate decision-making power in these sub-regional organisations belongs to the collective will of the Heads of State and Government who, except for in ECOWAS, take decisions by consensus. This contrasts with the PSC AU, which is a representative body, not always meeting at the level of Heads of State and Government, and not necessarily voting by consensus.

ECCAS. The Peace and Security Council (known by its French acronym COPAX) was established by the ECCAS Conference of Heads of State and Government in 1999 and further detailed in a Protocol in 2000.[162] COPAX is a decision-making platform with a broad peace and security mandate, bringing together the Conference of Heads of State and Government, the Council of Ministers of Foreign Affairs, the Defence and Security Commission and the General Secretariat. The Council of Ministers gives an opinion on the main political issues and prepares the decisions by the Conference. In practice, the Council's standby duties are assumed by the General Secretariat through the Undersecretary-General for Human Integration, Peace, Security and Stability. The Protocol gives the Conference the supreme power to decide

---

[157] Arts. 4(b), 5(1)(c) and 21(3)(h) Treaty on the Southern African Development Community (17 August 1992, in force 30 September 1993), 32 ILM (1993) 116, as amended in 2001, 2007, 2008 and 2009.

[158] Arts. 3(d), 6(i) and 163 Treaty establishing the Common Market for Eastern and Southern Africa (5 November 1993, in force 8 December 1994), 33 ILM (1994) 1067.

[159] Arts. 5(3)(f), 6(b), 123 and 124 Treaty for the establishment of the East African Community (30 November 1999, in force 7 July 2000), 2144 UNTS 255, as amended in 2006 and 2007.

[160] Arts. 6A(d), 7(g) and 18A Agreement establishing the Inter-Governmental Authority on Development (21 March 1996, in force 25 November 1996), IGAD/SUM-96/AGRE-Doc.

[161] On the PSC AU, see further Chapter 4.3.

[162] Protocol relating to the establishment of the Peace and Security Council of the African Union (9 July 2002, in force 26 December 2003), www.peaceau.org/uploads/psc-protocol-en.pdf.

on peacekeeping and other actions for the consolidation, promotion and restoration of peace and security. COPAX further comprises the ECCAS regional standby force and an early warning system.

ECOWAS. The ECOWAS Treaty calls upon its Member States to co-operate in establishing an appropriate peace and security mechanism, paying particular regard to the need to establish 'a regional peace and security observation system and peace keeping forces where appropriate'.[163] In 1999 ECOWAS established the Mechanism for Conflict Prevention, Management, Resolution, Peace-keeping and Security,[164] which is based on co-operation between the Authority of Heads of State and Government and the Mediation and Security Council. The Mediation and Security Council is composed of nine Member States, taking decisions by a two-thirds majority vote. When meeting at the level of Heads of State and Government, the Mediation and Security Council is mandated to take decisions on issues of peace and security on behalf of the Authority, including the decision to deploy political and military missions and approve their mandates and terms of reference. The Mechanism is further implemented through the ECOWAS regional standby force, the Defence and Security Commission, the Council of Elders, an early warning system and the ECOWAS Secretariat which includes a Deputy Executive Secretary for Political Affairs, Defence and Security.

SADC. In 1996 the SADC created the Organ on Politics, Defence and Security as an institutional framework to co-ordinate regional action in the area of politics, defence and security. With the 2001 amendment of the SADC's constituent treaty the Organ was incorporated in the SADC's institutional framework. The Protocol on Politics, Defence and Security Cooperation gives the Organ the express competence to develop peacekeeping capacity.[165] In consultation with the Summit Troika (i.e. the sitting, incoming and outgoing SADC Chairpersons), the Organ Troika (i.e. the sitting, incoming and outgoing Organ Chairpersons) is responsible for overall policy direction for the achievement of peace and security. As the Organ's main body, the Organ Troika can send a recommendation to undertake a Peace Operation to the SADC Summit of

---

[163] Art. 58(2)(f) ECOWAS Treaty (n. 156).
[164] Protocol relating to the Mechanism for Conflict Prevention, Management, Resolution, Peacekeeping and Security (adopted and provisionally in force 10 December 1999), https://academic.oup.com/jcsl/article-pdf/2399887/050231.pdf.
[165] Art. 2(2)(k) Protocol on Politics, Defence and Security (14 August 2001, in force 2 March 2004), www.sadc.int/files/3613/5292/8367/Protocol_on_Politics_Defence_and_Security2001.pdf.

Heads of State and Government. The Organ's work is further supported by the Ministerial Committee, the Inter-State Defence and Security Committee and the SADC regional standby force.

COMESA. Since 1999 COMESA has a Committee on Peace and Security, consisting of senior officials from the Ministries of Foreign Affairs. This Committee can recommend a Peace Operation to the Council of Ministers; the recommendation is forwarded to the Authority of Heads of State and Government for the final decision.[166] The Committee is assisted by a Committee of Elders and an early warning system.

EAC. According to the EAC Treaty, the Summit of Heads of State and Government 'shall review the state of peace, security and good governance'.[167] To this end its Member States will 'formulate a joint mechanism for the operationalisation of peace support operations within the context of the Charter of the United Nations, the Constitutive Act of the African Union and the Treaty' and 'conduct peace support operations within the Community under a conflict prevention, management and resolution framework'.[168] It has its own regional standby force, a Panel of Eminent Persons and an early warning system. For the purpose of the African Peace and Security Architecture (APSA), most EAC Member States contribute to the regional standby forces organised through a dedicated regional mechanism, called the East African Standby Force (EASF; see paragraph 4 of the Commentary to this Rule).[169] Although on paper EASF is distinct from EAC's own regional standby force, it is rather unclear whether the latter should be regarded as complementary to the EASF or as one of its competitors.[170]

IGAD. The IGAD Treaty assigns the Assembly of Heads of State and Government the function of monitoring political issues especially conflict prevention, management and resolution. The IGAD Council of Ministers may make recommendations and follow up in this area. Military advice is provided by an ad hoc panel of Chiefs of Defence Staff.

---

[166] L. Matshenyego Fisher, A. Sarjoh Bah, A. Mniema, H. Nguema Okome, M. Tamba, J. Frederiksen, A. Abdelaziz and R. Reeve, *African Peace and Security Architecture (APSA): 2010 Assessment Study* (2010), www.securitycouncilreport.org/atf/cf/%7B65BFCF9B-6D27-4E9C-8CD3-CF6E4FF96FF9%7D/RO%20African%20Peace%20and%20Security%20Architecture.pdf.

[167] Art. 11(3) EAC Treaty (n. 159).

[168] Art. 8 East African Community Protocol on Peace and Security (adopted and in force 15 February 2013), www.africa-platform.org/resources/eac-protocol-peace-and-security. The Conflict Prevention, Management and Resolution Mechanism, adopted pursuant to art. 4 of this Protocol, contains the details on Peace Operations and their organisation.

[169] *APSA* (n. 166), pp. 40 *et seq.*

[170] C. Hull, E. Skeppström and K. Sörenson, *Patchwork for Peace: Regional Capabilities for Peace and Security in Eastern Africa* (Swedish Defence Research Agency, 2011), p. 24.

The Secretariat's Division for Peace and Security is equipped with an early warning capacity.[171]

4. For a broader contextual understanding of the relevance and functioning of these sub-regional organisations, it is important to take into account their position within the continental peace and security architecture. Peace Operations authorised by the AU are carried out by the African Standby Force (ASF). The ASF consists of standby multi-disciplinary contingents with civilian and military components ready for rapid deployment at appropriate notice.[172] It comprises five multi-national brigades, each hosted by one of five African regions (i.e. central, west, south, east, north). The RECs in the central (ECCAS), western (ECOWAS) and southern (SADC) parts of the African continent play a dual role. First, within the confines of their geographic region and pursuant to their own constitutive instruments, these organisations may decide on sub-regional Peace Operations in one of their Member States. Second, these RECs contribute their regional standby force as components of the continental ASF. In the latter case, the authority to deploy a Peace Operation will be derived from the AU Constitutive Act and the PSC Protocol, rather than from the sub-regional organisation's own constituent instruments. RECs other than ECCAS, ECOWAS and SADC (some of which have significant overlaps in membership) contribute to the regional standby forces in central, west and south Africa, or contribute forces to regional mechanisms specifically set up for the purpose.[173] In practice, this means that most AMU Member States participate in the North African Regional Capability (NARC) regional mechanism, while most EAC and IGAD Member States contribute to the EASF (EAC; see paragraph 3 of the Commentary to this Rule). Member States of CEN-SAD and COMESA participate in the standby forces of sub-regional organisations or mechanisms covering their own respective regions.

---

[171] *APSA* (n. 166), pp. 24, 33.
[172] On the continental African Standby Force, see further Chapter 4.3.
[173] *APSA* (n. 166), pp. 40 *et seq.*

5

The Applicability of International Human Rights Law in Peace Operations

1. International human rights law (IHRL) is, in principle, applicable at all times, in peacetime as well as during armed conflict. It is, consequently, a legal regime that is, in principle, applicable in all Peace Operations, regardless of the character of the situation in which the Peace Force is deployed. However, IHRL was primarily developed to regulate the exercise of a State's powers towards individuals within its own territory, and a number of complex legal issues arise when one inquires whether IHRL applies to the conduct of personnel in international Peace Operations. A number of legal questions have not yet received any final response in jurisprudence or doctrine.

2. Peace Forces have an inherent role in the protection of human rights and the restoration of justice, whether expressly declared in the mandate or not. In Peace Operations, the significance of human rights obligations may be seen via three different aspects: (1) ideally, the mandate under which the operation is undertaken will make express provision requiring not only all parties to the conflict, but also the Peace Forces (where they are not among the parties to the conflict), to respect and protect human rights; (2) even when such commitment has not been expressly stated, Peace Operations are required to respect the law of the Host State including its obligations under international law of which human rights are part; and (3), finally, the human rights obligations of the Sending State and/or of the organisation under the control of which a Peace Operation is conducted may apply extraterritorially for acts committed within its jurisdiction.[1]

3. The present chapter addresses the legal basis and other general principles as to the applicability of IHRL in Peace Operations. How particular norms, such as provisions concerning the right to life or

---

[1] See B. F. Klappe, 'The Law of International Peace Operations', in D. Fleck (ed.), *The Handbook of International Humanitarian Law*, 3rd edn (Oxford University Press, 2013), pp. 619–625.

concerning liberty and security of person, apply is addressed in other chapters of this Manual.[2]

5.1 The human rights obligations that are applicable to a Peace Operation may be derived from the international obligations of the contributing States and/or from those of the international organisation undertaking the operation and may be based on treaty and/or customary law provisions.

1. This Manual applies to consensual Peace Operations regardless of their organisational structure, but the organisation of an operation may have an impact on the applicability of particular norms. International Peace Operations involve several actors, primarily the international organisation that undertakes the operation, the Troop Contributing Countries (TCCs) and the Host State. All of these actors have independent obligations under IHRL, and it must be determined in each particular operation to what extent the obligations of the respective actors apply. As a rule, a Peace Operation consists of national contingents or individuals which are placed at the disposal of an international organisation, but the precise status of an operation may vary under the law of the organisation. With regard to the UN, Peace Operations are ordinarily established as subsidiary organs of the organisation. National contingent forces and contributed individuals remain organs and agents of their TCCs, and as such they remain, in principle, bound by the obligations of their respective TCCs. The contingent forces may also acquire a status as part of a subsidiary organ of an organisation, and as such the contingents and contributed individuals will also be bound by the obligations of the organisation. In the case of NATO and the EU, a Peace Operation is not considered as a subsidiary organ of the organisation. Furthermore, as regards the EU, this notion does not exist in EU law, but an operation is nevertheless considered bound by the EU's obligations under international law, as well as by EU human rights law. Accordingly, the human rights obligations of Peace Forces will be derived from the obligations of the TCCs and those of the organisation, which may be applicable simultaneously. Whether these obligations apply de jure in a particular situation can be determined only by reference to the factual circumstances of that situation.

---

[2] See e.g. Chapter 12; Chapter 13.

2. However, the organisational structure of specific operations may imply that only one set of obligations applies. This is an exceptional scenario, but the EU's exercise of civil authority in Kosovo may be an example. Most EU civilian missions have individually seconded personnel as well as contract staff, and in such cases only the EU's human rights obligations would apply. Nevertheless, even if only one set of obligations were to apply de jure in a particular operation, it is recommended as best practice that each national contingent respects in full the obligations of both the relevant TCC and those of the organisation which has deployed the operation. It must be understood, however, that the UN is not bound by the individual obligations of the various TCCs, which may differ significantly. Apart from strict legal considerations, practical considerations make the creation of indeterminate multiple obligations unwarranted.

3. Human rights obligations of TCCs are based on the human rights treaties to which the State is a party, and on customary IHRL. International organisations are generally not parties to any human rights treaties. By way of exception, article 59(2) of the European Convention on Human Rights[3] allows the EU to accede to the Convention, and the EU is already a party to the UN Disabilities Convention.[4] However, some international organisations have human rights obligations under their constituent instrument or other provisions of their internal law (see e.g. article 6 of the EU Treaty, the EU Charter of Fundamental Rights[5] and, arguably, articles 1(3), 24(2), 55(c) and 56 of the UN Charter). Yet most international organisations are not bound by any detailed human rights treaty obligations. Human rights obligations for international organisations, which may differ as between such organisations, can nevertheless be based on customary IHRL.[6]

---

[3] Convention for the Protection of Human Rights and Fundamental Freedoms (4 November 1950, in force 3 September 1953), ETS 5, as amended by Protocol No. 14 (in force 1 June 2010) (ECHR). On the EU side, art. 6(2) Treaty on European Union (Consolidated Version), OJ 2016 No. C202, 7 June 2016, p. 13, provides that '[t]he Union shall accede to the [European Convention on Human Rights]'. However, in Opinion 2/13 of the Court (Full Court) of 18 December 2014, ECLI:EU:C:2014:2454, the EU Court of Justice ruled that the draft accession agreement of the EU to the Convention (see Final Report of the ad hoc Group 47+1 to the CDDH, Council of Europe Doc. 47+1(2013)008rev2) was incompatible with the EU Treaties. The requirements set out in that Opinion pose major challenges, and it remains to be seen whether the accession will in fact take place.

[4] UN Convention on the Rights of Persons with Disabilities (13 December 2006, in force 3 May 2008), 2515 UNTS 3.

[5] Charter of Fundamental Rights of the European Union, OJ 2016 No. C202, 7 June 2016, p. 389.

[6] See *Interpretation of the Agreement of 25 March 1951 between the WHO and Egypt*, Advisory Opinion, ICJ Reports 1980, 73, para. 37: 'International organizations are subjects of international

4. In addition to the question of applicability of the respective human rights obligations, questions of attribution may arise to determine responsibility for conduct in specific circumstances. This Manual addresses this issue in Part IV.

5. A Peace Force must also take into consideration the human rights obligations of the Host State; see Rule 5.5.

5.2 The human rights law obligations of a State undertaking or participating in Peace Operations apply towards all persons who are within the jurisdiction of that State, as exercised in particular through its contingent or its personnel.

1. While Peace Forces should respect human rights in all aspects of Peace Operations, a distinction must be drawn between human rights-related conduct which is practised as a matter of best practice and human rights obligations which must be complied with as a matter of law. In order for a Peace Force to have legal human rights obligations towards anyone, there must be a relevant nexus between the forces and the potential rights-holders. In human rights treaties, this nexus is often referred to as the exercise of "jurisdiction", but this term is not used in all the relevant treaties.[7] When the treaty itself does not express the relevant requirement, there may be some uncertainty with regard to when a particular individual is protected under the treaty. This Manual assumes, however, that there are sufficient references in human rights treaties to "jurisdiction" as the basis for the application of such treaties for it to be reasonable to conclude that jurisdiction will also form the basis for the application of treaties without such a reference, as well as for the application of customary IHRL.

2. "Jurisdiction" in human rights treaties is primarily territorial, in the sense that States are presumed to have human rights obligations within their own territory but not normally outside the territory. Practice from international human rights bodies has nevertheless accepted a notion of extraterritorial jurisdiction, meaning that a State is considered to exercise jurisdiction, and consequently to have human rights treaty obligations,

---

law and, as such, are bound by any obligations incumbent upon them under general rules of international law, under their constitutions or under international agreements to which they are parties.'

[7] For a thorough discussion, see M. Milanović, 'From Compromise to Principle: Clarifying the Concept of State Jurisdiction in Human Rights Treaties', 8 *Human Rights Law Review* (2008), pp. 411–448.

outside its own territory in exceptional circumstances, namely if it exercises authority or control over an individual or over a geographical area, regardless of whether this authority or control is exercised lawfully or unlawfully. This is now accepted by all but a very few objecting States and is the entry point for legal human rights obligations for Peace Forces, who operate outside the territory of their TCCs.

3. International practice makes a distinction between the exercise of jurisdiction over a territory, and the exercise of jurisdiction over an individual.

4. A State is considered to exercise jurisdiction over a territory if it exercises territorial control over an area outside its own territory. If Peace Forces acquire territorial control that is similar to that of an occupying force, then the requirements for extraterritorial application of the human rights obligations of TCCs are satisfied. More limited territorial control may also satisfy the requirements. IHRL may, for example, apply based on the territorial notion of "jurisdiction" when the Peace Force is exercising elements of governmental authority over a State's territory, or over part of it, either on behalf of the government or as part of a "transitional authority" and in areas where the Peace Force exercises physical control over an area, e.g. an established protected zone, demobilisation camp or buffer zone under its control.

5. With regard to jurisdiction over an individual, it is settled law today that a State exercises jurisdiction if State agents, such as military forces, bring an individual within their control, typically through capture and detention, irrespective of the purpose or duration of such detention. Accordingly, if a Peace Force detains an individual for a period of time, that individual will be within the jurisdiction of the element of that force that detained him. However, most situations where a Peace Force comes into contact with the civilian population, such as during observation of a peace line, monitoring of demilitarised zones, supervising prisoner exchanges between the former warring parties, supervising explosive ordnance disposal operations or distributing humanitarian relief supplies, will not usually bring affected individuals within the jurisdiction of the Peace Force that is undertaking such activities. The same would ordinarily apply for routine patrolling, even if incidental shooting occurs during the patrol.[8]

---

[8] Within the context of the ECHR (n. 3), the European Court of Human Rights (ECtHR) has developed case law that suggests that even incidental shootings may give rise to human rights

6. If an individual is within the jurisdiction of a State, the precise nature of the human rights that are owed will be determined by reference to the IHRL treaties that bind that State. Accordingly, if for example a person is within the jurisdiction of a State that is party to the International Covenant on Civil and Political Rights,[9] it is the rights and obligations as set forth in that instrument that will be applicable. This may be significant because relevant rights such as the right to life may be expressed differently as between some human rights treaties.

7. This Rule would not apply where, exceptionally, the structure of a Peace Operation is such that national contingents or contributed personnel are solely subject to the human rights obligations of the international organisation (see Rule 5.1 and accompanying Commentary).

5.3   Each State contributing personnel to a Peace Operation shall ensure that contributed personnel comply with the international human rights law obligations that bind that State and are relevant to that operation.

1. Every TCC has an independent obligation under IHRL to ensure that its armed forces comply with its human rights obligations during its participation in a Peace Operation. This follows from the tripartite obligation which is incumbent on all States parties to all human rights treaties to respect, to protect and to fulfil human rights. The obligation to *respect* human rights means that the State shall not interfere with anyone's enjoyment of their rights and freedoms. The obligation to *protect* human rights means that the State shall take active steps to protect individuals against such interference from other actors. Finally, the obligation to *fulfil* human rights means that the State shall take active feasible steps through legislation, administrative practice, budgetary allocations etc. to realise the human rights of everyone towards whom they have human rights duties and obligations. This tripartite obligation, which is similar to the obligation under international humanitarian law (IHL) 'to respect and to ensure respect for' the Geneva Conventions of 1949 in

---

obligations; see e.g. *Jaloud* v. *the Netherlands*, Application No. 47708/08, Judgment of 20 November 2014 [GC].

[9] International Covenant on Civil and Political Rights (16 December 1966, in force 23 March 1976), 999 UNTS 171.

all circumstances,[10] means that States must ensure, to the greatest extent possible, that their armed forces comply with their States' human rights obligations.

2. This Rule is to some extent tautological, in the sense that it requires personnel to comply with legally binding obligations. The key issue, which rather defies definition in a rule, is to determine which human rights obligations are legally binding and, consequently, must be complied with.

3. The UN Human Rights Committee has stated explicitly that the International Covenant on Civil and Political Rights applies to 'forces constituting a national contingent of a State Party assigned to an international peace-keeping or peace-enforcement operation'.[11]

4. Other human rights bodies have not expressed this with the same level of clarity with regard to consensual Peace Operations. However, the European Court of Human Rights has held TCCs responsible for the conduct of their troops in international military operations,[12] which demonstrates that the Convention is considered applicable in Peace Operations if the criteria for application are satisfied in the particular case. Domestic case law also supports this conclusion.[13]

5. It should be recalled that the scope of human rights obligations will vary depending on whether the Peace Force operates in a situation of armed conflict or in a situation other than armed conflict. For the former situation, see Rule 5.8.

6. This Rule applies to personnel who are contributed to a Peace Operation by States, and who are therefore participating in it as State agents. The Rule does not apply to personnel who are participating in a Peace Operation in their personal capacity (e.g. contracted staff who are not State agents).

---

[10] Common art. 1 Geneva Conventions (I–IV) on the (I) Wounded and Sick in Armed Forces in the Field, (II) Wounded, Sick and Shipwrecked Members of the Armed Forces at Sea, (III) Treatment of Prisoners of War and (IV) Protection of Civilian Persons in Time of War (12 August 1949, in force 21 October 1950), 75 UNTS 31, 85, 135, 287.

[11] UN Human Rights Committee, General Comment No. 31 on the Nature of the General Legal Obligation Imposed on States Parties to the Covenant, UN Doc. CCPR/C/21/Rev.1/Add.13 (2004), para. 10.

[12] See e.g. *Al-Skeini and Others* v. *the United Kingdom*, Application No. 55721/07, Judgment of 7 July 2011 [GC]; *Al-Jedda* v. *the United Kingdom*, Application No. 27021/08, Judgment of 7 July 2011 [GC]; *Jaloud* v. *the Netherlands* (n. 8).

[13] See e.g. *The Netherlands* v. *Hasan Nuhanović*, Supreme Court (Hoge Raad) of the Netherlands, Judgment of 6 September 2013, 53 ILM (2014) 516.

5.4 In conducting Peace Operations, an international organisation shall comply with its international human rights law obligations.

1. As a subject under international law, an international organisation has international legal rights and obligations, including in the field of human rights (see the Commentary to Rule 5.1). It must comply with these obligations in all its activities, including Peace Operations.

2. The IHRL obligations referred to in this Rule will include any human rights responsibilities that are provided for in its mandate and/ or that are otherwise imposed by the UN Security Council, in addition to human rights obligations based on customary international law and/or applicable international treaties.

3. While contemporary Peace Operations are regularly endowed with specific functions with regard to the protection of human rights, mandates are generally formulated without any specific reference to the human rights obligations of the Peace Operations. If any reference is made to IHRL, the reference usually covers the parties to the conflict and recognises rights that already apply rather than imposing new ones. However, such references may cover all forces in theatre, including a Peace Operation,[14] and they may specifically impose a requirement that the Peace Operation respects specified additional human rights beyond recognising already applicable rights.

4. As a measure to ensure compliance with human rights standards, the UN has adopted the Human Rights Due Diligence Policy.[15] This policy sets out measures that all UN entities must take in order to ensure that any support that they may provide to non-UN forces is consistent with the purposes and principles as set out in the UN Charter and with its responsibility to respect, promote and encourage respect for IHL, IHRL and international refugee law.

5. An international organisation may also unilaterally take upon itself other human rights obligations, including responsibilities with regard to ensuring that other actors that co-operate with the organisation during an operation respect their obligations.

---

[14] E.g. UNSC Res. 2134 (2014), para. 48.
[15] Human Rights Due Diligence Policy on United Nations Support to non-United Nations Security Forces, UN Doc. A/67/775–S/2013/110 (2013), Annex.

5.5   In accordance with the obligation to respect Host State law, there is an obligation to respect international human rights law applicable to the Host State.

1. One of the functions of Peace Forces is, frequently, to promote compliance by the Host State with IHRL rules that apply to it.[16] To achieve this aim, it is of fundamental importance that the Peace Forces themselves observe these rules during the operation, even if neither their TCCs nor the organisation is bound by some of these rules. Accordingly, a State that makes its forces available to a Peace Operation should ensure so far as possible that the foreseeable activities of the force will not contravene these obligations. Relevant documents such as detainee transfer agreements, for example, should incorporate safeguards. However, internal rules and international obligations of the Host State, including those aimed at respecting human rights, need not be observed where and to the extent that these rules are contrary to the international human rights obligations binding on the Peace Operation or on an individual TCC. This flows from the obligation of the Host State to respect the exclusively international status of the Peace Operation, as recognised in the Status of Forces Agreement (SOFA) or Status of Mission Agreement (SOMA), and thus to exempt the Peace Operation from the obligation to respect Host State laws that are inconsistent with its international status.

2. In case of conflict between the human rights obligations of the TCC and those of the Host State, the obligations of the former should have priority. Such conflicts of norms will, most likely, never consist of mutually exclusive norms, i.e. that conduct which is required for one actor is prohibited for another actor; a more realistic prospect is that a Peace Force finds itself in a situation where specific conduct is prohibited by human rights obligations that are binding on the force, while the same conduct is permitted for the Host State. An example may be use of the death penalty. In such cases, the Peace Force cannot circumvent its own human rights obligations by reference to an obligation to respect the human rights obligations of the Host State. The reverse situation, i.e. that a certain conduct is permissible for the Peace Force but prohibited by human rights obligations of the Host State, is unlikely to arise; but in such a situation the Peace Force should respect the more stringent obligations.

3. The responsibilities of a Peace Force to respect Host State law is discussed in more detail in Chapter 9.

---

[16] See Chapter 3; Chapter 17.

5.6   Interoperability issues may arise if the States contributing to a Peace Operation have divergent obligations under international human rights law. Applicable human rights obligations cannot be circumvented by reference to the fact that other actors in the same operation have different obligations.

1. The States contributing to a multi-national Peace Operation may be subject to differing human rights obligations by virtue of their participation in human rights treaties that either omit certain rights or express them differently. How any resulting operability issue is most conveniently to be addressed will depend on the particular circumstances. It may for example be appropriate for the Peace Force as a whole to accept, for the period indicated by the circumstances, application of the provision containing the most demanding human rights rules, such that all Sending States choose to comply with the most stringent provisions that bind any among them.

2. An alternative approach involves the use of caveats to applicable Rules of Engagement (ROE) or operational instructions such that a State that has the more stringent obligations under IHRL shall not engage in activities that would involve a potential breach of its obligations. While States should avoid national caveats to the greatest extent possible, in some cases they may be preferable to imposing the corresponding restriction on the entire Peace Force.

3. It follows that it is for States and their contributed personnel to be aware in advance of the mission of the potential for operational situations to cause interoperability difficulties due to differing IHRL obligations of the contributing States. It is for the contributing States to make arrangements to ensure that national human rights duties are complied with in such a manner as does not impede the accomplishment of the operational objectives and to seek to ensure that their contributed contingents and individuals are appropriately briefed as to their human rights obligations.

5.7   If a Peace Force considers that it may be unable to comply fully with its international human rights law obligations while discharging its duties in accordance with the mandate, the State or international organisation, as the case may be, should consider seeking to derogate from the relevant human rights provisions where possible.

1. States may, to the degree and in the circumstances provided for in the applicable human rights treaty, exclude the application of particular

rights in whole or in part by means of derogation. Any act of derogation must be in accordance with the terms of the treaty concerned.

2. Derogation by a State or an international organisation from human rights obligations may result in a perceived conflict between the actions of the force in derogating and one of the likely core objectives of the deployment, namely to establish or promote respect for the rule of law. Accordingly, a derogation should be considered only if it is impossible for the derogating State or Peace Force to comply with the relevant human rights norm while discharging its mandate, i.e. derogation should be undertaken only as a last resort. Moreover, the consistency between the human rights obligations of the Peace Force and its fulfilment of the mandate is one of the many matters that should be considered at the commencement of the mission.

3. Derogation from human rights treaties is generally permitted only during certain serious situations of public emergency, typically a 'public emergency which threatens the life of the nation'.[17] International practice does not provide a decisive response to the question of whether derogation is also permitted from a State's extraterritorial obligations, but the Group of Experts who prepared this Manual takes the position that derogation is permitted if the emergency requirement is satisfied in a Peace Force's area of deployment. In coming to this conclusion, the Experts noted that once it is accepted that a human rights treaty applies extraterritorially, including in situations that undoubtedly qualify as emergency situations, the impossibility to derogate would lead to an unrealistic and unworkable situation in which States would be required to apply the treaty in full in circumstances where it is impossible.

4. No TCC has ever attempted to derogate from human rights treaties during Peace Operations, but derogation should be considered in situations where the Peace Force is unable to comply with applicable human rights obligations while fulfilling its obligations under the mandate. Without prejudice to State practice, in the absence of a valid derogation, Peace Forces are legally bound to comply with applicable human rights obligations. It must be acknowledged that TCCs may be reluctant to accept the political costs of derogating from their human rights obligations, but such political considerations cannot set aside the legal obligations. In any case, the political costs would have to be weighed against the risk of having to apply human rights provisions in full, possibly resulting in greater risk to deployed forces and a reduced ability to

---

[17] Art. 4(1) International Covenant (n. 9).

address security threats. In addition, there are a number of arguments that could well reduce these perceived political costs. In particular, derogations are not contrary to human rights but are precisely the mechanism which human rights instruments provide to deal with emergencies.

5. Furthermore, the UN Security Council may authorise conduct which does not comply with the human rights obligations of TCCs. The legal basis for this is article 103 of the UN Charter, which states that, in case of conflict, the obligations under the Charter shall prevail over obligations under 'any other international agreement'.[18] There is now widespread agreement that this provision also applies to obligations in Security Council resolutions, but it remains an unsettled question whether it also applies to authorisations and not merely to obligations. The European Court of Human Rights has held that a resolution prevails only if it explicitly provides an obligation to act in a manner which does not comply with human rights treaties.[19] Other practice suggests that article 103 also applies to authorisations, and this is the prevailing view in legal literature.[20] There is, however, a presumption that the Security Council does not intend to permit or impose derogations from IHRL unless it says so explicitly, and an authorisation to take 'all necessary measures' should probably not be considered as an authorisation to take measures that violate applicable human rights obligations. Moreover, it has not been settled whether, in case of a derogation under a Security Council resolution, States would still need to follow the derogation procedures under the relevant human rights treaties. The prevailing view appears to be that a failure to do so would not prevent reliance on a derogation.[21] To avoid doubt, States should therefore consider derogations from human rights obligations to the extent that this is considered necessary to achieve the mandate.

6. One practical example of a situation where a Peace Force may need to consider a derogation concerns security detention. European

---

[18] See Rule 4.03 in N. Melzer and G. Gaggioli Gasteyger, 'Conceptual Distinction and Overlaps Between Law Enforcement and the Conduct of Hostilities', in T. D. Gill and D. Fleck (eds.), *The Handbook of the International Law of Military Operations*, 2nd edn (Oxford University Press, 2015), pp. 70–75.

[19] *Al-Jedda* v. *the United Kingdom* (n. 12). However, see the ECtHR's insistence on complying with the Convention even in case of binding Security Council obligations which may prevent this: *Al-Dulimi and Montana Management Inc* v. *Switzerland*, Application No. 5809/08, Judgment of 21 June 2016 [GC].

[20] E.g. K. Mujezinović Larsen, *The Human Rights Treaty Obligations of Peacekeepers* (Cambridge University Press, 2012).

[21] See, by analogy, *Hassan* v. *the United Kingdom*, Application No. 29750/09, Judgment of 16 September 2014 [GC] (derogation based on clear provisions of IHL applicable in international armed conflicts).

TCCs will be bound by the European Convention on Human Rights, which permits detention only for specific purposes; detention for security reasons is not included. If a State that is bound by this treaty wishes to detain an individual on the basis that he represents a security threat, the State needs to do this while ensuring compliance with the treaty. In the absence of explicit authority from the Security Council as discussed earlier, and except for internment in an international armed conflict or occupation in accordance with IHL, the State would then need to derogate to avoid any doubt.[22]

7. International organisations may need to consider derogations to the extent that they are bound by IHRL treaties or customary law – the EU is an important example, given its extensive treaty based human rights obligations.

8. It is unsettled in international law whether it is possible, or necessary, to derogate from international customary human rights obligations. As customary rules in this field are likely to be less detailed than conventional ones, especially compared to some provisions in the European Convention on Human Rights (cf. the detailed provisions in article 2 on the right to life, or in article 5 on the right to liberty and security), the rules may include sufficient flexibility to cover measures that would require derogation under human rights treaties. For this reason, this Rule applies only to human rights obligations that are based on treaty law. However, international organisations may need to consider derogating under customary law if they are unable to comply with a particular customary rule while fulfilling their obligations under the mandate. The position of the UN is that a Peace Force has no legal authority to derogate from human rights obligations, as it can only derogate to the extent that the Security Council has authorised it so to do. Consequently, with regard to the UN a derogation from human rights obligations needs to be done by the Security Council (see para. 5 of the Commentary to this Rule).

9. The Group of Experts who prepared this Manual recognises that the issue of extraterritorial derogations is contentious and that it is undecided whether and when a Peace Force may legally derogate from otherwise applicable human rights obligations. Therefore, the Rule stipulates that it applies only where such derogations are possible. To avoid legal uncertainties, States parties to a treaty should consider derogating as a group rather than unilaterally.

---

[22] See Rule 13.2 and accompanying Commentary.

5.8   When applicable simultaneously, international humanitarian law and human rights law are complementary. In case of collision between a norm of international humanitarian law and a norm of human rights law, the more specific norm applies in principle.

1. Decisions of the International Court of Justice and prevailing academic opinion recognise that IHRL applies at all times including when an armed conflict is taking place. States have, however, agreed rules that are specially designed to address the unusual circumstances of armed conflict. The Court has addressed how these two bodies of law should interrelate. In the *Nuclear Weapons* Advisory Opinion, the Court stated as follows:

> The Court observes that the protection of the International Covenant of Civil and Political Rights does not cease in times of war, except by operation of Article 4 of the Covenant whereby certain provisions may be derogated from in a time of national emergency. Respect for the right to life is not, however, such a provision. In principle, the right not arbitrarily to be deprived of one's life applies also in hostilities. The test of what is an arbitrary deprivation of life, however, then falls to be determined by the applicable lex specialis, namely, the law applicable in armed conflict which is designed to regulate the conduct of hostilities. Thus whether a particular loss of life, through the use of a certain weapon in warfare, is to be considered an arbitrary deprivation of life contrary to Article 6 of the Covenant, can only be decided by reference to the law applicable in armed conflict and not deduced from the terms of the Covenant itself.[23]

2. In the *Palestinian Wall* Advisory Opinion, the Court reaffirmed that, subject to any permissible derogation that a State may make, human rights protections do not cease during armed conflict. As to the relationship between the two bodies of law, the Court considered that three kinds of circumstance might arise. Some situations, it felt, may be exclusively matters for IHL, others may be exclusively matters for IHRL and yet others may have to be considered by reference to both bodies of law.[24] Thereafter, in the *Armed Activities (Democratic Republic of the Congo v. Uganda)* case, the Court appeared to characterise the two bodies of law as complementary in nature.[25]

---

[23] *Legality of the Threat or Use of Nuclear Weapons*, Advisory Opinion, ICJ Reports 1996, 226, para. 25.
[24] *Legal Consequences of the Construction of a Wall in Occupied Palestinian Territory*, Advisory Opinion, ICJ Reports 2004, 136, para. 106.
[25] *Armed Activities on the Territory of the Congo (Democratic Republic of the Congo v. Uganda)*, Judgment, ICJ Reports 2005, 168, para. 216.

3. In the case of *Hassan* v. *the United Kingdom*, the European Court of Human Rights has confirmed its view that 'international human rights law and international humanitarian law may apply concurrently'.[26]

4. It suffices for the purposes of the present Manual therefore to note that, according to current legal interpretations, if a Peace Force becomes involved in an armed conflict, IHRL and IHL should be viewed as complementary bodies of law. In determining which particular rules of law will apply to specific activities associated with the armed conflict, it should be recognised that some situations will call for the exclusive application of law of armed conflict rules, some will require the exclusive application of human rights norms, and some will be regulated by a combination of the two. In the latter case, it will need to be determined how IHL and IHRL rules interact when they both apply. In principle, the more specific rule will prevail (lex specialis) but there may also be cases where the more recent rule will prevail.

5. The interplay between the two legal regimes is relevant for a range of activities that are performed by Peace Forces, for example in cases involving detention of individuals that represent a security threat, or in combat operations that cause damage to civilians.[27]

5.9   In UN Peace Operations the UN Human Rights Due Diligence Policy and the UN Human Rights Screening Policy apply. Regional organisations and arrangements should consider applying similar policies.

1. In accordance with the Human Rights Due Diligence Policy[28] UN support can be provided to non-UN security forces. In such instances, it must not participate in situations where the supported forces violate human rights. Furthermore, the UN Human Rights Screening Policy outlines the principles and methodology by which the UN pursues human rights screening of personnel.[29] TCCs have to guarantee that none of their contributed troops are involved in human rights violations.

---

[26] *Hassan* v. *the United Kingdom* (n. 21), para. 77.
[27] Rule 5.8 is identical to Rule 4.02 in Melzer and Gaggioli Gasteyger (n. 18), pp. 63–70.
[28] See Human Rights Due Diligence Policy (n. 15).
[29] United Nations Policy, Human Rights Screening of United Nations Personnel, 11 December 2012.

6

The Applicability of International Humanitarian Law in Peace Operations

6.1 International humanitarian law applies to a Peace Operation, in particular to its forces, when the conditions for the application of this body of law are met, irrespective of the nature of the operation.

1. It is now generally accepted that Peace Operations as defined in this Manual may become bound by international humanitarian law (IHL). This is clear from a wide variety of statements and documents by States and international organisations. Reference may be made in particular to the practice of the UN. That a UN Peace Operation may become bound by IHL as a matter of principle when the conditions for the application of this body of law are met is clear from the promulgation of the UN Secretary-General's 1999 Bulletin on the Observance of IHL by UN Forces.[1] It is also reflected in many Status of Forces Agreements (SOFAs) concluded between the UN and Host States of Peace Operations.[2]

2. The potential applicability of IHL is not affected by the fact that forces involved in the hostilities are, or were originally, deployed as part of a Peace Operation, that a Peace Operation has been established or

---

[1] UN, Secretary-General's Bulletin on the Observance by United Nations Forces of International Humanitarian Law, UN Doc. ST/SGB/1999/13 (1999).
[2] Some of these include the wording that 'the United Nations shall ensure that [name operation] shall conduct its operation with full respect for the principles and rules of the international Conventions applicable to the conduct of military personnel. These international Conventions include the four Geneva Conventions of 12 August 1949 and their Additional Protocols of 8 June 1977 and the UNESCO Convention of 14 May 1954 for the Protection of Cultural Property in the Event of Armed Conflict.' See e.g. art. 6(a) Status of Forces Agreement between the United Nations and the Government of the Republic of South Sudan concerning the United Nations Mission in South Sudan (8 August 2011), www.un.org/en/peacekeeping/missions/unmiss/documents/unmiss_sofa_08082011.pdf. For a discussion of the application of IHL to Peace Operations, see T. Ferraro, 'The Applicability and Application of International Humanitarian Law to Multinational Forces', 95 *International Review of the Red Cross* (2013), pp. 561–612.

authorised by the Security Council or that the mandate of the operation is based on Chapter VII of the UN Charter. This is in accordance with the distinction between the jus ad bellum and the jus in bello. The rights and wrongs of the resort to the use of force, for example that one party is acting in connection with a Security Council mandate against an aggressor, have no bearing on the application of IHL.[3]

3. The separation between jus ad bellum and jus in bello is reflected in common articles 1, 2 and 3 of the four Geneva Conventions of 1949,[4] and in the Preamble to Additional Protocol I.[5] That separation leads to the conclusion that the law of armed conflict applies equally to all States, international organisations and armed groups involved as parties to an armed conflict irrespective of the legality, or otherwise, of the resort to force that initiated the armed conflict.[6] The relevant issue therefore becomes one of fact, namely, whether there is an international (IAC) or non-international armed conflict (NIAC) in existence (on this distinction, see Rule 6.2 and Commentary). The fact that a Peace Operation is undertaking military operations pursuant to a peacekeeping mandate does not preclude the possibility that the hostilities in which it is involved may constitute a basis to classify a situation as an armed conflict. Furthermore, if a Peace Operation does become a party to an armed conflict, the military operations that the Peace Operation carries out are constrained by the same body of law as that regulating the activities of the opposing parties to the armed conflict. The peace-related mandate of the Peace Operation does not entitle its members to act outside the law of armed conflict nor may it be used as a justification not to comply with IHL, unless the Security Council adopts a binding decision that would specifically override IHL pursuant to article 103 of the UN Charter.

---

[3] C. Greenwood, 'International Humanitarian Law and United Nations Military Operations', 1 *Yearbook of International Humanitarian Law* (1998), p. 14.
[4] Geneva Conventions (I–IV) on the (I) Wounded and Sick in Armed Forces in the Field, (II) Wounded, Sick and Shipwrecked Members of the Armed Forces at Sea, (III) Treatment of Prisoners of War and (IV) Protection of Civilian Persons in Time of War (12 August 1949, in force 21 October 1950), 75 UNTS 31, 85, 135, 287.
[5] Protocol (I) Additional to the Geneva Conventions of 12 August 1949, and relating to the Protection of Victims of International Armed Conflicts (8 June 1977, in force 7 December 1978), 1125 UNTS 4.
[6] *Ibid.*, preambular para. 5; L. C. Green, *The Contemporary Law of Armed Conflict*, 3rd edn (Manchester University Press, 2008), pp. 23–24; M. E. O'Connell, 'Historical Development and Legal Basis', in D. Fleck (ed.), *The Handbook of International Humanitarian Law*, 3rd edn (Oxford University Press, 2013), p. 1.

6.2   The conditions for the applicability of international humanitarian law to Peace Operations are those set out in international humanitarian law itself and established by practice. They do not differ from the conditions that apply to forces other than Peace Operations. Peace Operations which are the subject of this Manual are operations deployed to situations of non-international conflicts; different conditions apply for determining the existence of international armed conflicts and non-international armed conflicts.

1. Although the principle *that* IHL may apply to a Peace Operation is not controversial, this cannot be said for the question of *when* it applies to its forces. IHL applies to the parties to an armed conflict. Instruments of IHL themselves do not define the term "armed conflict". An authoritative definition was suggested by the International Criminal Tribunal for the former Yugoslavia in the *Tadić* case. The Tribunal held that an armed conflict exists 'whenever there is a resort to armed force between States or protracted armed violence between governmental authorities and organised armed groups or between such groups within a State'.[7] Although there is some debate on the precise threshold at which a situation becomes an armed conflict, it is understood that this determination must be made on the basis of the factual situation on the ground and on the fulfilment of criteria stemming from the relevant provisions of IHL.

2. A distinction must be made between IACs and NIACs.[8] The two situations are subject to distinct sets of rules of IHL, and the criteria for determining their existence are also different. Although an in-depth discussion of those criteria is outside the scope of this Manual, the following can be said.

3. In the words of article 2 common to the four Geneva Conventions of 1949, the law of IACs as codified in the Conventions applies to 'all cases of declared war or of any other armed conflict which may arise between two or more of the High Contracting Parties, even if the state of war is not recognised by one of them'. This could now be seen as part of customary international law which applies to IACs generally. The International Committee of the Red Cross (ICRC) Commentary further explains that 'any difference arising between two states and leading to

---

[7] *The Prosecutor* v. *Tadić*, Decision on Defence Motion for Interlocutory Appeal on Jurisdiction, IT-94-1, Appeals Chamber, 2 October 1995, para. 70.
[8] On the possibility of a NIAC becoming an IAC, see Rule 21.2, Commentary, para. 3.

the intervention of members of the armed forces is an armed conflict'.[9] As mentioned earlier, the International Criminal Tribunal for the former Yugoslavia held that an IAC exists whenever there is a 'resort to armed force between States'. These views adhere to the so-called "first-shot" theory, according to which the law of IACs applies from the first moment that force is used. This view is controversial; however, there is practice suggesting that some States and international organisations consider that a minimum threshold of violence must be crossed before there is an IAC.[10] It is generally considered that the word "State" as used earlier can be replaced with "international organisation".

4. According to the International Criminal Tribunal for the former Yugoslavia, the law of NIACs applies to situations of 'protracted armed violence between governmental authorities and organised armed groups or between such groups within a State'. Two basic requirements flow from this definition of a NIAC: the armed violence must be of sufficient intensity and the parties must be sufficiently organised. The following are indicative factors in assessing whether the requirement of intensity is satisfied: the number, duration and intensity of individual confrontations; the type of weapons and other military equipment used; the number of persons and type of forces partaking in the fighting; the number of casualties; the extent of material destruction; and the number of civilians fleeing combat zones. As far as the requirement of organisation is concerned, the following factors are relevant, with the understanding that State armed forces are presumed to be organised: the existence of a command structure and disciplinary rules and mechanism within the group; the existence of a headquarters; the fact that the group controls a certain territory; the ability of the group to gain access to weapons, other military equipment, recruits and military training; its ability to plan, co-ordinate and carry out military operations, including troop movements and logistics; its ability to define a unified military strategy and use military tactics; and its ability to speak with one voice and negotiate and conclude agreements such as ceasefires or peace accords. The aforementioned factors must not be understood as an exhaustive checklist. Rather, they are guidelines in distinguishing NIACs from situations in which violence

---

[9] T. Ferraro and L. Cameron, 'Article 2: Application of the Convention', in ICRC (ed.), *Commentary on the First Geneva Convention* (Cambridge University Press, 2016), p. 86, quoting J. S. Pictet (ed.), *Commentary on the Fourth Geneva Convention* (ICRC, 1958), pp. 20–21.

[10] For a detailed discussion, see A. Clapham, 'The Concept of International Armed Conflict', in A. Clapham, P. Gaeta and M. Sassòli (eds.), *The 1949 Geneva Conventions: A Commentary* (Oxford University Press, 2015), pp. 10–16.

occurs that do not go beyond internal disturbances and tensions such as riots, isolated and sporadic acts of violence, and other acts of a similar nature.

5. The applicability of IHL to Peace Operations will have to be determined on a case-by-case basis in light of the factual environment and the operationalisation of the mandate for the operation in question within that environment. Relevant factors in making that determination therefore include, inter alia, the relevant Security Council resolutions for the operation, the specific operational mandates, the role and practices actually adopted by the Peace Operation during the particular conflict, their Rules of Engagement (ROE) and operational orders, the nature of the arms and equipment used by the operation, the interaction between the operation and the parties involved in the conflict, any use of force between the operation and the parties to an armed conflict, the nature and frequency of such force, and the conduct of the alleged victim(s) and their fellow personnel.[11]

6. The requirements as to organisation of the armed group involved in the conflict and as to the intensity and protracted nature of the hostilities are of vital importance. Sporadic uses of force by a Peace Operation in exercising its right of self-defence against acts of the armed groups and uses of force in response to armed interference with, or otherwise in defence of, the mandate (also against the armed groups) would not necessarily amount to a NIAC involving the Peace Operation. Accordingly, sporadic action by the Peace Operation against the rebels or dissident forces will, in most cases, not be regulated by IHL.

7. It has also been suggested that, in case a Peace Operation supports one of the parties to a pre-existing NIAC, it could become a party even if the intensity criterion is not fulfilled by the operation. Rather, it could be sufficient that it provides military support (whether kinetic in nature or not) to one of the parties that is closely connected to the collective conduct of hostilities, in particular support that has a direct impact on the opposing party's ability to conduct its military operations.[12] This view is unsettled as a matter of law.

---

[11] Cf. mutatis mutandis *The Prosecutor* v. *Issa Hassan Sesay, Morris Kallon and Augustine Gbao*, Judgment, SCSL-04-15-T, Trial Chamber, 2 March 2009, para. 234.

[12] See ICRC, International Humanitarian Law and the Challenges of Contemporary Armed Conflicts, Report for the 32nd International Conference of the Red Cross and Red Crescent (2015), pp. 22–23; Ferraro (n. 2), pp. 583–584. It must be noted that this so-called "support-based approach" would only complement and not replace the determination of IHL applicability on the basis of the IHL classic criteria for armed conflict. It is used only when Peace Operations

8. In practice there seems to be a tendency for international organisations and States to be reluctant to consider that a Peace Operation has become a party to an armed conflict. This is understandable, because when a Peace Operation becomes a party to an armed conflict it is difficult to maintain that it is an impartial actor and States may have agreed to keep the peace but not to undertake hostilities. Impartiality is seen as a fundamental principle of Peace Operations, and its preservation is stressed in military doctrine. Another relevant factor is that, during an armed conflict, as a matter of IHL the forces of a party to the armed conflict may legitimately be attacked by the opposing party. From the perspective of the protection of members of a Peace Operation, it is thus preferable to maintain that they do not belong to a party to an armed conflict. Such policy considerations cannot change the applicable law, however.

9. The UN's view regarding when IHL applies to UN Peace Operations is set out in the Secretary-General's 1999 Bulletin on the observance by UN forces of IHL. The Bulletin applies 'when in situations of armed conflict [UN forces] are actively engaged therein as combatants, to the extent and for the duration of their engagement'.[13] This formulation is somewhat circular, by referring to "armed conflict" and "combatants". That there is a minimum threshold of intensity for a UN force to become a party to an armed conflict is confirmed by UN practice, State practice and the case law of domestic and international courts.[14] When a UN-led Peace Operation uses force in self-defence or in defence of the mandate on a non-systematic basis, this is considered to fall below the requisite threshold. Until now, the UN has never officially declared a UN Peace Operation to be a party to an armed conflict. The establishment of an "intervention brigade" as part of the UN Peace Operation in the Democratic Republic of the Congo has, however, led it to explicitly suggest that that operation could become such a party.[15]

---

are closely involved in a pre-existing NIAC but do not themselves meet the criterion of intensity derived from common art. 3 of the four Geneva Conventions of 1949. See also Rule 6.7, Commentary, para. 3.

[13] UNSG Bulletin (n. 1), Section 1.1.

[14] See e.g. *The Prosecutor* v. *C.K. and B.C.*, Military Court of Appeal (Militair Gerechtshof) of Belgium, Judgment of 17 December 1997, *Journal des Tribunaux* (1998), 286; *The Prosecutor* v. *Théoneste Bagosora et al.*, Judgment, ICTR-98-41-T, Trial Chamber, 18 December 2008; *Issa Hassan Sesay* (n. 11).

[15] Statement by Ms Patricia O'Brien, Legal Counsel of the UN, at the 36th Round Table of International Humanitarian Law, San Remo, Italy (2013), http://legal.un.org/ola/media/info_from_lc/POB-San-Remo-36th-Roundtable-5-September-2013.pdf.

Although, as discussed, the application of IHL must be determined on the basis of the facts and not statements of the organisation concerned, a statement made by the UN Legal Counsel at the occasion of the 36th Round Table of the International Institute of Humanitarian Law underscores that UN Peace Operations can become parties to an armed conflict.

10. IHL is frequently applied in Peace Operations as a matter of policy, even where it is not formally applicable. It is obvious that such application can relate only to those rules of IHL that impose limitations on the conduct of armed forces. Such policy-based application cannot affect the application of other rules of international law that apply de jure. If such other rules are more stringent, they take precedence over policy-based application of IHL prohibitions and restrictions. IHL also contains many rules that explicitly or implicitly grant authorisations to armed forces. The most important example is the underlying assumption that in an armed conflict it is legitimate to kill enemy combatants. Such authorisations apply only when IHL is applicable de jure.

6.3   International humanitarian law does not regulate the conduct of a Peace Operation deployed in the context of an armed conflict to which it does not become a party but members of that force shall benefit from the protections afforded to civilians by international humanitarian law.

1. The mere presence of a Peace Operation in an area where an armed conflict is taking place between third parties does not make the Peace Operation a party to that armed conflict. Except in the cases provided for in Rule 6.4, the members of such an operation benefit from the protections afforded to civilians by IHL. This is reflected in the Rome Statute of the International Criminal Court[16] and the Statute of the Special Court for Sierra Leone,[17] and supported by the case law of these Courts, as well as that of the International Criminal Tribunal for Rwanda.[18]

---

[16] Arts. 8(2)(b)(iii) and (e)(iii) Rome Statute of the International Criminal Court (17 July 1998, in force 1 July 2002), 2187 UNTS 90.

[17] Art. 4(b) Agreement between the United Nations and the Government of Sierra Leone on the establishment of a Special Court for Sierra Leone (with annexed Statute) (16 January 2002, in force 12 April 2002), 2178 UNTS 138.

[18] See further Chapter 21.

6.4 Members of the military component of a Peace Operation lose the protection from direct attack afforded to civilians if and for such time as the operation has become a party to the conflict. In cases where the Peace Operation has not become a party, individual members of a force lose such protection only to the extent that and for as long as they participate directly in hostilities.

1. Rule 6.2 deals with the criteria for IHL becoming applicable to a Peace Operation. During the period when that state of affairs pertains, the first sentence of Rule 6.4 applies. When these criteria are met, the operation becomes a party to the conflict. As a consequence, the members of its military contingents lose the protection afforded to civilians. The most important aspect of this protection is the protection from attack. Accordingly, the members of the military contingents of the Peace Operation can be made the object of attack at all times during which the Peace Operation continues to be involved as a party to the armed conflict. The fact that a Peace Operation has become a party to an armed conflict in no way affects the protected status of civilian personnel of the operation, i.e. personnel other than military contingent members, who remain protected from attack save in the exceptional circumstances discussed in Rule 6.8.

2. Individual members of an operation may also lose the protection from direct attack afforded to civilians without the force itself becoming party to an armed conflict. This is the case when they take a direct part in hostilities against a party to an armed conflict. This is the approach that was taken by the International Criminal Tribunal for Rwanda, the Special Court for Sierra Leone and the International Criminal Court. In cases in which accused before these tribunals were prosecuted for attacking UN peacekeepers, they inquired whether the peacekeepers were entitled to protection as civilians. To this end, they examined whether the peacekeepers were taking a direct part in hostilities at the time they were attacked. According to the tribunals, if that had been the case they would have become combatants[19] and as such legitimate targets for the duration of their participation in accordance with IHL.[20]

---

[19] The word "combatant" is used here in a colloquial sense to reflect that they are individuals who have involved themselves in the hostilities, not to signify that they have combatant status as that notion is reflected, for example, under art. 44 AP I (n. 5).

[20] See *Issa Hassan Sesay* (n. 11); *The Prosecutor* v. *Augustin Ndindiliyimana, Augustin Bizimungu, François-Xavier Nzuwonemeye and Innocent Sagahutu*, Judgment, ICTR-00-56-T, Trial Chamber, 17 May 2011.

3. The International Criminal Court extended this approach to military personnel in a Peace Operation led by the AU. The Pre-Trial Chamber concluded that personnel involved in peacekeeping missions enjoy protection from attack unless and for such time as they take a direct part in hostilities or in combat-related activities.[21]

4. On the basis of the above, the international tribunals have concluded that personnel participating in a Peace Operation enjoy the protection afforded to civilians. If such personnel take a direct part in the hostilities when the Peace Operation is not itself a party to the armed conflict, they lose their protection from attack for such time as they do so.

6.5   If the requisite conditions are met, the Peace Operation may become a party to the conflict. Depending on the factual circumstances, individual Troop Contributing Countries may become parties to the conflict in their own right.

1. This chapter refers to Peace Operations as parties to an armed conflict. This constitutes a loose use of the term "party", which is descriptive in nature. Peace Operations as such normally do not have an international legal personality of their own,[22] and therefore they cannot be a party to an armed conflict in the legal sense. There is some controversy over the question how to determine which actor is or which actors are the parties to an armed conflict in a specific case in which the conditions described in Rule 6.2 are met. Some States contributing troops to a Peace Operation that become involved in an armed conflict appear to consider that those troops are bound by all conventional obligations their Sending State has entered into and by customary international law binding that State. They consider that the Sending States become parties to the conflict in the sense of IHL, while other States disagree. According to the Group of Experts who prepared this Manual, both the organisation leading the operation and/or the Troop Contributing Countries (TCCs) may,

---

[21] *The Prosecutor* v. *Bahar Idriss Abu Garda*, Decision on the Confirmation of Charges, ICC-02/05-02/09, Pre-Trial Chamber I, 8 February 2010; *The Prosecutor* v. *Abdallah Banda Abakaer Nourain (Banda) and Saleh Mohammed Jerbo Jamus (Jerbo)*, Corrigendum of the 'Decision on the Confirmation of Charges', ICC-02/05-03/09, Pre-Trial Chamber I, 7 March 2011.

[22] It should be noted that UN Peace Operations do in fact have the capacity to conduct significant operational and legal transactions as 'subsidiary organs of the Security Council' by virtue of art. 29 UN Charter.

depending on the factual circumstances, become a party or parties to the conflict.

2. If the international organisation concerned has an international legal personality of its own, it is possible for that organisation to become a party to an armed conflict. If it does not have such a legal personality, then only the TCCs can become parties to the armed conflict.

3. In the former case, in which both the organisation and the TCCs are potential parties to the armed conflict, the Group of Experts who prepared this Manual considered that which actor or actors become a party to the conflict depends on whether the conduct in question can be attributed to the international organisation or to the TCCs. This question is closely linked to the command and control relationship within the operation concerned.[23] Such relationships vary between international organisations, and even between different Peace Operations led by one and the same international organisation. It is possible that both the international organisation and the TCCs become parties to the armed conflict.[24]

4. It may be noted that, in the case where a UN-led Peace Operation becomes involved in an armed conflict and the conduct of its troops can be attributed to the UN, it would not be the UN organisation as a whole but only the Peace Operation that would become a party to the armed conflict.

5. It is possible that a Peace Operation deployed to an armed conflict situation may undertake or be the subject of hostilities that fall below the armed conflict threshold. In such a situation, standards of international human rights law (IHRL) and internal regulations (such as ROE) would regulate the activities of the Peace Operation, which would be permitted to use force in self-defence. Nevertheless, in cases where the members of the military contingent are, on an individual basis, directly participating in hostilities between the parties to the conflict (without the Peace Operation itself becoming a party to such conflict), IHL would continue to regulate their conduct, in the same way as it would regulate the conduct of civilian members of the operation who participate directly in the hostilities. Under human rights standards the right to life, as reflected in

---

[23] Ferraro (n. 2), pp. 593–594; M. Zwanenburg, 'International Organisations v. Troop Contributing Countries: Which Should be Considered as the Party to the Armed Conflict During Peace Operations', *Proceedings of the 12th Bruges Colloquium, International Organisations' Involvement in Peace Operations: Applicable Legal Framework and the Issue of Responsibility, 20–21 October 2011* (College of Europe/ICRC, 2012), pp. 23–28. See further Chapter 4.2.

[24] ICRC (n. 12), pp. 23–24.

applicable IHRL treaties, may also provide an indication of whether a particular use of lethal force was lawful.

6. Importantly, however, members of the Peace Operation will have the protection afforded to civilians under IHL. They also have protected status under the UN Safety Convention,[25] where applicable.[26]

7. This does not preclude members of the Peace Operation from using force in the exercise of their inherent right to act in self-defence. Such use of force will not generally amount to participation in an armed conflict. That will arise only if the conditions referred to in the Commentary to Rule 6.4 apply. A Peace Operation is generally bound by the obligation to 'respect and ensure respect for' IHL.

6.6   International humanitarian law will determine the geographical scope of an armed conflict to which a Peace Operation is a party.

1. A Peace Operation may become a party to an armed conflict that, following such involvement, remains non-international in character. This might occur where, for example, a Peace Operation is mandated to assist the territorial government to restore a stable environment and governmental control over its territory, including through the use of force. While the law of NIAC will in principle apply throughout the territory of the State in which the NIAC is taking place,[27] the rules as to the conduct of hostilities will in practice be relevant only in areas where hostilities are actually taking place, and rules as to other activities associated with the armed conflict, such as detention, will be relevant only where those activities occur.[28]

---

[25] Convention on the Safety of United Nations and Associated Personnel (9 December 1994, in force 15 January 1999), 2051 UNTS 363. The Convention, inter alia, requires States parties to criminalise attacks on peacekeepers.

[26] See Arts. 8(2)(b)(iii) and (e)(iii) ICC Statute (n. 16).

[27] Art. 2 Protocol (II) Additional to the Geneva Conventions of 12 August 1949, and relating to the Protection of Victims of Non-International Armed Conflicts (8 June 1977, in force 7 December 1978), 1125 UNTS 610; Y. Sandoz, C. Swinarski and B. Zimmermann (eds.), *Commentary on the Additional Protocols of 8 June 1977 to the Geneva Conventions of 12 August 1949* (Martinus Nijhoff, 1987), pp. 1359–1360, para. 4490; *The Prosecutor* v. *Jean-Paul Akayesu*, Judgment, ICTR-96-4-T, Trial Chamber, 2 September 1998, para. 635.

[28] It may be noted that the UN's view of the application of IHL as set out in the Secretary-General's 1999 Bulletin (n. 1), given the wording 'to the extent and for the duration of [the UN Forces'] engagement', would lead to a much more geographically restricted application of IHL in respect of Peace Operations. For the Secretary-General's 1999 Bulletin, see Rule 6.2, Commentary, para. 9.

2. The participation of a Peace Operation in a NIAC does not alter the geographical application of the law of armed conflict throughout the country where the armed conflict is taking place. It is controversial how much further the geographical scope of application of IHL may extend.[29] There is broad support for the notion that IHL also applies in the territory of another State when a NIAC "spills over" into that State. It is unsettled, however, whether it would apply throughout that State's territory or only in the part where actual fighting is taking place. This question is in practice not very relevant for Peace Operations, because their mandate is generally limited to the territory of one Host State. It has also been contended that IHL applies in the territory of the TCCs, but this is contested.[30]

6.7 If a Peace Operation participates in a pre-existing non-international armed conflict, or if there is no pre-existing armed conflict, the law of non-international armed conflict starts to apply when the hostilities involving the Peace Operation satisfy the requirements of a non-international armed conflict. International humanitarian law ceases to apply when the armed conflict comes to an end or when circumstances requiring the continued application of international humanitarian law (such as the continued detention of members of an armed group) cease to exist, whichever is later.

1. In an IAC, IHL starts to apply to a Peace Operation from the moment that the force becomes a party to the armed conflict in accordance with the criteria in Rule 6.1.

2. Neither common article 3 nor Additional Protocol II explicitly addresses the temporal dimension to the application of the law of armed conflict to NIACs. If a Peace Operation becomes involved in a situation which did not previously amount to a NIAC, the law of NIACs will apply to the situation, and to the Peace Operation's participation in it, only when the criteria as to intensity, protracted hostilities and organisation, referred to in connection with Rule 6.2, have been satisfied.

---

[29] See generally M. Schmitt, 'Charting the Legal Geography of Non-International Armed Conflict', 90 *International Law Studies* (2014), pp. 1–19. See also V. Koutroulis, 'International Organizations Involved in Armed Conflict: Material and Geographical Scope of Application of International Humanitarian Law', *Proceedings of the 12th Bruges Colloquium* (n. 23), pp. 28–39.
[30] See Ferraro (n. 2), pp. 611–612; ICRC (n. 12), p. 14.

3. A view has been expressed that, if a Peace Operation becomes a party to a pre-existing NIAC, the law of NIAC will apply to the activities of the Peace Operation from the moment of its participation. According to this view, the extent or form of participation required depends on whether or not one accepts the "support-based theory". If one does, the decisive element will be the contribution made by the Peace Operation's action to the collective conduct of hostilities. Accordingly, military support having a direct impact on the opposing party's ability to conduct military operations will turn the Peace Operation into a party to the pre-existing NIAC.[31] However, views differ on this point and it is therefore not settled law.

4. A distinction should be drawn here between participation of the force as a party to the conflict, and the direct participation of individual members of the Peace Operation in the hostilities. Possible indicators that the force has become a party to the conflict may, for example, include: participation of its members in the fighting; official statements on behalf of the force that it has become a party to the conflict; involvement in the conflict by units of the Peace Operation as opposed to individuals.

5. In an IAC, IHL in principle ceases to apply on the general close of military operations.

6. In the case of a NIAC, it has been held that IHL continues to apply after the cessation of hostilities and until 'a peaceful settlement is achieved'.[32] However, this criterion does not provide sufficient practical guidance. The notion "peaceful settlement" should be interpreted as a situation where a factual and lasting pacification of the NIAC has been achieved. In this regard, it has been argued that a NIAC ceases to exist, and the applicability of IHL therefore comes to an end, only when at least one of the opposing parties to the conflict has disappeared or no longer meets the level of organisation required by IHL. A NIAC would also come to an end when the hostilities have ceased and there is no real risk of their resumption even though the level of organisation of the parties is still met. Taking into account that NIACs are often of a fluctuating nature, typified by temporary lulls in the armed violence or instability in the level of organisation of the non-State party to the conflict, the closest one may come to the requirement of a peaceful settlement suggested by the relevant international case law is by waiting for the complete

---

[31] For more details, see Ferraro (n. 2), pp. 583–587. See also Rule 6.2, Commentary, para. 7.
[32] *Tadić* (n. 7), para. 67.

cessation of all hostilities without real risk of resumption before assuming that a NIAC has come to an end.[33] It is also possible for a NIAC to come to an end through means other than a peaceful settlement such as through military defeat of one of the parties to the conflict.

6.8 Where international humanitarian law applies, it determines which persons are protected.

1. This Rule reflects the key protective role of IHL. It should be noted, however, that this body of law is not concerned exclusively with protection but also deals with the rights and duties of all persons who become involved in or who are affected by the conflict.

2. The status of the military members of a Peace Operation that is involved in an armed conflict was discussed in Rule 6.4. To recall, this Manual views them as members of the armed forces of a party to the conflict as soon as the Peace Operation becomes party to a conflict. From that moment they no longer enjoy the protections afforded to civilians.

3. Medical and religious personnel of armed forces or groups, however, are not regarded as fighters and are subject to special protection unless they take a direct part in hostilities.[34]

4. Civilian members of the Peace Operation remain civilians at all times. They are protected from attack, unless and for such time as they take a direct part in hostilities. This category includes, inter alia, unarmed military observers who remain deployed with the agreement of the Host State or of all the belligerent parties. It also includes civilian police, including formed police units, as they do not perform any combat functions. As a practical matter, it would be important in this case to ensure that military observers and civilian police, including members of formed police units, remain clearly distinguishable from the military contingents. This will ensure that they are identifiable as legally protected from attack by opposing forces, while national military contingents engaged in hostilities would not enjoy such protection.

5. In principle, the same applies to civilian contractors, including the personnel of private security companies who may be providing armed security services.

---

[33] ICRC (n. 12), p. 11.
[34] International Institute of Humanitarian Law, *The Manual on the Law of Non-International Armed Conflict* (2006), p. 4.

7

Implementing a Gender Perspective

7.1 Gender issues should be taken into account, in all mission aspects, including in Peace Operations. Participants in Peace Operations should consider gender issues in terms of both participation and substance.

1. Gender refers to both men and women and to the roles that society expects men and women to perform. In times of conflict and violence, taking gender issues into consideration refers to the knowledge and recognition that conflicts and violence can affect men and women very differently. For example, while women may be the predominant target of sexual violence, men and boys may also be subject to sexual abuse, with often overlooked protocols for reporting or addressing their suffering and experiences, especially in societies with a strong honour–shame culture. Similarly, while men and boys are more at risk of being recruited into armed groups[1] or more generally being pressured into committing violence (often because fighting is what is expected from men), women run the risk of not being equal beneficiaries of disarmament, demobilisation and reintegration (DDR) efforts or programmes, whether they have taken part in hostilities or served in support functions.

2. Gender in Peace Operations therefore presents its own specific challenges, both conceptual and practical, and considerations pertaining to gender form a complex web of cross-cutting issues. "Gender mainstreaming" is the interweaving of all these considerations at each stage of the conflict response: from early warning and prevention, through crisis management and peace support, to post-conflict reconciliation and reconstruction efforts. One such challenge relates to the fact that "gender" is often presented as being associated solely with women. This is because it has been recognised that women suffer disproportionately

---

[1] *Gender and Early Warning Systems: An Introduction* (OSCE ODIHR, 2009), www.osce.org/odihr/40269?download=true.

in conflict and that their role in the peace process has historically been neglected, but conflict affects both women and men. The policies, initiatives and tools for addressing gender issues that are placed at the disposal of Peace Operation planners and participants should therefore reflect the different approaches that are necessary to address the particular needs of men and women and girls and boys, respectively.

3. Conflicts often start because of real or perceived inequalities and yet conflicts further exacerbate inequalities. While frequently presented as a technical exercise, addressing gender inequalities is in principle a complex, often political issue,[2] which involves recourse to all bodies of law and is supplemented with additional specific instruments.

4. In October 2000, the Security Council adopted Resolution 1325 on Women, Peace and Security.[3] Building on previous commitments, it emphasises the importance of bringing gender perspectives to the heart of all UN conflict prevention, resolution, peacebuilding, peacekeeping, rehabilitation and reconstruction efforts. In this ground-breaking resolution, the Security Council shifted the narrative from the stereotype of women as victims, demanded institutional change including through representative gender equality, and expressed a willingness to incorporate civil society in consultations surrounding the planning and conduct of its missions. The resolution does not provide specific guidance on the components of a "gender perspective" and appears to be using gender and women's rights interchangeably. It offers a catalogue of aspects to be considered and areas to be covered by gender mainstreaming in the resolution of conflicts.

5. Security Council Resolution 1325 involves numerous bodies of law, engages with each stage of a Peace Operation, caters for the majority of the beneficiaries of Peace Operations, and applies in parallel with the structural gender issues that affect the institutions – national or international – that intervene in Peace Operations. Gender considerations comprise both the traditional prevention and protection efforts, but also a strong empowerment aspect which seeks to address representation shortcomings. Such shortcomings include the insufficient representation of women where decisions are made, where mandates are negotiated, where operations are planned and where missions are executed, as well as the insufficient representation of women in the implementation of the peace process in the Host State.

---

[2] *State of Affairs in Women, Peace and Security* (Knowledge Platform Security & Rule of Law/1325 Dutch NAP Partnership, 2015).
[3] UNSC Res. 1325 (2000).

6. Operationalising Resolution 1325 has therefore not always been an easy task, leading the UN Security Council to acknowledge again, in 2009, that 'women in situations of armed conflict and post-conflict situations continue to be often considered as victims and not as actors in addressing and resolving situations of armed conflict ... stressing the need to focus not only on protection of women but also on their empowerment in peacebuilding'.[4]

7. Gender mainstreaming in Peace Operations necessitates knowledge and understanding of the gender aspects of all bodies of applicable international law, and requires a conscious implementation of these aspects. Peace operations, in their multi-dimensional design and purpose, draw on a particularly diversified normative framework, which comprises provisions from the UN Charter, as well as other legal instruments on international human rights law (IHRL), international humanitarian law (IHL) and the web of topical and regional instruments to which the Host State and the Troop Contributing Countries (TCCs) may be party.[5]

8. With respect to IHRL, gender considerations arise in several aspects. One is the implementation of what is often only a formal equality in law between men and women. For Peace Operations, enforcing equality (whether an explicit part of the mandate or not) may be a challenge, as the level of equality provided under the relevant societal norms may fall short of the human rights obligations of either TCCs or the Host State. Further, the human rights obligations of TCCs and the Host State may not perfectly overlap.[6]

7.2 Discrimination based on gender is prohibited. Gender-based violence and especially violence against women are a form of gender-based discrimination and constitute a violation of international human rights law.

1. Clauses on non-discrimination within the instruments and protections available under IHRL apply to women and men alike.[7] Consequently, the rights of women, alongside those of men, are guaranteed by the universal

---

[4] UNSC Res. 1889 (2009), preambular para. 11.
[5] See e.g. UNSC Res. 2242 (2015), para. 7.
[6] See Chapter 5.
[7] Universal Declaration on Human Rights, UNGA Res. 217A (III) (1948); International Covenant on Civil and Political Rights (16 December 1966, in force 23 March 1976), 999 UNTS 171; International Covenant on Economic, Social and Political Rights (16 December 1966, in force 3 January 1976), 993 UNTS 4. All explicitly prohibit all discrimination on the basis of sex.

and regional instruments on human rights. Additionally, several women-specific human rights instruments exist. For example, the Convention on the Elimination of All Forms of Discrimination against Women[8] (CEDAW), an international treaty addressing discrimination against women overall, is often referred to as an international bill of rights for women. While CEDAW did not originally specify women's rights in conflict situations, it underscores women's participation in all contexts, and established the foundations for the Women, Peace and Security agenda.[9]

2. In 1993 the Vienna World Conference on Human Rights specifically recognised violence against women during armed conflict as a violation of human rights,[10] and the Committee in charge of implementing CEDAW has further adopted General Recommendation No. 30 which applies specifically in conflict and post-conflict situations.[11] Regional instruments provide additional women-specific protections of human rights,[12] some of which address specifically the situation of women in armed conflict.[13]

3. Gender-based violence has also been at the forefront of minority issues in conflict, with notable examples such as the massacre of thousands of Bosnian men and boys in Srebrenica, or the particularly violent and widespread sexual abuse of women in Rwanda. Such intersections between gender and other discriminations highlight the difficulties confronting the protection of human rights in conflict, as conflicts usually emerge where inequality has already reached a threshold of significance for the affected

---

[8] Convention on the Elimination of All Forms of Discrimination against Women (18 December 1979, in force 3 September 1981), 1249 UNTS 14.

[9] *Global Study on the Implementation of UNSCR 1325* (UN Women, 2015), p. 29.

[10] World Conference on Human Rights in Vienna, Vienna Declaration and Programme of Action (1993), para. 38: 'Violations of the human rights of women in situations of armed conflict are violations of the fundamental principles of international human rights and humanitarian law. All violations of this kind, including in particular murder, systematic rape, sexual slavery, and forced pregnancy, require a particularly effective response.'

[11] UN Committee on the Elimination of Discrimination against Women, General Recommendation No. 30 on Women in Conflict Prevention, Conflict and Post-Conflict Situations, UN Doc. CEDAW/C/GC/30 (2013).

[12] Such as the Protocol to the African Charter for Human and People's Rights on the Rights of Women, also known as the Maputo Protocol (11 July 2003, in force 25 November 2005), OAU Doc. CAB/LEG/66.6; Inter-American Convention on the Prevention, Punishment and Eradication of Violence Against Women, also known as the Convention of Belém do Pará (9 June 1994, in force 5 March 1995), 33 ILM (1994) 1354; Council of Europe Convention on Preventing and Combating Violence Against Women and Domestic Violence, also known as the Istanbul Convention (11 May 2011, in force 1 August 2014), CETS No. 210.

[13] For example, in 2014 the African Commission on Human and People's Rights adopted Resolution 283 on the situation of women and children in armed conflict, which calls upon its States parties to adopt different targeted practices in response to conflict-related and sexual and gender-based violence.

communities. This is also the case in matters of racial or religious discrimi-nation, where gender, gender identity or "sexualised" rights intersect even more deeply with these issues of inequality and discrimination.[14]

4. The concurrent TCC/Host State obligations under IHRL should be used to increase the opportunities to promote and protect the rights of women, and to protect against the detrimental effects of gender bias generally, including the preconceived roles for both sexes. In some instances, the Host State human rights apparatus might be anything from institutionally destroyed to particularly detrimental to women or sexual minorities, often supplemented by strong cultural and contextual impediments to gender equality and protections. In such instances it is useful to note that CEDAW calls on States to 'modify the social and cul-tural patterns of conduct of men and women, with a view to achieving the elimination of prejudices and customary and all other practices which are based on the idea of the inferiority or the superiority of either of the sexes or on stereotyped roles for men and women'.[15]

5. More than a decade after the milestone Resolution 1325, the Security Council unanimously adopted Resolution 2122 (2013)[16] and underscored the Security Council's desire to effectively augment the substantive equality provisions contained in Resolution 1325 and in the Women, Peace and Security agenda.[17] Its insistence on women's and girls' "empowerment and gender equality" resonates distinctly with IHRL, not only because it refers to topics such as promotion of the rule of law and threats to peace and security by terrorist acts, but also because the Security Council specifically addresses 'unequal citizenship rights, gender-biased application of asylum laws, and obstacles to registering and accessing identity documents', the differentiated impact on women and girls of forced displacement and enforced disappearance, as well as 'the need for access to the full range of sexual and reproductive health services, including regarding pregnancies resulting from rape, without discrimination'. In its substantive paragraphs, the Security Council resolution also calls for specific inclusion of provisions on women's

---

[14] See namely M. O'Flaherty, 'Sexual Orientation and Gender Identity', and D. Otto, 'Women's Rights', in D. Moeckli, S. Shah and S. Sivakumaran (eds.), *International Human Rights Law* (Oxford University Press, 2014), pp. 303–315 and 316–331.

[15] Art. 5(a) CEDAW (n. 8).

[16] UNSC Res. 2122 (2013).

[17] A. Swaine, 'Substantive New Normative Provisions on Women and Armed Conflict Concurrently Adopted by the United Nations Security Council and the CEDAW Committee', 18 *ASIL Insights* (2014), www.asil.org/insights/volume/18/issue/5/substantive-new-normative-provisions-women-and-armed-conflict.

participation in the electoral and political processes, and other reform programmes where these tasks are part of a Peace Operation's mandate; and addresses the obstacles to the realisation of their rights, 'including through gender-responsive legal, judicial and security sector reform'.[18]

6. Finally, other "thematic" instruments can also be effectively used to protect particularly vulnerable segments of the population such as women, children and minorities. While not always specifically developed to meet gender-related needs for protection, they have evolved to address situations where gender issues are at the forefront of their subject matter, often of relevance in conflict or post-conflict situations. For example, The UN Convention against Transnational Organized Crime[19] has been supplemented by a Protocol specifically seeking to prevent, suppress and punish trafficking in persons, especially women and children.[20] Similarly, the 2014 Arms Trade Treaty includes a provision requiring States to 'take into account the risk of the conventional arms ... being used to commit or facilitate serious acts of gender-based violence or serious acts of violence against women and children'.[21]

7. IHL, the law relating to the conduct of hostilities and the protection of persons not or no longer taking part in hostilities also offers and envisages different roles for men and women in armed conflict. These roles have certainly evolved; women are not the exclusive victims of rape, nor are men the only active participants in armed conflict. However, the most significant instruments on the laws of war do include specific requirements, aiming particularly towards the protection of women. The four Geneva Conventions of 1949,[22] for example, offer a range of protections for women. Some of them relate to the biological aspects of their sex, and refer to objectively female attributes such as being pregnant or nursing.[23] Caring for children, however, is something traditionally seen as inherently "feminine", and is recognised in the Geneva Conventions

---

[18] UNSC Res. 2122 (2013), paras. 4, 10.

[19] UN Convention against Transnational Organized Crime (15 November 2000, in force 29 September 2003), UNGA Res. 55/25 (2000).

[20] Protocol to Prevent, Suppress and Punish Trafficking in Persons, especially Women and Children (15 November 2000, in force 25 December 2003), UNGA Res. 55/25 (2000).

[21] Art. 7(4) Arms Trade Treaty (2 April 2013, in force 24 December 2014), UNGA Res. 67/234 (2013).

[22] Geneva Conventions (I–IV) on the (I) Wounded and Sick in Armed Forces in the Field, (II) Wounded, Sick and Shipwrecked Members of the Armed Forces at Sea, (III) Treatment of Prisoners of War and (IV) Protection of Civilian Persons in Time of War (12 August 1949, in force 21 October 1950), 75 UNTS 31, 85, 135, 287.

[23] Art. 89 Geneva Convention IV (n. 22).

under the phrase 'mothers with infants and young children', thus ignoring circumstances where the primary caregivers are men, and where these men require similar protections in order to ensure the protection and well-being of children.[24] It is therefore useful to make a more gender-neutral approach to achieve the best possible protection when IHL applies in Peace Operations.[25]

8. That increasing numbers of women are taking part in hostilities, for example, underlines the need to envisage protections within IHL that are tailored according to gender, both to implement fully the formal equality already enshrined in the Geneva Conventions, and to deliver specific protections for women ('all prisoners of war should be treated alike by the detaining power', 'without adverse distinction founded on sex', offering women treatment 'with all consideration due to their sex' but also 'as favourable as that granted to men').[26] Gender issues also arise in relation to detention and interrogation, where gender considerations should comprise issues such as separation of quarters, access and visits, family life, or protection against sexual or sexualised practices that may result in physical and psychological trauma and distress.[27]

9. The understanding of gender issues in relation to IHL has also evolved. The language of the Additional Protocols thus recognises a more inclusive approach towards the use of sexual violence in conflict. Attention shifts away from matters of "honour" or chastity for women, and there is a recognition that, while statistically women are disproportionately affected by rape and enforced prostitution, it remains a matter of personal dignity.[28] At the same time, the increase in violence against civilian populations has highlighted the widespread use of sexual violence in conflict, leading the Security Council to deplore the use of rape as a tactic of war,[29] and to seek to increase the measures for prevention and protection.

---

[24] *Ibid.*, art. 132. See also the prohibitions on executing women with young children in art. 76(3) Protocol (I) Additional to the Geneva Conventions of 12 August 1949, and relating to the Protection of Victims of International Armed Conflicts (8 June 1977, in force 7 December 1978), 1125 UNTS 4; art. 6(4) Protocol (II) Additional to the Geneva Conventions of 12 August 1949, and relating to the Protection of Victims of Non-International Armed Conflicts (8 June 1977, in force 7 December 1978), 1125 UNTS 610.

[25] See further Chapter 6.

[26] See art. 12 Geneva Convention I (n. 22); art. 12 Geneva Convention II (n. 22); arts. 14 and 16 Geneva Convention III (n. 22); art. 27 Geneva Convention IV (n. 22); art. 75 AP I (n. 24); art. 4 AP II (n. 24).

[27] See further Chapter 13.

[28] See, respectively, art. 76 AP I (n. 24) and art. 4(2)(e) AP II (n. 24).

[29] UNSC Res. 1820 (2008), para. 1; UNSC Res. 1888 (2009), para. 1; UNSC Res. 1889 (2009), para. 3; UNSC Res. 1960 (2010), para. 1.

10. Gender-based crimes can engage the criminal responsibility of individuals including in the context of Peace Operations.[30] However, as international criminal casework overall demonstrates, investigation and prosecution of gender-based and sexual violence committed during armed conflict are increasing, but still lag behind other crimes. The Security Council has repeatedly[31] called for action to end impunity, strengthen national and international capacity and punish perpetrators of conflict-related sexual violence, whether civilians or military personnel.[32] For example, the Rome Statute of the International Criminal Court (ICC) criminalises sexual violence when it amounts to genocide, crimes against humanity or war crimes.[33] It further provides for prosecution of sexual and gender-based violence under other crimes such as persecution or torture, and the Office of the Prosecutor has vowed to 'seek to highlight the gender-related aspects of other crimes within its jurisdiction', recognising that '[i]n conflict situations, acts of sexual and gender-based crimes rarely occur in isolation from other crimes'.[34]

7.3 A gender perspective should be taken into account throughout the life-cycle of a Peace Operation, from its inception and the development of its mandate to the performance of every task provided for in the mandate. Gender-specific indicators should also be included in the data collection and reporting requirements before, during and after a Peace Operation to provide a complete gender issues picture, to inform decision-making and to facilitate the learning of lessons.

1. As with Peace Operations, "gender" does not constitute a discrete topic operating within a single body of law, or where a single set of skills or expertise is required to effectively and efficiently carry out the

---

[30] See further Chapter 21.

[31] UNSC Res. 1325 (2000), para. 11, UNSC Res. 1820 (2008), para. 4, UNSC Res. 1889 (2009), para. 3, and UNSC Res. 2106 (2013), paras. 2 and 18, all emphasise States' responsibilities to put an end to impunity and to prosecute crimes against humanity and war crimes, including those related to sexual violence, but also to undertake the necessary legal and judicial reforms (UNSC Res. 1888 (2009), para. 5) and strengthen the rule of law and the capacity of civilian and military justice systems to address sexual violence in conflict and post-conflict situations (UNSC Res. 2106 (2013), para. 18).

[32] UNSC Res. 1888 (2009), para. 7.

[33] Arts. 7(1)(g), 8(2)(b)(xxii) and 8(2)(e)(vi) Rome Statute of the International Criminal Court (17 July 1998, in force 1 July 2002), 2187 UNTS 90.

[34] ICC, OTP Policy Paper on Sexual and Gender-Based Crimes (2014), pp. 6, 27.

gender-related aspects of the mandate or even of a task. Gender issues being human issues, they cut across each and every aspect of Peace Operations. The specific experiences, rights and roles of women and girls, men and boys must be included in preliminary analysis and assessments and thus be fed into the concrete strategies for the design of missions and the formulation and renewal of the mandate.[35] This comprises, but is not limited to, incorporating gender indicators in the early warning systems and gathering sex and age disaggregated data, as well as including a gender perspective in technical and financial assessments which would inform the scope of the mandate of the Peace Operation.

2. Mandates of Peace Operations sometimes expressly call for incorporation of gender perspectives into mission planning and operations. In addition, there are often provisions geared towards the specific protection of women and children as a particularly vulnerable part of the civilian population. In parallel, a number of other thematic resolutions demonstrated the Security Council's engagement with the protection of civilian populations at risk of particular forms of abuse that are exacerbated in conflict situations, and to which these populations are particularly vulnerable. Such resolutions aim to provide specific tools for and attention to, for example, the protection of children in armed conflict, or the prevention of sexual exploitation and abuse.[36] The mandate of the UN Multidimensional Integrated Stabilization Mission in the Central African Republic (MINUSCA), for example, lists not only references to specific gender-related activities, but also a requirement 'to take fully into account gender considerations as a cross-cutting issue throughout its mandate and to assist the Government of the CAR [Central African Republic] in ensuring the full and effective participation, involvement and representation of women in all spheres and at all levels, including in stabilisation activities, security sector reform and DDR and DDRR [disarmament, demobilisation, reintegration and repatriation] processes, as well as in the national political dialogue and electoral processes, through, inter alia, the provision of gender advisers, and further ... reporting by MINUSCA to the Council on this issue'.[37] This effectively establishes a provision for gender mainstreaming in dealings with the Host State, and an obligation to report back to the Security Council.

---

[35] UNSC Res. 2242 (2015), para. 7; Report of the High-Level Independent Panel on Peace Operations, Uniting Our Strengths for Peace: Politics, Partnership and People, UN Doc. A/70/95-S/2015/446 (2015), paras. 178, 257 *et seq.*

[36] See Chapter 14.2; Chapter 14.3.

[37] UNSC Res. 2149 (2014), para. 35.

3. Gender mainstreaming requires the application of a gender lens even to mandated tasks that are seemingly gender-neutral. For such tasks, policies and activities, success and lasting impact will also mean assessing and taking into account the different needs of their beneficiaries. One example of this concerns mainstreaming gender in demining and removal of unexploded ordnance. Consideration of gender in matters of surveying, clearance and victim assistance should inform decisions on and the activities carried out within the tasks pertaining to demining and removal of explosive remnants,[38] in order to ensure fuller protection of the categories of the population that are, because of their gender, engaged in activities presenting a higher risk of contact with unexploded ordnance, or who, if injured, risk further discrimination by the community.[39] For example, in certain countries boys are at higher risk of injury, because girls may not be allowed to play outside by themselves. If injured, however, girls are more likely to be faced with social exclusion and further discrimination.[40]

4. Mandates with DDR components must consider how men and women are affected differently in the immediate aftermath of an armed conflict, and in the DDR process. The overwhelming majority of DDR initiatives and mechanisms focus on men, as they traditionally compose the majority of the population engaged in hostilities. However, both men and women can transgress, willingly or unwillingly, the gender norms and roles prescribed in the community in which they live and evolve.[41] The most frequent examples include women who have participated in the hostilities, and who are overlooked by the DDR process or even stigmatised within their communities for having broken with the applicable stereotypes of victims, caregivers or supporters of the fighting men. Physical and psychological support for men, on the other hand, should consider the obstacles created by a stereotypical approach to manhood, toughness or the stigma of sexual abuse experienced by men and boys.

5. Further, design and implementation of DDR programmes must take into account measures to specifically address gender-related issues and traumas such as abduction and sexual and gender-based violations, as well as equal access to economic, educational and monetary opportunities arising from the DDR process. In order to ensure sustainable implementation

---

[38] UNSC Res. 1325 (2000), preambular para. 7, calls for 'all parties to ensure that mine clearance and mine awareness programmes take into account the special needs of women and girls'.
[39] *Gender Resource Package for Peacekeeping Operations* (UN DPKO, 2004), pp. 138–142.
[40] See further Chapter 18.
[41] C. Chinkin and H. Charlesworth, 'Building Women into Peace: The International Legal Framework', 27 *Third World Quarterly* (2006), pp. 937–957.

of their initiatives and measures, DDR programmes should involve women and women's groups as early as possible in the process and ensure the completeness and longevity of these efforts.[42]

6. Security Council Resolution 1325 discusses a multi-faceted gender approach to DDR relating specifically to women's issues. It encourages 'all those involved in the planning for disarmament, demobilization and reintegration to consider the different needs of female and male ex-combatants and to take into account the needs of their dependants', a provision also reflected in the UN Department of Peacekeeping Operations (DPKO) Gender Forward Looking Strategy.[43]

7. Gender considerations can be reflected in DDR via three angles: equality of treatment in DDR-related programmes and mechanisms, the different needs of women and men, and consultation and engagement with women on the broader DDR process.

8. When engaging in DDR, Peace Operations should foresee separate protocols for the demobilisation of women. Female fighters are often subject to sexual abuse and exploitation by fellow fighters, even when not specifically coerced into the war effort and community as "wives" for forced domestic labour or other conjugal duties. Placement in the same demobilisation facilities and programmes might result in continuing the abuse on women, or curtailing the effectiveness of the mental and physical healing process (for men and women alike) by perpetuating fear or shame through physical proximity.

9. In matters of overall reintegration, women – whether former fighters or dependants – should be systematically included in the mechanisms providing different types of support, from basic food and shelter, to opportunities for schooling or professional reinsertion. Gender considerations should guide the definition of the eligibility criteria for participation in DDR programmes. Status of the non-combatant abducted women and girls, or informal partnerships and their offspring, will establish the status of "dependant" for the purposes of DDR. Demobilisation camps and assembly areas should not separate families which consist of combatants and "camp followers" as this may render certain members of the family

---

[42] For example, UNSC Res. 2242 (2015), para. 15, calls for 'empowering women, including through capacity-building efforts, as appropriate, to participate in the design and implementation of efforts related to the prevention, combating and eradication of the illicit transfer, and the destabilizing accumulation and misuse of small arms and light weapons'.

[43] UNSC Res. 1325 (2000), para. 13; *Gender Forward Looking Strategy 2014–2018* (UN DPKO/DFS, 2014), p. 13.

more vulnerable.[44] In many instances, when DDR efforts are more decentralised or community-run, women and girls may also be set aside due to community non-acceptance, especially in instances of female combatants or in cases of rape or pregnancy.

10. The process of DDR often results in the demobilisation of large numbers of predominantly male ex-combatants. Violence arising from non-existent or inadequate psychological support, as well as economic competition for a labour market that may have also suffered from the conflict or where women may have been integrated, are among the frustrations and sources of tension between genders in post-conflict situations.[45]

11. Disarmament might result in the availability and proliferation of small arms and light weapons and is often the origin of more, albeit lower-intensity violence. Such violence may not be related to the conflict but is of criminal nature where women are at particular risk.[46] Small arms are reported to contribute to an increase in death by domestic violence and also to lead to an increased risk of sexual violence.[47] For men, especially boys, the risk of being recruited into local gangs operating on the criminal plane is greatly increased. Unresolved trauma due to their violent experiences may also lead to re-recruitment into armed groups and forces.[48]

12. DDR programmes with resettlement elements should be mindful of the local or customary laws on the rights of women to own, inherit or dispose of property. When male relatives are deceased or missing, women might also not be able to return to their family homes.[49]

13. Women's associations and informal networks should be included in the conception and implementation of the DDR process as they are likely to ensure the continuity of the reintegration process at the end of the formal DDR programmes. Women and women's networks have also historically played an important role in advocating disarmament. Consultations and engagement with women's groups can provide a

---

[44] *Women, Peace and Security: Study Submitted by the Secretary-General pursuant to Security Council Resolution 1325 (2000)* (UN, 2002), p. 131, paras. 401–412.

[45] *Ibid.*, p. 118, para. 361.

[46] Conflict-Related Sexual Violence: Report of the Secretary-General, UN Doc. S/2015/203 (2015), indicates that often abduction, arbitrary detention, torture, rape and other forms of sexual violence have increased in the post-war periods.

[47] H. Durham, 'International Humanitarian Law and the Protection of Women', in H. Durham and T. Gurd (eds.), *Listening to the Silences: Women and War* (Martinus Nijhoff, 2005), p. 105.

[48] *Gender Resource Package* (n. 39), p. 129.

[49] *Women, Peace and Security* (n. 44), p. 135, para. 416.

precious ally in public campaigning as well as a source of information on local threat perceptions, supply chains and caches or trade.[50]

14. Peace negotiations and the monitoring of the peace implementation process should comprise a twofold approach to gender mainstreaming if reflected in the mission mandate: (1) greater overall participation of women in the peace negotiation and implementation processes; and (2) the addressing of specific gender issues in the negotiation and drafting of the peace agreements.[51]

15. This approach is based on ideas of gender balance and representation as much as on substance. Early involvement of women in the peace negotiations should seek to further inform the negotiation agenda, the topics to be covered, and the structure and breadth of the peace agreement. The Women, Peace and Security package reiterates that parties 'should facilitate the equal and full participation of women at decision-making levels' during peace talks.[52]

16. Throughout the process, involved parties must keep in mind that a "gender perspective" in peace negotiations and agreements is not the same as adopting provisions mentioning women or gender.[53] The complexity of peace agreements reflects the multi-layered efforts towards reconciliation that must include specific attention to gender issues, including seeking justice,[54] demobilisation and interactions with customary law and local norms. Finally, '[I]f a peace agreement fails to note specifically the importance of gender equality, any measures proposed to promote gender equality in the implementation phase can be interpreted as beyond the scope of the peace mandate.'[55]

---

[50] *Ibid.*, p. 129, paras. 398–400.

[51] Windhoek Declaration and the Namibia Plan of Action on Mainstreaming a Gender Perspective in Multidimensional Peace Support Operations, UN Doc. A/55/138-S/2000/693 (2000), Annexes I–II, also noted in UNSC Res. 1325 (2000), para. 8(b), which further calls 'on all actors involved, when negotiating and implementing peace agreements, to adopt a gender perspective, including, inter alia ... [m]easures that support local women's peace initiatives and indigenous processes for conflict resolution, and that involve women in all of the implementation mechanisms of the peace agreements'.

[52] UNSC Res. 1325 (2000), paras. 1 and 8; UNSC Res. 2122 (2013), para. 7(c); UNSC Res. 2242 (2015), preambular para. 11.

[53] C. Bell and C. O'Rourke, 'Peace Agreements or Pieces of Paper? The Impact of UNSC Resolution 1325 on Peace Processes and Their Agreements', in S. Kuovo and Z. Pearson (eds.), *Gender and International Law* (Routledge, 2013), pp. 42–81.

[54] UNSG Report (2015) (n. 46), p. 25, para. 89, notes that '[i]n 2014, a number of ceasefire agreements that include specific provisions on CRSV [conflict-related sexual violence] continued to increase, with two new agreements signed (for CAR and South Sudan)'.

[55] *Women, Peace and Security* (n. 44), pp. 64–65, para. 201.

17. Taking into account gender considerations in the mandate of a Peace Operation when it foresees the facilitation of peace negotiations is therefore crucial. The inclusion of a so-called "equality clause"[56] in peace agreements might supply a useful checklist for subsequent constitutional efforts by providing a mandatory inclusion of human rights and equality considerations, as well as useful definitions or instructions for further implementation of international instruments.[57]

7.4 Troop Contributing Countries should be aware of the gender considerations in the areas of primary national responsibility such as force generation, training and discipline, and should strive to ensure that the appropriate levels of capacity and competence are met prior to deploying Peace Operations.

1. Gender awareness, programmes and tools should be mainstreamed also in the relevant national structures of TCCs as a matter of increasingly recognised best practice, even if not always as a matter of legal obligation. The primary responsibility lies with the TCCs to ensure that their troops have the necessary competencies to fully implement the operational mandate, including in its gender aspects, and some of the most relevant practices are listed next. Specifically, TCCs are responsible for working on increasing the number of female personnel (military or civilian) deployed in support of Peace Operations. The current level of deployment of female personnel has been highlighted as a particular shortcoming when it comes to mainstreaming gender in Peace Operations.[58] However, it is important to note that an increase in numbers of female personnel is not the only way to effectively and efficiently implement the provisions of Security Council Resolution 1325 and related resolutions.

2. TCCs are responsible for the pre-deployment training of their troops, and Resolution 1325 invites States to incorporate UN training guidelines

---

[56] An "equality clause" can, for example, define and prohibit discrimination, ensure that protections are mandatorily included in the subsequent drafting of a constitution or other legislation, and so forth.

[57] C. Chinkin, Peace Agreements as a Means for Promoting Gender Equality and Ensuring Participation of Women, EGM/PEACE/2003/BP.1 (2003), provides a useful review of many of the most notable peace agreements across four continents and spanning recent history.

[58] UNSC Res. 1820 (2008), para. 8; UNSC Res. 1888 (2009), para. 19; UNSC Res. 1960 (2010), para. 15; UNSC Res. 2106 (2013), para. 14; UNSC Res. 2122 (2013), para. 9; UNSC Res. 2242 (2015), para. 8.

on 'the protection, rights and particular needs of women, as well as on the importance of involving women in all peacekeeping and peace-building measures', in national military and civilian police training programmes. The resolution also urges States to increase support for gender-sensitive training efforts, including to those training efforts undertaken by UN Agencies and bodies.[59] Such training should be tailored to meet the specificities of the area of deployment and the particulars of the mission mandate and the conflict in question.

3. In addition, pre-deployment training must also comprise protocols on dealing with conflict-related sexual violence, exploitation and abuse when and where encountered, including when perpetrated by peacekeeping personnel. Furthermore, TCCs must prepare and provide adequate tools and means to investigate, report and punish such incidents.[60]

4. Finally, States should develop their own advisory capacity on gender issues in order efficiently to liaise with, or complement, the Gender Advisers of other actors within the peace effort, such as other States, international organisations, agencies of the Host State or civil society. In addition, the deployment of Women Protection Advisers may be appropriate in order to strengthen and co-ordinate assistance in matters of conflict-related sexual violence.[61]

---

[59] UNSC Res. 1325 (2000), paras. 6 and 7.
[60] UNSC Res. 1820 (2008), para. 8; UNSC Res. 1888 (2009), para. 3; UNSC Res. 1960 (2010), para. 15; UNSC Res. 2122 (2013), para. 9; UNSC Res. 2242 (2015), para. 9. See further Chapter 14.3; Chapter 16.
[61] UNSC Res. 1888 (2009), para. 12; UNSC Res. 2106 (2013), paras. 7 and 8; *Gender Forward Looking Strategy* (n. 43), p. 15.

8

Status of Forces and Status of Mission

8.1 Rights and obligations of an organisation deploying military and civilian personnel in a Peace Operation, and those of such personnel, should be specified in Status of Forces or Status of Mission Agreements. The immunity of personnel in the Host State and of Sending States' military personnel in any Transit State, which is based on customary international law and treaty law, is usually confirmed in Status of Forces or Status of Mission Agreements relating to Peace Operations.

1. A Status of Forces Agreement (SOFA) or Status of Mission Agreement (SOMA) should be concluded prior to each mission. It is a useful and for practical purposes necessary tool to regulate co-operation between Sending States and the Host State, but cannot be taken as the sole legal basis for defining the status of Peace Forces in the Host State.

2. The immunity of personnel participating in UN Peace Operations derives from customary international law and treaty law[1] as confirmed in SOFAs following the 1990 UN Model SOFA.[2] Certain doubts as to whether the immunity principle fully applies in the absence of a

---

[1] Privileges and immunities of the UN are fully recognised as a matter of customary law and are confirmed in art. 105 UN Charter and in the Convention on the Privileges and Immunities of the United Nations (13 February 1946, in force 17 September 1946), 1 UNTS 15 and 90 UNTS 327 (Corr.). The Convention addresses several classes of immunity: the UN as an organisation (arts. II and III, Sections 2–10), States (art. IV, Sections 11–16), senior and lower level officials of the UN (art. V, Sections 17–21) and experts on mission (art. VI, Sections 22–23).

[2] See UN Model Status of Forces Agreement for Peacekeeping Operations, UN Doc. A/45/594 (1990), paras. 5–15, 24–31 and 46–49. The UN Model SOFA provides for immunity ratione personae of the commander (para. 24) and of '[m]ilitary members of the military component of the United Nations peace-keeping operation [who] shall be subject to the exclusive jurisdiction of their respective participating States in respect of any criminal offences which may be committed by them in the [Host Country]' (para. 47(b)). It further provides for immunity ratione materiae of 'all members of the United Nations peace-keeping operation including locally recruited personnel … in respect of words spoken or written and all acts performed by them in their official capacity' (para. 46).

SOFA[3] are now removed by a more consistent UN SOFA practice.[4] Where SOFAs or SOMAs cannot be concluded or are not yet in force, the Security Council may decide that the UN Model SOFA be applied to the relevant UN operation provisionally. The Security Council may also declare a SOFA of a terminated operation provisionally applicable to a successor operation.[5] The immunity of all categories of personnel involved, civilian and military, is thus derived from the immunity of the UN itself, as members of Peace Operations are acting as agents of the UN. Missions deployed by organisations other than the UN have a similar immunity based on the immunity of the organisation. This does not exclude that military contingents, which are generally contributed by States retaining ultimate command and control over these contingents,[6] also enjoy State immunity as organs of their States, a status they do not lose with their assignment to the Peace Operation.[7] No practical problem has arisen from this double-rooted immunity status, as immunities spelled out in the SOFAs are based on and inspired by rules related to State immunity under customary law and there is agreement in Peace Operations between the international organisation involved and Troop Contributing Countries (TCCs) (which are not a party to the SOFA) to co-operate on the exercise of jurisdiction by these States (see paragraph 2 of the Commentary to Rule 8.2).

3. The position commonly shared today is that what is embodied in the UN Charter, the UN Privileges and Immunities Convention

[3] W. T. Worster, 'Immunities of United Nations Peacekeepers in the Absence of a Status of Forces Agreement', 47 *Military Law and the Law of War Review* (2008), pp. 277–376. See also S. J. Lepper, 'The Legal Status of Military Personnel in United Nations Peace Operations: One Delegate's Analysis', 18 *Houston Journal of International Law* (1995–1996), pp. 359–464; F. Rawski, 'To Waive or Not to Waive: Immunity and Accountability in UN Peacekeeping Operations', 18 *Connecticut Journal of International Law* (2002), pp. 103–132.

[4] The consistent practice of including immunity provisions in SOFAs and SOMAs is evidence of a broad acceptance of such immunity, such that it can now be considered as a principle of customary international law, and therefore applicable even in the absence of a specific agreement.

[5] See e.g. UNSC Res. 1320 (2000), para. 6, in respect of the UN Mission in Ethiopia and Eritrea (UNMEE), and UNSC Res. 2043 (2012), para. 7, noting the agreement between the Syrian government and the UN in respect of the UN Supervision Mission in Syria (UNSMIS), to be established under the command of a Chief Military Observer. Some of these decisions were taken under Chapter VII of the UN Charter. See UNSC Res. 1990 (2011), para. 4, to apply the SOFA for the UN Mission in Sudan (UNMIS) mutatis mutandis to the UN Interim Security Force for Abyei (UNISFA); UNSC Res. 1996 (2011), para. 26, to apply the UN Model SOFA mutatis mutandis to the UN Mission in the Republic of South Sudan (UNMISS).

[6] See Chapter 4.2.

[7] See M. Bothe, 'Peacekeeping', in B. Simma, D. E. Khan, G. Nolte and A. Paulus (eds.), *The Charter of the United Nations: A Commentary*, 3rd edn, 2 vols. (Oxford University Press, 2012), vol. I, pp. 1183–1184.

and the SOFAs has been so consistent that it may now be accepted as having created customary law for UN Peace Operations. Indeed, that status has never been contested in jurisprudence.[8] It may be referred to as "functional immunity", as it protects the official functions of the personnel involved rather than offering personal privileges not related to these functions. Functional immunity is understood to mean immunity in respect of words spoken or acts done in the course of and in relation to official functions. Moreover, military contingent members cannot be arrested and subjected to the Host State's jurisdiction in respect of criminal offences they may commit in the territory of the Host State. This personal immunity from the Host State's criminal jurisdiction, which is applicable only to military contingent personnel and not to civilian personnel, is additional to, and therefore goes beyond, functional immunity. As confirmed in State practice and jurisprudence, 'there is a right to immunity under international law, together with a corresponding obligation on the part of other States to respect and give effect to that immunity'.[9] This fully applies to the immunity of military contingent personnel participating in UN Peace Operations. The privileges and exemptions granted in this respect are for the benefit, and in the interests, of the operation and should be understood in the context of the founding provisions on privileges and immunities as set forth in article 105 of the UN Charter and the UN Privileges and Immunities Convention. The UN may waive the immunity of those civilian members of its operation who have abused their immunity, including for purposes of criminal prosecution by Host State authorities where it deems that to be warranted. On the other hand, military members who have abused their immunity, including by committing criminal offences, may be required to leave the Host State, but their immunity from the jurisdiction of the Host State remains.[10] In case of crimes committed by military contingent personnel, their Sending States have jurisdiction (see Rule 8.2).

4. The immunity of individual military personnel and other uniformed personnel, e.g. police officers, who are recruited directly by the international organisation and deployed to a Peace Operation, rather than

---

[8] See D. Fleck, 'The Legal Status of Personnel Involved in United Nations Peace Operations', 95 *International Review of the Red Cross* (2013), pp. 613–636.

[9] See *Jurisdictional Immunities of the State (Germany v. Italy: Greece intervening)*, Judgment, ICJ Reports 2012, 99, para. 56.

[10] See R. Higgins, *Problems and Process: International Law and How We Use It* (Clarendon Press, 1994), p. 94. Exceptional cases of abuse, such as crimes against humanity or war crimes, may warrant a different response.

by a Sending State, derive their immunity in the Host State exclusively from the immunity of the international organisation concerned.[11] Such personnel may therefore have their immunity waived by the organisation and be subjected to legal process, including criminal prosecution, by the Host State. Yet jurisdiction of the State of nationality over such personnel may still exist if that State has extraterritorial jurisdiction over the particular type of conduct. Hence TCCs do not have exclusive responsibility for the exercise of criminal jurisdiction over individually deployed military personnel or police personnel. With respect to police personnel, UN practice does not distinguish between individually deployed police officers and members of formed police units, as it considers both categories to be potentially subject to waiver of immunity by the organisation and possible prosecution by Host State authorities. As a general matter, however, TCCs and PCCs have particular responsibility for the good conduct of all their formed units and any individually deployed uniformed personnel.[12]

5. For locally recruited personnel, immunity status is expressly accorded in paragraph 28 of the UN Model SOFA, which refers to the privileges and immunities set forth in Sections 18 (a), (b) and (c) of the UN Privileges and Immunities Convention. This immunity is functional in character, and is in this sense no different from the functional immunity accorded to international civilian staff of a Peace Operation. The immunity can therefore be waived in accordance with the general criteria for waiver of the immunity of United Nations officials. The right and duty of the UN Secretary-General to consider such waiver of immunity are expressly stated in the UN Privileges and Immunities Convention.[13] For regional organisations similar rules apply.

---

[11] The controversial question whether the immunity of international organisations (other than the UN which is discussed in para. 2) is derived from treaty provisions rather than customary law (see M. Wood, 'Do International Organizations Enjoy Immunity Under Customary International Law?', 10 *International Organizations Law Review* (2014), pp. 287–318) is of minor relevance in this respect, as treaty regulation is available for Peace Operations conducted by regional organisations and the immunity of personnel participating in such operations is not denied in practice. See also N. Blokker, 'International Organizations: The Untouchables?', 10 *International Organizations Law Review* (2014), pp. 259–275; J. G. Lammers, 'Immunity of International Organizations: The Work of the International Law Commission', 10 *International Organizations Law Review* (2014), pp. 276–286; B. C. Rashkow, 'Immunity of the United Nations: Practice and Challenges', 10 *International Organizations Law Review* (2014), pp. 332–348.

[12] On the responsibility of the UN for ensuring compliance with the rule of law by all personnel participating in UN Peace Operations, see D. Fleck, 'Securing Status and Protection of Peacekeepers', in R. Arnold and G.-J. A. Knoops (eds.), *Practice and Policies of Modern Peace Support Operations Under International Law* (Transnational Publishers, 2006), pp. 144, 148, 155.

[13] Arts. V (Section 20) and VI (Section 23) UN Privileges and Immunities Convention (n. 1).

6. While the immunity of foreign visiting forces is sometimes restricted in SOFAs and SOMAs relating to the stationing of personnel in foreign countries for various tasks of international co-operation during normal peacetime and may then lead to concurrent jurisdiction with the Host State in certain cases,[14] members of Peace Operations should (and normally do) remain under the exclusive jurisdiction of their Sending States. This is because members of Peace Operations, unlike foreign military forces stationed in peacetime (e.g. for military training or exercises), are operating in a volatile environment where the rule of law, security and safety cannot be sufficiently ensured by the Host State, and subjecting them to Host State jurisdiction might put their operational impartiality in question.

8.2 Although Sending States' military personnel enjoying immunity are exempt from criminal jurisdiction in the Host State and any Transit State, the Sending State has jurisdiction over such personnel.

1. The most important effect of immunity is an exemption from jurisdiction.[15] This exemption applies to all criminal offences committed by Sending States' military personnel in the Host State and to all types of jurisdiction. No contrary agreement has been concluded in the practice of Peace Operations.[16]

2. Legal immunities vis-à-vis foreign States should not be misunderstood as offering impunity for any crimes or as avoiding responsibility in the event of wrongful acts committed by members of a mission. Where crimes have been committed by persons enjoying immunity, they may not be prosecuted by a foreign State, except under agreed rules establishing the consent of their Sending State to the exercise of jurisdiction.

---

[14] See e.g. art. VII Agreement between the Parties to the North Atlantic Treaty regarding the Status of Their Forces (19 June 1951, in force 23 August 1953), 199 UNTS 67; Agreement between the Member States of the European Union concerning the status of military and civilian staff seconded to the institutions of the European Union, of the headquarters and forces which may be made available to the European Union in the context of the preparation and execution of the tasks referred to in Article 17(2) of the Treaty on European Union, including exercises, and of the military and civilian staff of the Member States put at the disposal of the European Union to act in this context (EU SOFA), OJ 2003 No. C321, 31 December 2003, p. 6.

[15] J. Crawford, *Brownlie's Principles of Public International Law*, 8th edn (Oxford University Press, 2012), pp. 406–411.

[16] In EU civilian missions, at least in terms of legal texts, SOMAs provide in respect of civil jurisdiction that there might be local proceedings in relation to matters not arising from the performance of duties. Such proceedings are, however, unlikely to be undertaken in practice.

Criminal cases must be brought before national courts of the Sending State or before a competent international court. In recognition of this principle, the UN agrees with TCCs to co-operate in investigating acts of misconduct committed by members of the national contingent and to commit the TCC to the exercise of its jurisdiction over criminal offences.[17] Similar arrangements should be concluded for Peace Operations conducted by regional organisations.

3. Some Peace Operations military personnel are directly recruited by the UN or a regional organisation and deployed individually and not as part of a national contingent. Such personnel enjoy only functional immunity and are not subject to the exclusive jurisdiction of the State which has made them available to the organisation.

4. The obligation to make full reparation for any loss or injury wrongfully caused by personnel participating in Peace Operations should be observed as an essential part of such an operation. The international organisation and the Sending States involved should co-operate in the settlement of claims. The Host State may be involved as appropriate. Appropriate rules to implement this responsibility should be specified in agreements.[18]

8.3 For each Peace Operation, the responsibilities of the international organisation involved, the Troop Contributing Countries and the Host State should be clearly set out in appropriate form. Arrangements are usually concluded between the international organisation and the Sending States to facilitate the provision of national contingents.

1. The UN has developed models[19] for SOFAs and Memorandums of Understanding (MOUs) covering troop-contributing arrangements which can be tailored to the needs of the parties and circumstances. Negotiations should be concluded between the international organisation and the Host State and between the international organisation and Sending States respectively (see Rule 8.1 and accompanying Commentary).

---

[17] Art. 7quater and 7quinquiens Model Memorandum of Understanding between the United Nations and [participating State] contributing resources to [the United Nations Peacekeeping Operation], UNGA Res. 61/267 (2007) and UN Doc. A/C.5/69/18 (2014), Chapter 9.

[18] See Chapter 19; Chapter 20.

[19] See n. 2 and n. 17.

2. For EU Peace Operations, SOFAs or SOMAs are normally concluded with the Host State based on model texts. Sending States (except third States participating in an EU operation) are involved through the Council, which adopts the negotiating mandate for such agreements and makes the decisions as to their signature and conclusion. Relations between the EU and the Sending States are regulated in various EU acts and internal documents to which its Member States have agreed within EU bodies and in participation agreements with third States.[20] Pending the conclusion of a SOFA or SOMA, the EU usually seeks and obtains a unilateral declaration from the Host State guaranteeing the necessary protection and/or status.

3. When a NATO Non-Article 5 Crisis Response Operation (NA5CRO)[21] is mandated, a SOFA is the first legal instrument to be envisaged before physically deploying into a new theatre. In principle, NATO will negotiate such an agreement with the Host State where the Peace Operation is to be conducted, as well as with the States(s) that will provide parts of their territory for use for transit or as staging areas.[22] A SOFA deals with the legal status of the NATO forces, both the military and the civilian component, and that of non-NATO TCCs. It contains provisions concerning immigration, claims and other matters such as tax exemption on the import and export of material, supplies and goods for operational purposes. It notably also regulates criminal jurisdiction and the immunities and privileges of foreign forces, which are 'rooted in the concept of State immunity'.[23] SOFAs may provide the possibility for potential non-NATO TCCs involvement, but they do not deal with the practical arrangements relating to the actual participation in operations that still have to be clarified between NATO and each TCC. In most NATO/NATO-led operations and missions, multi-national forces may enter into arrangements with local authorities and/or with other TCCs in order to sustain their presence over time in a theatre of operations. Because TCCs as well as NATO itself will require the purchasing of goods and services inside or outside the theatre of operations, a number of MOUs or Technical Arrangements (TAs) are usually concluded within the

---

[20] For the EU model SOFA and SOMA, see on the one hand EU Council Docs. 12616/07 (2007), 11894/07 (2007), 11894/07 COR 1 (2007), and on the other hand EU Council Doc. 17141/08 (2008). These may be adapted to the specific case as necessary.

[21] NATO, Allied Joint Doctrine for Non-Article 5 Crisis Response Operations, AJP-3.4(A) (2010).

[22] NATO, Peace Support Operations, AJP-3.4.1 (2001), p. 4B-1.

[23] M. Prassé Hartov, 'NATO Status Agreements', 34 *NATO Legal Gazette* (2014), p. 46.

concept of NATO's Host Nation Support Policy.[24] This often translates into further arrangements between the parties involved covering logistic and financial support, and therefore a MOU may also be concluded between the NATO commander and the Host State regarding logistic support by the Host State.[25]

8.4 Matters pertaining to entry and exit, freedom of movement, exemption from customs and taxes, the right to operate equipment and engage in communications, logistic support, and safety and security should be addressed in the Status of Forces or Status of Mission Agreements and in associated arrangements with the Host State.

1. Core aspects of the arrangements with the Host State may be based on the UN Model SOFA.[26]

2. The freedom of movement of the Peace Operation should be confirmed in the SOFA with rights and obligations specified as appropriate.[27] The consent of the Host State to the deployment of a Peace Operation on its territory implies that the Host State will co-operate with the operation and will facilitate its operations. Freedom of movement is a key element of an operation's ability to perform its mandated tasks in an effective manner. Accordingly, practice has been to reflect the Host State's undertaking to permit and facilitate such freedom of movement in the SOMA or SOFA. Related components are: the right of the operation to import into the Host State free of taxes or customs duties all its equipment and supplies needed for operational purposes; the Host State's obligation to facilitate expedited clearance of such equipment and supplies from ports and customs warehouses; the Host State's obligation to allow the entry of mission personnel into and their exit from the Host State without any visa or immigration restrictions; and the Host State's obligation similarly to facilitate the entry and exit of contractors' personnel and equipment needed for the mission's operations. This entails that any necessary visas, permits and clearances of any kind must be granted without delay.

---

[24] See NATO, Allied Joint Doctrine for Host Nation Support, AJP-4.5 (2013), p. B-1.
[25] See further Chapter 11.
[26] See UN Model SOFA (n. 2).
[27] See *Ibid.*, paras. 12–14.

3. Obligations in relation to the safety and security of UN and associated personnel are addressed in the UN Safety Convention and in its 2005 Optional Protocol.[28] Limitations of these instruments have become apparent in recent practice:[29]

a.   Enforcement actions under Chapter VII of the UN Charter, 'in which any of the personnel are engaged as combatants against organised armed forces', are excluded from their scope of application (article 2 UN Safety Convention), since such operations are covered by international humanitarian law (IHL) and the Convention does not form part of the IHL regime;

b.   Peace Operations conducted by regional organisations are not covered by the scope of the Convention, since the Convention relates to United Nations and associated personnel only;

c.   Hardly any of the States hosting Peace Operations have ratified the Convention at the time of writing,[30] let alone the Optional Protocol.[31]

The SOFA concluded with the Host State often provides that relevant parts of the UN Safety Convention will be made applicable within the Host State. Relevant provisions may be included in the SOFA in accordance with Security Council and General Assembly resolutions.[32] Members of Peace Operations deserve and need every support by the international community as a whole. Host States must respect their role and must ensure that it is fully respected.

4. The Secretary-General has recently been tasked 'to take all measures deemed necessary to strengthen UN field security arrangements and improve the safety and security of all military contingents, police officers, military observers and, especially, unarmed personnel'.[33] What is first and foremost required is a clear criminalisation under the relevant national criminal law of any attack against peacekeepers however the conflict situation is to be defined, for as long as the peacekeepers are not engaged in hostilities to such an extent that they become lawful targets

---

[28] Convention on the Safety of United Nations and Associated Personnel (9 December 1994, in force 15 January 1999), 2051 UNTS 363; Optional Protocol to the Convention on the Safety of United Nations and Associated Personnel (8 December 2005, in force 19 August 2010), 2689 UNTS 59.

[29] See Fleck (n. 8), pp. 621–629.

[30] As of 1 July 2017, ninety-three States are parties to the UN Safety Convention (n. 28).

[31] As of 1 July 2017, thirty-one States are parties to the Optional Protocol to the UN Safety Convention (n. 28).

[32] See, for example, UNGA Res. 67/85 (2013), paras. 16 and 17.

[33] UNSC Res. 2086 (2013), para. 20.

under international humanitarian law. Precedents may be found in the provisions of national criminal law that penalise attacks against law enforcement officers; but the crime of attacking peacekeepers may require greater penalties. Adequate penalties also need to be available for attacks against humanitarian assistance personnel. The task here is for States to make adequate provision in their national legislation and to enforce the relevant rules.

9

Host State Law

9.1   Peace Operations and their members are subject to the Host State's laws while present or acting within its territory. In applying their national law to Peace Operations and their members, Host States must observe the relevant rules of international law governing the exercise of their jurisdictional competences, including any Status of Forces or Status of Mission Agreements, and any other applicable treaties or rules of customary law relating to immunities and privileges.

1. The principle of territorial sovereignty entitles every State to establish its jurisdiction over persons and entities present within its territory.[1] It follows that Peace Operations and their members are subject to the jurisdiction of the Host State during their presence within its territory and in relation to acts performed by them there.[2] The principle is reflected in Status of Forces Agreements (SOFAs), including agreements concluded in the context of Peace Operations. Such agreements commonly include a clause calling for respect for local law (see Rule 9.2).[3] They also commonly include provisions exempting foreign personnel from local civil and criminal jurisdiction. In doing so, SOFAs proceed on the assumption that such personnel are subject to the legal authority of the Host State in the first place.

---

[1] *Island of Palmas Case (the Netherlands/United States of America)*, Award of 4 April 1928, 2 RIAA 829, 838. Generally, see C. Ryngaert, *Jurisdiction in International Law*, 2nd edn (Oxford University Press, 2015).

[2] The territorial jurisdiction of the Host State, as it derives from the principle of State sovereignty, covers not only objects and individuals located in its territory, but also any events or activities taking place therein. Accordingly, events involving members of Peace Operations which take place on the Host State's territory are subject to its legal authority, even if the foreign personnel in question are no longer present within the Host State's territory.

[3] E.g. UN Model Status of Forces Agreement for Peacekeeping Operations, UN Doc. A/45/594 (1990), para. 6; art. 2(1) EU Draft Model Agreement on the status of the European Union-led forces between the European Union and a Host State, EU Council Docs. 12616/07 (2007), 11894/07 (2007) and 11894/07 COR 1 (2007).

2. The principle of territorial sovereignty constitutes the most comprehensive basis of jurisdiction among the different principles of State jurisdiction recognised by international law.[4] It entitles the Host State not only to lay down the law applicable within its territory, but also to enforce that law through executive action and through national courts. However, this does not mean that Peace Operations and their members are subject in all respects to the judicial and enforcement powers of the Host State during their presence within its territory. In applying and enforcing its laws, the Host State must comply with other applicable rules of international law governing the exercise of its territorial jurisdiction. These rules fall into two broad groups: treaty rules and rules of customary international law. First, the Host State must comply with any applicable international agreement granting Peace Operations, their constituent units and their members immunity from local jurisdiction. Such immunities may derive from agreements concluded specifically for the purposes of a particular mission, such as a SOFA.[5] However, they may also derive from agreements of a more general character, such as instruments defining the legal status of an international organisation involved in conducting the operation, such as the UN Privileges and Immunities Convention[6] in the context of UN-led Peace Operations. In addition, Host States must observe any exemptions from local jurisdiction recognised under customary international law. These include the immunities attaching to international organisations under customary international law, the rules of State immunity and the functional immunity enjoyed by State officials.[7]

9.2 Peace Operations and their members must respect the law of the Host State.

1. There can be little doubt that the principle of territorial sovereignty demands that Peace Operations and their members must respect the law of the Host State. As already noted, this duty is widely recognised

---

[4] In the famous words of Chief Justice John Marshall: 'The jurisdiction of the nation within its own territory is necessarily exclusive and absolute. It is susceptible of no limitation not imposed by itself' (*The Schooner Exchange* v. *McFaddon*, Supreme Court of the United States of America, Judgment of 24 February 1812, 11 US 116, 136).

[5] See further Chapter 8.

[6] Convention on the Privileges and Immunities of the United Nations (13 February 1946, in force 17 September 1946), 1 UNTS 15 and 90 UNTS 327 (Corr.).

[7] For further details, see A. Sari, 'The Status of Armed Forces in Public International Law: Jurisdiction and Immunity', in A. Orakhelashvili (ed.), *Research Handbook on Jurisdiction and Immunities in International Law* (Edward Elgar, 2015), p. 319.

in contemporary treaty practice. However, the exact scope of this duty, in particular the degree of submission it requires to local law, remains subject to debate. The question has not been authoritatively settled in international practice. This is because the interests of Troop Contributing Countries (TCCs) and of Host States diverge significantly on this issue. Whereas TCCs are generally inclined to interpret the duty to respect local law restrictively in order to minimise the exposure of their personnel to Host State jurisdiction, Host States tend to interpret the duty broadly in an attempt to maximise their legal authority over Peace Operations and their personnel.[8]

2. These diverging positions have given rise to two opposing schools of thought. The first adopts a principled perspective. It starts from the premise that territorial sovereignty is one of the fundamental principles of the international legal order and that the territorial principle constitutes the most established basis for the exercise of State jurisdiction. Limitations of these principles cannot be assumed lightly. According to this view, in the absence of international practice unequivocally pointing in the opposite direction, the duty to respect local law must be understood as a duty to obey the letter of local law.[9] Support for this position is drawn from the law of diplomatic relations, where the duty imposed by article 41(1) of the Vienna Convention on Diplomatic Relations[10] on diplomatic personnel to 'respect the laws and regulations of the receiving State' is commonly understood to entail a duty to obey local law. The opposing school of thought asserts that a duty to respect is not the equivalent of a duty to obey. It would be impractical to expect Peace Operations and their personnel to fully comply with the law of the Host State in all respects. All that is required is that they pay due regard to local norms and avoid, or at any rate minimise, any action which directly contradicts them.

3. One way to reconcile these two opposing positions is to recognise that Peace Operations and their members are bound to comply only with those local laws which are in fact applicable to them.[11] In particular,

---

[8] E. Denza, *Diplomatic Law: Commentary on the Vienna Convention on Diplomatic Relations*, 3rd edn (Oxford University Press, 2008), p. 461; I. Roberts (ed.), *Satow's Diplomatic Practice*, 6th edn (Oxford University Press, 2009), para. 9.55.

[9] D. W. Bowett, *United Nations Forces: A Legal Study of United Nations Practice* (Stevens, 1964), p. 388.

[10] Vienna Convention on Diplomatic Relations (18 April 1961, in force 24 April 1964), 500 UNTS 95.

[11] Indeed, some SOFAs expressly limit the scope of the duty to respect local law to what is compatible with the mandate and tasks of the operation. See art. 2 Agreement between the Republic of Bosnia and Herzegovina and the North Atlantic Treaty Organization (NATO) concerning the Status of NATO and its Personnel (23 November 1995), Appendix B to Annex 1A of the Dayton

matters falling within the internal administration of an operation and its national contingents must be considered the subject of the exclusive regulatory authority of the TCCs and the international organisation conducting the operation. This includes such matters as the employment of international staff, their conditions of service and the exercise of discipline. In fact, SOFAs concluded in the context of Peace Operations frequently allocate exclusive jurisdiction over military personnel to the TCCs.[12] Such matters therefore fall outside the jurisdictional competence of the Host State and the scope of its laws. While this approach narrows the gap between the two opposing schools of thought, in practice there is still a need for the parties to co-operate in good faith in order to reconcile their opposing interests. As stipulated by paragraph 6 of the 1990 UN Model SOFA, operational and unit commanders should take all appropriate steps in order to ensure that personnel under their command comply with local law to the greatest extent possible and that they do everything feasible to avoid openly violating local law. They should also consult and co-ordinate with the representatives of the Host State at the appropriate level on a regular basis to identify areas of concern and to seek practical solutions. In this respect, the Host State must bear in mind the international character and mandate, as well as the temporary nature, of the operation.

4. Particular difficulties may arise in situations where local law is found to be incompatible with generally recognised international standards, in particular with the requirements of international human rights law (IHRL). Such cases pose a significant legal and practical dilemma: should Peace Operations comply with the duty to respect local law at the expense of violating other applicable rules of international law or should they comply with those other international norms at the expense of failing to observe local law? The appropriate response will depend on the circumstances of each particular case, in particular on the nature and substance of the conflicting rules in question. It may be possible to diffuse any perceived impasse by reference to the international obligations of the Host State in situations where local law does not conform to those obligations. For example, Member States of the UN are required

---

Agreement, 35 ILM (1996) 102; art. 2 Military Technical Agreement between the International Security Assistance Force (ISAF) and the Interim Administration of Afghanistan (4 January 2002), 41 ILM (2002) 1032. See also UNMIK Regulation No. 2000/47 on the Status, Privileges and Immunities of KFOR and UNMIK and Their Personnel in Kosovo (2000), Section 2(2).

[12] See Chapter 8.

to give every assistance to the Organisation in any action it takes and to carry out the decisions of the Security Council in accordance with the Charter.[13] A mandate issued by the Security Council should therefore be given precedence over any incompatible provisions of Host State law. A cogent argument can also be made that the duty to respect local law does not absolve Peace Operations and their constituent units from their obligation to respect IHRL.[14] For example, a rule of Host State law which directly conflicts with norms of IHRL or international humanitarian law (IHL) would not be applicable to the Peace Operation or its personnel. Obligations of TCCs under either of those bodies of law would take precedence over the duty to respect Host State law. For example, a detainee could not be transferred to Host State custody where this would conflict with general norms, such as the prohibition of torture or inhumane treatment, or with specific obligations of individual TCCs, such as the obligation, for States which have abolished the death penalty, not to render a person into the custody of a State where the death penalty will be imposed.

5. An equally difficult question is what positive steps Peace Operations and their constituent units must undertake to discharge their obligation to ensure respect for human rights. As a minimum, they should escalate concerns within their chain of command and also raise these concerns, if appropriate, with the authorities of the Host State, in line with the principles laid down in the United Nations Human Rights Due Diligence Policy.[15] Whether further steps ought to be taken will depend on the operation's mandate and the nature and degree of authority it exercises within the Host State. Where Peace Operations administer territory, for example, they may be in a position, and thus under a duty, to take additional measures to ensure that local laws comply with international standards. Where necessary, the organisation conducting the mission and/or the TCCs should consider concluding agreements with the Host State to ensure their continued ability to comply with their international obligations.

---

[13] Arts. 2(5) and 25 UN Charter.

[14] That seems to be the implication of *Al-Saadoon and Mufdhi* v. *the United Kingdom*, Application No. 61498/08, Judgment of 2 March 2010.

[15] Human Rights Due Diligence Policy on United Nations Support to non-United Nations Security Forces, UN Doc. A/67/775–S/2013/110 (2013), Annex.

Sending State Law

10.1 While the rights and duties of a Peace Operation in the Host State are primarily determined at the international level, Sending States retain certain powers and responsibilities.

1. The international status of any Peace Operation and the execution of its mandate require Troop Contributing Countries (TCCs) in the first place to exercise rights and to comply with obligations determined at the international level. Such rights and obligations will derive from the mandate as established through relevant Security Council resolutions, a decision of the regional organisation engaged in that operation and any agreements between the organisation conducting the mission and the Host State.[1] Their implementation may be further regulated in internal rules of the international organisation, such as the Principles and Guidelines for United Nations Peacekeeping Operations.[2]

2. The Sending States retain, however, certain powers and responsibilities that directly relate to the conduct of their national contingents. National contingents of a Peace Operation remain subject to the prescriptive jurisdiction and usually to the enforcement jurisdiction of the Sending State. This does not mean that national law generally applies extraterritorially. Rather, the territorial validity of national law is generally limited to the territory of the State. International law, however, permits States to exercise prescriptive jurisdiction extraterritorially on the basis of several recognised principles. One of these is the competence of a State to regulate and control the conduct of its organs and officials.[3] The application of a Sending State's national law in Peace Operations is an expression of this

---

[1] See Chapter 3.

[2] UN, United Nations Peacekeeping Operations: Principles and Guidelines (2008), www.un.org/en/peacekeeping/documents/capstone_eng.pdf.

[3] See M. Bothe, 'Peacekeeping Forces', in R. Wolfrum (ed.), *Max Planck Encyclopedia of Public International Law* (Oxford University Press, 2016), para. 48, www.mpepil.com.

competence; it mainly relates to personnel administration, labour law, discipline and criminal jurisdiction.[4] Sending States generally retain exclusive jurisdiction over their military personnel in Peace Operations and enjoy immunity for their official acts on the basis of Status of Forces Agreements (SOFAs) or Status of Mission Agreements (SOMAs) and customary international law.[5] Criminal and disciplinary investigations will therefore follow the national law of the Sending State, without prejudice to reporting obligations owed to the international organisation conducting the mission and the duty to respect Host State law.[6] The TCCs will usually raise the exercise of exclusive jurisdiction over their military personnel as a condition for their participation in a mission. This is partly due to their aforementioned competence over their officials and partly to their obligations to ensure discipline, oversight and compliance by military personnel and officials with their legal obligations under national and international law.[7]

3. In certain fields the law of the Sending State may provide higher standards than those applicable in the international organisation or the Host State. This may become relevant for the conduct of certain national contingents in a Peace Operation, particularly in the fields of human rights,[8] environmental protection and safety regulations.

4. To the extent that the performance of the mandate allows for actions which conflict with its national law, a TCC will be able to undertake such action only if it provides a legal basis through appropriate legislation. Failing such a legal basis, TCCs will need to enter a national caveat to the performance of such tasks.

10.2 In enforcing their jurisdiction in the territory of third States, Sending States must observe the relevant rules of international law governing the exercise of their jurisdictional competences, including any applicable treaties and rules of customary international law.

1. While international law permits the exercise of prescriptive jurisdiction by Sending States in the territory of third States,[9] different rules

---

[4] F. Seyersted, 'Jurisdiction over Organs and Officials of States, the Holy See and Intergovernmental Organisations', 14 *International and Comparative Law Quarterly* (1965), pp. 31–82 (Part I) and pp. 493–527 (Part II).
[5] See Chapter 8.
[6] See Chapter 9.
[7] See Chapter 21.
[8] See Chapter 5.
[9] E.g. in *Cyprus v. Turkey*, Application Nos. 6780/74 and 6950/75, Decision on Admissibility, 26 May 1975, para. 8, the European Commission of Human Rights held that 'authorised agents of a State, including diplomatic or consular agents and armed forces', remain under the jurisdiction of their Sending States.

govern the exercise of enforcement jurisdiction under such circumstances. As the Permanent Court of International Justice has pointed out in the *Lotus* case, a State 'may not exercise its power in any form in the territory of another State' without being entitled by a permissive rule of international law to do so.[10] While Sending States may exercise their prescriptive jurisdiction over their national contingents present in the territory of the Host State without special permission, they may take steps to enforce their domestic laws against members of their own contingent or against third parties, for example by carrying out an investigation or imposing disciplinary measures, only if specifically authorised to do so under international law. Such permissive rules fall into two groups.

2. First, SOFAs and other applicable international instruments may entitle Sending States to exercise their enforcement jurisdiction within the Host State. The 1990 UN Model SOFA, for instance, directs Sending States to take appropriate disciplinary action against their military personnel and implies that Sending States are entitled to arrest military members of their national contingents.[11] The arrangements detailing the legal status of the International Security Assistance Force (ISAF) stipulated that ISAF and supporting personnel remained at all times 'subject to the exclusive jurisdiction of their respective national elements in respect of any criminal or disciplinary offences which may be committed by them on the territory of Afghanistan'.[12] The arrangements also imposed an obligation on the Interim Administration of Afghanistan to assist the ISAF Sending States in the exercise of their respective jurisdictions.[13] By agreeing to facilitate the exercise of the exclusive jurisdiction enjoyed by ISAF contributing nations over their personnel, the Interim Administration clearly consented to the exercise of enforcement measures by those nations within the territory of Afghanistan. International human rights law (IHRL) and, where applicable, international humanitarian law (IHL) require States to conduct effective investigations in situations where obligations under those bodies of law may impinge. For example, any use of force must be monitored and reported upon, and any potential violations must be investigated. Provision should therefore

---

[10] *The Case of the S.S. Lotus (France v. Turkey)*, Judgment (1927), PCIJ Series A, No. 10, 18-19. See also *Re Bolton and Another, Ex parte Beanne*, High Court of Australia, Judgment of 9 April 1987, 162 CLR 514, 519.

[11] UN Model Status of Forces Agreement for Peacekeeping Operations, UN Doc. A/45/594 (1990).

[12] Military Technical Agreement between the International Security Assistance Force (ISAF) and the Interim Administration of Afghanistan (4 January 2002), 41 ILM (2002) 1032, Annex A, Section 1(3).

[13] *Ibid.*

be made in SOFAs to enable Sending States to comply with these obligations and to exercise the necessary enforcement powers in the territory of the Host State.

3. Second, customary international law permits Sending States to take measures necessary for maintaining discipline and for the internal administration of their national contingents in the territory of the Host State. State practice shows that national armed forces' laws and regulations routinely enable the authorities of Sending States to take disciplinary measures against members of their armed forces abroad.[14] It also demonstrates that Sending States routinely exercise those powers which are reasonably necessary to ensure the continued functioning of their military contingents as an effective military unit in the territory of the Host State.[15] These customary rules may usefully complement any corresponding rules laid down in SOFAs. However, in the interests of legal certainty, it is advisable to specify what enforcement measures Sending States may take in the territory of the Host State in express terms, rather than fall back on the rules of customary international law.

---

[14] See R. Liivoja, 'An Axiom of Military Law: Applicability of National Criminal Law to Military Personnel and Associated Civilians Abroad' (Dissertation, Helsinki, 2011), pp. 159–222; F. Adaka, 'The Enforcement of Military Justice and Discipline in External Military Operations: Exploring the Fault Lines', 47 *Military Law and the Law of War Review* (2008), pp. 253–265.

[15] E.g. *Shooting Range Extension Case*, Supreme Administrative Court (Verwaltungsgerichtshof) of Kassel, Germany, Judgment of 26 January 1984, 86 ILR (1984) 533, 534.

Troop Contributing Country Memorandums of Understanding and Other Instruments and Regulations

11.1 The international organisation or lead State undertaking a Peace Operation can conclude an arrangement with a Troop Contributing Country to set out the administrative, logistical and financial terms and conditions which govern the contribution of personnel, equipment and services provided by the Troop Contributing Country to the organisation. Generally, such an arrangement is called a Memorandum of Understanding. In accordance with the intention of the participants, the arrangement can be legally binding.

1. At the request of an international organisation, States contribute personnel, equipment and services to the organisation to assist it in carrying out its mandate. In order to establish the administrative, logistical and financial terms and conditions which govern the contribution of support provided by the Troop Contributing Country (TCC) to the organisation, the organisation and the TCC can conclude a Memorandum of Understanding (MOU).[1] Such arrangements contain details of the personnel, major equipment and self-sustainment services that the TCC will provide including the reimbursement rates that apply. Other subjects which can be covered are, inter alia, the command and control (C2) structure, the transfer of authority, standards of conduct, discipline and the exercise of jurisdiction by the TCC, responsibility for third party claims, accountability and the settlement of disputes.[2] The parties may conclude supplementary arrangements, such as a Technical (TA) or Implementing Arrangement (IA), to the MOU. Such arrangements do not have a prescribed form.

---

[1] For the UN, see the Manual on Policies and Procedures concerning the Reimbursement and Control of Contingent-Owned Equipment of Troop/Police Contributors Participating in Peacekeeping Missions, UN Doc. A/C.5/69/18 (2015) (COE Manual).
[2] *Ibid.*, Chapter 9.

2. With regard to the exercise of disciplinary and jurisdictional authority retained by the TCC,[3] it is through a MOU that the international organisation undertaking the Peace Operation may oblige the TCC to exercise its exclusive jurisdiction. To obtain this commitment via a MOU is important, since the TCC is not party to the Status of Forces Agreement (SOFA) concluded between the international organisation and the Host State, in which arrangement the exclusive right to exercise jurisdiction by the contingents is laid down.

3. An arrangement between the international organisation undertaking a Peace Operation and a TCC can be legally binding,[4] depending on the intention of the participants in the arrangement. If that intention is not addressed explicitly in the arrangement, the extent to which treaty language is used in the arrangement can be taken into consideration when assessing whether the parties intended the arrangement to be legally binding. A clear and precise statement of the intent and purpose of the participants as to the scope, status and content of the arrangement is therefore desirable in order to prevent a situation in which one participant assesses the document as legally binding and the other does not.

4. The UN considers the arrangements it concludes with a TCC to be legally binding.[5] In that regard, when an arrangement provides for major logistical support by a TCC to the UN, the arrangements made are laid down in a "Letter of Assist" which is considered to be a quasi-commercial agreement. NATO, however, considers the support arrangements it concludes to be non-legally binding arrangements. As to the EU, the relations with Member States as TCCs are addressed in horizontal internal documents. The EU does not have TCC MOUs with its Member States, and with third States it has fully fledged international agreements.[6] A TCC may provide support to another TCC, such as medical, logistical, technical and in extremis[7] support, to enable it to fulfil its mandated tasks. The TCCs may enter into an arrangement to set out the terms and conditions governing such provision of support. Such an arrangement

---

[3] See Chapter 4.2.

[4] See e.g. art. II Memorandum of Understanding on Cooperation in the Area of Peace and Security between the African Union, the Regional Economic Communities and the Coordinating Mechanisms of the Regional Standby Brigades of Eastern African and Northern Africa (2008), www.peaceau.org/uploads/mou-au-rec-eng.pdf.

[5] COE Manual (n. 1), p. 8.

[6] Cf. Appendix VI.

[7] A situation of such exceptional urgency that immediate action must be taken to minimise imminent loss of life or catastrophic degradation of the political or military situation; see United States, Joint Special Operations Task Force Operations, JP 3-05.1 (2007), GL-11.

will also be legally binding if the participants in the arrangement intend for it to create legal relations. If the international organisation undertaking the Peace Operation assumes certain responsibilities in relation to such arrangements, they become trilateral in character. For example, in UN-led operations, the UN may agree to cover the cost of equipment supplied by one TCC to another TCC, or the maintenance thereof.

11.2 Support and services to the international organisation or lead State undertaking a Peace Operation and/or to the Troop Contributing Countries may be provided by the Host State authorities as well as by civilian international contractors. The administrative, logistical and financial terms and conditions regarding the provision of such support and services should be set forth in an arrangement and/or a contract.

1. If the international organisation and/or TCCs rely on Host State support in connection with a Peace Operation, arrangements and/or contracts are usually concluded with the Host State authorities and/or civilian contractors. Such arrangements and/or contracts set out the administrative, logistical and financial terms governing the provision of support by the Host State authorities or civilian international contractors to the international organisation and/or TCCs. In UN-led operations, major requirements for supplies and services are often procured through a commercial contract with an international contractor, on the basis of either a global systems contract or a specific bidding exercise. Especially those Peace Operations which are conducted in remote areas can benefit from Host State support and/or support from a contractor. Supplies and services so provided for may, inter alia, include fuel, water, food, medical services, waste removal and use of buildings and facilities. Arrangements which elaborate on Host State support and the employment of international contractors generally flow from or are within the framework of a SOFA.[8]

2. In accordance with the intentions of the international organisation and/or TCCs on the one hand and the Host State authorities on the other hand, bilateral arrangements between them may address any

---

[8] See further Chapter 8.

topic which they deem necessary, such as the transfer of detainees,[9] in the arrangement mentioned earlier or in a separate arrangement.[10]

11.3 Apart from mission-specific arrangements, non-mission-specific policies, guidelines and instruments providing operational and technical standards are employed by international organisations conducting Peace Operations to secure the interoperability of the contingents.

1. In a Peace Operation, the ability of the contingents to operate together using harmonised standards, doctrines, procedures and equipment is essential for the international organisation undertaking the Peace Operation to fulfil its mandated tasks. Therefore, policies, guidelines[11] and instruments consisting of operational and technical standards, such as standard operating procedures[12] and Standardisation Agreements,[13] which have been developed and adopted by the international organisation, need to be applied by the TCCs.

[9] See, for example, the Arrangement for the Transfer of Detainees between the Canadian Forces and the Ministry of Defence of the Islamic Republic of Afghanistan (18 December 2005).

[10] See further Chapter 13.

[11] For example, the Capstone Doctrine. See UN, United Nations Peacekeeping Operations: Principles and Guidelines (2008), www.un.org/en/peacekeeping/documents/capstone_eng.pdf.

[12] Standing instructions on how to implement a specific task, process or activity, or how to achieve a desired result. These provide institutional recognition of best practice methods or steps to be followed unless ordered otherwise. See UN, 'Peacekeeping Resources Hub', http://research.un.org/en/peacekeeping-community/Guidance. For the NATO definition, which is quite similar, see NATO, Glossary of Terms and Definitions, AAP-06 (2016), p. 128.

[13] A NATO standardisation document that specifies the agreement of Member States to implement a standard, in whole or in part, with or without reservation, in order to meet an interoperability requirement. See NATO Glossary (n. 12), p. 93.

PART III

Conducting a United Nations (Mandated) Peace Operation

The Use of Force

12.1 The use of force by members of a Peace Force may be permitted in accordance with the mandate or in self-defence.

1. The circumstances in which a Peace Force may lawfully use force when undertaking its mandated tasks are limited to circumstances in which the use of force is strictly necessary as a means to achieve the tasks provided for in the mandate or in self-defence. Likewise, the degree of force that may then be used is subject to the limitations prescribed by law. Unnecessary use of force is incompatible both with the mandate, which may include any decisions made by the relevant organisation in connection with the performance of the mandate, and with applicable international and domestic law. While the Rules set out in this chapter are mainly relevant for military members of a Peace Force, they may apply also to other personnel of Peace Operations, in particular to members of formed police units, with the exception of Rule 12.6 when relevant. Rule 12.8 will also apply primarily to the military members of the Peace Operation, although police units may have instructions which resemble Rules of Engagement (ROE) in some respects.

12.2 The mandate may authorise the use of necessary and proportionate force for the achievement of tasks, purposes and objectives set out in the mandate when circumstances require the use of force.

1. As to mandates generally, see Chapters 3 and 4. In this context, the "mandate" will include any decisions made by the competent organs of the organisation conducting the operation which are intended to provide additional guidance and authority in carrying out the mandate.

2. The terms of a mandate may authorise the use of force up to and including lethal force for the performance of tasks that are set out in the mandate and in any other decisions based on the mandate by the organisation conducting the operation when circumstances require that force be employed to perform those tasks. Such authorisation can be either explicit or implicit, e.g. the use of "necessary means" to accomplish a particular objective. If that is the case, the Peace Force will not be acting in breach of its mandate or of international law if the specified degree of force is used in strict compliance with such limitations as the mandate and any relevant related decisions prescribe. However, any such use of force will need to comply with any additional body of national or international law that applies in the circumstances.

3. If the terms of the mandate can properly be regarded as providing legal authority to use force in situations which are not specifically addressed by applicable domestic and international human rights law (IHRL), the mandate shall constitute sufficient authority for the use of the degree of force it permits in the circumstances it specifies and as such the use of force in these circumstances will not be "arbitrary". In practice, however, it is extremely unlikely that a mandate will be intended to exclude the modalities of actual force application, in particular the requirement that force be used only when necessary and in a proportionate manner, and IHRL requirements will govern the actual implementation of lethal force whenever it is applicable (see Rule 12.5).[1] Hence, any force employed will generally be subject to the requirements of necessity and proportionality as set out in paragraph 2 of the Commentary to Rule 12.3. In situations where the mandate provides for the Peace Force to engage in hostilities in the context of an armed conflict, or the Peace Force becomes a party to an armed conflict, the rules relating to the conduct of hostilities under the law of armed conflict will determine the outer limits of permissible force under those circumstances (see Rule 12.6).

4. Following the High-Level Independent Panel on United Nations Peace Operations recommendation, UN missions should not be mandated to conduct counter-terrorism operations and, where a UN mission operates in parallel with counter-terrorism forces, the respective role of each must be clearly delineated.[2]

---

[1] See Chapter 5.
[2] Report of the High-Level Independent Panel on United Nations Peace Operations, Uniting Our Strengths for Peace: Politics, Partnership and People, UN Doc. A/70/95-S/2015/446 (2015), paras. 116–126.

12.3 Members of a Peace Force have the inherent right to use such force as is necessary and proportionate in personal self-defence or in defence of others.

1. The right to use force in personal self-defence or in defence of others is inherent in the sense that it is not dependent on the status of those involved as members of a Peace Force or on a specific authorisation in the mandate. The self-defence aspect of the Rule is based on the right of any person to take such proportionate action as is required by the circumstances to defend him- or herself against a credibly perceived imminent threat of death or serious bodily injury, including abduction, until such threat is removed or eliminated. The reference to 'defence of others' reflects the right of a member of a Peace Force to use necessary and proportionate force to defend another person or persons against a credibly perceived imminent threat of death or serious bodily injury. As with the case of personal self-defence, this right lasts until the threat is removed or eliminated. Accordingly, if, for example, a member of a Peace Force perceives that force must be used to protect mission-associated personnel against an imminent threat of death or serious injury, the peacekeeper will be justified in using such force as is necessary and proportionate for that purpose.

2. Necessity in these circumstances (self-defence and performance of the mandate) means that force may be used while the threat persists or while the situation requires and until it is extinguished; with respect to the use of lethal force, necessity requires that no other alternatives are feasibly available. It may be possible to satisfactorily address the threat confronting members of a Peace Force or others by the use of available non-lethal force. In general, whenever possible, force should be preceded by an appropriate warning and should be used in a graduated manner. These criteria apply to any use of force, lethal or non-lethal. If it is apparent to the members of the Peace Force that non-lethal force would suffice, the force actually used should to the maximum extent possible under the circumstances be limited to non-lethal force. However, if the threat is perceived by them as being of imminent death or serious bodily injury, lethal force may be directly used. Proportionality in this context means that intensity of the harm inflicted on the perpetrator must not be excessive in relation to the intensity of the harm threatened by the perpetrator. Clearly this also applies in reaction to an ongoing unlawful use of force directed against members of the Peace Force, mission personnel or others.

3. The necessary and proportionate use of force does not require that a threat involving the use of a weapon be met with the use of the same kind of weapon in self-defence. Indeed, if a peacekeeper is threatened by a person not using a weapon, proportionate and necessary action in self-defence may, depending on the circumstances, involve the use of a weapon by the peacekeeper.

4. States have different legislation on self-defence and the defence of others. As personnel of a Peace Operation have to comply with the domestic law of their Sending State,[3] where that law does not provide for the use of force in defence of others, this will need to be provided for in the ROE. Likewise, if domestic law requires that persons should seek an avenue of escape or avoid putting themselves in harm's way as a requirement for invocation of self-defence, the ROE should set out the conditions in which self-defence would be applicable in such circumstances. In such cases, Sending States (Troop Contributing Countries (TCCs) and/or Police Contributing Countries (PCCs)) should ensure that such ROE authority can be given under their domestic legal system and should enact legislation to that effect if necessary. Such ROE may also have the benefit of promoting a common baseline to act in the defence of others for the entire Peace Operation.

5. The domestic law of the Host State will also be relevant in all cases where the use of force is not provided for in the mandate. In such cases, where Host State law does not provide for the defence of others, it may be considered advisable to obtain explicit Host State consent allowing the Peace Force to act in the defence of others. However, a mandate which is issued by the Security Council will have precedence over any provisions of Host State law which directly conflict with it. Additionally, where immunity from Host State law is provided for, it would preclude the application of Host State law relating to the use of force which conflicts with the mandate.

12.4   Members of a Peace Force may have the right to use necessary and proportionate force in defence of mission-essential property or in the maintenance of their right to move freely.

1. The mandate may explicitly provide for the use of force to defend mission-essential property or to secure and maintain the right of members

---

[3] See Chapter 10.

of the Peace Force to move freely within the theatre of operations in the performance of their duties in connection with the Peace Operation. To the extent that it does so, this would provide a sufficient justification for the use of necessary and proportionate force in defence of property that is essential to the successful accomplishment of the mission or in securing and maintaining freedom of movement against those who would seek to forcibly interfere with it, sometimes referred to as "spoilers".

2. In the absence of an explicit reference in the mandate to the use of force to defend mission-essential property or to secure and maintain freedom of movement, force used for such purposes will be lawful only to the extent that it complies with applicable domestic law, including ROE where incorporated therein. There are some States whose domestic law will permit the use of lethal force in defence of property per se or to secure or maintain freedom of movement, while other States' domestic law permits the use of lethal force only if there is a concomitant threat of death or serious bodily injury arising from or associated with the damage, destruction or removal of the relevant property or from the denial of or interference with freedom of movement.

3. If the use of force for defence of mission-essential property and to ensure freedom of movement does not relate to direct danger to life, such authorisation should be included in the applicable ROE, and States should consider adopting such authorisation into their domestic law. Defence of property may include essential property which, while not directly pertaining to the mission, is essential for the safety, security or extraction of mission personnel and for the performance of the mission. The use of lethal force by a UN Peace Force 'in defence of the mandate' will be permissible only to the extent that the circumstances come within those discussed in this chapter. These specifically authorised instances of use of force include cases where a UN Peace Operation is tasked, as part of its mandate, to 'protect United Nations personnel, installations and equipment'.[4] It is, indeed, not necessarily self-defence when a unit carries out specifically mandated tasks of protecting UN installations and equipment in general, e.g. warehouses for storage of humanitarian goods, etc.

4. Property that is considered to be mission-essential should as far as possible be specified and designated as such in applicable ROE or related guidance.[5]

---

[4] See the various UNSC Resolutions on the UN Operation in Côte d'Ivoire (UNOCI).
[5] For a discussion of ROE in relation to the use of force, see Rule 12.8 and accompanying Commentary.

12.5   Where international human rights law is applicable, that body of law will determine the circumstances and manner in which force may be employed.

1. As to the application of IHRL generally to Peace Operations, see Chapter 5. Human rights law will apply as a matter of law only if the affected individuals are within the jurisdiction of the international organisation or of a Sending State at the relevant time.[6]

2. The use of lethal force in Peace Operations is informed in particular by the right to life. This right is, inter alia, codified in article 6 of the International Covenant on Civil and Political Rights. Article 6(1) provides: 'Every human being has the inherent right to life. This right shall be protected by law. No one shall be arbitrarily deprived of his life.'[7] A deprivation of life is arbitrary: when there is no legal basis for the use of lethal force; when it occurs under a law which does not strictly control and limit the circumstances when lethal force may be employed; if it would have been reasonable to take precautionary measures, such as the issue of a warning with an opportunity to surrender; or if the force used exceeds what is necessary in the circumstances to maintain, restore or impose law and order. The right to life is recognised as a norm of customary law, which means it applies also to States that are not party to the Covenant, whether or not they are party to any other treaty that codifies the right to life. It also applies to international organisations conducting Peace Operations. When applying the right to life to Peace Operations, the particular context is likely to be relevant, including the fact that troops operate extraterritorially and often in a non-permissive environment.

3. Necessary and proportionate lethal force in defence of another person would come within article 6 of the Covenant as not being arbitrary,[8]

---

[6] Art. 2(1) International Covenant on Civil and Political Rights (16 December 1966, in force 23 March 1976), 999 UNTS 171; art. 1 Convention for the Protection of Human Rights and Fundamental Freedoms (4 November 1950, in force 3 September 1953), ETS 5, as amended by Protocol No. 14 (in force 1 June 2010) (ECHR). As to jurisdiction for the purposes of IHRL, see Rule 5.2 and accompanying Commentary.

[7] Note that other human rights provisions may qualify the right to life in different and sometimes more specific terms. See in this regard for example art. 2 ECHR (n. 6), which lists specific grounds on which lethal force may be used. Moreover, in the jurisprudence of the European Court of Human Rights it has been decided that 'any use of force must be "no more than absolutely necessary", that is to say it must be strictly proportionate in the circumstances': *Nachova and Others* v. *Bulgaria*, Application Nos. 43577/98 and 43579/98, Judgment of 6 July 2005 [GC], para. 94. However, though the language may differ, the degree of care that is required when using lethal force is likely to be interpreted similarly under the respective human rights provisions.

[8] See explicitly art. 2(2)(a) ECHR (n. 6).

and the same may apply to non-lethal force associated with other kinds of Peace Force activity, such as action to put down civil disturbances in the Peace Force's zone of operations or action to prevent detained persons escaping from lawful custody.[9] However, such operations must be carefully planned and the force used must be strictly necessary and proportionate. This implies the need for appropriate training of relevant deployed personnel and the careful drafting of applicable ROE. The obligation to protect the right to life implies a procedural duty to conduct a thorough, independent investigation into deprivations of life and into deaths from other than natural causes attributable to State agents, private persons or persons unknown, an obligation which has obvious implications for the staffing and resourcing of Peace Operations.

4. The jurisprudence of the European Court of Human Rights makes it clear that the relevant operation must have been carefully planned and controlled with a view to seeking to avoid the need to take life, all available information must be carefully considered, the use of lethal force must be strictly proportionate to the accomplishment of the objective, and all possible precautions must have been carefully taken with a view to avoiding the requirement to resort to lethal force whenever possible and with a view to minimising the loss of life.[10]

5. What is non-arbitrary, strictly proportionate and absolutely necessary will depend, inevitably, on the circumstances of the particular situation and on the reasonable appreciation of the security personnel dealing with the situation as to the practical options that are then available to them. Careful consideration and planning may not be feasible if a violent and dynamic situation is unfolding. However, if the general security situation is such that events of that nature ought to have been anticipated, a failure to make appropriate arrangements in advance, coupled with the use of lethal force in circumstances where lesser force would be appropriate, may constitute a breach of the right to life.

6. Accordingly, care will be required and all viable non-lethal options should be pursued. If the use of lethal force is the only viable way of addressing the situation, the amount of force used, the time period during which it is used and the locations where it is used must be those

---

[9] See explicitly *Ibid.*, art. 2(2)(b) and (c).

[10] See *McCann and Others* v. *the United Kingdom*, Application No. 18984/91, Judgment of 27 September 1995 [GC], para. 212. See further *Andronicou and Constantinou* v. *Cyprus*, Application No. 25052/94, Judgment of 9 October 1997; *Gül* v. *Turkey*, Application No. 22676/93, Judgment of 14 December 2000. Note also *Isayeva* v. *Russia*, Application No. 57950/00, Judgment of 24 February 2005, paras. 190, 191 and 200.

which are absolutely necessary and objectively proportionate to the circumstances. Consequently, lethal force may be used only for as long as the situation unavoidably requiring the use of such force exists and not thereafter.

12.6 A Peace Operation that becomes involved as a party to an armed conflict must comply with international humanitarian law when undertaking operations in connection with that conflict. In situations involving the conduct of hostilities against targets under the law of armed conflict, the rules of the law of armed conflict relating to the conduct of hostilities will apply. The use of force outside the context of hostilities will, in general, be governed by rules provided by other applicable bodies of law, in particular international human rights law.

1. The intended scope of this Manual does not include a restatement of the law of armed conflict rules on the use of force.[11] The purpose of the present Rule is therefore simply to state that the action in relation to an armed conflict that can be taken by a Peace Force that becomes involved in that armed conflict is subject to the rules of the law of armed conflict without prejudice to any other applicable body of law. However, as a general matter, the rules relating to the conduct of hostilities under the law of armed conflict will apply when force is used by one party against another party to that conflict or against civilians who directly participate in hostilities. The use of force outside the context of hostilities will generally have to comply with the more restrictive rules relating to law enforcement. For the general relationship between the two bodies of law, see Chapters 5 and 6.

12.7 A Peace Operation should be appropriately equipped to enable it to adjust the degree and nature of force that it employs to suit as closely as possible the requirements of foreseeable security situations.

1. It is not appropriate to expect a Peace Force to equip itself for circumstances that cannot reasonably be foreseen as likely to arise. However, if, for example, a Peace Force can reasonably expect to encounter demonstrations and rioting while undertaking its mandate, to equip that force

---

[11] See further Chapter 6.

exclusively with lethal weapons would render it more likely that a use of force which results in loss of life will be regarded as in breach of the right to life on the basis that required planning did not take place to minimise the likely need to resort to lethal force.[12]

2. Those planning a Peace Operation should therefore consider the provision of equipment that will facilitate the use of lesser degrees of force where the circumstances of the Peace Operation, or of the planned Peace Operation, render this appropriate. Such equipment might include tear gas, rubber bullets, water cannon, truncheons and other reasonably available non-lethal options.

3. It should be recalled that, while the use of riot control agents as a method of warfare is prohibited to States parties to the Chemical Weapons Convention,[13] the use of such agents by a Peace Force would be permitted outside an armed conflict or when an armed conflict is taking place in which it is not participating. Similarly, while the use of expanding bullets is prohibited in international armed conflicts (IACs), and in most circumstances in non-international armed conflicts (NIACs), such use may be permissible in appropriate circumstances under domestic law by a Peace Force that is not a party to an armed conflict, for example, in hostage rescue scenarios.

4. To the extent that the Secretary-General's 1999 Bulletin[14] is stated to apply the law of armed conflict to situations falling short of armed conflict, the Bulletin has the status of a statement of policy. It should, however, be borne in mind that the terms of the Bulletin will not affect the applicability of domestic human rights law and IHRL.

12.8 Where the use of force is authorised beyond self-defence under Sending State law, Rules of Engagement should be issued by an authority superior to the Peace Force. The restrictions on the use of force referred to in this chapter should be reflected in such issued Rules of Engagement.

1. The content of ROE does not have the status of law as such; they are orders or directives that define the circumstances under which force

---

[12] See e.g. *Güleç* v. *Turkey*, Application No. 21593/93, Judgment of 27 July 1998.

[13] Convention on the Prohibition of the Development, Production, Stockpiling and Use of Chemical Weapons and on Their Destruction (13 January 1993, in force 29 April 1997), 1974 UNTS 45.

[14] UN, Secretary-General's Bulletin on the Observance by United Nations Forces of International Humanitarian Law, UN Doc. ST/SGB/1999/13 (1999).

may be used and that constitute the sole operational authority for the use of force.[15] ROE are therefore a tool enabling a superior authority to discharge its responsibility to control the use of force by forces that have deployed pursuant to the superior authority's instructions. They may be crafted to provide for escalation, de-escalation or maintenance of the operational situation and may disclose to the receiving commander information as to the political goals to be achieved by the operation as well as the authorisations and restrictions with which military action must comply. Operational staff in NATO and EU operations will generally develop ROE for an operation. Other organisations may follow a different procedure. These will be based primarily on operational requirements but legal and policy input will also be provided. Any authorisations provided in ROE must reflect the scope of authority set out in the mandate. Hence, while ROE may restrict the circumstances in which specific authorisations may be carried out, for example by requiring subordinate commanders to seek authorisation from higher authority for the performance of specific tasks allocated in the mandate, they may not exceed the scope of authority provided for in the mandate.

2. Although reflecting operational, policy and legal limitations, ROE must be crafted so as to ensure that action by members of the Peace Force complies with the international and domestic law limitations on the circumstances in which force, and specifically lethal force, may be used. ROE take the form of a profile of rules reflecting actions that the Peace Force is permitted at a particular time to undertake. That profile may be expected to change from time to time as the prevailing circumstances dictate. In NATO and EU practice the Military Commander with overall responsibility for the operation will submit a request for the profile of ROE that is considered to be required, in the prevailing operational circumstances, to facilitate the success of the operation. This ROE request, sometimes called a "ROEREQ", will be considered by the superior authority which in due course decides upon and issues the ROE for the operation in the form of an ROE authorisation, or "ROEAUTH". Each of the granted rules is selected from lists of possible military actions that are grouped

---

[15] See International Institute of Humanitarian Law, *Sanremo Handbook on Rules of Engagement* (2009), p. 1, para. 3: 'ROE are issued by competent authorities and assist in the delineation of the circumstances and limitations within which military forces may be employed to achieve their objectives ... they provide authorization for and/or limits on, among other things, the use of force, the positioning and posturing of forces, and the employment of certain specific capabilities. In some nations, ROE have the status of guidance to military forces; in other nations, ROE are lawful commands.'

according to particular categories of activity. While there may be divergent interpretations of particular ROE terms, such as "hostile act" and "hostile intent", what is critical is that, irrespective of the precise terms employed, members of the Peace Force consulting applicable ROE receive clear guidance that accords with the legal restrictions on the use of force that are referred to earlier in this Manual and that apply to them. The UN follows a somewhat different procedure, establishing ROE at the outset of a mission designed to meet all possible contingencies for the duration of the mandated period which can, in principle, be altered only with specific new authorisation by the authority establishing the operation.

3. Where the legal obligations and restrictions applicable to particular personnel or units within the Peace Force differ, for example because of differing Sending State legal provisions or interpretations, these differences should be reflected in supplementary instructions that are issued to the particular personnel or units.

4. Furthermore, a TCC can for legal or other reasons narrow the ROE applicable to its forces by issuing national restrictions on them, e.g. on the performance of certain tasks, generally referred to as "caveats", but such caveats may not be more permissive than the ROE applicable to the force as a whole. Additionally, subordinate commanders may restrict, but not broaden, the ROE authorised by higher authority.

5. The lawful use of force in self-defence cannot be restricted by ROE. However, the different interpretations of States as to the scope of self-defence imply the risk that force contingents may respond inconsistently in given situations. The aim of a multi-national command is to overcome difficulties posed by such inconsistent interpretations so that the Peace Force commander can have assurance that the forces under his/her command will respond appropriately to uncertain future events, and the careful crafting of ROE is one way of seeking to achieve that consistency.[16]

12.9 Planners of Peace Operations should put in place arrangements for post-incident investigations to be undertaken. Such investigations should be either administrative or disciplinary in nature, depending on what is known as to the circumstances.

1. It is widely recognised that the obligation to protect the right to life implies a procedural duty to investigate deprivations of life and deaths from other than natural causes attributable to State agents, private

---

[16] The EU uses "confirmatory ROE" for this purpose.

persons or persons unknown.[17] The obligation is to conduct a thorough independent investigation into all of the relevant circumstances pertaining to the incident giving rise to the death(s). The investigation should seek to determine whether the force used was appropriate, should seek to identify those responsible and should support any punishment awarded. The investigators should be institutionally and practically independent of those potentially implicated, and should take into account surrounding features such as planning and the control of those involved in using the force.[18] The obligation implies, inter alia, the availability of investigators, of associated specialists, of personnel to secure the scene and of the basic facilities required to undertake such investigations.

[17] Consider for example *McKerr* v. *the United Kingdom*, Application No. 28883/95, Judgment of 4 May 2001, para. 111.
[18] Consider *Ibid.*, paras. 112 and 113. See further *McCann* (n. 10), para. 150; *Kaya* v. *Turkey*, Application No. 22535/93, Judgment of 28 March 2000, para. 124.

Detention

13.1 Detention of persons during Peace Operations must not be arbitrary.

1. The first Rule of this chapter[1] reflects the basic principle underlying both international humanitarian law (IHL)[2] and international

---

[1] This chapter draws mainly upon:

 – the Copenhagen Principles and Guidelines on the Handling of Detainees in International Military Operations (2012), http://um.dk/en/~/media/UM/English-site/Documents/Politics-and-diplomacy/Copenhangen%20Process%20Principles%20and%20Guidelines.pdf (Copenhagen Principles). These were developed through the Copenhagen Process meetings, at which participants (representatives of a number of States and observers from some international organisations), while not seeking to create new legal obligations or authorisations under international law, confirmed the desire to develop principles to guide the implementation of the existing obligations with respect to detention in international military operations. They are intended to apply to international military operations in the context of non-international armed conflicts and Peace Operations; they are not intended to address international armed conflicts. They do not affect the applicability of international law to military operations conducted by States or international organisations; the obligations of their personnel to respect such law, or the applicability of international and national law to non-State actors. The Commentary was not approved by the participants but was issued under the sole responsibility of the Chairman of the process. See the introductory part to the Principles and Guidelines, as well as Principles 1 and 16 and the Commentary thereto;
 – J. Kleffner, 'Operational Detention and the Treatment of Detainees', in T. D. Gill and D. Fleck (eds.), *The Handbook of the International Law of Military Operations* (Oxford University Press, 2010), pp. 465–479;
 – UN DPKO/DFS, Interim Standard Operating Procedures on Detention in United Nations Peace Operations, DPKO/DFS SOP Ref. 2010.06 (2010) (UN ISOP);
 – the United Nations (revised) Standard Minimum Rules for the Treatment of Prisoners, UNGA Res. 70/175 (2015) (Mandela Rules); and
 – J. Pejic, 'Procedural Principles and Safeguards for Internment/Administrative Detention in Armed Conflict and Other Situations of Violence', 87 *International Review of the Red Cross* (2005), pp. 375–391, which reflects the official position of the International Committee of the Red Cross (ICRC). See ICRC, International Humanitarian Law and the Challenges of Contemporary Armed Conflicts, Report for the 30th International Conference of the Red Cross and Red Crescent (2007), 30IC/07/8.4 (2007), p. 11 and Annex 1, www.icrc.org/eng/assets/files/other/ihl-challenges-30th-international-conference-eng.pdf.

[2] See e.g. J.-M. Henckaerts and L. Doswald-Beck, *Customary International Humanitarian Law*, vol. I, *Rules* (Cambridge University Press, 2005), Rule 99, pp. 344–352. See also ICRC, Strengthening International Humanitarian Law Protecting Persons Deprived of Liberty: Concluding Report,

human rights law (IHRL)[3] rules in relation to deprivation of liberty. Furthermore, under IHRL it has been recognised that the core of the right not to be deprived of liberty arbitrarily is non-derogable.[4]

2. Paragraph 8 of the UN Interim Standard Operating Procedures (ISOP) also confirms this principle. The Commentary to the Copenhagen Principles treats this principle as part of the requirement that detention must be 'conducted in accordance with applicable international law'.

3. The jurisprudence and opinions of international human rights bodies have by now formed a consolidated position confirming that when a person is detained, even extraterritorially, he/she is within the jurisdiction of the detaining State or organisation.[5]

4. The Rules that follow set out more detailed provisions aiming to ensure that this basic Rule is respected.

5. Detention for the purposes of this chapter refers to deprivation of liberty by a Peace Operation of persons other than personnel of the operation. It does not cover restrictions of liberty that do not amount to a deprivation of liberty.[6] States have different views as to when and under what circumstances a restriction of liberty amounts to detention. In any

---

32IC/15/XX (2015), pp. 15 and 28, http://rcrcconference.org/wp-content/uploads/2015/04/32IC-Concluding-report-on-persons-deprived-of-their-liberty_EN.pdf.

[3] See e.g. art. 9 International Covenant on Civil and Political Rights (16 December 1966, in force 23 March 1976), 999 UNTS 171 (ICCPR), which explicitly states, inter alia, that '[n]o one shall be subjected to arbitrary arrest or detention'; art. 7(3) American Convention on Human Rights (21 November 1969, in force 18 July 1978), 1144 UNTS 123 (ACHR); art. 6 African Charter on Human and Peoples' Rights (27 June 1981, in force 21 October 1986), 1520 UNTS 217 (ACHPR); art. 5(1) Convention for the Protection of Human Rights and Fundamental Freedoms (4 November 1950, in force 3 September 1953), ETS 5, as amended by Protocol No. 14 (in force 1 June 2010) (ECHR) as interpreted by the European Court of Human Rights (ECtHR), e.g. in *Hassan* v. *the United Kingdom*, Application No. 29750/09, Judgment of 16 September 2014 [GC], para. 105.

[4] See, for the ICCPR (n. 3), UN Human Rights Committee, General Comment No. 29: Article 4: Derogations during a State of Emergency, UN Doc. CCPR/C/21/Rev.1/Add.11 (2001), paras. 11 and 14–16, as well as General Comment No. 35: Article 9: Liberty and Security of Person, UN Doc. CCPR/C/GC/35 (2014), paras. 65–68. See also Inter-American Court of Human Rights, *Habeas Corpus in Emergency Situations*, OC-8/87, Advisory Opinion of 30 January 1987, and *Judicial Guarantees in States of Emergency*, OC-9/87, Advisory Opinion of 6 October 1987. The ECtHR's *Hassan* v. *UK* judgment (n. 3) also appears to reflect this view, see paras. 99–110.

[5] See Rule 5.2 and accompanying Commentary. See e.g. General Comment No. 35 (n. 4), para. 63. See also Kleffner (n. 1), p. 468.

[6] The distinction between deprivation of liberty and restrictions thereof is, inter alia, reflected in art. 5(1) and (3) Protocol (II) Additional to the Geneva Conventions of 12 August 1949, and relating to the Protection of Victims of Non-International Armed Conflicts (8 June 1977, in force 7 December 1978), 1125 UNTS 610 (AP II) and in Copenhagen Principles 1 to 3 (n. 1) and the accompanying Commentary (especially Commentary 1.4 where reference is made to 'restrictions of liberty' not amounting to detention in situations such as roadblocks and checkpoints). For the ICCPR (n. 3), compare arts. 9 and 12 (and see also General Comment No. 35 (n. 4), para. 5), and for the ACHR (n. 3) arts. 7 and 22. For the ECHR (n. 3), see art. 5 thereof in contrast with art. 2 of Protocol No. 4 to the ECHR (16 September 1963, in force 2 May 1968), ETS 46. See also Kleffner (n. 1), pp. 465–466.

case, even persons whose liberty of movement has only been restricted shall at all times be humanely treated as required by applicable international law, as to which see Rule 13.14.

13.2 Detention may take place only on grounds recognised in applicable international law.

1. The first element to the avoidance of arbitrary detention is of a substantive nature: detention can be justified only on a limited number of grounds.[7] Either these grounds may be defined directly in international law, or international law may require that they be defined in domestic law.

2. Some IHRL instruments also set out the accepted grounds for detention, notably article 5 ECHR. By contrast, others do not and merely prohibit arbitrary deprivation of liberty combined with a reference to grounds established by law.[8]

3. The Human Rights Committee has expressed the view that: 'Any substantive grounds for arrest or detention must be prescribed by law and should be defined with sufficient precision to avoid overly broad or arbitrary interpretation or application.'[9] The European Court of Human Rights has held that the requirement that detention must take place 'in accordance with a procedure prescribed by law'[10] means that any such law must be defined with sufficient clarity and must be accessible and foreseeable in its application.[11]

4. The most established ground for detention is detention related to prosecution for a criminal offence, whether it be pre-trial or post-conviction detention.[12] However, this is not the only acceptable ground for detention. For example, detention may also be justified when a number of conditions are met in the context of controlling immigration[13] and on account of mental health or for preventing the spreading of infectious diseases.[14] Detention may also be permissible in case of non-compliance with the lawful order of a court or in order to secure the fulfilment of a specific obligation prescribed by law.[15] Furthermore, and this is

---

[7] See also Pejic (n. 1), p. 383; Kleffner (n. 1), pp. 469–473.

[8] See e.g. art. 9(1) ICCPR (n. 3); art. 7(2) ACHR (n. 3); art. 6 ACHPR (n. 3).

[9] General Comment No. 35 (n. 4), para. 22.

[10] Art. 5(1) ECHR (n. 3).

[11] E.g. *Hassan and Others* v. *France*, Application Nos. 46695/10 and 54588/10, Judgment of 4 December 2014, para. 59.

[12] E.g. art. 9(3) ICCPR (n. 3); art. 5(1)(a) and (c) ECHR (n. 3).

[13] See art. 5(1)(f) ECHR (n. 3); General Comment No. 35 (n. 4), para. 18, in relation to the ICCPR (n. 3).

[14] See art. 5(1)(e) ECHR (n. 3); General Comment No. 35 (n. 4), para. 19, in relation to the ICCPR (n. 3).

[15] See art. 5(1)(b) ECHR (n. 3).

particularly relevant for Peace Operations, security reasons can constitute a valid reason for detention, but only very exceptionally.[16] By contrast, detention as punishment for the legitimate exercise of rights as guaranteed by human rights treaties is prohibited,[17] as is detention based on the inability to fulfil a contractual obligation.[18]

5. Permissible grounds for detention under IHRL may be laid down in international law rather than, or in addition to, domestic law.[19] However, any such international law provisions, such as a treaty or Security Council resolution, would need to meet the requisite quality of law, i.e. be sufficiently precise, accessible and foreseeable. There may be international law provisions that meet these conditions as regards the grounds for detention, but see Rule 13.4 as to the procedural safeguards.[20] As regards Security Council resolutions, a general authorisation to take 'all necessary measures' would not meet these requirements[21] but more specific language explicitly authorising detention for specified reasons could meet these requirements.[22] Similar considerations apply to any legal acts adopted by regional organisations in relation to detention in Peace Operations conducted by those organisations, and to any international agreements covering detention in Peace Operations, such

---

[16] General Comment No. 35 (n. 4), para. 15. See further n. 22 and para. 12 of the Commentary to this Rule in relation to the ECHR (n. 3), which does not list this as a ground for detention. See also para. 6 of the Commentary to this Rule.

[17] See General Comment No. 35 (n. 4), para. 17, in relation to the ICCPR (n. 3).

[18] Art. 11 ICCPR (n. 3); art. 7(7) ACHR (n. 3); art. 1 Protocol No. 4 to the ECHR (n. 6).

[19] See e.g. *Hassan and Others* v. *France* (n. 11), paras. 58 and 61–66; *Medvedyev and Others* v. *France*, Application No. 3394/03, Judgment of 29 March 2010 [GC], paras. 79–80. This may even include unwritten law, provided that it is accessible and foreseeable; see *Korbely* v. *Hungary*, Application No. 9174/02, Judgment of 19 September 2008 [GC], para. 70.

[20] E.g. in *Hassan and Others* v. *France* (n. 11) the ECtHR accepted the adequacy of the grounds for detention, which had their international law basis in UNSC Res. 1816 (2008) *juncto* arts. 101 and 105 UN Convention on the Law of the Sea (10 December 1982, in force 16 November 1994), 1833 UNTS 397, albeit together with domestic French law (paras. 61–66) but it held that there was no law defining the precise conditions of detention and applicable safeguards (paras. 67–72).

[21] See also Rule 5.7, Commentary, paras. 5–6.

[22] Some Security Council resolutions have explicitly granted detention authority: see e.g. UNSC Res. 169 (1961), para. 4 (on the Congo); UNSC Res. 837 (1993), para. 5 (on the perpetrators of attacks against UNOSOM II in Somalia); UNSC Res. 1638 (2005), para. 1 (concerning former President Charles Taylor of Liberia). See also UNSC Res. 1546 (2004), para. 10 (on Iraq) *juncto*, the letter of the US Secretary of State annexed to this resolution. The latter, which provided for 'internment where this is necessary for imperative reasons of security', was not adequate to derogate from art. 5 ECHR (n. 3), which does not provide for "security detention". See also *Al-Jedda* v. *the United Kingdom*, Application No. 27021/08, Judgment of 7 July 2011 [GC], paras. 100–109. See also para. 12 of the Commentary to this Rule.

as detainee transfer agreements or Status of Forces Agreements (SOFAs) that include provisions on detention.[23]

6. Personnel of a Peace Force may also be able to rely on provisions of Host State law where these provide for a citizen's arrest.

7. By contrast to IHL treaty rules applicable in international armed conflicts (IACs),[24] IHL treaty rules applicable in non-international armed conflicts (NIACs) do not define any permissible grounds for detention. They only provide for a number of fundamental guarantees that must be respected towards all persons who do not take a direct part or who have ceased to take part in hostilities, including those detained,[25] while adding some specific safeguards for those 'deprived of their liberty for reasons related to the armed conflict, whether they are interned or detained'[26] and for the prosecution and punishment of criminal offences 'related to the armed conflict'.[27]

8. It is a matter of debate whether customary IHL applicable to NIACs provides an authority to detain. The UK courts, at first instance and on appeal, have rejected this in the *Serdar Mohammed* case.[28] However, in Resolution 1 on 'Strengthening International Humanitarian Law Protecting Persons Deprived of Their Liberty' adopted by the thirty-second International Conference of the Red Cross and Red Crescent in December 2015, one of the recitals states that the Conference was 'mindful that deprivation of liberty is an ordinary and expected occurrence in armed conflict,

---

[23] For an example of a detainee transfer agreement adopted as a fully fledged international agreement, see the Agreement between the European Union and the Central African Republic concerning detailed arrangements for the transfer to the Central African Republic of persons detained by the European Union military operation (EUFOR RCA) in the course of carrying out its mandate, and concerning the guarantees applicable to such persons, OJ 2014 No. L251, 23 August 2014, p. 3.

[24] Geneva Conventions (I–IV) on the (I) Wounded and Sick in Armed Forces in the Field, (II) Wounded, Sick and Shipwrecked Members of the Armed Forces at Sea, (III) Treatment of Prisoners of War and (IV) Protection of Civilian Persons in Time of War (12 August 1949, in force 21 October 1950), 75 UNTS 31, 85, 135, 287. See especially arts. 21 and 118 Geneva Convention III on prisoners of war and arts. 42 and 78 Geneva Convention IV on internment of civilians when 'the security of the Detaining Power makes it absolutely necessary' or for 'imperative reasons of security'.

[25] See common art. 3(1) Geneva Conventions I–IV (n. 24); art. 4 AP II (n. 6).

[26] See art. 5 AP II (n. 6).

[27] See *Ibid.*, art. 6.

[28] *Serdar Mohammed and Others* v. *Secretary of State for Defence* and *Yunus Rahmatullah and the Iraqi Civilian Claimants* v. *Ministry of Defence and Foreign and Commonwealth Office*, Court of Appeal of England and Wales, Civil Division, Judgment of 30 July 2015, [2015] EWCA Civ 843, especially paras. 164–253, upholding [2014] EWHC 1369 (QB) and [2014] EWHC 3846 (QB) on this point. Note that the UK Supreme Court on further appeal found a power to detain pursuant to Security Council resolutions where detention is necessary for imperative reasons of security and that art. 5(1) of the ECHR (n. 3) should be read as accommodating detention under that power: *Abd Ali Hameed Al-Waheed* v. *Ministry of Defence* and *Serdar Mohammed* v. *Ministry of Defence*, Supreme Court of the United Kingdom, Judgment of 17 January 2017, [2017] UKSC 2, 56 and 57.

and that under [IHL] States have, in all forms of armed conflict, both the power to detain, and the obligation to provide protection and to respect applicable legal safeguards'.[29] This suggests that States consider that IHL does provide a power to detain in NIACs. This was also the view of nearly all members of the Group of Experts who prepared this Manual, without prejudice to the scope and modalities of this power to detain.

9. Even if customary IHL applicable in NIACs includes the power to detain, it would need to specify which categories of person could be detained and on what grounds. Given the absence in NIACs of combatant and prisoner of war status,[30] it is arguably legally necessary, and at least highly desirable, that the grounds for detention in NIACs, whether status- or conduct-based, be defined in relevant domestic law or other rules of international law. This is all the more so in the light of the impact of IHRL.

10. The position taken in the Manual on the relationship between IHL and IHRL is set out in Rule 5.8, which states that '[w]hen applicable simultaneously, international humanitarian law and human rights law are complementary. In case of collision between a norm of international humanitarian law and a norm of human rights law, the more specific norm applies in principle'. The Commentary to this Rule adds (Rule 5.8, para. 4) that 'it will need to be determined how IHL and IHRL rules interact when they both apply. In principle, the more specific rule will prevail (lex specialis) but there may also be cases where the more recent rule will prevail'. The Commentary to Copenhagen Principle 4 states that '[w]here a person is detained in situations of armed conflict the lex specialis will be international humanitarian law. That law may be supplemented or informed by human rights law depending on the detaining authority's legal obligations'.

11. Whereas for IACs it is generally accepted that the IHL rules on detention are lex specialis and in principle[31] take precedence over IHRL rules, including as regards the grounds for detention,[32] it is questionable

---

[29] ICRC, Resolution 1 on Strengthening International Humanitarian Law Protecting Persons Deprived of Their Liberty, 32IC/15/R1 (2015).

[30] See e.g. the brief identification of different State views on whether detention of members of armed groups in NIACs could be based exclusively on their status or requires an individual threat assessment in ICRC (n. 2), p. 29.

[31] There may be specific points on which IHRL contains more specific and/or more recent rules that may prevail. For example, States that have accepted an absolute prohibition on the death penalty under IHRL including in times of armed conflict cannot impose such a penalty even where IHL would allow for this.

[32] *Hassan v. UK* (n. 3), paras. 100–107 (on the question of principle) and paras. 108–111 (application in the case at hand).

whether the same holds true for detention in NIACs because, as already explained, even if IHL were to provide a detention authority in NIACs it fails to set out clear grounds for detention.[33] In NIACs, it is therefore arguably necessary for the grounds for detention to be laid down by domestic law or other rules of international law, such as regulations of an international organisation or an international agreement, such as a SOFA or transfer agreement.[34]

12. Furthermore, a specific issue under the ECHR is that "security detention" does not correspond to any of the detention grounds permitted under article 5 ECHR.[35] Therefore, States parties to the ECHR may need to have recourse to a derogation under article 15 of the ECHR and/or an overriding Security Council detention authority in order to be able to perform security detentions, whether outside the context of an armed conflict or of members of armed groups or other persons for reasons related to a NIAC. As indicated in Rule 5.7 and the accompanying Commentary, the Group of Experts who prepared this Manual takes the position that derogation is permitted if the emergency requirement is satisfied in a Peace Force's area of deployment and that derogation should be considered in situations where the Peace Forces are unable to comply with article 5 of the ECHR while fulfilling their obligations under the mandate.[36]

13.3 When circumstances justifying detention have ceased to exist, a detainee must be released.

1. This Rule is self-explanatory. As detention must be based on specific grounds and factual circumstances corresponding to such grounds, detention must cease when those circumstances no longer exist.[37]

2. This Rule is, for example, reflected in Copenhagen Principle 4. The Commentary to this Principle provides further guidance on what a prompt release means in this context, and implies a prompt release whenever circumstances justifying detention have ceased to exist.

---

[33] E.g. in *Hassan* v. *UK* (n. 3) the ECtHR appears to have limited its deference to IHL detention grounds to detention in the context of IACs (para. 104, final sentence).

[34] Compare General Comment No. 35 (n. 4), paras. 64–66; Kleffner (n. 1), pp. 467–469.

[35] See e.g. *Hassan* v. *UK* (n. 3), para. 97. Obviously, this does not in any way affect the legality of detentions for the purposes of criminal prosecution.

[36] See Rule 5.7, Commentary, paras. 5–6, which also identifies the conditions under which a UNSC resolution could be regarded as taking precedence over art. 5 ECHR (n. 1) under art. 103 UN Charter.

[37] See also Pejic (n. 1), pp. 382–383; Kleffner (n. 1), p. 469.

3. Paragraph 7 of the UN ISOP provides that '[a]ny person detained by [UN] personnel shall be released or handed over ... as soon as possible'. This is further developed in paragraphs 73 to 91 of the UN ISOP. Those paragraphs set a relatively short detention period (48 hours, possibly extended by 24 hours for transit or handover), except in certain cases of detention for criminal prosecution, and provide that '[a] detained person shall be released as soon as the detention is no longer warranted in accordance with the Mission-specific military rules of engagement or policy directives ... and within the time limits set forth in paragraphs 7, 73, 74 and 75'.[38]

13.4   Detention must be subject to procedural safeguards in accordance with applicable international law. These safeguards include in particular the possibility promptly to challenge the lawfulness of detention and the requirement that there shall be an appropriate periodic review at least every six months. Both the initial and the subsequent periodic reviews should in principle be undertaken by a court but shall in any event be undertaken by an impartial and independent authority.

1. A second element in avoiding arbitrary detention is of a procedural nature: detention must be accompanied by procedural safeguards.[39]

2. However, the precise nature and extent of those safeguards differ under IHRL and IHL, and there is no universal agreement on what the minimum procedural safeguards are in some cases, notably as regards security detention in NIACs. This is closely linked to the interaction between IHL and IHRL in NIACs as regards deprivation of liberty (explained in Rule 13.2 in relation to the grounds for detention).

3. This Rule sets out the principle that there must be procedural safeguards and specifies one of the most essential safeguards, namely that there must be impartial and independent review of detention. Other procedural safeguards are set out in the Rules that follow.

4. Under IHRL, detention requires prompt judicial control and the possibility to challenge the lawfulness of detention.[40] This may be subject to derogations but an appropriate impartial and independent review must be ensured. However, neither State practice nor the jurisprudence of human rights bodies has established any precise and generally

---

[38] UN ISOP (n. 1), para. 76.
[39] See art. 9(1) ICCPR (n. 3); art. 5(1) ECHR (n. 3); art. 7(2) ACHR (n. 3). See also Pejic (n. 1), pp. 383 and 384–391.
[40] See art. 9(3)–(4) ICCPR (n. 1); art. 5(3)–(4) ECHR (n. 1); art. 7(5)–(6) ACHR (n. 1). See also the UN Human Rights Committee's General Comment No. 35 (n. 4), paras. 39–48.

applicable minimum content that must be respected. In those circumstances, the applicable minimum standards may differ depending on which – especially regional – human rights treaties apply. The Human Rights Committee's General Comment No. 35 on article 9 ICCPR provides some guidance in this respect.[41]

5. IHL contains hardly any rules on procedural safeguards applicable in NIACs, and the International Committee of the Red Cross (ICRC) is working on this topic.[42]

6. Copenhagen Principle 12 calls for 'a prompt initial review' and periodic review 'by an impartial and objective authority'. The ICRC also identifies a prompt and subsequent periodic review by 'an independent and impartial body'.[43]

7. In this context, independence does not necessarily require review by a judicial body. Independence and impartiality will depend on the composition and autonomy of the reviewing body but also on its authority, in particular its authority to issue binding decisions.[44]

13.5 Persons detained are to be promptly informed of the reasons for their detention in a language that they understand.

1. The right to be promptly informed of the reasons for detention is well established under IHRL.[45] For IHL, see e.g. article 75(3) of Additional Protocol I.[46] This Rule is included in paragraph 10 of the UN ISOP.[47]

---

[41] General Comment No. 35 (n. 4), paras. 15, 45 and 65–66.

[42] For a detailed analysis, see ICRC (n. 2). By contrast, internment of civilians in IACs and occupations requires periodic review (at least twice yearly in a Party's own territory: art. 43 Geneva Convention IV (n. 24)) and if possible every six months in occupied territory (art. 78); such reviews may be of an administrative nature (arts. 41–42 and 78). This was acknowledged by the ECtHR in *Hassan* v. *UK* (n. 3), para. 33.

[43] Pejic (n. 1), pp. 385–386, 386–387 and 388–389.

[44] See e.g. the UN Human Rights Committee's General Comment No. 35 (n. 4), para. 45 ('Exceptionally, for some forms of detention, legislation may provide for proceedings before a specialized tribunal, which must be established by law and must either be independent of the executive and legislative branches or enjoy judicial independence in deciding legal matters in proceedings that are judicial in nature'); *Hassan* v. *UK* (n. 3), para. 106 ('Whilst it might not be practicable, in the course of an international armed conflict, for the legality of detention to be determined by an independent "court" in the sense generally required by article 5 § 4 ... nonetheless ... the "competent body" should provide sufficient guarantees of impartiality and fair procedure to protect against arbitrariness').

[45] See e.g. art. 9(2) ICCPR (n. 3) ('Anyone who is arrested shall be informed, at the time of arrest, of the reasons for his arrest and shall be promptly informed of any charges against him'); art. 7(4) ACHR (n. 3); art. 5(2) ECHR (n. 3).

[46] Protocol (I) Additional to the Geneva Conventions of 12 August 1949, and relating to the Protection of Victims of International Armed Conflicts (8 June 1977, in force 7 December 1978), 1125 UNTS 4.

[47] Orally when detention commences and at the earliest practical time in writing. See also Pejic (n. 1), p. 384.

13.6   Persons detained are to be promptly informed of their rights and should have access to legal assistance where feasible.

1. The Human Rights Committee's General Comment No. 35 states that '[d]etainees should be promptly informed of their rights, in a language they understand', and that prompt and regular access should be given to independent lawyers.[48]

2. The ICRC considers that '[a]n internee/administrative detainee should be allowed to have legal assistance' and that '[a]n internee/administrative detainee and his or her legal representative should be able to attend the proceedings in person'.[49]

13.7   Additional rights apply in relation to criminal proceedings including the principles of legality and fair trial.

1. Both IHRL[50] and IHL[51] provide for additional rights in respect of criminal proceedings.[52] Both IHL[53] and IHRL[54] limit, and in some cases exclude, the death penalty.

13.8   Detained persons are to be promptly registered by the detaining authority, which must keep records while protecting personal data.

1. Registration and keeping of adequate records[55] are essential for the proper application of detention rules, e.g. to ensure respect for applicable

---

[48] General Comment No. 35 (n. 4), para. 58.

[49] Pejic (n. 1), pp. 388 and 389.

[50] E.g. arts. 14 and 15 ICCPR (n. 3); art. 6 ECHR (n. 3); arts. 8 and 9 ACHR (n. 3); art. 7 ACHPR (n. 3).

[51] E.g. common art. 3(1)(d) Geneva Conventions I–IV (n. 24); art. 6 AP II (n. 6); Henckaerts and Doswald-Beck (n. 2), Rule 100, pp. 352–371 ('No one may be convicted or sentenced, except pursuant to a fair trial affording all essential judicial guarantees' – in both IACs and NIACs), Rule 101, pp. 371–372 (principle of legality – nullum crimen sine lege), and Rule 102, pp. 372–374.

[52] See also the UN Human Rights Committee's General Comment No. 2 (n. 4), in particular para. 16, and the Commentary to Copenhagen Principle 13 (n. 1).

[53] E.g. art. 6(4) AP II (n. 6) for NIACs.

[54] E.g. art. 6 ICCPR (n. 3); Second Optional Protocol to the ICCPR, aiming at the abolition of the death penalty (15 December 1989, in force 11 July 1991), 1642 UNTS 414; Protocols No. 6 (28 April 1984, in force 1 March 1985), ETS 114 and 13 (3 May 2002, in force 1 July 2003), ETS 187 to the ECHR on the abolition of the death penalty; art. 4 ACHR (n. 3); Protocol to the ACHR to abolish the death penalty (8 June 1990, in force 28 August 1991), OASTS 73.

[55] For IHL, see e.g. Henckaerts and Doswald-Beck (n. 2), Rule 123, pp. 439–442: 'The personal details of persons deprived of their liberty must be recorded.' See also Copenhagen Principle 8 (n. 1); UN ISOP (n. 1), paras. 10, 13, 49, 50 (including registration of items taken from detainees), 79, 88, 91 and 92; Mandela Rules 6–10 (n. 1).

time limits. It is also crucial to ensure accountability, whether it be to prove that applicable rules have been correctly applied, or to address any violations of those rules.[56]

2. The right to privacy under IHRL requires that personal data of detainees be adequately protected,[57] and IHL[58] also requires this to some extent.[59]

3. It is also required that detainees be held in a designated and acknowledged place of detention.[60]

13.9 Access to detainees must be given to the International Committee of the Red Cross in accordance with international humanitarian law where applicable. Such access to the International Committee of the Red Cross should also be given in non-international armed conflicts and where warranted in other situations. Access to detainees must also be given to such competent human rights bodies as have a right of access and may be given to other relevant organisations where appropriate. The International Committee of the Red Cross and competent human rights bodies, as well as other relevant organisations where appropriate, should accordingly be notified of any detention.

1. As regards IHL, in NIACs, '[T]he ICRC may offer its services ... with a view to visiting all persons deprived of their liberty for reasons related to the conflict in order to verify the conditions of their detention and to restore contacts between those persons and their families.'[61]

2. Paragraphs 12 and 96 of the UN ISOP provide for notification to and access for the ICRC irrespective of the applicable law for all detentions covered by those standard operating procedures.

---

[56] See e.g. Commentary, para. 1 to Copenhagen Principle 8 (n. 1).

[57] Protection of personal data requirements has been founded on IHRL provisions on the right to private life, notably under art. 17 ICCPR (n. 3) (see e.g. UN Human Rights Committee, General Comment No. 16: Article 17: Right to Privacy, UN Doc. HRI/GEN/1/Rev.9 (Vol. I) (1988), para. 10) and art. 8 ECHR (n. 3). Specific data protection rules may go further – see e.g. the Council of Europe Convention for the Protection of Individuals with regard to Automatic Processing of Personal Data (28 January 1981, in force 1 October 1985), ETS 108; art. 8 Charter of Fundamental Rights of the European Union, OJ 2016 No. C202, 7 June 2016, p. 389, and related EU legislation.

[58] See e.g. the protection against public curiosity in art. 13 Geneva Convention III (n. 24).

[59] See also Commentary 4 to Copenhagen Principle 8 (n. 1); UN ISOP (n. 1), para. 30 (protection from exposure to public curiosity).

[60] See Copenhagen Principle 10 (n. 1) and Commentary 4 to 6 thereto; General Comment No. 35 (n. 4), para. 58; Pejic (n. 1), pp. 384–385.

[61] Henckaerts and Doswald-Beck (n. 2), Rule 124(B), pp. 442–445. See also Pejic (n. 1), p. 391.

3. Copenhagen Principle 11 provides that in NIACs 'and where warranted in other situations, the detaining authority is to notify the ICRC or other impartial humanitarian organisation of the deprivation of liberty, release or transfer of a detainee. Detaining authorities are to provide the ICRC or other relevant impartial international or national organisations with access to detainees.'

4. Given that IHRL applies to detentions in Peace Operations, access must be granted to competent human rights bodies. The qualifications 'competent' and 'which have a right to access' mean that such access is legally required only where the relevant body has competence under the applicable human rights instrument or other rules of international law (e.g. obligations in the framework of the UN) and where that competence includes a right of access.

5. The Human Rights Committee's General Comment No. 35 states that '[i]ndependent and impartial mechanisms should be established for visiting and inspecting all places of detention'.[62]

6. Access may be given to other relevant organisations where appropriate. This could include international organisations or nongovernmental organisations. The determination of when such access is appropriate will be made by the Peace Operation.

13.10   Any right to consular and diplomatic protection of detainees which have a nationality other than that of the Host State shall be respected in accordance with the Vienna Conventions on Diplomatic and Consular Relations.

1. Pursuant to article 36(1)(b) of the Vienna Convention on Consular Relations,[63] a foreign national who is detained must be informed that he/she is entitled to contact the consular post of his/her State of nationality. Furthermore, 'consular officers shall have the right to visit a national of the sending State who is in ... detention, to converse and correspond with him and to arrange for his legal representation' unless the detainee opposes this.[64] States may exercise diplomatic protection in relation to their nationals abroad and, pursuant to article 3(1)(b) of the Vienna Convention on

---

[62] General Comment No. 35 (n. 4), para. 58.
[63] Vienna Convention on Consular Relations (24 April 1963, in force 19 March 1967), 596 UNTS 262.
[64] *Ibid.*, art. 36(1)(c).

Diplomatic Relation,[65] the functions of a diplomatic mission include '[p]rotecting in the receiving State the interests of the sending State and of its nationals, within the limits permitted by international law'.

2. Paragraph 56 of the UN ISOP provides that a foreign national[66] shall be informed of the right to communicate with the appropriate embassy, consular official or diplomatic representative and that the latter will be granted access for the purposes of such communication.

3. The Human Rights Committee's General Comment No. 35 states that '[d]etained foreign nationals should be informed of their right to communicate with their consular authorities, or, in the case of asylum seekers, with the Office of the United Nations High Commissioner for Refugees'.[67]

13.11   Detainees shall have a right to contact their families and the outside world as appropriate.

1. Rule 105 of the ICRC Customary IHL Study states that '[f]amily life must be respected as far as possible' and applies this rule to both IACs and NIACs. Rule 126 of the same Study provides that '[c]ivilian internees and persons deprived of their liberty in connection with a non-international armed conflict must be allowed to receive visitors, especially near relatives, to the degree practicable'.

2. Copenhagen Principles 10 and 11 provide that '[p]ersons detained are to be permitted to have appropriate contact with the outside world including family members as soon as reasonably practicable. Such contact is subject to reasonable conditions relating to maintaining security and good order in the detention facility and other security considerations' and that '[w]here practicable, the detainee's family is to be notified of the deprivation of liberty, release or transfer of a detainee'.

3. According to paragraphs 16 and 17 of the UN ISOP, this includes making reasonable efforts to notify the person designated by the detainee of the detention and location thereof, allowing the detainee to communicate orally or in writing with designated family members and other representatives, as well as allowing a reasonable number of visits by both of the latter consistent with operational and security requirements.[68]

---

[65] Vienna Convention on Diplomatic Relations (18 April 1961, in force 24 April 1964), 500 UNTS 95.
[66] Presumably this means a person with a nationality different from that of the Host State.
[67] See n. 4, para. 58.
[68] See also Pejic (n. 1), pp. 389–390. See also General Comment No. 35 (n. 4), para. 58, on keeping an accessible register as well as giving access to independent medical personnel and lawyers and to family members.

13.12   Detainees shall have the right to bring a complaint or to make a submission relating to any aspect of their detention.

1. Copenhagen Principle 14 provides that '[d]etainees or their representatives are to be permitted to submit, without reprisal, oral or written complaints regarding their treatment or conditions of detention. All complaints are to be reviewed and, if based on credible information, be investigated by the detaining authority.'

2. This right is also recognised by the ICRC[69] and is reflected in paragraphs 70–72 of the UN ISOP and Mandela Rules 56–57.

13.13   Where applicable, detainees shall have the right to compensation in case of an unlawful arrest.

1. This right exists under article 9(5) of the ICCPR and article 5(5) of the ECHR.

13.14   All persons detained will in all circumstances be treated humanely and with respect for their dignity without any adverse distinction founded on race, colour, religion or faith, political or other opinion, national or social origin, sex, birth, wealth or other similar status. Torture, and other cruel, inhuman or degrading treatment or punishment, is prohibited.

1. The prohibition of torture and of other cruel, inhuman or degrading treatment or punishment under IHRL is absolute.[70] This prohibition obviously applies also to detainees.[71] As indicated in the Commentary to Rule 13.1, the prohibition also applies in relation to persons whose liberty has only been restricted.

2. Given its absolute nature, this prohibition under IHRL continues to apply when IHL applies. In addition, various IHL rules contain similar prohibitions and require humane treatment of detainees.[72] These rules

---

[69] See also Pejic (n. 1), p. 389.
[70] See e.g. arts. 7 and 4(2) ICCPR (n. 3); art. 5 and 27(2) ACHR (n. 3); arts. 3 and 15(2) ECHR (n. 3). Art. 5 ACHPR (n. 3) does not qualify or condition this prohibition in any way either.
[71] See e.g. art. 10(1) ICCPR (n. 3); General Comment No. 35 (n. 4), para. 58.
[72] See e.g. common art. 3 Geneva Conventions I–IV (n. 24); Henckaerts and Doswald-Beck (n. 2), Rules 87–88 and 90, pp. 306–311, 315–319.

are reflected in paragraph 19 of the UN ISOP[73] and in Mandela Rules 1 and 43.

3. The prohibition of discrimination also applies.[74]

4. Physical force is not to be used against a detained person except in circumstances where such force is necessary and proportionate, in particular to prevent escape or to prevent a detainee from harming him-/herself or others, or from destroying property.[75]

13.15   Detaining authorities are responsible for providing detainees with adequate conditions of detention including food and drinking water, accommodation, access to open air, safeguards to protect health and hygiene, and protection against the rigours of the climate and the dangers of military activities. Wounded and sick detainees are to receive the medical care and attention required by their condition.

1. This Rule copies Copenhagen Principle 9.[76] Furthermore, the Human Rights Committee's General Comment No. 35 states that '[p]rompt and regular access should be given to independent medical personnel'.[77]

13.16   A State or international organisation may transfer a detainee to another State or authority only in compliance with the transferring State's or international organisation's international law obligations. It must ensure that the detainee who is to be transferred is not subject to a real risk of treatment that would breach international law obligations concerning humane treatment and due process. This may require adequate ex ante assurances followed by ex post monitoring, as well as capacity building.

1. The first sentence is copied from Copenhagen Principle 15. The second sentence reflects Commentary paragraph 4 thereto.

---

[73] See also Kleffner (n. 1), pp. 473–475.

[74] See e.g. UN ISOP (n. 1), para. 18; Mandela Rule 2 (n. 1).

[75] See e.g. UN ISOP (n. 1), paras. 26–29; Mandela Rules 47–49 (n. 1). Furthermore, as regards searches and questioning, see UN ISOP (n. 1), respectively paras. 43–47 and 41–42.

[76] See for further details of each of these elements the Commentary thereto as well as the UN ISOP (n. 1), paras. 20–21 (food and water), 22 (safety), 23–25 (health and hygiene), 30–32 (privacy and separate accommodation) and 33–40 (medical services); Pejic (n. 1), p. 390; Mandela Rules (n. 1), 12–17 (accommodation), 18 (hygiene), 19–21 (clothing and bedding), 22 (food and water), 23 (exercise and sport) and 24–35 (health care).

[77] See n. 4, para. 58.

2. Both IHL and IHRL impose limitations and/or conditions on transferring detainees to a third party. As regards IHL, obligations of *non-refoulement* have been read implicitly into common article 3 to the four Geneva Conventions of 1949.[78] As regards IHRL, limitations on transfers primarily result from the prohibition of torture, inhuman and degrading treatment, and have repeatedly been confirmed in the jurisprudence of human rights bodies.[79] Limitations may also result from treaty obligations excluding the death penalty[80] or from other fundamental rights such as the right to a fair trial.[81] The EU Charter of Fundamental Rights has an explicit transfer limitation rule in its article 19(2).

3. Furthermore, under international refugee law the principle of *non-refoulement* is well established, although it has a somewhat more narrow scope.[82] See, in particular, article 33 of the Refugees Convention.[83]

4. The limitations applicable under IHRL, IHL and refugee law are not identical. Where two or three of the bodies of law apply simultaneously, all the applicable limitations must be respected.

5. Before delving further into the legal requirements for transfers of detainees, it is worth mentioning why such transfers may be necessary. Essentially, it is often the best available course of action, notably where (i) release would pose a security threat and/or lead to impunity and (ii) prolonged detention by a Peace Operation itself is not a feasible option,

---

[78] Compare the explicit provisions on transfer in IACs: see art. 12 Geneva Convention III (n. 24); art. 45 Geneva Convention IV (n. 24).

[79] See e.g. for the ICCPR (n. 3), UN Human Rights Committee, Communication No. 470/1991, *Kindler v. Canada*, UN Doc. CCPR/C/48/D/470/1991 (1993), para. 6.2; General Comment No. 31 on the Nature of the General Legal Obligation Imposed on States Parties to the Covenant, UN Doc. CCPR/C/21/Rev.1/Add.13 (2004), para. 12; General Comment No. 35 (n. 4), para. 57. For the ECHR (n. 3), see *Soering v. the United Kingdom*, Application No. 14038/88, Judgment of 26 June 1989; *Saadi v. Italy*, Application No. 37201/06, Judgment of 28 February 2008 [GC]; *Trabelsi v. Belgium*, Application No. 140/10, Judgment of 4 September 2014.

[80] See e.g. *Al-Saadoon and Mufdhi v. the United Kingdom*, Application No. 61498/08, Judgment of 2 March 2010, especially paras. 115–123 (the risk of the death penalty is an obstacle to transfer).

[81] See e.g. *Ibid.*, para. 149.

[82] See Rule 14.4.6, Commentary, para. 4.

[83] UN Convention relating to the Status of Refugees (28 July 1951, in force 22 April 1954), 189 UNTS 137. Art. 33 states: '1. No Contracting State shall expel or return ("refouler") a refugee in any manner whatsoever to the frontiers of territories where his life or freedom would be threatened on account of his race, religion, nationality, membership of a particular social group or political opinion. 2. The benefit of the present provision may not, however, be claimed by a refugee whom there are reasonable grounds for regarding as a danger to the security of the country in which he is, or who, having been convicted by a final judgement of a particularly serious crime, constitutes a danger to the community of that country.' For the extended scope of application of the Refugees Convention, see Protocol relating to the Status of Refugees (31 January 1967, in force 4 October 1967), 606 UNTS 267.

including because of limitations under IHRL.[84] This is particularly the case where a person is detained for violation of Host State law and in which circumstance he or she can often only be prosecuted by the Host State, in which case a Peace Operation may lack a legal basis for prolonged detention. Moreover, most Peace Operations are temporary and, when they stop, the question of what to do with persons who still need to be detained will in any event need to be addressed. Furthermore, a variety of other reasons may also lead to transfer being the best available option, including mandate restrictions, resource limitations and/or concerns about the sovereignty of the Host State.

6. The reason why detainee transfers may nevertheless pose challenges, even where they may be the best course of action, is that there have often been concerns about whether the receiving party will treat transferred detainees correctly. This challenge arises especially where the Host State has a poor human rights record and/or does not have fully functioning law enforcement and judicial authorities. Such situations have often been addressed through a dual track approach comprising transfer arrangements and assurances in combination with capacity-building support to Host States.

7. Turning back now to the legal requirements, the key consideration is that, before the transfer and acting in good faith, there must be an overall assessment of whether the person concerned would face a real risk of a violation of the aforementioned rights.[85]

8. Where transfer arrangements or agreements are concluded, or assurances are given in another way, this does not in itself mean that no such risk exists but is one element to be taken into account. The content of any such arrangement/agreement will impact on how much weight can be given to it. One important element in this respect is the inclusion of provisions on monitoring, which may include a right to visit transferred detainees and to ensure that relevant actors may have access to them.[86]

9. In this respect, Copenhagen Principle 15 states that '[w]here the transferring State or international organisation determines it appropriate to request access to transferred detainees or to the detention facilities of the receiving State, the receiving State or authority should facilitate such access for monitoring of the detainee until such time as the detainee has

---

[84] See also Copenhagen Principle 13 (n. 1).
[85] See e.g. Commentaries 3 and 4 to Copenhagen Principle 15 (n. 1); UN ISOP (n. 1), para. 80.
[86] For further guidance, see the case law cited in nn. 79–81.

been released, transferred to another detaining authority, or convicted of a crime in accordance with the applicable national law'. The Commentary thereto adds that '[s]ome States currently undertake monitoring of detainees that they have transferred. Such monitoring is often dealt with in bilateral agreements or arrangements. Current practice suggests that monitoring may last at least until the detainee has been released or convicted of a crime in accordance with applicable law.' Transfer agreements/ arrangements may require that the ICRC be allowed to visit transferred detainees but any such visits will be negotiated by and take place in accordance with ICRC working modalities and cannot replace a post-transfer monitoring mechanism conducted by the transferring authority.

10. Furthermore, when transfer of a detainee is envisaged, the detainee should be informed thereof and should be able to challenge the envisaged transfer before it is carried out.[87] Transfers must also be duly registered and documented.[88]

11. Finally, where the conditions for the transfer of a person are not met but the Peace Operation is not authorised or able to lawfully keep the person in detention, and releasing the person would pose a serious risk to the life and physical integrity of other persons, the Peace Operation will need to decide which course of action poses the least risk to the life and physical integrity of other persons.

13.17   Detaining authorities should develop and implement standard operating procedures and other relevant guidance regarding the handling of detainees. Such guidance should reflect the different categories of detainees and the rules applicable to each of them.

1. The first sentence is copied from Copenhagen Principle 5.

2. The development and implementation of such procedures are important since the legal framework may not always be clear or complete by itself and personnel of a Peace Operation need to have clear and sufficiently detailed instructions to ensure that any detained person is treated correctly.

3. The UN ISOP provide a significant level of detail (set out in more than one hundred paragraphs), also refer to mission-specific Rules of

---

[87] The requirements as regards the body before which this challenge can be brought should be the same as those for the body before which the lawfulness of detention may be challenged (see Rule 13.4 and accompanying Commentary).

[88] See Rule 13.8 and accompanying Commentary. See also UN ISOP (n. 1), paras. 85–88.

Engagement (ROE), SOFAs or Status of Mission Agreements (SOMAs), policy directives and applicable international law, and provide that a Head of Mission (HOM) and his/her delegate may issue supplemental guidance.[89] The UN ISOP, in paragraphs 14–16, also provide for the designation of a Detention Focal Point in every mission reporting directly to the HOM with a right to access, a right to inquire into any detention matters and a right to provide advice thereon to the HOM or any other mission personnel.

4. Furthermore, given that there may be important differences in the rules applicable to different kinds of detainee, before embarking on deployment it should be determined which kinds of detainee an operation may have to handle. In the context of Peace Operations covered in this Manual, the categories of detainees could include in particular:

a. members of an armed group involved in a NIAC or persons who had engaged in acts constituting direct participation in hostilities;
b. persons detained in connection with criminal prosecution and/or who are serving a sentence;
c. persons other than members of an armed group involved in a NIAC or persons who had engaged in acts constituting direct participation in hostilities but who are detained for security reasons inside or outside the context of armed conflict;
d. voluntary or protective detainees.

5. Both IHL and IHRL require that different kinds of detainee may need to be segregated.[90] This is also reflected in paragraphs 31–32 of the UN ISOP.

---

[89] UN ISOP (n. 1), para. 3.
[90] See e.g. art. 10(2) and (3) ICCPR (n. 3). IHL, inter alia, requires separate detention of men and women in a number of cases; see e.g. art. 5(2)(a) AP II (n. 6).

The Protection of Civilians

14.1   GENERAL

1. Chapter 14 addresses various aspects pertaining to the protection of civilians (POC) in Peace Operations and is divided in several sub-chapters. This first sub-chapter describes the notion of POC in greater detail. General rules are provided which aim to further the protection of civilians, including in Peace Operations where POC is not expressly stipulated in the mandate. The following sub-chapters are devoted either to particularly vulnerable segments of the civilian population, i.e. children (sub-chapter 14.2) or refugees and other forcibly displaced persons (sub-chapter 14.4), or to enduring problems in relation to POC, i.e. sexual exploitation and abuse (SEA) (sub-chapter 14.3).

14.1.1   In Peace Operations civilians are entitled to protection.

1. The protection of civilians is of paramount concern to Peace Operations. As affirmed by the UN Secretary-General, '[a]ll United Nations peace operations today have the obligation to advocate the protection of civilians'.[1] In recent years regional organisations and arrangements have developed their own policies in this area.[2] Legal duties to protect civilians are chiefly to be found in international human rights law (IHRL) and international humanitarian law (IHL). The applicability of these areas of law to Peace Operations is discussed in Chapters 5 and 6. The norms most relevant to the protection of civilians are the right to life

---

[1] Report of the Secretary-General, The Future of United Nations Peace Operations: Implementation of the Recommendations of the High-Level Independent Panel on Peace Operations, UN Doc. A/70/357-S/2015/682 (2015), para. 17.
[2] E.g. NATO, Policy for the Protection of Civilians (2016), www.nato.int/cps/en/natohq/topics_135998.htm; EU Concept on Protection of Civilians (PoC) in EU-led Military Operations, EU Council Doc. CSDP/PSDC 114 (2015).

(found in IHRL), the principle of distinction (in IHL) and the prohibition of ill-treatment and torture (in IHRL and IHL). It is a matter of debate whether a Security Council mandate to protect civilians who are under an imminent threat of attack gives rise to a separate legal obligation to protect them.[3]

2. The protection of civilians includes 'activities undertaken to improve the security of the population and people at risk and to ensure the full respect for the rights of groups and the individual recognised under regional instruments ... and international law, including humanitarian, human rights and refugee law'.[4] It also involves the question of how to conduct a Peace Operation while respecting the rights of civilians.

14.1.2 The protection of civilians is a Host State responsibility. Peace Operations have an important role to play in supporting governments to fulfil that responsibility. When the protection of civilians is prejudiced, a Peace Operation should use all means available to it to protect civilians who are under imminent threat.

1. Host governments bear the primary responsibility for the protection of civilians. This duty is not diminished by the fact that a Peace Operation or other protection actors are present on the ground. Promoting POC is, however, also a moral obligation of the UN. The responsibility of the Host State does not weaken the duty of a Peace Operation to act within its capabilities when said government is not able or willing to protect its citizens. Civilians under threat look to the Peace Operation for assistance and protection. The core principles of UN peacekeeping are to be applied progressively and with sufficient flexibility as to meet new challenges. They should never serve as justification for failing to protect civilians.[5] Nor should national law be invoked as a justification in this regard. Therefore, Troop Contributing Countries (TCCs) should adopt legislation enabling POC.

---

[3] S. Wills, 'International Responsibility for Ensuring the Protection of Civilians', in H. Willmot, R. Mamiya, S. Sheeran and M. Weller (eds.), *The Protection of Civilians* (Oxford University Press, 2016), pp. 228–234.

[4] See AU, Draft Guidelines for the Protection of Civilians in African Union Peace Support Operations (2012), p. 5, www.peaceau.org/uploads/draft-au-poc-guidelines-english.pdf.

[5] Report of the High-Level Independent Panel on Peace Operations, Uniting Our Strengths for Peace: Politics, Partnership and People, UN Doc. A/70/95-S/2015/446 (2015), paras. 82, 85.

2. Peace Operations that are given a mandate to protect civilians must do all they can to protect civilians under threat.[6] The absence of a formal mandate does not relieve the Peace Force of the task of rendering assistance to persons in need. The obligation to protect civilians is then assumed. Peace Forces who witness violence against civilians are required to do what they can to stop it in accordance with basic UN principles and consistently with 'the perception and the expectation of protection of civilians created by a peace operation'.[7] In certain situations, a proactive approach is required on the part of the Peace Operation.

3. The first UN peacekeeping operation with a specific mandate to use force to protect civilian populations was the UN Assistance Mission in Sierra Leone (UNAMSIL), 1999–2005.[8] Today, the overwhelming majority of UN peacekeeping missions have a mandate to protect civilians.[9] Peace Operations can support POC through advocacy, monitoring IHRL compliance, endeavours to strengthen the rule of law and political involvement with the parties to the conflict. Their physical presence on the ground has a deterrent effect and promotes proactive action.[10] There have been efforts to reinforce international protection frameworks. These include, inter alia, the rise in human rights and protection-related mandates for Peace Operations, the Responsibility to Protect (R2P) as elaborated in the World Summit Outcome of 2005,[11] and the UN Secretary-General's Human Rights Up Front initiative.[12]

4. Within the Special Committee on Peacekeeping Operations,[13] the protection of civilians received special attention in reports from 2009 and thereafter.[14] The Departments of Peacekeeping Operations (DPKO) and of Field Support (DFS) have discussed the actual implementation of the mandate to protect civilians. The DPKO, the DFS and the UN Office

---

[6] *Ibid.*, para. 83.
[7] See the Report of the Panel on United Nations Peace Operations, UN Doc. A/55/305-S/2000/809 (2000), para. 62 (Brahimi Report), in reaction to the Report of the Independent Inquiry into the actions of the United Nations during the 1994 genocide in Rwanda, UN Doc. S/1999/1257 (1999).
[8] See UNSC Res. 1270 (1999), operative para. 14.
[9] High-Level Panel (n. 5), para. 90.
[10] *Ibid.*, para. 83.
[11] 2005 World Summit Outcome, UNGA Res. 60/1 (2005).
[12] High-Level Panel (n. 5), para. 84.
[13] Special Committee on Peacekeeping Operations, GA/C34, www.un.org/en/peacekeeping/ctte/CTTEE.htm.
[14] Reports of the Special Committee on Peacekeeping Operations, UN Docs. A/63/19 (2009), A/64/19 (2010), A/65/19 (2011), A/66/19 (2012).

for the Coordination of Humanitarian Affairs (OCHA) have engaged in a complete study of the implementation of the mandate in order to develop an operational concept for POC with a view to, on the one hand, guiding the deployment efforts of Peace Operations and, on the other hand, organising the training of military personnel.

5. Since the intervention in Libya, the Security Council has taken the protection of civilians forward by authorising in March 2013 the deployment of an Intervention Brigade in the UN Stabilization Mission in the Democratic Republic of the Congo (MONUSCO) with the mandate to 'ensure ... effective protection of civilians under threat of physical violence'.[15]

14.1.3 Protection mandates must be sufficiently realistic and form part of a broader political strategy. The Security Council should be kept informed about what is needed to deal with threats to civilians, and Troop and Police Contributing Countries should provide the required resources and apply their leverage to respond to threats against civilians.

1. In 2009 it was emphasised that resources needed to be allocated to POC in UN peacekeeping operations.[16] Frank assessments of threats to civilians must drive capability requirements and planning. Adequate infantry and enhanced mobility assets are needed so that armed peacekeepers can deliver physical protection.[17] Deployment strategies, operational concepts and communication plans should be revised when resources are not provided, and the international command must be advised promptly on the expected impacts on mandate implementation, including on how the mandate should be amended.[18]

2. There should be sustained communication between missions and host authorities concerning all threats to civilians. This includes juvenile protection, sexual violence and all matters pertaining to the protection of women and girls, as well as men and boys.[19]

3. All military and police personnel should have received guidance and scenario-based training on POC prior to deployment.

[15] UNSC Res. 2098 (2013).
[16] UNSC Res. 1894 (2009).
[17] High-Level Panel (n. 5), para. 92, 93.
[18] *Ibid.*, para. 95.
[19] *Ibid.*, para. 97.

14.1.4   Whenever a Peace Operation is mandated to protect civilians, the protection task should be reflected in the operation's Rules of Engagement.

1. Rule 1.8 of the UN Master List of Numbered Rules of Engagement authorises the use of force up to and including deadly force to defend any civilian who is in need of protection against a hostile act or hostile intent when competent authorities are not in a position to render immediate assistance.[20]

14.1.5   Whenever a Peace Operation is not expressly mandated to protect civilians, the operation's Rules of Engagement should allow for the possibility of carrying out tasks related to the protection of civilians.

1. This Rule is derived from the fact that the absence of a formal mandate does not relieve peacekeeping forces of the task to render assistance to persons in need. The Rules of Engagement (ROE) should therefore not hamper the performance of the protection task in circumstances requiring the Peace Operation to carry out such a task.

14.1.6   Special protection and assistance must be given by the Peace Operation to particularly vulnerable groups of individuals requiring special attention.

1. Mandates of contemporary Peace Operations carry the evidence of what the Security Council describes as its 'progressive consideration … of the protection of civilians in armed conflict as a thematic issue'. Such consideration emerged as a systematic inclusion of POC in peacekeeping mandates. It should, however, be noted that children and armed conflict (CAAC) mandates in resolutions of the Security Council are older than the concept of POC. These older mandates consider the protection of children as an IHL and peace and security issue, rather than through the lens of vulnerability.[21]

2. When mandated to protect civilians, Peace Forces should seek to understand the specific needs for protection that the different groups might have. These specific needs are based, inter alia, on their gender and age, and are also context- and country-specific. To that end Peace Operations should incorporate advisers on protection of civilians, child

---

[20] See V. Holt and T. Berkman, *The Impossible Mandate? Military Preparedness, the Responsibility to Protect and Modern Peace Operations* (Stimson Center, 2006), pp. 83–86.
[21] The issue of CAAC is further addressed in Chapter 14.2.

protection and women's protection working together with the mission's human rights component.

3. The failures to protect civilians in the conflicts of the 1990s coincided with the specific plight of women in Rwanda and in Bosnia and Herzegovina where they were subjected to systematic sexual violence.[22] The Security Council adopted Resolution 1325 (2000) a year after it had adopted thematic resolutions on POC including children in armed conflict, highlighting the disproportionate suffering inflicted on women, and also underlining the role of women as actors and agents in the peace process.[23] The importance of both protection of women in armed conflict and the full involvement of women in the prevention and resolution of armed conflict is reasserted and articulated in the Aide Memoire on issues pertaining to POC in armed conflict,[24] which also highlights the categories of measures that should be implemented within each distinct area.

4. Gender-based violence against civilians is any violence that stems from the social expectations that a community has of men and women. The terminology of many mandates thus provides for 'protection of civilians ... and especially women and children' because of the systematic and widespread violence against these two vulnerable groups. Protection of civilians against gender-based violence refers, for example, to the widespread and systematic use of rape and other forms of sexual violence against women and girls, including abductions and sexual enslavement. However, it also refers to the forced recruitment into the armed groups or forces, where the civilian victims are predominantly men and boys. Men and boys are also more at risk of extrajudicial killings.

5. In some conflict-afflicted areas, women and girls may represent the majority of the civilians. It is therefore essential that the availability of appropriate gender expertise be ensured in all relevant functional units, and especially in the units and structures in charge of the implementation of the POC mandate.

6. Even in the absence of actual hostilities in areas with civilian populations, many other gender-based threats against civilians, especially against women and girls, persist. Rape and other forms of sexual abuse can be a frequent occurrence during the post-conflict stabilisation

---

[22] *Preventing Conflict, Transforming Justice, Securing the Peace: A Global Study on the Implementation of United Nations Security Council Resolution 1325* (UN Women, 2015), p. 326.

[23] UNSC Res. 1325 (2000).

[24] Statement by the President of the Security Council, Aide Memoire for the consideration of issues pertaining to the protection of civilians in armed conflict, UN Doc. S/PRST/2010/25 (2010), Annex, pp. 15–16.

phase, for example with the release of large numbers of men as a result of the demobilisation process. For men and boys, the risk of being drawn into urban violence and crime often accompanies the lack of economic opportunities in the immediate aftermath of the conflict. Over the years, it has been recognised that a gender-sensitive strategy in policing sets the standard for national counterparts and fosters a more effective approach towards protecting civilians.[25]

7. In addition, Peace Forces should be mindful that the route to effective POC is not only through military means or physical interposition. In the context of Peace Operations with a POC mandate, Peace Forces should take into account the whole range of protection issues relating to women and girls and the necessary interventions to address them – including women's leadership and empowerment – in the planning of activities under the POC mandate.[26] Women's involvement in the POC process – be it through participation and representation in the force or through consultations – brings an additional, gender-sensitive perspective on how threats are perceived, and can increase both the military and non-military effectiveness of the force in the execution of its POC mandate.[27]

8. The strategic threat assessment process should take into account the characteristics that make certain populations more vulnerable to certain threats. The most notable characteristics are gender and age, but they include status as refugees or internally displaced persons (IDPs), religion and ethnicity. The threat assessment should be combined with an inclusive local consultation process with the host government, with non-governmental organisations and with women and youth organisations in order to identify the threats posed to them and their vulnerabilities, differing as these do as between men and women.[28] The POC strategy should also be accompanied by a credible and gender-specific messaging with respect to deliverables and local expectations, in order to ensure good expectations management and avoid putting the civilian population at further risk by creating unreasonable expectations.

---

[25] High-Level Panel (n. 5), para. 165.

[26] *Global Study* (n. 22), p. 157 (Recommendations).

[27] With UNSC Res. 2122 (2013) on women, peace and security, the Security Council '[e]xpresses its intention to increase its attention to women, peace and security issues in all relevant thematic areas of work on its agenda, including in particular Protection of civilians in armed conflict, Post-conflict peacebuilding, The promotion and strengthening of the rule of law ... Peace and Security in Africa, Threats to international peace and security caused by terrorist acts, and Maintenance of international peace and security'.

[28] UN DPKO/DFS, Policy on the Protection of Civilians in United Nations Peacekeeping, DPKO/DFS Ref. 2015.07 (2015), pp. 25 *et seq.*

14.2 CHILDREN

1. A significant segment of the civilian population, and a particularly vulnerable one, is the children who find themselves exposed to the violence and abuse associated with armed conflict. The impact of armed conflict on children includes physical attacks and violence towards them, including conflict-related sexual violence, their vulnerability during evacuation or life as internally displaced children, their situation with respect to life in camps, and issues associated with asylum or nationality. A particularly significant issue concerns the various types of association between children and the parties to the conflict, especially the recruitment and use of child soldiers.

14.2.1 Children must be protected, at all times and without discrimination, from the direct and indirect impact of armed conflict. This protection stems from the rules and principles of all bodies of applicable law, generally, and from a set of specific measures for the protection of children in armed conflict.

1. Children are entitled to the protections required by their status as minors as guaranteed in all universal instruments on international human rights law (IHRL). These protections must be given without discrimination and must include special measures for assistance and protection.[29]

2. The Convention on the Rights of the Child (CRC), an instrument that has been nearly universally ratified, establishes that children have the right to such protection and care as are necessary for their well-being, including the right to have their basic needs met. This reflects children's rights to both survival and development.[30] The CRC defines a child as 'every human being below the age of eighteen years unless under the law applicable to the child, majority is attained earlier'[31] and draws from the rights and protections of multiple bodies of law.

3. According to article 38 of the CRC, States parties must respect international humanitarian law (IHL) and all provisions which are relevant to the child, and must protect and care for children affected

---

[29] See specifically art. 24(1) International Covenant on Civil and Political Rights (16 December 1966, in force 23 March 1976), 999 UNTS 171; art. 10(3) International Covenant on Economic, Social and Cultural Rights (16 December 1966, in force 3 January 1976), 993 UNTS 4.

[30] Arts. 3 and 6 Convention on the Rights of the Child (20 November 1989, in force 2 September 1990), 1577 UNTS 44 (CRC).

[31] Art. 1 CRC (n. 30).

by armed conflict. Thus, children under 15 should not be forced or recruited to take part in hostilities or to join the armed forces. In addition, article 39 of the Convention requires that governments provide for physical and psychological recovery and social reintegration of children who are victims of any form of conflict-related neglect and abuse.[32]

4. Following the Machel Report on the impact of armed conflict on children,[33] the disproportionate suffering of children was highlighted, and within a year the Security Council had created the mandate of a Special Representative and appointed the first Special Representative for Children in Armed Conflict. In the following years the situation of children affected by war was placed on the Security Council agenda.[34] In 2000, with Resolution 1314, the Security Council reaffirmed that 'the deliberate targeting of civilians, including children, and the committing of systematic, flagrant and widespread violations of international humanitarian and human rights law, including that relating to children, in situations of armed conflict may constitute a threat to peace and security'.[35] In parallel, this special respect and protection in armed conflict have also been restated in the Optional Protocol to the Convention on the Rights of the Child on the involvement of children in armed conflict which further raises the age for direct participation in armed conflict to 18 and establishes a ban on compulsory recruitment for children under 18.[36] Finally, the protection of children in war is also part of customary international law and applicable to both international (IACs) and non-international armed conflicts (NIACs).[37]

5. As of 2001, the Security Council had requested that the UN Secretary-General identify and list parties to conflicts that recruit and use children,[38] and called for dialogue with parties to conflicts that

---

[32] *Ibid.*, arts. 38 and 39; arts. 23, 24, 38, 50, 76 and 89 Geneva Convention IV on the Protection of Civilian Persons in Time of War (12 August 1949, in force 21 October 1950), 75 UNTS 287.

[33] Report of the Expert of the Secretary-General, Impact of Armed Conflict on Children, UN Doc. A/51/306 (1996) (Machel Report).

[34] UNSC Res. 1261 (1999) and Res. 1314 (2000).

[35] UNSC Res. 1314 (2000), para. 9.

[36] Optional Protocol to the Convention on the Rights of the Child on the Involvement of Children in Armed Conflict (25 May 2000, in force 12 February 2002), 2173 UNTS 222 (CRC Optional Protocol).

[37] J.-M. Henckaerts and L. Doswald-Beck, *Customary International Humanitarian Law*, vol. I, *Rules* (Cambridge University Press, 2005), Rule 135, pp. 479–482; art. 70(1) Protocol (I) Additional to the Geneva Conventions of 12 August 1949, and relating to the Protection of Victims of International Armed Conflicts (8 June 1977, in force 7 December 1978), 1125 UNTS 4 (AP I); art. 4(3) Protocol (II) Additional to the Geneva Conventions of 12 August 1949, and relating to the Protection of Victims of Non-International Armed Conflicts (8 June 1977, in force 7 December 1978), 1125 UNTS 610 (AP II).

[38] UNSC Res. 1379 (2001), para. 16.

recruit or use children to develop 'clear, time-bound Action Plans to end the practices'.[39] Shortly thereafter the Security Council requested the Secretary-General to devise a systematic and comprehensive monitoring and reporting mechanism to provide timely, accurate and reliable information on the recruitment and use of children and other violations committed against children affected by armed conflict, and endorsed the Monitoring and Reporting Mechanism proposed by him.[40] The Mechanism provides for the systematic gathering of information on grave violations against children, which is included in the annual Report of the Secretary-General on Children and Armed Conflict (CAAC) as well as in country-specific reports.[41] It is triggered when parties in situations of armed conflict are listed in the annexes of the annual Report of the Secretary-General on CAAC. The mechanism seeks to monitor and influence the conduct of all parties to conflict, including State and non-State parties,[42] by strengthening and systematising the practice of reporting, focusing primarily on the six grave violations.

6. Deliberate attacks on schools and hospitals are among the grave violations, and emphasis has been placed in Security Council Resolution 1998 (2011)[43] on avoiding their use in a manner that would be inconsistent with their protected status, or that might endanger both the safety of children and teachers, and the future development of children in conflict-affected areas through education. In 2015, many States adopted the Safe Schools Declaration, which endorsed the Guidelines for Protecting Schools and Universities from Military Use during Armed Conflict.[44] Although not legally binding, these Guidelines detail the applicable provisions of IHRL

---

[39] UNSC Res. 1460 (2003), para. 4.

[40] Respectively UNSC Res. 1539 (2004) and 1612 (2005).

[41] The most serious violations of children's rights during armed conflicts have been identified by the UN Secretary-General and have been clustered into six groups based on their egregious nature and the severity of their consequences on the lives of children. These are: (1) recruitment and use of children; (2) killing or maiming of children; (3) sexual violence against children; (4) attacks against schools or hospitals; (5) abduction of children; and (6) denial of humanitarian access for children. See Office of the Special Representative of the Secretary-General for Children and Armed Conflict (OSRSG CAAC), The Six Grave Violations Against Children During Armed Conflict: The Legal Foundation, Working Paper No. 1 (2009, updated 2013), p. 9, https://childrenandarmedconflict .un.org/publications/WorkingPaper-1_SixGraveViolationsLegalFoundation.pdf.

[42] OSRSG CAAC, UNICEF and DPKO, Monitoring and Reporting Mechanism Guidelines (2012), p. 5, www.unicefinemergencies.com/downloads/eresource/docs/2.6%20Child%20Protection/ MRM%20Guidelines%20English.pdf.

[43] Reiterated in UNSC Res. 2225 (2015), para. 7; UNSC Res. 2143 (2014), para. 6; UNSC Res. 2068 (2012), para. 2.

[44] *Guidelines for Protecting Schools and Universities from Military Use during Armed Conflict* (GCPEA, 2014).

and IHL and provide good practices and guidance on reducing the impact of armed conflict on education, particularly in relation to military use.[45]

7. International law has strengthened the understanding of the acceptable minimum age for direct participation in hostilities, and in many instances has raised it. In general, many international instruments prohibit the recruitment and use of children as soldiers when they are under the age of 18,[46] but if certain safeguards are in place voluntary recruitment of children under the age of 18 may be permitted.[47] In any event, however, that the recruitment (conscripting or enlisting) of children under age 15 as well as their general participation in hostilities are strictly prohibited by international law[48] and constitute a war crime[49] is increasingly recognised through international criminal law and jurisprudence.[50]

14.2.2 Peace Forces should ensure that roles and responsibilities with respect to the protection of children in armed conflict are clear for all areas of the mandate and that planning, conducting and reporting on the mission reflect the children's specific needs for protection.

1. The Security Council notes that 'the best interests of the child as well as the specific needs and vulnerabilities of children should be considered when planning and carrying out actions concerning children in situations of armed conflict'.[51]

---

[45] Report of the Special Representative of the Secretary-General for CAAC, UN Doc. A/70/162 (2015), para. 20.

[46] A few examples include art. 3 CRC Optional Protocol (n. 36); The Paris Commitments to Protect Children from Unlawful Recruitment or Use by Armed Forces or Armed Groups (2007), para. 4, www.unicefinemergencies.com/downloads/eresource/docs/2.6%20Child%20Protection/ pariscommitments_en.pdf; art. 22 African Charter on the Rights and Welfare of the Child (11 July 1990, in force 29 November 1999), OAU Doc. CAB/LEG/24.9/49.

[47] Art. 3 CRC Optional Protocol (n. 36).

[48] Art. 77(2) AP I (n. 37): 'The Parties to the conflict shall take all feasible measures in order that children who have not attained the age of fifteen years do not take a direct part in hostilities and, in particular, they shall refrain from recruiting them into their armed forces'; art. 4(3) AP II (n. 37): 'Children shall be provided with the care and aid they require, and in particular: ... (c) children who have not attained the age of fifteen years shall neither be recruited in the armed forces or groups nor allowed to take part in hostilities'; art. 38 CRC (n. 30).

[49] According to art. 8(2)(b)(xxii) and 8(2)(c)(vii) Rome Statute of the International Criminal Court (17 July 1998, in force 1 July 2002), 2187 UNTS 90, it constitutes a war crime to '[conscript or enlist] children under the age of fifteen years into the national armed forces or using them to participate actively in hostilities'.

[50] See *The Prosecutor* v. *Thomas Lubanga Dyilo*, Judgment, ICC-01/04-01/06-2842, Trial Chamber, 14 March 2012; *The Prosecutor* v. *Charles Ghankay Taylor*, Judgment, SCSL-03-01-T-1283, Trial Chamber, Judgment, 26 April 2012. See generally Chapter 21.

[51] UNSC Res. 2225 (2015), preambular para. 16.

2. Child protection in UN-authorised operations must therefore be addressed pursuant to all child protection guidance and relevant Security Council resolutions on CAAC.[52] According to the Department of Peacekeeping Operations (DPKO)/Department of Field Support (DFS) Policy on Protection of Civilians, this includes, but is not limited to, mainstreaming of child protection into all mission components, child protection training of all peacekeeping personnel, monitoring and reporting of grave violations against children, dialogue with parties to the conflict to end grave violations against children, and release of children from armed forces and groups.[53]

3. While it is highly unlikely that a Peace Force would be involved in the recruitment and use of child soldiers, Peace Forces may experience many other practical concerns with respect to the special measures for child protection or the treatment of children for association with armed groups. For example, in matters of detention, in addition to the general protections against arbitrary detention provided by international law,[54] and recalling that children are usually victims rather than perpetrators, the Security Council further reiterates that no child should be deprived of his/her liberty unlawfully or arbitrarily, and '[e]ncourages Member States to consider non-judicial measures as alternatives to prosecution and detention ... taking into account that deprivation of liberty of children should be used only as a measure of last resort and for the shortest appropriate period of time, as well as to avoid wherever possible the use of pre-trial detention for children'.[55] In addition, children's disarmament, demobilisation and reintegration (DDR) into society call for tailored measures, 'including through adequate education and training',[56] alongside other alternatives that balance accountability with children's special status by virtue of their age and the forced nature of their association.[57]

4. Children, irrespective of their gender, are particularly at risk of sexual exploitation and abuse. Security Council Resolution 2225 (2015) calls for 'the continued implementation by United Nations peacekeeping

---

[52] UNSC Res. 1261 (1999), 1314 (2000), 1370 (2001), 1460 (2003), 1539 (2004), 1612 (2005), 1882 (2009), 1998 (2011), 2068 (2012), 2143 (2014) and 2225 (2015).

[53] UN DPKO/DFS, Policy on the Protection of Civilians in United Nations Peacekeeping, DPKO/DFS Ref. 2015.07 (2015), p. 8.

[54] See Chapter 13.

[55] UNSC Res. 2225 (2015), preambular para. 17 and operative para. 6.

[56] UNGA Res. 51/77 (1997), para. 25.

[57] OSRSG CAAC, Children and Justice During and in the Aftermath of Armed Conflict, Working Paper No. 3 (2011), p. 28, https://childrenandarmedconflict.un.org/publications/Working Paper-3_Children-and-Justice.pdf.

operations of the Secretary-General's zero-tolerance policy on sexual exploitation and abuse and ... full compliance of their personnel with the United Nations code of conduct ... and urges Troop Contributing Countries to continue taking appropriate preventive action, such as mandatory pre-deployment child protection training including on sexual exploitation and abuse, and to ensure full accountability in cases of such conduct involving their personnel'.[58]

5. Respect for the rights of children is the responsibility of each involved State. Respect for children's rights is therefore a question of the concurrent obligations of the State Parties to the applicable IHRL treaties, whether a Host State or a Troop Contributing Country (TCC).[59] The TCCs, however, have the primary responsibility to ensure that education and training for individuals preparing for deployment includes the relevant CAAC awareness and standard operating procedures.[60] In addition, and because the monitoring and reporting mechanism operates on multiple levels from country level to the Security Council level, UN-mandated forces (through the Special Representative of the UN Secretary-General (SRSG) or Force Commander (FC)) should contribute to the collection and transmission of accurate and verifiable monitoring and reporting information. These tasks are often carried out by the Child Protection Advisers and conducted in co-ordination with other mission components, such as human rights or police and military observers, but also other UN entities and relevant local actors.[61]

6. Measures to protect children against all forms of abuse in armed conflict are at the intersection of many other thematic approaches to peace and security. For instance, the Women, Peace and Security agenda[62] provides for additional attention on gender perspectives in protecting children, as boys and girls are subject to different forms of violence and their overall needs in an armed conflict may differ.[63]

---

[58] UNSC Res. 2225 (2015), para. 16. See further Chapter 14.3; Chapter 16.
[59] See Chapter 5.
[60] UNSC Res. 2143 (2014), para. 20: 'recommends further that United Nations entities and United Nations peacekeeping troop and police-contributing countries undertake targeted and operational trainings for the preparation of United Nations mission personnel including troop and police contingents on their contribution in preventing violations against children so as to give all mission personnel the ability to effectively recognize, report and respond to violations and abuses committed against children and to successfully support child protection activities for better implementation of their respective mandates'.
[61] UNSC Res. 2143 (2014), preambular paras. 15–16; UNSC Res. 2225 (2015), para. 13.
[62] See UNSC Res. 1325 (2000) on women, peace and security, and related resolutions.
[63] See Chapter 7.

7. Similarly, when involved in the negotiation of peace agreements, Peace Forces should ensure the inclusion of child protection and, if applicable, reintegration in all peace negotiations and processes,[64] taking into account age assessment mechanisms and corresponding measures. A Peace Force mandate may also include the support of local security forces, which should then include training and support for preventing and combating violations against children in armed conflict, including through consultation on the development and implementation of action plans, as required by Security Council Resolution 1612 (2005) and related resolutions.[65]

8. The work of international organisations other than the UN in this respect is crucial, as in many instances these international organisations will operationalise the provisions of the CAAC resolutions in Peace Operations, through internal policies and guidelines, specific action plans and co-operation agreements.[66] The Security Council has recognised these efforts to mainstream child protection mechanisms in all peace and security activities of the AU[67] and in the EU Guidelines on Children in Armed Conflict,[68] as well as in NATO's Military Guidelines on CAAC.[69]

---

[64] UNSC Res. 2225 (2015), para. 9; UNSC Res. 2143 (2014), para. 9.

[65] UNSC Res. 1612 (2005), para. 7, calls for States to 'develop and implement action plans without further delay, in close collaboration with United Nations peacekeeping missions and United Nations country teams, consistent with their respective mandates and within their capabilities'.

[66] On the work carried out with international organisations such as the AU, the EU, NATO and the League of Arab States, see CAAC Report (n. 45), paras. 52–55.

[67] UNSC Res. 2143 (2014), preambular para. 17, referring to the Declaration between the Office of the Special Representative of the Secretary-General on CAAC and the Peace and Security Department of the African Union Commission (2013).

[68] EU Council Doc. 287/1/08 REV1 and 10019/08 (2008).

[69] NATO, Military Guidelines on CAAC, MCM-0016-2012 (2012).

14.3   COMBATING SEXUAL EXPLOITATION AND ABUSE

14.3.1   Sexual exploitation and abuse by military, police and civilian personnel of [UN] Peace Operations missions are prohibited.

1. The UN rules that specifically prohibit and set standards for combating sexual exploitation and abuse (SEA) are set out in the UN Secretary-General's Bulletin of 2003 entitled 'Special Measures for Protection from Sexual Exploitation and Sexual Abuse'.[70] The rules are binding for all staff of the UN, including staff of separately administered organs and programmes of the UN (Section 2.1).[71] The term "sexual exploitation" is defined in the 2003 Bulletin as 'any actual or attempted abuse of a position of vulnerability, differential power, or trust, for sexual purposes, including, but not limited to, profiting monetarily, socially or politically from the sexual exploitation of another'; and the term "sexual abuse" as 'the actual or threatened physical intrusion of a sexual nature, whether by force or under unequal or coercive conditions' (Section 1). In short, forbidden are sexual relations with minors under 18 years of age and sexual relations in exchange for assistance, food, goods, services or money (often referred to as "transactional sex"). Strongly discouraged are sexual relations with "beneficiaries of assistance" since these are based on inherently unequal power dynamics (Section 3).[72] The Secretary-General's 2003 Bulletin furthermore underlines that 'sexual exploitation and sexual abuse violate universally recognized international legal norms and standards and have always been unacceptable behaviour and prohibited conduct for United Nations staff. Such

---

[70] UN, Secretary-General's Bulletin, Special Measures for Protection from Sexual Exploitation and Sexual Abuse, UN Doc. ST/SGB/2003/13 (2003).

[71] For further reading on the binding nature of the document, see B. Oswald, H. Durham and A. Bates, *Documents on the Law of UN Peace Operations* (Oxford University Press, 2010), pp. 10, 433. See also R. S. Burke, *Sexual Exploitation and Abuse by UN Military Contingents: Moving Beyond the Current Status Quo and Responsibility Under International Law* (Brill Nijhoff, 2014), pp. 29–61.

[72] However, there is confusion and resistance to the 2003 UNSG Bulletin (n. 70) with regard to its provisions relating to sexual relationships, which are strongly discouraged as it has been held that not all sexual relations between UN personnel and nationals are exploitative or non-consensual. More clarification on the interpretation of this provision may be needed. See UN Office of Internal Oversight Services, Evaluation Report: Evaluation of the Enforcement and Remedial Assistance Efforts for Sexual Exploitation and Abuse by the United Nations and Related Personnel in Peacekeeping Operations, IED-15-001 (2015), pp. 23, 27 (OIOS Report 2015). See also O. Simic, *Regulation of Sexual Conduct in UN Peacekeeping Operations* (Springer, 2012).

conduct is prohibited by the United Nations Staff Regulations and Rules' (Section 3.1).[73]

2. In addition to the rules in the 2003 Bulletin, a comprehensive strategy to combat SEA by UN peacekeeping personnel was developed following the 2005 report of the Secretary-General's Special Advisor on SEA by UN peacekeeping personnel, His Royal Highness Prince Zeid Ra'ad Zeid al-Hussein.[74] The Zeid Report identified a number of reforms to better confront SEA by peacekeepers, which led to the adoption of several measures to address SEA on three levels: (1) prevention, (2) enforcement and (3) remedial action. This "three-pronged" strategy underlines the zero-tolerance policy of the UN with regard to SEA by peacekeeping personnel and has been stressed by all subsequent Secretaries-General. According to former Secretary-General Ban Ki-moon: 'The United Nations, and I personally, are profoundly committed to a zero-tolerance policy against sexual exploitation or abuse by our own personnel. This means zero complacency. When we receive credible allegations, we ensure that they are looked into fully. It means zero impunity.'[75] The UN's approach to addressing SEA is now so advanced that other international organisations, such as the AU and NATO, have consulted with the UN on how best to deal with SEA.[76] Therefore, while dealing with the UN's strategy to combat SEA, this chapter offers Rules which should be followed in all Peace Operations, regardless of the international organisation or lead State. This applies to

---

[73] See, inter alia, art. 27 Geneva Convention IV on the Protection of Civilian Persons in Time of War (12 August 1949, in force 21 October 1950), 75 UNTS 287; art. 4 Protocol (II) Additional to the Geneva Conventions of 12 August 1949, and relating to the Protection of Victims of Non-International Armed Conflicts (8 June 1977, in force 7 December 1978), 1125 UNTS 610; UN Staff Regulations and Rules, UN Doc. ST/SGB/2017/1 (2017), Regulation 1.2; UN, Secretary-General's Bulletin on the Observance by United Nations Forces of International Humanitarian Law, UN Doc. ST/SGB/1999/13 (1999), Section 7; several rules in 'We Are United Nations Peacekeeping Personnel', www.un.org/en/peacekeeping/documents/un_in.pdf; UN, Ten Rules/Code of Personal Conduct for Blue Helmets, www.un.org/en/peacekeeping/documents/ten_in.pdf, Rule 4.

[74] A Comprehensive Strategy to Eliminate Future Sexual Exploitation and Abuse in United Nations Peacekeeping Operations, UN Doc. A/59/710 (2005) (Zeid Report 2005). See also Chapter 7, in which ways of gender mainstreaming on all these three levels are provided, including employing more women in peacekeeping missions.

[75] See UN, Conduct and Discipline, www.un.org/en/peacekeeping/issues/cdu.shtml.

[76] J. Stern, Reducing Sexual Exploitation and Abuse in UN Peacekeeping: Ten Years After the Zeid Report, Stimson, Civilians in Conflict, Policy Brief No. 1 (2015), p. 20. For further reading on the AU "zero-tolerance policy" in line with the UN policy on SEA, see e.g. AU, 'Letter to Human Rights Watch', 19 October 2014; AU, Press Release: The African Union Releases the Key Findings and Recommendations of the Report of Investigations on Sexual Exploitation and Abuse in Somalia (2015).

the prohibition set forth in Rule 14.3.1, as well as to the best practices set forth in Rules 14.3.2 to 14.3.5.

3. The aforementioned developments, leading the UN to explicitly prohibit SEA and implement a strategy to combat it, were the result of numerous allegations of SEA by UN peacekeepers making international headlines. Two of the first missions to have become known for SEA by peacekeepers towards the local population were the UN missions in Somalia in 1992 and Cambodia in 1992–1993. Since then, many more such incidences of SEA have come to light and include missions in Kosovo, Bosnia and Herzegovina, East Timor, Eritrea, Mozambique, Sierra Leone, Liberia, Cote d'Ivoire, Haiti, Sudan, South Sudan, Guinea, Rwanda, the Democratic Republic of the Congo, the Central African Republic and Burundi. Thus, despite regulation since 2003 that prohibits and aims to eradicate SEA, SEA allegations continue to persist.[77] SEA may take the form of rape, enforced prostitution, forced oral sex or any other form of SEA, targeting both women/girls and men/boys of the local population in the Host State alike.[78] According to a 2015 UN Office of Internal Oversight Services (OIOS) evaluation report on SEA by peacekeepers over the period 2008–2013, there has been an overall decline of SEA allegations since 2009 (480 SEA allegations were received by the UN) but, nevertheless, SEA allegations persist, with a slight increase in 2013.[79] According to the study, SEA allegations involving minors (under 18 years old) accounted for over one-third (36 per cent).[80] The largest number of allegations involved military personnel, followed by civilians and then the police.[81] Civilians acccounted for a percentage disproportionate to their numbers (33 per cent of SEA allegations, while they constitute only 17 per cent of mission personnel).[82] The missions that have accounted for the highest number of SEA allegations are also the largest missions: the

---

[77] In addition, recently more attention was given to the issue of sexual violence against humanitarian workers by other humanitarian workers as one humanitarian worker, Megan Nobert, spoke out. She had been raped by another humanitarian worker who worked for a sub-contractor employed by a UN agency. However, under the applicable rules, the agency has no responsibility for the actions of the employees of its vendors. See for more information on this issue M. Nobert, 'Aid Worker: I Was Drugged and Raped by Another Humanitarian in South Sudan', *Guardian*, 29 July 2015. See also Nobert's organisation at Report the Abuse, www.reporttheabuse.org.

[78] Only recently more attention has been given to boys as victims of SEA by peacekeeping personnel. See, inter alia, S. Sengupta, 'Allegations Against French Peacekeepers Highlight Obstacles in Addressing Abuse', *New York Times*, 25 May 2015.

[79] OIOS Report 2015 (n. 72), pp. 8–9.

[80] *Ibid.*

[81] *Ibid.*, pp. 9–10.

[82] *Ibid.*, p. 9.

missions in Haiti (MINUSTAH), Democratic Republic of the Congo (MONUSCO), Liberia (UNMIL), Sudan (UNMIS) and South Sudan (UNMISS).[83] The OIOS concluded in this report, but also in its earlier reports, that there are serious problems of SEA by peacekeepers in the missions. According to another study, which evaluated thirty-six international peacekeeping missions by the UN, NATO, AU and the Economic Community of West African States (ECOWAS) active in the years 1999–2010, it has been submitted that SEA have been more frequently reported under the following circumstances: in situations with lower levels of battle-related deaths; in larger operations; in more recent operations, in particular after 2005 (which could in part be due to a higher focus on SEA in these years); where the State hosting the mission is less developed; and where the conflict involved high levels of sexual violence.[84]

4. Peacekeepers make enormous contributions to and sacrifices for the cause of peace and security, including by protecting civilians from conflict-related sexual violence by, for instance, militia or government forces,[85] which may rise to the level of war crimes, crimes against humanity or genocide.[86] However, when they are themselves involved in SEA of the local population, this causes enormous physical, psychological and socio-economic harm to the victims, families and societies concerned. In addition, it taints the reputation, credibility and legitimacy of UN personnel, Troop Contributing Countries (TCCs) and Police Contributing Countries (PCCs). For example, SEA by peacekeepers may affect local development and relations between local women and men and it may involve an

---

[83] *Ibid.*, pp. 8–9 (with MONUSCO accounting for 45 per cent – 214 allegations – of all peacekeeping-related SEA allegations). See for similar statistics T. Awori, C. Lutz and P. J. Thapa, Final Report: Expert Mission to Evaluate Risks to SEA Prevention Efforts in MINUSTAH, UNMIL, MONUSCO, and UNMISS (2013) (Final Report 2013).

[84] R. Nordas and S. C. A. Rustad, 'Sexual Exploitation and Abuse by Peacekeepers: Understanding Variation', 39 *International Interactions* (2013), pp. 511–534.

[85] A number of UNSC resolutions have recognised conflict-related sexual violence as a security issue that demands a security response, i.e. mandating peacekeepers to intervene against sexual violence. See UNSC Res. 1325 (2000), 1820 (2008), 1888 (2009), 1960 (2010) and 2106 (2013). See also A.-M. de Brouwer, 'Conflict-Related Sexual Violence: Achievements and Challenges in International Criminal Law and the Role of the Military', 108 *Militair Rechtelijk Tijdschrift* (2015), pp. 53–73. See furthermore Chapter 14.4, for ways to prevent conflict-related sexual violence of refugees, including through "firewood patrols" by peacekeepers.

[86] Under certain circumstances, sexual violence may amount to war crimes (in particular when committed as part of a plan or policy or as part of a large-scale commission of such crimes), crimes against humanity (when committed as part of a widespread or systematic attack against a civilian population) or genocide (when committed with a specific intent to destroy a certain group). See e.g. arts. 6, 7 and 8 Rome Statute of the International Criminal Court (17 July 1998, in force 1 July 2002), 2187 UNTS 90. For further reading, see A.-M. de Brouwer, *Supranational Criminal Prosecution of Sexual Violence: The ICC and the Practice of the ICTY and ICTR* (Intersentia, 2005).

increased risk of the spread of diseases, such as HIV/AIDS, and unwanted pregnancies. Similarly, when SEA by peacekeepers take place, a mission can no longer credibly advise the government on adherence to standards of international human rights law (IHRL) while its own personnel are violating IHRL. In sum, SEA by peacekeepers of the local population are widely considered as one of the most devastating departures from the UN's ideals.

14.3.2   Prevention should be part of the [UN's three-pronged] strategy to combat all forms of misconduct, including sexual exploitation and abuse. Prevention of sexual exploitation and abuse should take place through, inter alia, training, awareness-raising activities and practical preventive measures.

1. The first prong of the strategy, prevention of SEA, includes components both of internal and external information-sharing and of risk reduction. Internally, prevention through information-sharing includes training to all peacekeepers on SEA. In the 2005 Zeid Report it was held that inadequate training was a very important factor contributing to SEA by peacekeepers.[87] To date, training is considered to be one of the most effective ways to prevent SEA.[88] Since 2005, training on SEA by peacekeepers is mandatory for all personnel arriving on peacekeeping missions.[89] Pre-deployment training takes place for all international civilian staff (by the Department of Peacekeeping Operations, DPKO), military personnel (by the TCC) and police personnel (by the PCC).[90] The Conduct and Discipline Unit (CDU) at UN Headquarters assists TCCs and PCCs with SEA training by developing and sharing training modules, including through video and e-learning.[91] In addition, the Conduct and Discipline Teams (CDTs) in field missions – which are overseen by the CDU – provide direct induction, refresher and ongoing training in missions and work together with CDU to incorporate mission-specific information in training modules. The core conduct and discipline training in missions covers

---

[87] Zeid Report 2005 (n. 74), p. 62.

[88] *Peacekeepers and Sexual Violence in Armed Conflict* (Geneva Centre for the Democratic Control of Armed Forces, 2006).

[89] See Conduct in UN Field Missions, https://conduct.unmissions.org.

[90] *Ibid.*

[91] *Ibid.* See also Stern (n. 76), p. 13. Note also the UN's video called 'To Serve with Pride: Zero Tolerance for Sexual Exploitation and Abuse', which was made to raise awareness among UN and related personnel about the impact of acts of sexual exploitation and abuse on individuals and communities and provides information about the obligations of all people serving the UN to refrain from such acts. See Conduct in UN Field Missions: Multimedia Resources, https:// conduct.unmissions.org/multimedia.

a range of topics including: 'the [CDT] mandate and functions; Code of Conduct and core values; definitions and types of misconduct; examples of sexual exploitation and abuse and consequences; individual and management responsibilities; obligations to report misconduct; disciplinary and administrative procedures; and the rights and responsibilities of the peacekeeping personnel'.[92]

2. Externally, prevention of SEA through information-sharing includes outreach by the CDTs in the field to the local population and the broader public, including local government officials, relevant civil society organisations, international organisations and non-governmental organisations.[93] The aim of the outreach is to educate the local population about what is considered to be SEA and where they can report instances of SEA by peacekeepers. The range of awareness-raising measures undertaken in field missions includes poster campaigns, newsletters, brochures, websites and radio broadcasts.[94]

3. A third approach to the prevention of SEA involves measures in the field that aim to reduce the risk of SEA by peacekeepers by implementing practical measures to that effect. Such measures include: 'restrictions of movement, curfews, requiring soldiers to wear uniforms outside barracks, designating off-limits areas, instituting non-fraternization policies, increased patrols around high [risk] areas and decentralization of conduct and discipline [CDT] personnel into locations with a potentially high risk of misconduct'.[95] Another way to reduce the risk of SEA by peacekeepers is by vetting UN personnel applying to work in field missions. The CDU's Misconduct Tracking System is used for this purpose.

4. Although it is difficult to measure the impact of the aforementioned preventive measures on the actual reduction/prevention of SEA by peacekeepers, the UN prevention strategy has been held to be "robust" and significant progress has been made over the years in developing and conducting training, reaching out to communities and implementing practical measures that reduce the risk of SEA.[96] It has been held that further improvements in the training and screening of all categories of peacekeepers could still be made.[97]

---

[92] See Conduct in UN Field Missions: Prevention, https://conduct.unmissions.org/prevention.
[93] Ibid.
[94] Ibid.
[95] Ibid.
[96] Stern (n. 76), p. 20.
[97] See, inter alia, Ibid.; Report of the Secretary-General, Special Measures for Protection from Sexual Exploitation and Sexual Abuse, UN Doc. A/69/779 (2015).

14.3.3   Enforcement of [UN] standards of conduct should be part of the [UN's three-pronged] strategy to combat all forms of misconduct, including sexual exploitation and abuse. Enforcement of the prohibition of sexual exploitation and abuse should take place through, inter alia, investigation and, where such exploitation or abuse is proved, administrative action and/or disciplinary measures.

1. Except for military contingents, investigating SEA is in principle carried out by OIOS, which is independent of the peacekeeping mission (following a recommendation in the Zeid Report). All SEA-related offences fall under category 1 cases, seen by the UN as "high-risk", "complex matters" and "serious criminal cases".

2. When allegations of SEA concerning civilian personnel are substantiated, the UN decides on the measures to be taken.[98] In most cases, the relevant personnel are dismissed from service, while some cases are referred to national authorities for prosecution.[99] When allegations of SEA involving military and police personnel occur, the UN may repatriate the individuals concerned and ban them from future peacekeeping operations. The UN has thus only administrative jurisdiction over them. Disciplinary sanctions and any other judicial actions remain the responsibility of the national jurisdiction of the individual involved. This similarly applies to members of military contingents deployed on peacekeeping missions and experts on mission (civilian police and military observers). This was found to be problematic in the Zeid Report because TCCs are reluctant to admit publicly to acts of wrongdoing, which could lead to impunity of perpetrators for SEA. The responsibility for investigating an allegation of SEA and taking subsequent disciplinary action rests with the TCC, in accordance with the revised Memorandum of Understanding (MOU) (following recommendations in the Zeid Report), endorsed by the General Assembly in 2007.[100] The TCC involved must then report back to the CDU on the outcome of misconduct investigations and actions taken. The CDU and field

---

[98] According to the 2003 UNSG Bulletin (n. 70), SEA constitute acts of serious misconduct and are therefore grounds for administrative action or disciplinary measures, including summary dismissal (Sections 3.2(a) and 3.3).

[99] OIOS Report 2015 (n. 72), p. 19.

[100] Report of the Special Committee on Peacekeeping Operations and its Working Group on the 2007 resumed session, UN Doc. A/61/19 (Part III) (2007) endorsed by UNGA (UN Doc. A/RES/61/26 B). Note furthermore the UN Model Status of Forces Agreement for Peacekeeping Operations, UN Doc. A/45/594 (1990), which stipulates that TCCs have the exclusive responsibility to discipline and criminally sanction their military contingents.

mission teams track actions taken through the Misconduct Tracking System, a global database and confidential tracking system for all allegations of misconduct.[101] In all instances involving personnel who are not staff members, the UN can take only limited action against such personnel (e.g. repatriation and barring from future missions) and must rely on Member States to take disciplinary action.[102]

3. One of the main recommendations in the Zeid Report was to have greater recourse to the Host State for investigations and prosecutions of UN officials and experts on mission. However, as these people have functional immunity, it was recommended that functional immunity should be more easily waived by the UN Secretary-General to allow the Host State to investigate and prosecute where appropriate. A Group of Experts, established after the Zeid Report, concluded in their report on accountability that waiving immunity should be a priority, given that the Host State is where the crimes took place and thus where the witnesses and evidence are to be found.[103] Holding the trial in the Host State would also have the most concrete impact on the affected victims. However, despite these benefits, the UN is unlikely to waive immunity in order to enable the Host State to exercise criminal jurisdiction if the Host State's legal system is dysfunctional or if the ability of the local justice system to guarantee fair trials is in doubt. Given that peacekeeping operations are typically operating in a conflict, quasi-conflict or post-conflict context, such concerns are often present.[104]

4. Significant barriers continue to impede enforcement of SEA allegations and include long delays in investigation, muliple actors having distributed responsibilities, and wide variations in sanctions.[105] Given the UN's lack of competence over disciplinary and criminal matters, the UN is dependent on Member States for investigation and prosecution purposes.

[101] Note furthermore that the 2003 UNSG Bulletin (n. 70) states that UN personnel have a duty to report all concerns or suspicions of SEA and that the UN's whistleblower policy protects staff members who report in good faith from retaliation.

[102] See also 2003 UNSG Bulletin (n. 70), Section 6. For a more elaborate exploration of issues related to enforcement, see Chapters 9, 10, 11, 19, 20 and 21.

[103] Report of the Group of Legal Experts on Ensuring the Accountability of United Nations Staff and Experts on Mission with Respect to Criminal Acts Committed in Peacekeeping Operations, UN Doc. A/60/980 (2006).

[104] For further reading, see C. Ferstman, Criminalizing Sexual Exploitation and Abuse by Peacekeepers, USIP Special Report 335 (2013), pp. 6–8.

[105] OIOS Report 2015 (n. 72); Final Report 2013 (n. 83).

14.3.4   Remedial action should be part of the [UN's three-pronged] strategy to combat sexual exploitation and abuse. Remedial action should take place through assistance and support and includes, inter alia, medical, legal, psycho-social and immediate material care as well as the facilitation of the pursuit of paternity and child support claims.

1. The third prong, remedial action, involves assistance to complainants, victims and children born as a result of SEA by UN and related personnel by making use of pre-existing local services and networks in the Host State. This commitment was laid down in a 2007 General Assembly Resolution entitled 'UN Comprehensive Strategy on Assistance and Support to Victims of Sexual Exploitation and Abuse by United Nations Staff and Related Personnel'.[106] Pre-existing service organisations, including community-based organisations, intergovernmental organisations and non-governmental organisations, work together with an in-mission UN focal point – the CDT – to provide for assistance to victims of SEA (Purposes 11–13).

2. The main purpose of the Strategy is to ensure that complainants, victims and children born as a result of SEA by UN staff and related personnel receive appropriate assistance and support in a timely manner (Purpose 1). Assistance includes medical, legal, psycho-social and immediate material care (including food, clothing and shelter) as well as the facilitation of the pursuit of paternity and child support claims, all depending on the individual needs and their recognition of victimhood (as complainant, victim or child born as a result of SEA) (Principles 6–8). All assistance should be provided in a manner that does not increase their trauma, cause further stigmatisation or exclude or discriminate against other victims of SEA (Principle 9). In cases of referral, the process needs to be simple, safe and with respect for the need for confidentiality, dignity and non-discrimination (Principle 11). The Strategy makes explicit that the assistance shall in no way diminish or replace the individual responsibility for acts of SEA (which rests with the perpetrators) and that it is not intended as a means for compensation (Purpose 3). The provision of any assistance and support by the UN

---

[106] UNGA Res. 62/214 (2008). The commitment of the UN and other intergovernmental organisations and non-governmental organisations to providing assistance to victims of SEA by their personnel was, moreover, laid down in a 'Statement of Commitment on Eliminating Sexual Exploitation and Abuse by UN and Non-UN Personnel' the year before. This statement was issued at a 2006 high level conference on eliminating SEA by UN and non-governmental organisation personnel and hosted by the DPKO, UN Office for the Coordination of Humanitarian Affairs (OCHA), UN Development Programme (UNDP) and UN Children's Fund (UNICEF).

is furthermore not an acknowledgement of the validity of the claims or an indication of acceptance of responsibility by the alleged perpetrator (Purpose 14).

3. Those who can receive assistance are thus complainants, victims and children born as a result of SEA by UN and related personnel. Complainants are defined as 'persons who allege ... that they have been, or are alleged to have been, sexually exploited or abused by United Nations staff or related personnel, but whose claim has not yet been established through a United Nations administrative process or Member States' processes' (Principle 5c). To receive assistance as a complainant, the person should officially register the allegation in accordance with the procedures of the relevant organisation.[107] Victims are 'persons whose claims that they have been sexually exploited or abused by United Nations staff or related personnel have been established through a United Nations administrative process or Member States' processes' (Principle 5d). Children born as a result of sexual exploitation and abuse are 'children who are found by a competent national authority to have been born as a result of acts of sexual exploitation and abuse by United Nations staff or related personnel' (Principle 5e).

4. The assistance mechanism will serve complainants, victims and children born as a result of SEA by UN staff and related personnel, so that assistance and support remain consistent regardless of the agency, department or organisation associated with the SEA (Principle 4). "Related personnel" includes 'consultants, individual contractors, United Nations Volunteers, experts on mission and contingent members' (Principle 5f).

5. In 2015, the OIOS concluded that the UN has performed 'very poorly' on assistance to victims of SEA as very few have been assisted.[108] Their data suggest that, to date, only 26 out of (only) 217 identified SEA victims (12 per cent) have been referred for assistance, and of those little is known of the assistance provided to them.[109] As for paternity claims in relation to SEA, such allegations have been totally unsuccessful to date, partly due to difficulties related to evidence gathering (DNA testing).[110] Lack of funding and lack of a strong organisational victim

---

[107] See also Conduct in UN Field Missions: Remedial Action, https://conduct.unmissions.org/remedial-action.
[108] OIOS Report 2015 (n. 72), p. 23.
[109] *Ibid.*, p. 24.
[110] *Ibid.*, p. 26.

assistance structure are among the main reasons for the poor record on effective remedial action to address SEA by UN personnel and related personnel.[111] As victims of SEA should be assisted 'reliably', 'quickly' and 'in a timely manner', formulations used in the 2007 General Assembly Resolution cited earlier, based on these findings the OIOS expressed its 'serious concern' as to the state of affairs on victim assistance to date, many years since the adoption of the resolution.[112]

14.3.5   The [UN] prevention, enforcement and remedial action strategies to combat sexual exploitation and abuse should be continuously evaluated and where necessary further strengthened.

1. The UN continuously strives to improve and strengthen its zero-tolerance policy on SEA in all three areas of its strategy to combat SEA by peacekeeping personnel: prevention, enforcement and remedial action. Such measures include, inter alia, those that bring about speedier investigations of SEA and improve accountability, and the establishment of a trust fund for assistance to victims of SEA.

2. Ten years after the Zeid Report and twelve years after the Secretary-General's 2003 Bulletin, the OIOS concluded in 2015 that, 'despite continuing reductions in reported allegations, that are partly explained by underreporting, effectiveness of enforcement against sexual exploitation and abuse is hindered by a complex architecture, prolonged delays, unknown and varying outcomes, and severely deficient victim assistance'. Since 2003, the UN has worked to evaluate and improve its zero-tolerance policy on SEA, in particular in light of continuing reports on SEA by peacekeepers, the most recent involving the mission in the Central African Republic.[113]

3. On the basis of the Secretary-General's report on SEA of February 2015 (on special measures for protection from SEA), as adopted by the

---

[111] *Ibid.*, pp. 24, 26, 28. See also Stern (n. 76); Report of the Secretary-General, Implementation of the United Nations Comprehensive Strategy on Assistance and Support to Victims of Sexual Exploitation and Abuse by United Nations Staff and Related Personnel, UN Doc. A/64/176 (2009).

[112] OIOS Report 2015 (n. 72), p. 27.

[113] See e.g. UN News Centre, 'Fresh Allegations of Sexual Abuse Made Against UN Peacekeepers in Central African Republic', 5 January 2016; UN News Centre, 'Ban Vows to Act Quickly After Report Finds UN Failed to Respond "Meaningfully" to Central African Republic Abuse Allegations', 17 December 2015. Note that, in light of the history of allegations of SEA by troops in the Central African Republic, the then Special Representative for the Central African Republic was requested to resign by the UN Secretary-General.

General Assembly in May 2015, the UN has committed itself to implementing over forty proposals from this report.[114] In September 2015, the Secretary-General furthermore released his report, 'The Future of UN Peace Operations', which sets out his agenda for strengthening UN peacekeeping, and also again highlights some of the most pertinent measures to combat SEA by peacekeepers.[115] Furthermore, what becomes apparent from these reports is that, for effectively combating SEA by peacekeepers, Member State commitment and involvement are crucial.

4. Some of the most important measures to strengthen the UN's zero-tolerance policy of SEA concern, in the area of prevention, the development of a mandatory e-learning programme on SEA for all field personnel and expanding the vetting of all personnel to ensure that they do not have a history of sexual misconduct during prior service in the United Nations.

5. In the area of enforcement, proposals relate to: establishing immediate response teams in peacekeeping missions to gather and preserve evidence within 72 hours of receipt of an allegation for use in investigations; adopting a six-month timeline for completion of investigations of SEA and calling on Member States to adhere to the same timeline and to embed national investigation officers in their contingents; developing an enhanced complaint reception framework to ensure mechanisms within communities where people can come forward, in confidence, to raise complaints regarding UN personnel; strengthening managerial and leadership accountability, including by developing leadership accountability frameworks on conduct and discipline, including sexual exploitation and abuse (this may e.g. result in a finding of misconduct or serious misconduct and repatriation of the commander without the possibility of further service in field missions);[116] strengthening administrative measures against all members of staff found to have committed SEA, including withholding entitlements; suspending pay to TCCs and PCCs in connection with suspects on the basis of credible evidence; repatriating contingents where there is a demonstrated pattern of abuse or non-response to allegations of misconduct and consider terminating the deployment of uniformed personnel where there is a documented

---

[114] UNSG Report 2015 (n. 97).

[115] The Future of United Nations Peace Operations: Implementation of the Recommendations of the High-Level Independent Panel on Peace Operations, UN Doc. A/70/357-S/2015/682 (2015).

[116] Note that the 2003 UNSG Bulletin (n. 70) also stipulates such obligations for commanders in Section 4.

pattern of non-compliance with United Nations standards of conduct; publicly disclosing the nationality of personnel contributed by Member States being investigated for SEA; and adding the issue of SEA onto the agenda of meetings of the Security Council to highlight developments in this area and to take the initiative to follow up on reported cases. Member States' commitment is extremely important for accountability purposes, and the UN has called on them to hold courts martial as a measure of visible accountability and to finalise an international treaty to ensure accountability of United Nations personnel in connection with crimes committed in peacekeeping operations.[117]

6. In the area of remedial action, an important proposed measure is establishing a trust fund to provide support and assistance to complainants, victims and children born as a result of SEA, and Member States are called on to financially support such a fund.

7. Since the allegations of SEA by peacekeepers in 2015, most notably in the Central African Republic, a number of measures have been put in place, including the appointment by the Secretary-General of a High-Level Independent Panel on Peace Operations to review the SEA allegations in the Central African Republic.[118] Other measures have also been put in place, including the establishment of a new position, namely a Special Coordinator on Improving the United Nations Response to Sexual Exploitation and Abuse.[119] The Secretary-General's report of 16 February 2016 included the nationalities of the alleged perpetrators for the first time.[120] The Security Council also renewed its commitment

---

[117] See also Ferstman (n. 104). See further for thoughts on setting up an International Tribunal for SEA by UN peacekeepers and staff: *Preventing Conflict, Transforming Justice, Securing the Peace: A Global Study on the Implementation of United Nations Security Council Resolution 1325* (UN Women, 2015), and the report from the UK House of Lords Select Committee, Sexual Violence in Conflict: A War Crime (2016). In addition, in case the SEA rise to the level of genocide, crimes against humanity or war crimes, it could be argued that the perpetrators could be prosecuted before an international criminal tribunal or court, such as the International Criminal Court. See, on this matter, e.g. M. O'Brien, 'Sexual Exploitation and Beyond: Using the Rome Statute of the International Criminal Court to Prosecute UN Peacekeepers for Gender-Based Crimes', 11 *International Criminal Law Review* (2011), pp. 803–827; Burke (n. 71), pp. 179–230 (the latter also discussing avenues to hold the TCC or UN accountable).

[118] The following report was the result: M. Deschamps, H. B. Jallow and Y. Sooka, Taking Action on Sexual Exploitation and Abuse by Peacekeepers: Report of an Independent Review on Sexual Exploitation and Abuse by International Peacekeeping Forces in the Central African Republic (2015).

[119] UN News Centre, 'Seasoned Official Appointed to Coordinate UN Efforts to Curb Sexual Abuse by Peacekeepers', 8 February 2016.

[120] Report of the Secretary-General, Special Measures for Protection from Sexual Exploitation and Sexual Abuse, UN Doc. A/70/729 (2016).

to stronger measures against wrongdoers. In Security Council Resolution 2272 (adopted in March 2016), the Council endorsed the Secretary-General's decision to repatriate an entire military or police unit where 'there is credible evidence of widespread or systemic sexual exploitation and abuse by that unit'.[121] The Secretary-General also requested the replacement of troops from a State 'whose personnel are the subject of an allegation or allegations of sexual exploitation and abuse' and which has failed to act appropriately in response.[122] On 6 January 2017, the UN announced its plan to create a high level task force to develop a strategy to further strengthen the UN response to SEA.[123]

---

[121] UNSC Res. 2272 (2016), para. 1.

[122] *Ibid.*, para. 2.

[123] UN News Centre, 'New Task Force to Develop Strategy to Strengthen UN Response to Sexual Exploitation and Abuse', 6 January 2017. On this new strategy, see further Rule 16.6, Commentary, para. 4.

14.4 REFUGEES AND OTHER FORCIBLY DISPLACED PERSONS

14.4.1 International refugee law is specialised human rights law. Unlike international human rights law, international refugee law does not allow for derogation in time of public emergency or conflict; it applies in full in time of peace and in time of war.

1. International refugee law applies irrespective of the existence of armed conflict,[124] and in that sense it differs from international humanitarian law (IHL) which applies only in times of armed conflict. However, the applicability of international refugee law in Peace Operations depends on the question whether the Host State involved is a party to the relevant treaties,[125] in particular the 1951 Convention Relating to the Status of Refugees,[126] the 1967 Protocol Relating to the Status of Refugees[127] and/ or the 1969 Organisation of African Unity (OAU, now AU) Convention on the Specific Aspects of Refugee Problems in Africa.[128]

2. In addition, international refugee law applies in Peace Operations that are conducted under the banner of the UN. The Security Council has consistently emphasised the importance of international refugee law in its resolutions on Peace Operations,[129] and regularly calls on Peace Operations to act in compliance with international refugee law.[130]

---

[124] J. C. Hathaway, *The Rights of Refugees Under International Law* (Cambridge University Press, 2005), p. 261.

[125] This is without prejudice to the application of norms of international refugee law having the status of customary international law; see e.g. Rule 14.4.6.

[126] UN Convention Relating to the Status of Refugees (28 July 1951, in force 22 April 1954), 189 UNTS 137 (Refugees Convention). As of 1 July 2017, the Refugees Convention has 145 States parties.

[127] Protocol Relating to the Status of Refugees (31 January 1967, in force 4 October 1967), 606 UNTS 267 (Refugees Protocol). As of 1 July 2017, the Refugees Protocol has 146 States parties.

[128] Convention Governing the Specific Aspects of Refugee Problems in Africa (10 September 1961, in force 20 June 1974), 1001 UNTS 45 (AU Refugees Convention). As of 1 July 2017, the AU Refugees Convention has forty-six African States parties.

[129] See in particular UNSC Res. 1208 (1998), in which reference is made to the Report of the Secretary-General on Protection for Humanitarian Assistance to Refugees and Others in Conflict Situations, UN Doc. S/1998/883 (1998). See also, among many other resolutions, UNSC Res. 1265 (1999), 1778 (2007), 1894 (2009), 834 (2008) and 2149 (2014), para. 42. The Security Council consistently notes that the legal framework for Peace Operations in armed conflicts is provided by IHL, international human rights law and international refugee law.

[130] See recently e.g. UNSC Res. 1996 (2011), para. 3(b)(iv); UNSC Res. 2085 (2012), para. 18; UNSC Res. 2147 (2014), para. 5(d); UNSC Res. 2227 (2015), para. 33. Note that resolutions concerning operations based on Chapter VII of the UN Charter are also used in this chapter in order to extract general principles with regard to the treatment of refugees and internally displaced persons: apart from the fact that operations may comprise both peacekeeping and peace

Peace Forces should therefore be cognisant of the ratio and substance of international refugee law.[131]

3. In addition, international obligations in the field of international refugee law of the Sending State of the Peace Forces may be applicable if they exercise effective control over refugees in a particular area.[132]

4. When a Peace Operation has been charged with an interim administration mandate,[133] the mission assumes the international obligations of the State, supplemented by specific obligations set out in the mandate and international rules accepted by the UN.[134]

14.4.2   Refugees are persons who have been forced to flee their country of origin. They are entitled to international protection.

1. It is important to note that refugees are defined in various ways. They are defined in the main universal treaty, the Refugees Convention, as any person who:

> As a result of events occurring before 1 January 1951 and owing to well-founded fear of being persecuted for reasons of race, religion, nationality, membership of a particular social group or political opinion, is outside the country of his nationality and is unable or, owing to such fear, is unwilling to avail himself of the protection of that country or who, not having a nationality and being outside the country of his former habitual residence

---

enforcement, the nature of a Peace Operation has no direct bearing on the scope and content of the rights of refugees.

[131] This need is recognised by the Security Council, which clearly states that UN peacekeeping and other relevant missions should provide for the dissemination of information about international refugee law (UNSC Res. 1674 (2006), para. 17) and underlines the importance of personnel being trained in international refugee law (UNSC Res. 1270 (1999), para. 1).

[132] Regional international human rights courts and bodies have consistently ruled that "effective control" serves as an exception to the territorial application of human rights and refugee law. A minority of States oppose this position, but see Rule 14.4.6 and Chapter 5. It should be added that, under domestic law, protection of refugees by Peace Operations may also be equated with protection by individual States; see e.g. art. 7(1)(b) Directive 2011/95/EU of 13 December 2011 on standards for the qualification of third-country nationals or stateless persons as beneficiaries of international protection, for a uniform status for refugees or for persons eligible for subsidiary protection, and for the content of the protection granted (recast), OJ 2011 No. L337, 20 December 2011, p. 9 (Qualification Directive).

[133] See for instance the UN Transitional Administration for Eastern Slavonia, Baranja and Western Sirmium (UNTAES), UNSC Res. 1037 (1996); UN Transitional Administration in East Timor (UNTAET), UNSC Res. 1272 (1999); UN Transitional Authority in Cambodia (UNTAC), UNSC Res. 745 (1992); UN Mission in Kosovo (UNMIK), UNSC Res. 1244 (1999).

[134] See e.g. UNSC Res. 1244 (1999), para. 11(k), deciding that the main responsibilities of the international presence are, inter alia, '[a]ssuring the safe and unimpeded return of all refugees and displaced persons to their homes in Kosovo'; similarly, UNSC Res. 1037 (1996), para. 11(d).

as a result of such events, is unable or, owing to such fear, is unwilling to return to it.[135]

The temporal and the (optional) geographical limitations of the Refugees Convention have been removed by the Refugees Protocol: the Refugees Convention now applies to refugees worldwide.[136]

2. An important regional treaty is the AU Refugees Convention. It comprises, next to the definition from the Refugees Convention, a second, categorically different one:

> The term refugee shall also apply to every person who, owing to external aggression, occupation, foreign domination or events seriously disturbing public order in either part or the whole of his country of origin or nationality, is compelled to leave his place of habitual residence in order to seek refuge in another place outside his country of origin or nationality.[137]

Considering those categorically differing definitions, it is important to identify which one applies in the Host State.

3. The Office of the United Nations High Commissioner for Refugees (UNHCR), charged with providing international protection to refugees and seeking durable solutions to the problem of refugees (see Rule 14.4.10), recognises in addition to individuals who meet the criteria of the Refugees Convention definition those who are:

> outside their country of nationality or habitual residence and unable to return there owing to serious and indiscriminate threats to life, physical integrity or freedom resulting from generalized violence or events seriously disturbing public order.[138]

The mandate of the UNHCR, in other words, comprises refugees as defined in the Refugees Convention and, beyond those, refugees who flee from serious and indiscriminate threats to life or freedom. As a result, there may be a discrepancy between the obligations of States pertaining to refugees – when these are confined to refugees in the sense of the Refugees Convention – and "mandate" refugees, i.e. those who fall within the wider definition of UNHCR.

---

[135] Art. 1(A)(2) Refugees Convention (n. 126).
[136] Art. 1(2) Refugees Protocol (n. 127). States could, when becoming a party to the Refugees Convention, opt to confine their obligations to Europe, and hence to European refugees; see art. 1(B)(1) Refugees Convention (n. 126). Turkey is the only State party that has explicitly retained the geographical limitation after signing the Protocol on the basis of art. 1(3) Refugees Protocol (n. 127).
[137] Art. 1(2) AU Refugees Convention (n. 128).
[138] *Resettlement Handbook*, revised edn (UNHCR, 2011), p. 81.

14.4.3 Recognition of refugee status is a declaratory and not a constitutive act. The right to international protection – including the protection that is prescribed by the Refugees Convention – is therefore not conditional on status determination.

1. A person is a refugee as soon as he/she fulfils the criteria contained in the applicable refugee definition, whether formally recognised as a refugee or not. Recognition of this refugee status does not therefore make him/her a refugee but declares this person to be one.[139] Refugee status may be determined on an individual basis but also on a collective, prima facie basis (for instance, in case of large numbers of refugees originating from one particular State) on the basis of readily apparent, objective circumstances in the country of origin.[140]

2. This Rule means that Peace Forces should treat persons with protection claims as refugees except when proven otherwise or when an exclusion clause is applicable (see Rule 14.4.4). Refugee rights can be denied only after a careful refugee status determination procedure.[141]

14.4.4 A person who satisfies the criteria contained in the refugee definition of the Refugees Convention must be excluded from the benefits of this status when there are serious reasons for considering that (a) he/she has committed a crime against peace, a war crime or a crime against humanity, as defined in the international instruments drawn up to make provision in respect of such crimes; (b) he/she has committed a serious non-political crime outside the State of refuge prior to his/her admission to that country as a refugee; or (c) he/she has been guilty of acts contrary to the purposes and principles of the UN.

1. These exhaustively enumerated grounds for exclusion[142] are laid down in article 1(F) of the Refugees Convention and reflect the concerns of the

---

[139] UNHCR, Handbook and Guidelines on Procedures and Criteria for Determining Refugee Status under the 1967 Convention and the 1967 Protocol Relating to the Status of Refugees, HCR/1P/ENG/REV.3 (2011), para. 28.

[140] UNHCR, Guidelines on International Protection No. 11: Prima Facie Recognition of Refugee Status, HCR/GIP/15/11 (2015).

[141] Refugee status determination is usually carried out by the authorities of the State hosting the refugees or alternatively by UNHCR officials. UNHCR has published a Handbook (n. 139), supplemented by a series of guidelines on international protection intended to guide governments, legal practitioners, decision-makers and the judiciary, as well as UNHCR staff carrying out refugee status determination in the field.

[142] A categorically different and highly specific exclusion clause is laid down in art. 1(D) Refugees Convention (n. 126), which stipulates that the Convention shall not apply to persons who are at present receiving protection or assistance from organs or agencies of the UN other than UNHCR. This has so far been applied only to Palestinian refugees under the protection of the UN Relief and Works Agency for Palestine Refugees in the Near East (UNRWA).

drafters of the Convention in the wake of World War II: only those deserving international protection should be entitled to the benefits of the Convention, and those who do not should not be able to avoid prosecution.[143] They are also applied by UNHCR.

2. Substantive guidance in the context of crimes against peace, war crimes and crimes against humanity should be drawn from international instruments.[144] Of particular importance in that respect are the Rome Statute of the International Criminal Court[145] and the Statutes of the International Criminal Tribunals for the former Yugoslavia[146] and for Rwanda.[147] Terrorist acts are considered to be serious non-political crimes since they are likely to be disproportionate to any avowed political objective.[148]

3. Those who are excluded from refugee status are ordinary aliens: they do not enjoy any special protection on the basis of the relevant refugee law instruments.[149]

14.4.5 A person ceases to be a refugee when demonstrating no further need for international protection. This happens if (i) he/she voluntarily re-avails himself of the protection of his/her country of nationality; (ii) having lost his/her nationality, he/she voluntarily re-acquires it; (iii) he/she acquires a new nationality, and enjoys the protection of his/her new nationality; or (iv) he/she voluntarily re-establishes him-/herself in the country which he/she left or outside which he/she remained owing to fear of persecution. Alternatively, a person ceases to be a refugee when the circumstances in connection with which this status has been recognised have ceased to exist.

1. Refugee status is in principle a temporary status, i.e. for the duration of need. In article 1(C) the Refugees Convention enumerates exhaustively

---

[143] The AU Refugees Convention (n. 128) comprises comparable exclusion clauses in art. 1(5).

[144] UNHCR, Background Note on the Application of the Exclusion Clauses: Article 1F of the 1951 Convention relating to the Status of Refugees (2003), paras. 23–36. See also UNHCR, Guidelines on International Protection: Application of the Exclusion Clauses: Article 1F of the 1951 Convention Relating to the Status of Refugees, HCR/GIP/03/05 (2003).

[145] Rome Statute of the International Criminal Court (17 July 1998, in force 1 July 2002), 2187 UNTS 90.

[146] Statute of the International Criminal Tribunal for the Former Yugoslavia, annexed to UNSC Res. 827 (1993) (as amended).

[147] Statute of the International Criminal Tribunal for Rwanda, annexed to UNSC Res. 955 (1994) (as amended).

[148] UNHCR Guidelines (n. 144), paras. 15, 26.

[149] They may be forcibly returned to their country of origin unless *refoulement* prohibitions that are part of international human rights law bar such return. On *refoulement*, see Rule 14.4.6.

when the Convention may cease to apply.[150] The relevant provisions indicate that the person concerned no longer satisfies the criteria of the definition as a result of acts that demonstrate he/she is no longer unable or unwilling to avail him- or herself of the protection of the country of origin or that the person has acquired that of another State. However, so-called "go and see" visits to the country of origin – reconnaissance – that may be organised by UNHCR in the framework of voluntary repatriation operations (on which see Rule 14.4.15) do not result in loss of refugee status.

2. When the circumstances in connection with which the refugees were recognised as refugees have ceased to exist, cessation of refugee status is warranted.[151] In such a change of circumstances in the country of origin, there is no longer need to provide international protection, and the (former) refugee may consequently be returned to his/her country of origin. This provision has effect regardless of the volition of the (former) refugee concerned.

3. The mandate of UNHCR includes similar cessation clauses, which define when the High Commissioner's competence shall cease to apply with respect to refugees who are of the High Commissioner's concern.[152] However, in case of voluntary repatriation operations, UNHCR must nonetheless be regarded as entitled to insist on the High Commissioner's legitimate concern over the outcome of any return that he/she has assisted, and should be given direct and unhindered access to returnees (see also Rule 14.4.14). This should be considered as inherent in his/her mandate.[153]

14.4.6 A refugee is protected against expulsion *(refoulement)* in any manner whatsoever to the frontiers of territories where his/her life or freedom would be threatened on account of his/her race, religion, nationality, membership of a particular social group or political opinion.

1. The principle of *non-refoulement* is the most important norm of international refugee law. In the absence of a subjective right to be granted

---

[150] The AU Refugees Convention (n. 128) comprises comparable clauses in art. 1(4).

[151] See art. 1(C)(5) and (6) Refugees Convention (n. 126).

[152] Chapter II, para. 6(A) UNHCR Statute, UNGA Res. 428 (V) (1950).

[153] Conclusion of the Executive Committee of the High Commissioner's Programme on Voluntary Repatriation, No. 40 (XXXVI) (1985), sub (l). In practice this responsibility, and access to returnees, is included in the voluntary repatriation agreements UNHCR concludes with countries of origin and countries of refuge; cf. the model agreement included in *Handbook on Voluntary Repatriation: International Protection* (UNHCR, 1996).

asylum, its ongoing observation secures asylum for the refugee.[154] It prohibits the expulsion of refugees to territories where their life or freedom would be threatened.

2. The prohibition of *refoulement* is a treaty obligation,[155] and in addition a norm of customary international law. This means that under all circumstances Peace Forces are obliged to examine the risk of *refoulement*, in particular in case of relocation of refugees.

3. The applicability of the principle of *non-refoulement* is not dependent on determination of status, and it consequently also applies to those who seek asylum, and whose status has not yet been determined. States are bound to observe this principle at their borders, and even outside their territory if they have effective control over the persons concerned.[156] The prohibition includes indirect (or chain) *refoulement*, which means that States are also responsible for the conduct of States to which they forcibly return refugees and the possibility of subsequent expulsion.

4. The principle of *non-refoulement* is also part of international human rights law (IHRL) and IHL in which it has a different substantive and personal scope. The principle of *non-refoulement* in IHRL does not include a condition of nexus to a persecution ground and is thus broader in its scope of protection than its refugee law counterpart. It merely focuses on the severity of the treatment awaiting the person concerned in another State or jurisdiction, to wit, torture or inhuman and degrading treatment or punishment.[157] Therefore, even when international refugee

---

[154] Granting asylum is not a hostile act: 'The grant of asylum to refugees is a peaceful and humanitarian act and shall not be regarded as an unfriendly act by any Member State'; art. 2(2) AU Refugees Convention (n. 128). See also Rule 13.16, which applies the principle of *non-refoulement* to Peace Operations.

[155] Art. 33(1) Refugees Convention (n. 126); art. 2(3) AU Refugees Convention (n. 128).

[156] For instance, a state vessel on the high seas; see *Jamaa and Others* v. *Italy*, Application No. 27765/09, Judgment of 23 February 2012 [GC]. It is generally accepted that "effective control" serves as an exception to the territorial application of human rights and refugee law; see e.g. *Haitian Center for Human Rights* v. *United States*, Report No. 51/96, Case 10.675, Decision of 13 March 1997, paras. 156–158; UNHCR, *Extraterritorial Application of* Non-Refoulement *Obligations under the 1951 Convention relating to the Status of Refugees and its 1967 Protocol*, Advisory Opinion, 26 January 2007, www.unhcr.org/4d9486929.pdf. See also *Al-Jedda* v. *the United Kingdom*, Application No. 27021/08, Judgment of 7 July 2011 [GC]; *Al-Skeini and Others* v. *the United Kingdom*, Application No. 55721/07, Judgment of 7 July 2011 [GC]. These last two cases dealt with human rights violations by the United Kingdom during the war in Iraq. The United States, however, holds the minority position that human rights generally do not apply extraterritorially.

[157] See art. 3 Convention Against Torture and Other Cruel, Inhuman or Degrading Treatment or Punishment (10 December 1984, in force 26 June 1987), 1465 UNTS 85; art. 7 International Covenant on Civil and Political Rights (16 December 1966, in force 23 March 1976), 999 UNTS

law does not apply or excludes a person from refugee status, IHRL may bar forcible return. In IHL it is not allowed to transfer a protected person 'to a country where he or she may have reason to fear persecution for his or her political opinions or religious beliefs'.[158] This prohibition applies to persons protected by the fourth Geneva Convention of 1949 during, and under specific circumstances for a sustained period after, an international armed conflict (IAC).

14.4.7   Refugees must not suffer adverse consequences on account of their formal nationality.

1. Article 3 of the Refugees Convention provides that the Convention shall be applied without discrimination as to race, religion or country of origin. The exemption from exceptional measures such as internment as enemy aliens is illustrative: 'With regard to exceptional measures which may be taken against the person, property or interests of nationals of a foreign State, the Contracting States shall not apply such measures to a refugee who is formally a national of the said State solely on account of such nationality.'[159]

2. In time of war or other grave exceptional circumstances, a State may take provisional measures which it considers to be essential to its national security in the case of a particular person, but only pending a determination that the person concerned is in fact a refugee and that the continuance of such measures is necessary in his/her case in the interests of national security.[160] If a rationing system exists, which applies to the population at large and regulates the general distribution of products in short supply, refugees shall be accorded the same treatment as nationals.[161]

---

171. Important regional examples can be found in art. 3 Convention for the Protection of Human Rights and Fundamental Freedoms (4 November 1950, in force 3 September 1953), ETS 5 as amended by Protocol No. 14 (in force 1 June 2010); art. 5 African Charter on Human and Peoples' Rights (27 June 1981, in force 21 October 1986), 1520 UNTS 217. The prohibition of *refoulement* under IHRL is a peremptory (jus cogens) norm of customary international law, which means that the prohibition is absolute: no derogation or exceptions are possible. See further Chapter 5.

[158] Art. 45 Geneva Convention IV on the Protection of Civilian Persons in Time of War (12 August 1949, in force 21 October 1950), 75 UNTS 287. See further Chapter 6.

[159] Art. 8 Refugees Convention (n. 126).

[160] *Ibid.*, art. 9.

[161] *Ibid.*, art. 20.

14.4.8   Refugees are entitled to the human rights listed in the Refugees Convention. These rights are geared to enabling refugees to become self-reliant in the Host State.

1. Beyond the key protection against forced return, the Refugees Convention comprises many social and economic rights, which become applicable with the passage of time and are geared to enabling self-reliance in the country of refuge. The Convention consists of an incremental structure of entitlement that proceeds from the different levels of attachment of the refugee with the country of asylum over time. Those levels are: being within the jurisdiction of the country of refuge, physical presence, lawful presence, lawful stay and durable residence. The standard of compliance varies from comparable standards – most favoured national treatment, same treatment as aliens, same treatment as nationals – to absolute rights.[162] The rights include, inter alia, freedom of religion, the right to association, access to courts, housing, public education[163] and freedom of movement in the country of refuge.[164]

14.4.9   Persons who are displaced within their country of nationality or habitual residence are not refugees: they have not crossed an international border, and therefore do not qualify as refugees in any definition. They are internally displaced persons who remain subject to the jurisdiction of their country of nationality or habitual residence.

1. Common to all refugee definitions is the requirement of "alienage", i.e. the requirement of having crossed an international border. Those who may otherwise find themselves in a comparable situation as refugees but have not crossed an international border are internally displaced persons (IDPs) who remain under the jurisdiction of their own country. They consequently do not enjoy protection on the basis of international refugee law but derive protection from IHRL and IHL, similar to any citizen or habitual resident of the country concerned.[165]

2. Best practices with regard to the treatment of IDPs have been developed under the guidance of the UN. In 1998, the Guiding Principles on

---

[162] See Hathaway (n. 124).
[163] Respectively arts. 6, 15, 16, 21 and 22 Refugees Convention (n. 126).
[164] *Ibid.*, art. 26. On camps and settlements near borders, see Rule 14.4.11.
[165] M. Jacques, *Armed Conflict and Displacement: The Protection of Refugees and Displaced Persons Under International Humanitarian Law* (Cambridge University Press, 2012), p. 16.

Internal Displacement were adopted by the UN Commission on Human Rights.[166] Although a set of non-binding principles, they restate to a large extent existing principles of conventional and/or customary international law particularly in so far as they are applied in situations of armed conflict. The UN Guiding Principles tailor these rights to the predicament of IDPs, and include the right to be protected against grave crimes; the right to know the fate and whereabouts of missing relatives, including access to their grave sites; the right to family reunification; the right to be issued all documents necessary for the enjoyment and exercise of their legal rights; the right not to be discriminated against as a result of their displacement; and the right of international humanitarian organisations to offer their services in support of IDPs.[167]

3. In 2009, the AU Convention for the Protection and Assistance of Internally Displaced Persons in Africa was adopted.[168] The Convention restates some of the UN Guiding Principles and includes specific provisions on protection and assistance to IDPs in situations of armed conflict: members of armed groups shall, inter alia, be prohibited from carrying out arbitrary displacement, restricting the freedom of movement of IDPs, recruiting children, kidnapping, recruiting, abducting or engaging in hostage taking, sexual slavery and trafficking in persons especially women and children.[169] In addition, States have a positive obligation under the AU IDP Convention to protect IDPs against harm, including starvation and sexual and gender-based violence.[170] It also obliges States to secure satisfactory conditions of safety, dignity and security in the camps in the form of adequate food, water, shelter, medical care, sanitation and education and to ensure the right to seek safety in another part of the State and to be protected against forcible return to or resettlement in any place where their life, safety, liberty and/or health would be at risk.[171]

---

[166] UN Commission on Human Rights, Guiding Principles on Internal Displacement, UN Doc. E/CN.4/1998/53/Add.2 (1998). In 2006, the UN Commission on Human Rights was replaced by the Human Rights Council.

[167] Ibid., respectively Principles 11(2), 16(1), 16(4), 17, 20(2), 22 and 25(2).

[168] African Union Convention for the Protection and Assistance of Internally Displaced Persons in Africa, also known as the Kampala Convention (22 October 2009, in force 6 December 2012), www.refworld.org/docid/4ae572d82.html (AU IDP Convention). As of 1 July 2017 the AU IDP Convention has twenty-seven African States parties.

[169] Ibid., art. 7.

[170] Ibid., art. 9(1).

[171] Ibid., art. 9(2)(a), (b) and (e).

14.4.10   States are obliged to co-operate with the United Nations High Commissioner for Refugees in the exercise of his/her functions.

1. States are bound to co-operate with UNHCR in the exercise of his/her functions either on the basis of specific instruments such as the Refugees Convention and the AU Refugees Convention or on the basis of the UN Charter.[172]

2. The UNHCR is a subsidiary organ of the General Assembly,[173] and has been charged to provide international protection to refugees and to pursue durable solutions for them:[174] either local integration (in the country of refuge), voluntary repatriation (to the country of origin) or resettlement in a third State.

3. The UNHCR is a highly operational agency with an extensive presence in the field:[175] most Peace Operations will therefore include collaboration with UNHCR, and the Security Council commonly calls for such co-operation.[176] UNHCR's humanitarian activities may be linked to the military in two ways: peacekeepers may be mandated to ensure the secure delivery of assistance to the victims of the conflict in question, and military resources may be used to augment the capacity of UNHCR to implement UNHCR's mandate.[177] The mandate of UNHCR provides that its work shall be of an entirely non-political character: it shall be humanitarian and social and shall relate, as a rule, to groups and categories of refugees.[178] These characteristics may present UNHCR with a humanitarian dilemma in the sense that associating with the civil and military components of integrated missions may be seen as compromising its independent, impartial and neutral role.[179] Quick-impact projects undertaken by military components of missions designed to win the hearts and minds of the local population that

---

[172] Cf. art. 35(1) Refugees Convention (n. 126); arts. 2(5), 56, 57, 104 UN Charter; art. 2 Refugees Protocol (n. 127); art. 8 AU Refugees Convention (n. 128) (see also art. 7 on co-operation of the national authorities with the Organisation of African Unity (OAU, now AU)).

[173] Established by UNGA Res. 319 (IV) (1949). It functions in accordance with its Statute; see n. 152.

[174] UNHCR Statute (n. 152), Chapter I, para. 1.

[175] UNHCR's presence in the field is usually governed by so-called "co-operation agreements" with the Host State.

[176] See e.g. UNSC Res. 1778 (2007), para. 2(c).

[177] *Working with the Military* (UNHCR, 1995), para. 3.1.

[178] UNHCR Statute (n. 152), Chapter I, para. 2.

[179] B. Deschamp, Victims of Violence: A Review of the Protection of Civilians Concept and its Relevance to UNHCR's Mandate, UNHCR PDES/2010/11 (2010), para. 63; *Working with the Military* (n. 178), para. 3.3.

include the same or similar activities undertaken by humanitarian actors may have the same effect.[180]

4. Although UNHCR's original mandate does not specifically cover IDPs, it has de facto incorporated this group in its mandate.[181]

14.4.11   Refugee camps and settlements must be located away from the border.

1. Refugees tend to seek refuge in neighbouring States, and they often settle close to the border of their country of origin. The proximity of refugee camps to the border may pose various problems: the camps may harbour combatants (sometimes referred to as "refugee warriors"), or the camps may be used as recruiting grounds, or as rear bases to achieve military purposes in the country of asylum or in the country of origin. Camps should not be located in close proximity to the border but should be located at a reasonable distance from the border of their country of origin of the refugees residing there.[182] This responsibility derives from the obligation of a State not to allow knowingly its territory to be used for acts contrary to the rights of other States.[183] The AU Refugees Convention stipulates in this respect:

> Signatory States undertake to prohibit refugees residing in their respective territories from attacking any State Member of the OAU, by any activity likely to cause tension between Member States, and in particular by use of arms, through the press, or by radio.[184]

2. Supporting the relocation of refugee camps that are in close proximity to the border may be part of the mandate of a Peace Operation.[185]

---

[180] V. Holt and G. Taylor, *Protecting Civilians in the Context of UN Peacekeeping Operations. Successes, Setbacks and Remaining Challenges* (UN, 2009), p. 71.

[181] For instance within the framework of the Global Protection Working Cluster Group; see *Handbook for the Protection of Internally Displaced Persons* (2010).

[182] See UNSC Res. 1208 (1998), para. 4. UNHCR recommends a minimum of 50 kilometres, unless the situation calls for a larger distance: *Operational Guidelines on Maintaining the Civilian and Humanitarian Character of Asylum* (UNHCR, 2006), p. 43.

[183] See *Corfu Channel Case* (*the United Kingdom* v. *Albania*), Judgment, ICJ Reports 1949, 4. See also Declaration on Principles of International Law concerning Friendly Relations and Cooperation among States in Accordance with the Charter of the United Nations, UNGA Res. 2625 (XXV) (1970), Annex.

[184] Art. 3(2) AU Refugees Convention (n. 128). See also UNSC Res. 1208 (1998).

[185] See e.g. UNSC Res. 1778 (2007), para. 2(c); UNSC Res. 1861 (2009), paras. 6(c) and 23; UNSC Res. 1923 (2010), para. 8(ii); UN Doc. S/2009/535 (2009), para. 16.

14.4.12   The civilian and humanitarian character of refugee camps and settlements and sites with internally displaced persons must be secured.

1. The Host State is primarily responsible for the security and civilian character of the refugee camps,[186] and the Security Council regularly calls on States to respect and maintain the civilian and humanitarian nature of refugee camps and IDP sites.[187] Ensuring the civilian character of refugee camps by means of demilitarisation, i.e. separating combatants from refugees, is part of this obligation[188] but the camps must also be protected against external influences in the context of violence emerging from any of the parties engaged in the conflict.[189] Part of this task is to prevent the recruitment of refugees by armed groups.[190]

2. Peacekeepers may be called upon to help promote the civilian character of refugee camps and settlements by providing force protection and patrolling,[191] as well as providing support to enhance governance systems in the settlements, including improved community policing, enhancement of State authority, civilian patrols and police training.[192]

3. The duty to secure the civilian and humanitarian character of camps may also entail the separation of refugees from other persons who do not qualify for the international protection afforded to refugees or otherwise do not require international protection.[193] Combatants and other armed elements are not eligible for international protection

---

[186] UNSC Res. 1208 (1998), para. 3; UNHCR, The Security, Civilian and Humanitarian Character of Refugee Camps and Settlements: Operationalizing the 'Ladder of Options', UN Doc. EC/50/SC/INF.4 (2000), para. 5; UNHCR's Executive Commission, Conclusion 94 (LIII) (2002) (Conclusion on the Civilian and Humanitarian Character of Asylum), sub (a).

[187] UNSC Res. 1674 (2006), para. 14; UNSC Res. 1778 (2007), preamble; UNSC Res. 1834 (2008), preamble; UNSC Res. 1861 (2009), preamble and para. 23; UNSC Res. 1923 (2010), preamble.

[188] UNSC Res. 1778 (2007); UNSC Res. 1923 (2010), para. 3(ii). See also AU Refugees Convention (n. 128), preamble.

[189] See e.g. UNSC Res. 2211 (2015), para. 9(a).

[190] See e.g. UNSC Res. 1778 (2007), para. 2(f) (on the recruitment of children); UNSC Res. 1834 (2008), para. 11; UNSC Res. 1861 (2009); UNSC Res. 1923 (2010), paras. 8(vi), 23 (recruitment of children).

[191] UN Doc. S/2012/486 (2012), para. 58. In South Sudan, restoring the civilian character of the refugee camps included supporting the verification of a weapons-free camps campaign: UN Doc. S/2013/140 (2013), para. 62. On protection, see further Rule 14.4.13.

[192] UN Doc. S/2012/820 (2012), para. 64.

[193] UNSC Res. 1208 (1998), para. 6. See by way of illustration the benchmark (for withdrawal of the Peace Operation) set for peacekeepers in Chad regarding demilitarisation of camps for refugees and internally displaced persons: UN Doc. S/2009/359 (2009), Annex I.

until it has been established that they have genuinely and permanently renounced military or armed activities.[194]

4. The AU IDP Convention explicitly prohibits violating the civilian and humanitarian nature of the places where IDPs are sheltered and prohibits members of armed groups from infiltrating such places.[195]

14.4.13 Refugee camps and camps for internally displaced persons and their immediate surroundings must be protected.

1. The physical protection of refugees in refugee camps and settlements is the responsibility of the Host State.[196] Peace Operations may involve assistance in the protection of refugee and IDP camps,[197] for instance by active patrolling of civilians in camps,[198] maintaining law and order,[199] sensitisation activities to combat violence against women and girls[200] and policing camps.[201] On occasion it may also entail maintaining a presence inside refugee and IDP camps and demilitarised zones around and inside such camps, in order to promote the re-establishment of confidence and to discourage violence, in particular by deterring the use of force.[202] Worth mentioning is the installation of free emergency call centres to facilitate the direct access of refugees and IDPs to national security forces.[203]

2. Peace Forces may be assigned human rights and monitoring missions in refugee camps. Such missions may include verification exercises to collect and verify reports of child recruitment.[204]

3. The need for protection may extend beyond camp boundaries, for instance when refugees and IDPs, often female, need to gather wood,

---

[194] UNHCR Guidelines (n. 140), para. 22. See Rule 14.4.15, Commentary, para. 3.

[195] Art. 7(5)(i) AU IDP Convention (n. 169).

[196] See e.g. Second Report of the Secretary-General on Security in the Rwandese Refugee Camps, UN Doc. S/1995/65 (1995), para. 40. In Chad, peacekeepers were involved in the creation and training of a local security force meant to protect refugees and IDPs: UNSC Res. 1778 (2007), paras. 1, 2(a) and (b), 5, 6 (a)(i); UN Doc. S/2009/359 (2009), paras. 26, 28.

[197] UNSC Res. 1706 (2006), para. 9(b); UNSC Res. 1778 (2007), para. 6(a)(i); UNSC Res. 1861 (2009), para. 7(a)(i).

[198] UNSC Res. 2003 (2011), para. 3; UNSC Res. 2147 (2014), para. 4(a)(i); UNSC Res. 2228 (2015), para. 4; UNSC Res. 2155 (2014), paras. 4(a)(ii), 12.

[199] UNSC Res. 1778 (2007), para. 5; UNSC Res. 1927 (2010), para. 4; UNSC Res. 2070 (2012), para. 6; UNSC Res. 2180 (2014), para. 22.

[200] UN Doc. S/2008/601 (2008), para. 39; UN Doc. S/2009/535 (2009), para. 31.

[201] UNSC Res. 1944 (2010), para. 12; UNSC Res. 2180 (2014), para. 22.

[202] UNSC Res. 1706 (2006), paras. 8(d), 9(d).

[203] UN Doc. S/2010/409 (2010), para. 13; UN Doc. S/2010/217 (2010), para. 20.

[204] UN Doc. S/2008/760 (2008), paras. 29–30; UN Doc. S/2009/535 (2009), paras. 30, 34, 36; UN Doc. S/2009/199 (2009), paras. 40, 44; UN Doc. S/2010/409 (2010), para. 41.

water and other basic resources outside the perimeters of the camp, in order to protect them against murder, rape, assault and theft of their property.[205] In Darfur the practice of "firewood patrols" was developed by peacekeeping troops.[206]

14.4.14   Unhindered access of refugees and internally displaced persons to humanitarian assistance must be secured.

1. The Security Council has underlined 'the importance of safe and unhindered access of humanitarian personnel to civilians in armed conflict, including refugees and internally displaced persons, and the protection of humanitarian assistance to them'.[207] Peace Operations may be called upon to provide logistical and security support to humanitarian agencies to secure access to refugee camps and IDP settlements.[208] The duty to protect refugees and IDPs may include the protection of humanitarian convoys and assistance, such as food transport and aid for refugees by UNHCR.[209] Peace Operations may be called upon to provide protection, for example escorts, to facilitate relief operations to refugee camps.[210]

2. The AU IDP Convention obliges States to allow rapid and unimpeded passage of all relief consignments and personnel to IDPs.[211] It prohibits the impeding of humanitarian assistance or the passage of relief consignments, equipment and personnel to IDPs, the attacking or otherwise harming of humanitarian personnel and resources or other materials adopted for the assistance or benefit of IDPs and the destruction, confiscation or diversion of such materials, in each case by members of armed groups.[212]

---

[205] *Sudan: Firewood Patrols for IDPs* (Norwegian Refugee Council, 2006).
[206] *Ibid.*; E. Patrick, 'Sexual Violence and Firewood Collection in Darfur', 27 *Forced Migration Review* (2007), p. 40.
[207] UNSC Res. 751 (1992), para. 14; UNSC Res. 775 (1992); UNSC Res. 794 (1992), para. 10; UNSC Res. 814 (1993); UNSC Res. 1265 (1999), para. 7; UNSC Res. 1509 (2003), paras. 3(k), 8; UNSC Res. 2149 (2014), para. 42. See also e.g. UNGA Res. 62/95 (2007), para. 2.
[208] See e.g. UN Doc. S/2009/535 (2009), para. 17. On freedom of movement, see further Chapters 8 (esp. Rule 8.4); 12 (esp. Rule 12.4). On freedom of movement over air and water, see Chapter 15.
[209] See on humanitarian assistance, UNGA Res. 46/182 (1991); *Compilation of United Nations Resolutions on Humanitarian Assistance: Selected Resolutions of the General Assembly, Economic and Social Council and Security Council Resolutions and Decisions* (UN Office for the Coordination of Humanitarian Affairs, 2009); UN Doc. S/2014/708 (2014), para. 16.
[210] UN Doc. S/2014/708 (2014), para. 58; UN Doc. S/2014/821 (2014), para. 57.
[211] Art. 5(7) AU IDP Convention (n. 169).
[212] *Ibid.*, art. 7(5)(g) and (h).

14.4.15 Refugees can return to their country of origin only on a voluntary basis. Both refugees and internally displaced persons have the right to return to their place of origin.

1. Since refugees are entitled to protection against forced return, return can take place only on a voluntary basis.[213] When the circumstances that gave rise to flight are improving, UNHCR may organise the voluntary return of refugees to their country of origin. Voluntary repatriation operations usually take place on the basis of voluntary repatriation agreements UNHCR concludes with the country of origin and the country of refuge. Those agreements emphasise the voluntary nature of return, comprise the modalities for return in safety and dignity, freedom of choice of destination, and assurances upon return,[214] as well as many practical issues such as the right to bring property including livestock into the country free of customs duties, charges and tariffs. On the basis of such an agreement, usually a tripartite commission is established consisting of representatives of the parties to the agreement to address practical issues such as identifying border-crossing points.

2. UN peacekeeping mandates often address the return of refugees,[215] in terms of 'the creation of conditions conducive to the voluntary, safe, dignified and sustainable return of refugees and internally displaced persons'.[216] These mandates may include rather specific tasks such as

---

[213] Unlike the Refugees Convention (n. 126), the AU Refugees Convention (n. 128) includes an article (art. 5) on voluntary repatriation.

[214] See e.g. art. 10(1) Model Voluntary Repatriation Agreement, Annex 5 to *UNHCR Handbook* (n. 153): 'The Government of (country of origin) shall issue, together with other relevant parties, general amnesties, formal guarantees or public assurances to encourage the refugees to voluntarily repatriate without any fear of harassment, intimidation, persecution, discrimination, prosecution or any punitive measures whatsoever on account of their having left, or remained outside of (country of origin).'

[215] E.g. those of UN Operation in Mozambique (UNOMOZ); UN Transitional Authority in Cambodia (UNTAC); UN Multidimensional Integrated Stabilization Mission in the Central African Republic (MINUSCA); UN Mission in Sierra Leone (UNAMSIL); UN Assistance Mission for Rwanda (UNAMIR).

[216] UNSC Res. 1674 (2006), para. 16; UNSC Res. 1778 (2007), para. 1; UNSC Res. 1868 (2009), para. 4(f); UNSC Res. 1917 (2010), para. 6(c); UNSC Res. 1925 (2010), para. 12(g); UNSC Res. 2041 (2012), para. 7(d). Some resolutions call for 'support' for returning refugees and IDPs, without explaining what this particular support might entail; see e.g. the call on UNAMSIL in UNSC Res. 1346 (2001), para. 8; UNSC Res. 1370 (2001), para. 8; UNSC Res. 1470 (2003), para. 16; UNSC Res. 1508 (2003), para. 10. UNHCR explains what the contribution of the military may consist of in this respect: repair of roads and bridges and other engineering tasks, or mine clearing and the collection and disposal of weapons and explosives, monitoring ceasefires, supervising border crossings and assisting in the demobilisation of militias: *Working with the Military* (n. 178), para. 4.6. The voluntary return and resettlement in secure and sustainable conditions of a critical mass of IDPs were formulated as one of the benchmarks of withdrawal in a

confidence-building broadcasts preceding return,[217] escorting returnees from the border to reception centres and onwards,[218] providing security during return,[219] clearing of mines from repatriation routes,[220] patrolling routes used by refugees and IDPs to return to their communities,[221] helping with the repatriation and resettlement of refugees and displaced persons,[222] facilitating the voluntary return of refugees and IDPs,[223] assisting UNHCR in the provision of logistical support for the repatriation of refugees,[224] monitoring the process of repatriation of refugees and resettlement of displaced persons to verify that it is carried out in a safe and orderly manner,[225] ensuring the maintenance of IHRL by monitoring,[226] co-ordinating international efforts towards the protection of returnees,[227] patrolling areas of return[228] and contributing to defusing local tensions and promoting reconciliation in these areas.[229]

Peace Operation in Africa: UNSC Res. 1861 (2009), paras. 1, 25; UN Doc. S/2009/199 (2009), para. 60 (IDPs and refugees in UN Doc. S/2009/535 (2009), para. 52).

[217] Cf. the activities of Radio UNAMIR (UN Doc. S/1995/297 (1995), para. 5) and Radio UNMIL (UN Doc. S/2014/123 (2014), para. 67; UN Doc. S/1995/678 (1995), para. 6). Of a similar purport is a cross-border communication strategy aimed at encouraging refugees to return: UN Doc. S/2012/964 (2012), para. 27.

[218] 1991 Agreement on a Comprehensive Political Settlement of the Cambodia Conflict (Paris Agreement) (text in Annex to UN Doc. A/46/608-S/23177 (1991), Annex 2 (art. XII entitled 'Repatriation and Resettlement of Displaced Cambodians')). The UN Transitional Authority in Cambodia (UNTAC) was established by UNSC Res. 745 (1992) to implement the mandate envisaged in the Paris Agreements. The second Paris Agreement was the Agreement concerning the Sovereignty, Independence, Territorial Integrity and Inviolability, Neutrality and National Unity of Cambodia. See also UN Doc. S/2014/342 (2014), para. 51; UN Doc. S/2013/761 (2013), para. 53.

[219] UN Doc. S/2012/506 (2012), para. 47.

[220] Ibid. Assistance may also consist of road construction: UN Doc. S/2008/601 (2008), para. 31 (road construction as a quick impact project); UN Doc. S/2006/159 (2006), para. 34 (rehabilitation of roads).

[221] UN Doc. S/2011/807 (2011), para. 28.

[222] UNSC Res. 897 (1994), para. 2(e); UNSC Res. 997 (1995), para. 3(b); UNSC Res. 1029 (1995), para. 2(a); UNSC Res. 1470 (2003), para. 16; UNSC Res. 1508 (2003), para. 10; UNSC Res. 2149 (2014), para. 30(c).

[223] UNSC Res. 1509 (2003), para. 6; UNSC Res. 1706 (2006), para. 9(a).

[224] UNSC Res. 1029 (1995), para. 2(c). One example is making trucks available to UNHCR to facilitate the pre-positioning of food and non-food items in areas of return: UN Doc. S/2005/177 (2005), para. 64.

[225] UNGA Res. 872 (1993), para. 3(f); similarly, and in co-operation with UNHCR, UNSC Res. 1037 (1996).

[226] UNSC Res. 2155 (2014), para. 4(a)(vi).

[227] UNSC Res. 1509 (2003), para. 3(l); UNSC Res. 1706 (2006), para. 9(b).

[228] UN Doc. S/2014/342 (2014), para. 51; UN Doc. S/2013/761 (2013), para. 53.

[229] UN Doc. S/2010/529 (2010), paras. 33, 35 (inter-community dialogue project); UN Doc. S/2010/409 (2010), para. 51; UN Doc. S/2010/217 (2010), para. 39 (reconciliation ceremonies between refugees, IDPs in return villages), para. 41 (creation of a local vigilance committee). Worth adding are the sensitisation messages broadcast by Radio UNTAC. For examples of

3. Reference should be made to the reverse situation: the repatriation of former combatants, prisoners of war and foreign elements from the area of operations to the country of origin.[230] Their return is not mandatory in the sense that they may have a well-founded fear of persecution in their country of origin, and in that case they may be entitled to protection as refugees,[231] provided they are not excluded from that status on the basis of article 1(F) of the Refugees Convention (see Rule 14.4.4).

4. The AU IDP Convention vests States parties with the duty to seek lasting solutions to the problem of displacement by promoting and creating satisfactory conditions for voluntary return, local integration or relocation on a sustainable basis and in circumstances of safety and dignity.[232] This entails, inter alia, that States should enable IDPs to make a free and informed choice on whether to return, integrate locally or relocate and should co-operate with third parties in providing protection and assistance in the course of finding sustainable solutions.[233]

5. Both returnees and IDPs have the right to return to their place of origin by virtue of IHRL.

---

dialogues, see M. Y. A. Zieck, *UNHCR and Voluntary Repatriation of Refugees: A Legal Analysis* (Martinus Nijhoff, 1997), pp. 319, 321. See also Z. Mei, *Radio UNTAC of Cambodia: Winning Ears, Hearts and Minds* (White Lotus, 1994).

[230] Cf. UNSC Res. 1925 (2010), para. 12(j); UNSC Res. 2149 (2014), para. 30(g). In another operation, the peacekeepers worked with traditional leaders and the local authorities on reconciliation efforts, including the establishment of property dispute committees: UN Doc. S/2005/560 (2005), para. 22.

[231] By way of illustration, see UN Doc. S/2004/536 (2004), para. 27, on an estimated 500–2,000 ex-combatants who were to be given the option to be repatriated or to remain as refugees.

[232] Art. 11(1) AU IDP Convention (n. 169).

[233] *Ibid.*, art. 11(2) and (3).

15

Aerial and Maritime Dimensions of Peace Operations

1. This chapter deals with the aerial and maritime dimensions of consensual Peace Operations as defined in this Manual. It will consider the law relating to aircraft and vessels participating in or directly supporting such operations and, in particular, the rules of conventional and customary international law relating to aerial and maritime passage in international and national waters and airspace and the rights of third States in relation to vessels and aircraft bearing their nationality. Attention will also be devoted to how the rules as to the use of force apply to the maritime and aerial dimensions of such operations.

2. In view of the focus of this chapter and of the Manual as a whole upon Peace Operations, naval and air operations in the more general sense will not be addressed. Consequently, there will be no discussion of the individual or collective right of national self-defence by States in the naval and aerial context, of evacuation of nationals or of the law relating to maritime interdiction/interception beyond what is strictly relevant to Peace Operations. Likewise, the fact that the law of naval warfare forms a sub-regime within the law of armed conflict applicable to international armed conflicts (IACs) will not be discussed. The law of naval operations which has developed in recent decades as a subset of operational law will be addressed only within the aforementioned contexts.

15.1 All activities by Peace Operations in the maritime and aerial domains must be conducted in accordance with applicable international law.

1. Naval and aerial assets can be used directly in the context of Peace Operations when the mandate calls specifically or implicitly for their employment in performing specific tasks. They may also be used in support of any other Peace Operation in so far as is required by the prevailing circumstances and compatible with the mandate and with applicable

222

international law. There have been a number of Peace Operations with a maritime and/or aerial component.[1] For example, maritime operations were conducted in the framework of the UN Transitional Authority in Cambodia (UNTAC) (e.g. eradication of weapons smuggling), UN Temporary Executive Authority (UNTEA) in West New Guinea/West Irian (e.g. law enforcement), UN Observer Group in Central America (ONUCA) in the Gulf of Fonseca (e.g. prevention of cross-border infiltration and arms transfers) and UN Transitional Administration in East Timor (UNTAET) (e.g. protection of offshore resources).[2] The most significant example to date is the UN Interim Force in Lebanon (UNIFIL) Maritime Task Force deployed since October 2006. Turning to aerial operations, unmanned aerial vehicles have been used in missions such as the UN Mission in Sudan (UNMIS) in Sudan and UN Stabilization Mission in the Democratic Republic of the Congo (MONUSCO) for the purpose of surveillance and reconnaissance, and conventional manned aircraft, fixed wing or rotary, are often employed in Peace Operations for various purposes.[3]

2. A variety of maritime and aerial tasks can be entrusted to a Peace Operation: supporting land operations, protecting installations, protecting shipping in transit, sea mine clearance, search and rescue, interdicting vessels of interest, information sharing, stabilisation operations, capacity building and personnel evacuation.[4] In carrying out these tasks Peace Operations must comply with applicable international law.[5] The latter may include, inter alia: UN Security Council resolutions, in particular those providing the mandate; treaties, in particular the UN Convention on the

---

[1] See generally A. B. Siegel, 'An Examination of Maritime Peace Support Operations', in J. J. Wirtz and J. A. Larsen (eds.), *Naval Peacekeeping and Humanitarian Operations* (Routledge, 2009), pp. 97–109; R. Stephens Staley, *The Wave of the Future: The United Nations and Naval Peacekeeping* (Lynne Rienner Publishers, 1992); J. Ginifer, 'A Conceptual Framework for UN Naval Operations', in M. C. Pugh (ed.), *Maritime Security and Peacekeeping* (Manchester University Press, 1994), pp. 55–73; J. Ginifer, 'The UN at Sea? The New Relevance of Maritime Operations', 1 *International Peacekeeping* (1994), pp. 320–335; R. McLaughlin, *United Nations Naval Peace Operations in the Territorial Sea* (Martinus Nijhoff, 2009).
[2] *United Nations Peacekeeping Missions Military Maritime Task Force Manual* (2015), p. 9; J. A. Koops, 'United Nations Observer Group in Central America (ONUCA)', in J. A. Koops, N. MacQueen, T. Tardy and P. D. Williams (eds.), *The Oxford Handbook of United Nations Peacekeeping Operations* (Oxford University Press, 2015), p. 308; L. Savadogo, 'Les navires battant pavillon d'une organisation internationale', 53 *Annuaire français de droit international* (2007), pp. 649–652.
[3] UNSC Res. 1706 (2006), para. 8(b) and (e); UNSC Res. 2098 (2013), para. 12(c); K. P. Apuuli, 'The Use of Unmanned Aerial Vehicles (Drones) in United Nations Peacekeeping: The Case of the Democratic Republic of Congo', 18 *ASIL Insights* (2014), www.asil.org/insights.
[4] *United Nations Manual* (n. 2), p. 16.
[5] For an overview of various legal issues, see F. J. Hampson, 'Naval Peacekeeping and the Law', in Pugh (n. 1), pp. 190–213.

Law of the Sea (UNCLOS),[6] other applicable treaties relating to the law of the sea and the Convention on International Civil Aviation;[7] customary international law, in particular customary principles and rules of the law of the sea and air law; and other possible elements of the mandate, including the scope of consent of the Host State. Status of Forces Agreements (SOFAs) and transit agreements with third States may also be relevant. The Security Council may determine to authorise action under Chapter VII of the Charter which departs from specific rules contained in treaties and customary law in so far as these are not of a peremptory nature.[8] In doing so the Council can authorise action which exceeds the limitations laid down in UNCLOS or other applicable treaties. In situations involving the use of force, the mandate will set out the parameters in which vessels may be diverted or boarded and to what extent force may be used in order to enforce compliance. Alongside these parameters, the relevant legal regimes relating to how force must be employed will be incorporated into the Rules of Engagement (ROE) for conducting the operation. These may include international humanitarian law (IHL) in so far as applicable, international human rights law (IHRL), for example in the context of maritime law enforcement situations, and relevant national law.

15.2   Vessels and aircraft conducting, or operating in support of, Peace Operations enjoy the freedoms of navigation and overflight in and above the high seas and the exclusive economic zone. These freedoms must be exercised in accordance with international law.

1. The high seas freedoms of navigation and overflight form part of customary international law as reflected in UNCLOS.[9] Their application extends to the exclusive economic zone.[10] The exercise of these freedoms is subject to due regard obligations in relation to third States and/or the coastal State.[11]

---

[6] United Nations Convention on the Law of the Sea (10 December 1982, in force 16 November 1994), 1833 UNTS 397.

[7] Convention on Civil Aviation (7 December 1944, in force 4 April 1947), 15 UNTS 295, as amended by the Protocol relating to an amendment to the Convention on Civil Aviation [3bis] (10 May 1984, in force 1 October 1998), 23 ILM (1984) 705.

[8] See further Chapter 3.

[9] Art. 87(1)(a) and (b) UNCLOS (n. 6). See also art. 12 Convention on Civil Aviation (n. 7): 'Over the high seas, the rules in force shall be those established under this Convention.'

[10] Art. 58(1) UNCLOS (n. 6).

[11] *Ibid.*, arts. 58(3), 87(2).

15.3   Vessels engaged in, or in support of, Peace Operations enjoy the right of innocent passage in the territorial sea, archipelagic waters and certain international straits, the right of archipelagic sea lanes passage in archipelagic waters where applicable and the right of transit passage in certain international straits. These rights must be exercised in accordance with international law.

1. These navigational rights form part of customary law as reflected in several provisions of UNCLOS.[12] The conditions under which the said rights may be exercised are regulated in the aforementioned provisions. Archipelagic sea lanes passage and transit passage encompass both navigation by sea and overflight. The exercise of these rights is subject to due regard obligations in relation to third States and/or the coastal State. There is no right of overflight in airspace superjacent to the territorial sea, above archipelagic waters where air routes have not been designated or above international straits subject to a regime of non-suspendable innocent passage.

15.4   States exercise full sovereignty over their internal waters as well as the airspace above their land territory and territorial sea. A Peace Operation may operate in the internal waters or national airspace of a State only with its consent, unless provided otherwise in a Security Council resolution adopted pursuant to Chapter VII of the UN Charter.

1. The sovereignty of a State over its internal waters and national airspace is enshrined in customary international law as reflected in UNCLOS, the customary law of the sea and the Convention on Civil Aviation.[13] Consequently, a Peace Operation may operate vessels and aircraft in these areas only with the consent of the relevant State and subject to any conditions it may decide to impose. If the use of unmanned aerial vehicles or other forms of remote surveillance in national airspace is sanctioned by the Host State, the mandate and associated agreements will normally set out the conditions for operation of aircraft and permitted activities in national airspace. In any case, due regard should be paid to the sovereignty of the Host State and to the rights of its nationals including the right to privacy. For UN Peace Operations, for example, all collected data and images become UN property and are governed by the applicable UN regimes.[14]

---

[12] *Ibid.*, arts. 17–19, 37–45, 52–54.
[13] *Ibid.*, arts. 2(1), 8; arts. 1–2 Convention on Civil Aviation (n. 7).
[14] *Performance Peacekeeping: Final Report of the Expert Panel on Technology and Innovation in UN Peacekeeping* (2014), pp. 108–109.

15.5   The territorial sea is a maritime zone where the coastal State exercises sovereignty subject to the regime of innocent passage under customary international law as reflected in the UN Convention on the Law of the Sea. Vessels conducting, or in support of, a Peace Operation may operate in the territorial sea of a coastal State only in accordance with the regime pertaining to innocent passage or with the consent of the Host/coastal State if the right of innocent passage does not cover the envisaged activities, unless provided otherwise in a Security Council resolution adopted pursuant to Chapter VII of the UN Charter.

1. In accordance with customary international law, State sovereignty extends to the territorial sea and the airspace above it.[15] The exercise of sovereignty over the territorial sea by the coastal State is subject to limitations under international law,[16] of which the right of innocent passage is the most significant.

2. Owing to the coastal State's sovereignty over the territorial sea, a Peace Operation may operate in these waters only in accordance with the regime of innocent passage. Innocent passage provides for continuous and expeditious passage through the territorial sea and for the avoidance of any activity prejudicial to the legal order or security of the coastal State. In practice, this would preclude any type of (military) activity not directly connected to the safe navigation of the vessel(s) in question.[17]

3. Consent of the coastal State must be obtained if the envisaged activities of vessels engaged in a Peace Operation traversing the territorial sea are inconsistent with the right of innocent passage. In this regard, the maritime operations conducted in the framework of the International Force for East Timor (INTERFET) are instructive as to the importance of designing a detailed navigational regime. Australia, the lead nation, concluded a SOFA with Indonesia enabling freedom of movement for INTERFET aircraft and ships throughout East Timor. The SOFA further provided that access to a certain island would be possible 'by air and sea through designated corridors'. The aerial corridor was established through informal agreement, whereas the parties never set the co-ordinates of the maritime corridor. As a result, INTERFET units had to navigate in accordance with a less generous regime under the general rules of

---

[15] Art. 2(1) and (2) UNCLOS (n. 6); *Military and Paramilitary Activities in and against Nicaragua (Nicaragua v. United States of America)*, Merits, ICJ Reports 1986, 14, para. 212.

[16] Art. 2(3) UNCLOS (n. 6).

[17] *Ibid.*, arts. 17, 18 and 19. See K. Aquilina, 'Territorial Sea and the Contiguous Zone', in D. Attard, M. Fitzmaurice and N. A. Martínez Gutiérrez (eds.), *The IMLI Manual on International Maritime Law*, 3 vols. (Oxford University Press, 2014), vol. I, pp. 38–51.

the law of the sea. Additionally, the need to navigate through Indonesia's territorial sea and archipelagic waters coupled with restrictive national maritime policies of certain participating INTERFET units complicated operations. The intricate navigational situation led INTERFET Headquarters to issue a policy document setting out the legal status of relevant waters and applicable navigational rights.[18]

4. Acting under Chapter VII of the UN Charter, the Security Council may in its mandate exempt a Peace Operation from the application of this Rule, or it may decide that the normally applicable regime shall continue to apply. The relationship between the UN Interim Force in Lebanon (UNIFIL) Maritime Taskforce and the Lebanese government is noteworthy in that the Security Council chose that the consent requirement would continue to apply. Accordingly, UNIFIL may conduct activities in the areas of maritime operations located in the territorial sea only with the Lebanese government's consent.[19] There have also been instances of the Security Council specifically allowing UN Member States to operate in the territorial sea of a specified third State in the context of maritime interdiction, blockades or embargoes.[20]

15.6   The coastal State possesses sovereign rights and jurisdiction but does not exercise sovereignty in its maritime zones beyond the territorial sea. A Peace Operation is not required to obtain the consent of the coastal State in order to operate in maritime zones beyond the territorial sea.

1. The coastal State may have other maritime zones beyond the territorial sea with respect to which it possesses sovereign rights and jurisdiction over specific matters but does not exercise sovereignty. In the contiguous zone the coastal State may exercise the control necessary to prevent and punish infringement of its customs, fiscal, immigration or sanitary laws and regulations.[21] As to the continental shelf and the exclusive economic zone, the coastal State enjoys sovereign rights and jurisdiction, inter alia,

---

[18] F. Rogers, 'The International Force in East Timor – Legal Aspects of Maritime Operations', 28 *University of New South Wales Law Journal* (2005), pp. 571–572, 576–578.

[19] UNSC Res. 1701 (2006), paras. 11(f), 14; M. D. Fink, 'De Maritieme Taakgroep UNIFIL te Libanon', 101 *Militair Rechtelijk Tijdschrift* (2008), p. 107.

[20] E.g. UNSC Res. 820 (1993), para. 29: 'Reaffirms the authority of States acting under paragraph 12 of resolution 787 (1992) to use such measures commensurate with the specific circumstances as may be necessary under the authority of the Security Council to enforce the present resolution and its other relevant resolutions, *including in the territorial sea* of the Federal Republic of Yugoslavia (Serbia and Montenegro)' (emphasis added).

[21] Art. 33 UNCLOS (n. 6).

in relation to the protection and utilisation of natural resources.[22] To the extent that the Peace Operation does not engage in activities that touch upon these matters, it may operate in these maritime zones without the consent of the coastal State. Peace Operations are required to abide by applicable due regard obligations in relation to third States and/or the coastal State.

15.7   Flag States exercise exclusive jurisdiction over ships flying their flag on the high seas. Save in exceptional circumstances as regulated under international law, vessels conducting a Peace Operation may not board a ship without the consent of the flag State. A Security Council resolution adopted pursuant to Chapter VII of the UN Charter may provide an exception to this Rule.

1. The principle of exclusive flag State jurisdiction on the high seas is part of customary international law as reflected in UNCLOS.[23] Exceptions to this Rule can be generally placed in two categories: the right of visit and the right of hot pursuit. The exercise of these rights is subject to strict conditions as detailed in UNCLOS and other applicable rules of international law.[24]

2. The practice of the Security Council generally respects and follows the principles of the law of the sea.[25] This includes the principle of exclusive jurisdiction of the flag State. In several instances where the Security Council has empowered UN Member States to carry out actions at sea in furtherance of international peace and security it has refrained from

---

[22] See generally Part II, Section 4, Part V and Part VI *Ibid.*

[23] *Ibid.*, art. 92(1).

[24] *Ibid.*, arts. 110–111. See N. M. Poulantzas, *The Right of Hot Pursuit in International Law*, 2nd edn (Martinus Nijhoff, 2002); E. Papastavridis, *The Interception of Vessels on the High Seas* (Hart Publishing, 2014).

[25] D. R. Rothwell and T. Stephens, *The International Law of the Sea*, 2nd edn (Hart Publishing, 2016), p. 283. On UN Security Council practice with respect to maritime interdiction, embargoes and blockades, see R. McLaughlin, 'United Nations Mandated Naval Interdiction Operations in the Territorial Sea?', 51 *International and Comparative Law Quarterly* (2002), pp. 249–278; N. Klein, *Maritime Security and the Law of the Sea* (Oxford University Press, 2012), pp. 276–285; A. H. A. Soons, 'A "New" Exception to the Freedom of the High Seas: The Authority of the UN Security Council', in T. D. Gill and W. P. Heere (eds.), *Reflections on Principles and Practice of International Law* (Martinus Nijhoff, 2000), pp. 205–221; G. P. Politakis, 'UN-Mandated Naval Operations and the Notion of Pacific Blockade: Comments on Some Recent Developments', 6 *African Journal of International and Comparative Law* (1994), pp. 173–208; L. E. Fielding, *Maritime Interception and UN Sanctions* (Austin & Winfield, 1997); H. B. Robertson, 'Interdiction of Iraqi Maritime Commerce in the 1990–1991 Persian Gulf Conflict', 22 *Ocean Development and International Law* (1991), pp. 289–299.

deviating from the aforementioned principle.[26] Nonetheless, on several occasions the Security Council has invoked its power under Chapter VII of the Charter and authorised the boarding of vessels by third States, in particular with respect to the situations in Southern Rhodesia,[27] Iraq–Kuwait,[28] former Yugoslavia,[29] Haiti[30] and more recently Libya.[31] Maritime interdiction in the context of Peace Operations cannot be justified as a collective security measure if the pertinent UN Security Council resolution has not directly authorised such action.[32]

15.8   In the conduct of Peace Operations, force may be applied only in conformity with the mandate and applicable international law. In carrying out maritime interdiction/interception measures, force may be used only where the mandate has specifically authorised its use and as a last resort to enforce compliance. Boarding of vessels and detention of persons, in so far as authorised under the mandate, must be conducted in conformity with applicable international law. The use of force in the aerial dimension of Peace Operations must comply with the mandate and with applicable international law. The latter precludes, in most circumstances, the use of force against civil aircraft in flight. Any use of force must be strictly necessary and proportionate.

1. The part of this Rule relating to the use of force in conducting maritime interception/interdiction is derived from the case law of the International Tribunal for the Law of the Sea (ITLOS) as it applies to constabulary action at sea.[33] It draws upon earlier precedents as well as substantial State practice. The conditions under which force is to be used have been detailed by the ITLOS as follows: 'The normal practice used to stop a ship at sea is first to give an auditory or visual signal to stop, using

---

[26] E.g. UNSC Res. 1874 (2009), paras. 11–13; UNSC Res. 1540 (2004); UNSC Res. 1718 (2006), para. 8(a) and (f).
[27] UNSC Res. 221 (1966), para. 5.
[28] UNSC Res. 665 (1990), para. 1.
[29] UNSC Res. 787 (1992), para. 12; UNSC Res. 820 (1993), para. 29.
[30] UNSC Res. 917 (1994), para. 10.
[31] UNSC Res. 1973 (2011), paras. 13–15.
[32] D. Guilfoyle, 'Interdicting Vessels to Enforce the Common Interest: Maritime Countermeasures and the Use of Force', 56 *International and Comparative Law Quarterly* (2007), pp. 69–82.
[33] *The M/V 'SAIGA' (No. 2) Case (Saint Vincent and the Grenadines* v. *Guinea)*, Judgment, ITLOS Reports 1999, 10, para. 155; *The M/V 'Virginia G' Case (Panama/Guinea-Bissau)*, Judgment, ITLOS Reports 2014, 4, paras. 359–360. See also *Corfu Channel Case (the United Kingdom* v. *Albania)*, Judgment, ICJ Reports 1949, 4, 22.

internationally recognized signals. Where this does not succeed, a variety of actions may be taken, including the firing of shots across the bows of the ship. It is only after the appropriate actions fail that the pursuing vessel may, as a last resort, use force. Even then, appropriate warning must be issued to the ship and all efforts should be made to ensure that life is not endangered.'[34]

2. If a vessel is boarded in the context of maritime interception/interdiction that has been mandated as part of the Peace Operation, all persons must be treated with respect for their dignity and in conformity with applicable international law and the mandate. If persons are detained for any reason, the Rules relating to detention will apply.[35] Temporary confinement of the crew of a boarded vessel may be carried out if the safety of the boarding team or the effective inspection of the vessel would otherwise be compromised.

3. With regard to the aerial domain, forces conducting Peace Operations must refrain from resorting to the use of weapons against civil aircraft in flight other than in the very exceptional circumstances reflected in the final sentence of article 3bis(a) of the Convention on Civil Aviation and, in case of interception, the lives of persons on board and the safety of the aircraft must not be endangered.[36]

4. The rules and principles of general international law, which include the right of self-defence, continue to apply at sea[37] and in the air. Likewise, the rules and principles of the law of the sea treaties and air law treaties and the customary law of the sea and of the air apply to all actions undertaken at sea and in the air in the context of a Peace Operation in so far as they are applicable under the circumstances, unless a Security Council mandate under Chapter VII of the Charter expands or creates exceptions to what is required or permitted pursuant to these rules and principles.

---

[34] *M/V 'SAIGA' (No. 2)* (n. 33), para. 156. On the use of force at sea, see K. Neri, *L'emploi de la force en mer* (Bruylant, 2012); O. Corten, *Le droit contre la guerre*, 2nd edn (Pedone, 2014), pp. 73–79; P. Jimenez Kwast, 'Maritime Law Enforcement and the Use of Force: Reflections on the Categorisation of Forcible Action at Sea in the Light of the *Guyana/Suriname* Award', 13 *Journal of Conflict and Security Law* (2008), pp. 49–91.

[35] See Chapter 13.

[36] Art. 3bis Convention on Civil Aviation (n. 7).

[37] See the penultimate preambular paragraph to UNCLOS (n. 6): 'Affirming that matters not regulated by this Convention continue to be governed by the rules and principles of general international law'; Y. Tanaka, *The International Law of the Sea*, 2nd edn (Cambridge University Press, 2015), p. 175.

16

Monitoring Compliance in the Field of Conduct and Discipline

16.1 Setting the standards for conduct and discipline in UN Peace Operations is a shared responsibility of the UN, Troop Contributing Countries and Police Contributing Countries.

1. This chapter will almost exclusively deal with monitoring conduct and discipline in UN-conducted operations. Other regional organisations conducting UN-mandated operations such as the AU, EU and NATO do not have a specific organisational element to monitor conduct and discipline. The final Rule in this chapter (Rule 16.8) addresses non-UN Peace Operations. Since 1948 more than 71 UN peacekeeping operations have been initiated and, in 2017, 16 operations conducted by the UN are ongoing with a total number of personnel of approximately 112,000.[1]

2. The UN expects all categories of peacekeeping personnel[2] to uphold and respect principles set out in the Charter, such as human rights and respect for all cultures, to adhere to the highest standards of behaviour and to conduct themselves in a professional and disciplined manner at all times.[3] UN staff members are governed by the standards of conduct set out in the UN Staff Regulations and Rules[4] and other

---

[1] See 'Fact Sheet United Nations Peacekeeping Operations', 31 May 2017, www.un.org/en/peacekeeping/documents/bnote0517.pdf: troops 79,471; police 12,254; military observers 1,569; civilian personnel 15,319 (international 5,043; local 10,276); UN Volunteers 1,587; 1,987 staff officers. The total number of personnel serving in 16 peacekeeping operations is approximately 112,000; the number of States contributing uniformed personnel is 128.

[2] UN officials (both national and international); UN Volunteers; individual military and police personnel, members of formed police units, and other government-provided personnel with the legal status of experts on mission; members of military contingents and military staff officers; consultants or individual contractors of the UN.

[3] Art. 101(3) UN Charter: '[t]he paramount consideration in the employment of the staff and in the determination of the conditions of service shall be the necessity of securing the highest standards of efficiency, competence, and integrity'.

[4] UN Staff Regulations and Rules, UN Doc. ST/SGB/2017/1 (2017). There are several other policy documents that incorporate the UN standards of conduct. Some apply to all UN personnel, and others have been developed for specific categories of personnel, for example, civilian, military and

administrative issuances.[5] Staff members are not to discriminate against individuals or groups of individuals or abuse the power and authority vested in them and are to uphold the highest standards of efficiency, competence and integrity. The concept of integrity includes, but is not limited to, probity, impartiality, fairness, honesty and truthfulness in all matters affecting their work and status. Staff members are bound to respect those standards of conduct through the signing of their offer of appointment and the related employment contract with the UN.[6] For UN Volunteers, the standards of conduct are contained in the UN Volunteers Conditions of Service,[7] which forms part of the offer letter issued by the UN Volunteers Programme for each Volunteer, through which they are bound.

3. Individual military and police personnel and members of formed police units, as well as some other government-provided personnel, are deployed by Police Contributing Countries (PCCs) with the legal status of experts on mission. They individually sign an undertaking upon commencement of service with the UN, through which they agree to be bound by the provisions contained in this undertaking.[8]

4. Conduct and discipline of members of military contingents and military staff officers are governed by the Memorandum of Understanding (MOU) concluded between the Troop Contributing Country (TCC) and the UN for the deployment of military contingents and military staff officers. Through this MOU, Member States agree that, while their military personnel remain subject to the exclusive jurisdiction of respective TCCs, they will comply with UN standards of conduct and other such documents adopted by the UN that regulate the conduct[9] of this category of personnel. Specific substantive rules for contingent members

---

police personnel. For an overview, see Conduct in UN Field Missions: UN Standards of Conduct: Documents, https://conduct.unmissions.org/documents-standards.

[5] Standards of conduct for the international civil service, contained in Report of the International Civil Service Commission for 2012, UN Doc. A/67/30 (2012), Annex IV. These (revised) standards of conduct were approved by the General Assembly with effect from 1 January 2013: UNGA Res. A/RES/67/257 (2012).

[6] Art. I, Regulation 1.2(b) UN Staff Regulations and Rules (n. 4).

[7] *International UN Volunteer Handbook: Conditions of Service* (United Nations Volunteers Programme, 2015), Chapter 2, www.un.org/en/ethics/pdf/International_UN_Volunteer_Conditions_of_Service_2015.pdf.

[8] See Regulations governing the Status, Basic Rights and Duties of Officials other than Secretariat Officials, and Experts on Mission, UN Doc. ST/SGB/2002/9 (2002).

[9] Art. 7quinquiens and Annex H Model Memorandum of Understanding between the United Nations and [participating State] contributing resources to [the United Nations Peacekeeping Operation], UNGA Res. 61/267 (2007), and UN Doc. A/C.5/69/18 (2014), Chapter 9.

are stated in assenting or refuting form, inter alia: 'We will always conduct ourselves in a professional and disciplined manner; understand the
mandate and mission and comply with their provisions.'[10] The Ten Rules
of the Code of Personal Conduct for Blue Helmets[11] summarise the rules
in soldierly language, and military personnel are supposed to carry the
rules, translated in their national language, in their pockets. In addition
to UN-initiated internal rules, national contingents are bound by national
laws and national military codes of the Sending State.[12] Moreover, contingents through provisions in the Status of Forces Agreement (SOFA) will
have to respect the laws of the Host State.[13] The conduct of operations is
furthermore regulated by international law, and it is now widely accepted
and encouraged that soldiers involved in Peace Operations apply, whenever force is employed, the principles of humanity, military necessity, proportionality and distinction as a matter of policy. In an attempt to address
the issue and for the purpose of setting out fundamental principles and
rules of international humanitarian law (IHL) that apply to forces conducting operations under UN command and control, the UN Secretary-
General issued a Bulletin in 1999.[14] Shortly after its promulgation, the
Bulletin triggered questions in the legal community on the threshold for
the application of the Bulletin.[15] Other relevant bodies of law include
international human rights law (IHRL) and national laws, including military criminal law and disciplinary law of the TCCs and of Host States.
Training and practical instruction on how to apply rules in particular on
the use of force such as Rules of Engagement (ROE), using real-time scenarios, should be an ongoing process at all levels.

5. For individual UN consultants and contractors, agreements signed
between them and the UN contain provisions on the obligation to
respect the UN standards of conduct. While not UN personnel, corporate contractors agree that: '[t]he Contractor shall be responsible for

---

[10] For an overview of all rules, see nn. 4–8.
[11] UN, Ten Rules/Code of Personal Conduct for Blue Helmets, www.un.org/en/peacekeeping/
documents/ten_in.pdf.
[12] See Chapter 10.
[13] See Chapter 9.
[14] UN, Secretary-General's Bulletin on the Observance by United Nations Forces of International
Humanitarian Law, UN Doc. ST/SGB/1999/13 (1999). Section 1 of the Bulletin states that the
fundamental principles and rules of IHL set out in the Bulletin are applicable to UN forces when
in situations of armed conflict they are actively engaged therein as combatants, to the extent and
for the duration of their engagement. They are accordingly applicable in enforcement actions or in
peacekeeping operations when the use of force is permitted in self-defence.
[15] For a detailed discussion, see Chapter 6.

the professional and technical competence of the personnel it assigns to perform work under the Contract and will select reliable and competent individuals who will be able to effectively perform the obligations under the Contract and who, while doing so, will respect the local laws and customs and conform to a high standard of moral and ethical conduct'.[16] These General Conditions of Contract have a binding effect on employees of the UN contractors.

6. The UN has adopted a three-pronged strategy in addressing misconduct through prevention, enforcement and remedial action.[17] Implementing this strategy forms part of the exercise of the conduct and discipline functions. *Prevention* is aimed at ensuring that misconduct does not occur in the first place and is, accordingly, of critical importance in the reduction of acts of misconduct. Prevention includes activities such as raising awareness, including through public communication, training and outreach, vetting of personnel, maintaining conduct and discipline and adopting preventive measures that relate to the particular circumstances of a field mission, as well as ensuring the welfare and recreation of personnel.[18] *Enforcement* encompasses activities associated with actions taken in response to instances of alleged misconduct reported in a field mission. Prompt and consistent enforcement is essential to the goal of ensuring that the UN standards of conduct are respected. Without such enforcement, there is no accountability for violations of the UN standards of conduct and possible criminal acts.[19] *Remedial action* is the third prong of the UN strategy for addressing misconduct.[20] The purpose of the Strategy is to ensure that victims of sexual exploitation and abuse (SEA) by UN staff and related personnel receive appropriate assistance and support in a timely manner.[21] It also enables the UN system to facilitate, co-ordinate and provide assistance and support to victims of SEA, by calling for the establishment of a SEA Victim Assistance Mechanism in every country in which the UN operates. Assistance and support are provided to complainants, victims and children born as a result of SEA.

---

[16] UN General Conditions of Contracts for the Provision of Goods and Services (2012), para. 2.1, www.un.org/Depts/ptd/about-us/conditions-contract.

[17] See UN DPA/DPKO/DFS, Policy on Accountability for Conduct and Discipline in Field Missions, Ref. 2015.10 (2015).

[18] *Ibid.*, Chapter D, para. 10.5.

[19] *Ibid.*, Chapter D, para. 10.6.

[20] This applies in instances involving SEA and concerns the implementation of all aspects of the UN Comprehensive Strategy on Assistance and Support to Victims of Sexual Exploitation and Abuse by UN Staff and Related Personnel, UNGA Res. 62/214 (2008).

[21] See further Chapter 14.3.

These include but are not limited to medical, legal, psychological and social services.

16.2   The UN, Troop Contributing Countries and Police Contributing Countries have a shared responsibility for pre-deployment training and "in-mission" training on conduct and discipline issues.

1. Conduct and discipline issues are an essential component of pre-deployment and in-mission induction training, which is mandatory for all civilian, military and police personnel. Pre-deployment training is the mechanism for ensuring that staff and troops that deploy to Peace Operations are prepared to respect the UN's standards of conduct.[22] Pre-deployment training for all international civilian staff is conducted by the Integrated Training Service of the Department of Peacekeeping Operations (DPKO).[23] TCCs and PCCs are responsible for providing mandatory pre-deployment training for military and police personnel. This training is usually delivered by peacekeeping training institutions operating on a national or regional/sub-regional basis. The DPKO and the Department of Field Support (DFS) have established the capacity to function as a hub for matching Member States' training capacity to needs. The Conduct and Discipline Unit (CDU) at UN Headquarters is responsible for helping TCCs and PCCs to improve their pre-deployment training. The CDU, in co-ordination with the Integrated Training Service, is training the trainers on the Core Pre-Deployment Training Module on conduct and discipline, and strengthening the instructors' understanding of the standards and best practices in conduct and discipline training methodologies and materials. In co-operation with Integrated Training Mission Cells, Conduct and Discipline Teams (CDTs) in field missions provide direct induction, refresher and ongoing training in missions and work with UN Headquarters to incorporate mission-specific information in training modules. Mission-based awareness-raising initiatives form a significant part of the strategies of the CDTs to prevent SEA. The teams seek to raise awareness by reaching out

---

[22] Outlined in Report of the Secretary-General, The Future of United Nations Peace Operations: Implementation of the Recommendations of the High-Level Independent Panel on Peace Operations, UN Doc. A/70/357–S/2015/682 (2015).

[23] See UN Peacekeeping Resource Hub, http://research.un.org/en/peacekeeping-community/Training.

to host populations, including local government officials, relevant civil society organisations, international organisations and non-governmental organisations. The wide range of awareness-raising measures undertaken in field missions includes poster campaigns, newsletters, brochures, websites and radio broadcasts. Prevention measures at field level include restriction of movement, curfews, requiring soldiers to wear uniforms outside barracks, designating off-limits areas, non-fraternisation policies and increased patrols around high risk areas and decentralisation of CDT personnel into locations with a potentially high risk of misconduct.

16.3   Monitoring compliance with standards of conduct and discipline is a responsibility of the UN and managers and commanders at all levels.

1. Addressing misconduct involves ensuring that mechanisms are in place so that complaints of misconduct are received and assessed, that administrative investigations conducted by the UN are completed promptly and professionally and that necessary and appropriate follow-up action including public awareness activities is promptly taken. The UN is responsible for taking appropriate action with respect to its staff members when they are alleged to have engaged in misconduct, as well as for reporting to, and requesting appropriate action by, Member States and other employers, as applicable, when their personnel serving in field missions are found to have engaged in misconduct. The UN may also refer to Member States instances where any of their contributed personnel are alleged to have engaged in misconduct which constitutes a crime under national laws. It may also refer cases involving the settlement of claims, including paternity and child support claims, to them. In these cases, effective co-ordination and sharing of evidence between the UN investigative entity and the national investigators are essential for a successful prosecution.

2. The UN is accountable to its Member States for measures taken to implement its three-pronged strategy in addressing misconduct by personnel serving in field missions, including through the production of detailed reports on these matters by the Secretary-General or the Special Committee on Peacekeeping Operations.[24]

---

[24] See e.g. Report of the Secretary-General, Special Measures for Protection from Sexual Exploitation and Sexual Abuse, UN Doc. A/70/729 (2016); Report of the Special Committee on Peacekeeping Operations, UN Doc. A/69/19 (2015), Chapter V.E.

16.4   Managers and commanders are to ensure that personnel under their command or supervision are aware of the UN standards of conduct and are aware that they have an obligation to report misconduct by their subordinates.

1. Millions of soldiers, police officers and civilian staff have been serving during the past decades in UN Peacekeeping Operations worldwide.[25] They have often operated under extreme circumstances. During these missions, they may have encountered extremist groups and suicide attackers and may have witnessed death and injury of fellow soldiers and indiscriminate attacks on the civilian population. It is under these circumstances that peacekeepers may overreact to situations and engage in misconduct. They may have lost sight of what action is warranted in the circumstances, questioning the need to adhere to rules when it appears to them that other actors do not. Of vital importance is the role of leaders, both managers and commanders. They must ensure that personnel under their command or supervision are aware of the UN standards of conduct,[26] including by ensuring attendance at training sessions. They must also ensure compliance with the UN standards of conduct by personnel under their command or supervision, must identify potential risks of misconduct and must implement appropriate measures to address such risks. Leaders should be able to anticipate difficulties before they arise and prevent inappropriate actions before they happen. If they fail in that primary task, they still have an option to redress the situation, using their authority to intervene and stop inappropriate behaviour. If despite these measures inappropriate behaviour takes place, managers and commanders have the responsibility to report the misconduct and to take necessary disciplinary action.[27]

2. Despite large-scale deployments of troops, comparatively limited numbers of commanders and soldiers have been prosecuted and convicted for inappropriate or criminal behaviour. Although these numbers are limited, these events attract considerable attention in the media, primarily because of the seriousness of any incident of uniformed troops abusing power and using force against unarmed civilians. It is particularly unacceptable because of the widely held notion that uniformed troops are specifically sent to protect civilians against any form of violence. Media attention has also grown due to the omnipresence of mobile

---

[25] Annual turnover of over 150,000 personnel in UN peacekeeping operations.

[26] See UN DPA/DPKO/DFS (n. 17), Chapter E, para. 14.1.

[27] See Information Circular on Reporting of Suspected Misconduct, UN Doc. ST/IC/2005/19 (2005).

phones and cameras on the battlefield, used by soldiers and civilians alike, which has enabled virtually instantaneous reports of violent events to be transmitted across the world.

3. In 2015 in UN Peacekeeping Operations a total of 919 cases of misconduct were reported.[28] There is no ground to believe that large numbers of cases are not reported as international media and human rights organisations follow military operations with close scrutiny. A variety of plausible reasons could explain the relatively small percentage[29] of peacekeepers that have been found to have engaged in misconduct during UN peacekeeping operations.

4. From a positive point of view, the increased attention given to conduct and behaviour during recruit training/initial training and during pre-deployment training has borne fruit. Continued training during deployment is a priority of many commanders. Specific training packages on IHL, IHRL, conduct and discipline, and ROE have been developed over the years and are used widely by armed forces. In addition, armed forces have set minimum training standards before units or individuals are to be deployed. The effect is strengthened by the increased awareness of political leaders, commanders and soldiers that good conduct and behaviour are a force-multiplier and a precondition for winning respect from the local population and, conversely, that ill-disciplined forces can rapidly and gravely undermine the mission's prospects of success. The behaviour of soldiers is also directly linked to force protection and safety of the unit, which is a prerequisite for bringing the mission to a successful conclusion.

16.5   Managers and commanders must be held accountable in terms of performance regarding the exercise of their conduct and discipline functions.

1. The arrests, the subsequent trials and the convictions of senior political leaders and military commanders since the establishment of international courts and tribunals (including the International Criminal

---

[28] See Conduct in UN Field Missions: Investigations, https://conduct.unmissions.org/enforcement-investigations; 603 cases involved category I cases (serious misconduct), 303 cases involved category II cases (minor misconduct). For an explanation of categories of misconduct, see Rule 16.7, Commentary. Of sixty-nine reported cases of sexual exploitation and abuse, eighteen were substantiated, twenty-five were unsubstantiated and twenty-six were pending. See Conduct in UN Field Missions: Other Misconduct, https://conduct.unmissions.org/other-misconduct-introduction.

[29] This figure is 0.007 per cent, based on a total of 125,097 peacekeepers deployed in 2015. See 'Fact Sheet United Nations Peacekeeping Operations', 31 December 2015, www.un.org/en/peacekeeping/archive/2015/bnote1215.pdf.

Court) have contributed to a consciousness at all levels that soldiers and civilians alike have to abide by the rules and serve as a warning and a deterrent to commanders and soldiers. Practices for the maintenance of discipline and the handling of disciplinary and criminal cases vary widely. Managers and commanding officers must report misconduct by their subordinates and they are to be held accountable in terms of their performance regarding the exercise of their conduct and discipline functions.[30] Such reports shall be made to the Head of the respective civilian, police or military component, for onward transmission to the Head of Mission (HOM) and his/her supporting CDT or Conduct and Discipline Focal Point, and then to the supporting CDT. Reports can also be made directly to the Office of Internal Oversight Services (OIOS).[31] Commanders or managers may be tempted to suppress a report of misconduct, believing that it may discredit them and their unit. This temptation must be resisted. There is still the question whether a prompt and thorough professional investigation into relevant facts and circumstances is possible. Operational circumstances, ongoing skirmishes in the area, logistical impediments to transporting forensic experts to the scene, and the availability of independent witnesses and interpreters may each have serious impacts on the reliability of such an investigation.

2. Examples of cover-ups have attracted worldwide attention. What started as involvement in a humanitarian mission in Somalia in December 1992 quickly transformed into a black page in Canadian UN peacekeeping history as a result of the misconduct of a handful of soldiers, lacking appropriate leadership. In March 1993, a 16-year-old Somali teenager, Shidane Abukar Arone, sneaked into the Canadian compound and was caught and incarcerated. Subsequently soldiers of the Canadian Airborne Regiment beat their captive to death. During the course of the night, about a dozen other paratroopers became aware of the beating, but failed to intervene.[32] In the aftermath, it became apparent that military personnel and Department of National Defence civilian officials at all levels had been less than forthcoming with information about the incident. The repercussions included a Commission of Inquiry,[33] military prosecutions

---

[30] See UN DPA/DPKO/DFS (n. 17), Chapter E, para. 14.3.

[31] *Ibid.*, para. 14.2, and see Rule 16.7.

[32] See D. J. Bercuson, 'Up from the Ashes: The Re-professionalization of the Canadian Forces After the Somalia Affair', 9 *Canadian Military Journal* (2009), pp. 31–39.

[33] Dishonoured Legacy: The Lessons of the Somalia Affair, Report of the Commission of Inquiry into the Deployment of Canadian Forces to Somalia (1997), https://qspace.library.queensu.ca/handle/1974/6881.

of soldiers involved in the incident,[34] administrative measures against the military leadership involved, the disbanding of the Canadian Airborne Regiment[35] and the resignations of the Chief of Defence Staff and the Defence Minister.[36] The Somalia Inquiry made a total of 157 specific recommendations including a complete overhaul of the military justice system and the removal of military police from the chain of command, both of which were implemented. It also recommended the use of civilian courts to try soldiers, which was not implemented, but remains a live issue in Canadian military justice.

3. In UN Peacekeeping Operations accountability for HOMs is achieved through provisions included in the "Compact" signed between them and the Secretary-General. In addition ad hoc reports may also lead to holding senior leaders to account.[37] For all other managers and commanding officers, performance in the exercise of the conduct and discipline functions shall be evaluated through performance appraisal mechanisms, including e-performance tools for staff members and end-of-mission reports or other applicable mechanisms for military and police personnel.[38]

16.6   The UN and Member States have an important role to ensure compliance in the field of conduct and discipline. The UN has taken measures to strengthen the Organisation's role in the areas of prevention, enforcement and remedial action, in particular in cases of sexual exploitation and abuse.

1. Allegations of misconduct, human trafficking and SEA by UN peacekeeping personnel have been made in many missions, from the early

---

[34] Two were charged as a result of the killing: one tried to hang himself, but succeeded only in doing himself irreparable brain damage. The other was imprisoned for five years. One other soldier was also convicted of aiding the two. One company commander was court-martialled and convicted of encouraging the "Rambo-like" atmosphere that formed the context of the killing.

[35] On 23 January 1995, Canadian Defence Minister David Collenette announced the disbanding of the regiment after the broadcast of several videotapes showing soldiers making racist comments and taking part in brutal hazing rituals.

[36] See H. Schneider, Washington Post Foreign Service, 9 October 1996. At the inquiry, the Chief of Defence Staff was critical of his subordinates but rejected demands that he accept responsibility himself. That position opened him to repeated criticism from retired generals and defence analysts and, according to polls, a loss of public support as well.

[37] In 2015 the UN Secretary-General asked a HOM to resign after he allegedly failed to take action to follow up adequately on allegations of sexual abuse in the mission. In another mission in 2016, the Secretary-General asked for the immediate replacement of the Force Commander, following a situation where the mission did not respond effectively to extreme violence against civilians, allegedly due to his lack of leadership.

[38] See UN DPA/DPKO/DFS (n. 17), Chapter E, para. 14.3.

1990s onwards.[39] Following allegations of sexual exploitation in West Africa in 1993, the Secretary-General promulgated a Bulletin which states explicitly that the exchange of money, employment, goods or services for sex and sex with persons under 18 years of age are prohibited.[40] The high number of allegations of SEA involving peacekeepers uncovered in the Democratic Republic of the Congo in 2004 prompted a re-thinking of the UN's approach to this problem in peacekeeping missions. In March 2005, a report on the subject was released[41] and, subsequently, the Special Committee on Peacekeeping Operations adopted the framework for a comprehensive strategy to address SEA and other forms of serious misconduct in peacekeeping missions, which is set out in its 2006 landmark report on the subject.[42] The report resulted in a range of activities to address potential gaps in the accountability framework, and to bring about a systemic change in order to ensure accountability of all categories of UN peacekeeping personnel for, inter alia, SEA. The activities also aimed to develop a legal framework enabling, in addition to disciplinary measures imposed by the UN (also referred to as the Organisation), criminal prosecution of the UN officials and experts on mission in respect of criminal acts committed by them while serving in peacekeeping missions.

2. The Special Committee on Peacekeeping Operations[43] recommended that the capacity of the DPKO/DFS to 'address all cases of misconduct including sexual exploitation and abuse' should be strengthened. Conduct and Discipline Officers in the field perform functions that are pivotal to this integrated approach, and their routine functions encompass all reports of misconduct. The finalisation in 2007 of revisions to the UN Model MOU[44] has enhanced the certainty of enforcement action in cases of wrongdoing on the part of military contingent members.

3. Different categories of peacekeeping personnel are subject to the Organisation's disciplinary system to varying degrees, and misconduct contrary to the prohibitions of the Bulletin may concurrently constitute a criminal offence warranting the institution of criminal proceedings. While directly employed UN staff in peacekeeping missions are subject

---

[39] See also Chapter 14.3; Chapter 19.

[40] UN, Secretary-General's Bulletin, Special Measures for Protection from Sexual Exploitation and Sexual Abuse, UN Doc. ST/SGB/2003/13 (2003).

[41] A Comprehensive Strategy to Eliminate Future Sexual Exploitation and Abuse in United Nations Peacekeeping Operations, UN Doc. A/59/710 (2005).

[42] UN Doc. A/59/19/Rev.1 (2005).

[43] Report of the Secretary-General, Comprehensive Report of Conduct and Discipline Including Full Justification of All Posts, UN Doc. A/62/758 (2008).

[44] See UN Model MOU (n. 9).

to the full range of disciplinary measures provided in Staff Regulations and Staff Rules, the Organisation's ability to discipline UN police officers, members of formed police units, UN military observers and members of military contingents i.e. troops extends at the most to their repatriation on disciplinary grounds. For all categories of peacekeeping personnel, the UN relies on Member States, usually the TCCs or the States of nationality of the suspect in case of international civilian staff or local staff members, to conduct criminal proceedings for offences committed by them while serving with the UN. The General Assembly has requested the Secretary-General 'to bring credible allegations that reveal that a crime may have been committed by UN officials and experts on mission to the attention of the States against whose nationals such allegations are made, and to request from those States an indication of the status of their efforts to investigate and, as appropriate, prosecute crimes of a serious nature, as well as the types of appropriate assistance States may wish to receive from the Secretariat for the purposes of such investigations and prosecutions'.[45]

4. The Secretary-General's new strategy[46] to improve the Organisation's system-wide approach to preventing and responding to SEA focuses on four main areas of action. The first part is to elevate the voice of victims themselves and put their rights and dignity at the forefront. With greater benefit of the knowledge and support of external experts and organisations, the UN will take up the cause of victims from allegation to judgment. The UN will also tangibly improve the medical, social, legal and financial assistance provided to them, where appropriate. The UN will encourage fast-tracking of cases through better advocacy and through the full power and tools at the disposal of the UN. Member States and other partners are expected to support these efforts.[47] Second, the UN will work to end impunity for those guilty of SEA. The UN will seek to establish greater transparency on reporting and investigations, as well as on administrative and judicial processes and outcomes, including clarifying limitations on the UN to ensure criminal accountability. The Organisation will work with Member States on their own efforts to act more swiftly on credible allegations, promote greater transparency in national judicial and administrative processes, and achieve justice and closure for victims.

---

[45] UNGA Res. 62/63 (2008), para. 9.
[46] Report of the Secretary-General, Special Measures for Protection from Sexual Exploitation and Abuse: A New Approach, UN Doc. A/71/818 (2017).
[47] Ibid., Chapter II, para. 13(a).

The UN will reinforce these objectives within the UN system with concrete steps towards creating a culture of prevention, pursuing initiatives designed to reconnect all personnel to the core values of the UN, raise awareness and training, and strengthen standards for hiring and retention.[48] Third, the UN will build a truly multi-stakeholder network to support efforts to prevent and respond to SEA. The UN will engage more directly and continuously with civil society, as well as with external experts and organisations. The UN will seek the advice and help of those from outside the Organisation, drawing on the wisdom of local communities and leaders, as well as of acknowledged experts and organisations around the world. The Organisation will seek expertise especially from those countries directly involved and with experience in UN peace and humanitarian operations.[49] Lastly, the UN will reorient its approach to strategic communications to raise awareness worldwide regarding the problem of SEA, to address the stigma and discrimination that victims face, and to promote the UN as a global platform for sharing best practices in prevention and response. The UN will also expand the use of technology and new media at all levels to aid in preventive efforts and to increase transparency across the Organisation in combating SEA.[50] Prevention is considered to be the backbone of the Organisation's response and includes risk assessment, training, community outreach, awareness training and vetting of personnel. E-learning initiatives will be accessible system-wide to facilitate training.[51] In the area of pre-deployment training, core training materials are made available, and TCCs and PCCs are to provide the· UN Secretariat with a certificate to show that they have complied with the requirement to deliver training materials to all members of contingents and formed police units.[52]

5. It is critical for the integrity of the Organisation to ensure that former UN personnel found to have engaged in misconduct do not re-enter the Organisation. Exchange of information between UN entities remains a challenge due to the internal legal framework and recruitment-related policies, the size of the workforce and the variety of categories

---

[48] *Ibid.*, Chapter II, para. 13(b).
[49] *Ibid.*, Chapter II, para. 13(c).
[50] *Ibid.*, Chapter II, para. 13(d).
[51] *Ibid.*, Chapter IV.B, para. 50.
[52] Report of the Secretary-General, Special Measures for Protection from Sexual Exploitation and Abuse, UN Doc. A/69/779 (2015); 2016 UNSG Report (n. 24); 2015 UNSG Implementation Report (n. 22).

of personnel and of mechanisms used for their recruitment.[53] A vetting mechanism already in place is a confidential Misconduct Tracking System maintained by the DFS to vet personnel for prior misconduct while in the service of the Organisation. The system will be expanded to include all UN Agencies, Funds and Programmes. The OIOS (see Rule 16.7) has made several recommendations for improved effectiveness in the battle against misconduct.[54] One recommendation is for the DPKO/DFS to revise the MOU, defining minimum investigative standards and protocols to be followed by TCCs, requiring their compliance and defining the investigation competencies and experience of National Investigating Officers. The MOU should further include a target period for completing investigations and identify an appropriate role for the Host State.

16.7   Investigation and administrative action are responsibilities for the UN, Troop Contributing Countries and Police Contributing Countries.

1. The investigative responsibilities of the OIOS are limited by its mandate[55] and by the fact that TCCs have exclusive criminal jurisdiction over their contingents. Investigation activities cover resources, activities and personnel of the UN Secretariat and its Offices and Departments at all duty stations and locations, including peacekeeping operations and special political missions. OIOS does not investigate cases that do not implicate civilian or uniformed personnel, funds or activities of the Organisation. Misconduct is classified into two broad categories, according to the relative seriousness of the contravention and the risk to the Organisation.[56] OIOS investigations focus on the most serious violations, such as fraud, corruption, criminal activities, SEA, outside activities, serious theft, procurement irregularities, conflicts of interest, embezzlement, gross mismanagement and waste of UN resources. This category is referred to as category I ("serious matters").[57] OIOS will not normally investigate personnel matters, traffic incidents, simple thefts, contract

---

[53] 2015 UNSG Report (n. 52), para. 39.
[54] UN Office of Internal Oversight Services, Evaluation Report: Evaluation of the Enforcement and Remedial Assistance Efforts for Sexual Exploitation and Abuse by the United Nations and Related Personnel in Peacekeeping Operations, IED-15-001 (2015), para. 73.
[55] See UN Doc. A/48/218B (1994).
[56] See the Report of the Office of Internal Oversight Services on Strengthening the Investigation Functions in the United Nations, UN Doc. A/58/708 (2004); UNGA Res. 59/287 (2005).
[57] OIOS Investigations Manual, Chapter 1, para. 1.3.1, https://oios.un.org/resources/2015/12/7KKtL7Id.pdf.

disputes, office management disputes, basic misuse of equipment or staff, prohibited conduct by staff and basic mismanagement issues. These matters are usually referred to as category II ("routine matters"), and allegations may be investigated by the Special Investigation Unit, Military Police, UN Police and ad hoc panels.[58] The Office of Human Resources Management in the Department of Management takes decisions concerning disciplinary measures for civilian personnel. When allegations of serious misconduct involving military and police personnel occur, the UN may repatriate the individuals concerned and ban them from future peacekeeping operations. Disciplinary sanctions and any other judicial actions remain a national responsibility. Members of military contingents deployed on peacekeeping missions remain under the exclusive jurisdiction of their national government. The responsibility for investigating an allegation of misconduct and taking subsequent disciplinary action rests with the TCC, in accordance with the revised UN Model MOU, endorsed by the General Assembly in 2007.[59] The TCC involved must then report back to the UN on the outcome of misconduct investigations and on actions taken.

16.8   As regards non-UN Peace Operations, the responsibility for setting the standards for conduct and discipline, for pre-deployment training and "in-mission" training on conduct and discipline issues and for monitoring and enforcing compliance with these standards, including through investigation and administrative action, is shared between the regional organisation or arrangement conducting the operation and the Troop Contributing Countries and Police Contributing Countries. Commanders and civilian hierarchy at all levels are to ensure that personnel under their command or supervision are aware of the applicable standards of conduct and reporting obligations and must monitor compliance with these standards at their level and within the scope of their responsibilities. They must be held accountable for their performance regarding the exercise of these conduct and discipline functions.

1. The Rules and Commentary in this chapter have focused on UN Peace Operations. In other Peace Operations, these various responsibilities

---

[58] *Ibid.*
[59] See UN Model MOU (n. 9).

will also be shared between the regional organisation or arrangement concerned and the TCCs/PCCs but the precise way in which these responsibilities are shared may differ between the various organisations or arrangements.

2. In case of mandates adopted by the UN Security Council, the mandate establishing a non-UN lead mission will as a rule emphasise the need for the new force to act in full compliance with applicable IHL, IHRL and international refugee law.[60] In his report[61] the Secretary-General calls upon the Security Council to ensure that, when it authorises the deployment of non-UN international forces, it calls for States to take preventive measures, ensure both the accountability of perpetrators and remedies for victims in collaboration with the victims' rights advocate, co-operate with the UN in monitoring, investigating and reporting allegations, and keep the UN informed of progress and outcomes. States should be required, prior to deployment, to adhere to arrangements similar to those in place for UN TCCs/PCCs, which could include measures such as adopting standards of conduct and policies containing clear prohibitions and measures in cases of breaches, ensuring risk assessments and training, screening of personnel, holding perpetrators accountable, ensuring rapid and effective investigations and co-operating with the victims' rights advocate.

3. In specific situations, following a new Security Council resolution, non-UN troops may come under operational command and control of a newly established UN lead peacekeeping mission. From then on, the UN mission leadership will have a more prominent role when it comes to the responsibility for troop behaviour. A so-called "re-hatting process" is developed to ensure new troops adhere to the UN standards of conduct and discipline. Since 1999, the UN has been re-hatting[62] troops that operated initially under a Security Council resolution authorising regional organisations[63] or ad hoc coalitions[64] to stabilise a specific country. Important steps to ensure compliance with rules for conduct and discipline are to measure the overall readiness of units in terms of operational capabilities, logistics and training. This will include assessment and

---

[60] See e.g. UNSC Res. 2127 (2013), para. 33.

[61] See 2008 UNSG Report (n. 43).

[62] The transfer of uniformed military and police personnel deployed by non-UN Peace Operations to a succeeding UN Peace Operation. Re-hatting refers to the change of berets or helmets worn by personnel of the non-UN operation to the UN colours.

[63] The AU in Burundi, Sudan, Mali and the Central African Republic; the Economic Community of West African States (ECOWAS) in Sierra Leone, Liberia and Côte d'Ivoire.

[64] International Force in East Timor (INTERFET) and Multinational Interim Force in Haiti (MIFH).

advisory visits and pre-deployment visits to potential TCCs and PCCs or to the area where troops are deployed. The Human Rights Due Diligence Policy on UN support to non-UN security forces[65] requires the UN to conduct a risk assessment and to identify and ensure implementation of mitigating measures before it provides support to non-UN security forces. Since 2012, the policy on human rights screening of UN personnel[66] has required the UN to obtain certification from TCCs/PCCs that none of its nominated personnel has been convicted of, or is under investigation for, criminal offences or for violation of human rights.

[65] The Human Rights Due Diligence Policy was endorsed by the Secretary-General in July 2011, and was transmitted to the General Assembly and Security Council in March 2013. See Human Rights Due Diligence Policy on United Nations Support to non-United Nations Security Forces, UN Doc. A/67/775–S/2013/110 (2013), Annex.

[66] The Human Rights Screening Policy was approved by the Secretary-General's Policy Committee in Decision No. 2012/18 (2012).

17

Promotion of the Rule of Law

17.1   Respect for the rule of law is fundamental to the proper functioning of all States and societies. Accordingly, where a Peace Operation is deployed to a country in which either the rule of law has broken down or respect for it is otherwise impaired, taking action to establish and thereafter maintain the proper functioning of the essential rule of law institutions and to foster respect for them and for the laws, procedures and proceedings associated with them is critical to the success of the Peace Operation.

1. All States and societies rely for their efficient operation on the idea that there are particular rules that bind the members of that society and with which the society must comply. It is not necessarily the case that all members of the society are bound by the same rules. Thus, a number of States, for example, have a specific set of laws that apply only to the members of their armed forces. The fact that certain members of the society are bound by rules that are special to them or are exempt from rules that do not apply to them may not necessarily adversely affect the notion that the society as a whole is bound by the law; in general laws should, however, be clear, just and evenly applied and should protect individual rights. What is, however, of fundamental importance is that the legal arrangements under which the society operates, including for example its constitutional arrangements, the rights of its citizens, their access to courts, the procedural arrangements applying in those courts and the interaction between citizens and various organs of the State such as the police and security services, shall command the general respect of the population as a whole.[1]

---

[1] 'For the United Nations, the rule of law refers to a principle of governance in which all persons, institutions and entities, public and private, including the State itself, are accountable to laws that are publicly promulgated, equally enforced and independently adjudicated, and which are consistent with international human rights norms and standards. It requires, as well, measures to ensure

2. The rule of law is generally defined as a system in which the following four universal principles are upheld:[2]

1. The government and its officials and agents, individuals and private entities are accountable under the law;
2. The laws are clear, publicised, stable and just; are applied evenly; and protect fundamental rights, including the security of persons and property;
3. The process by which the laws are enacted, administered and enforced is accessible, fair and efficient;
4. Justice is delivered in a timely way by competent, ethically sound and independent officials who are of sufficient number, have adequate resources and reflect the makeup of the communities they serve.

3. Individual citizens may from time to time commit breaches of the law. These occurrences do not usually undermine this notion of the rule of law. Indeed, it is usually the role of the police and security services to deal with such legal breaches. The effective implementation of the rule of law, therefore, requires a general, not necessarily universal, acceptance by the population that the relevant institutions, and their personnel, are generally operating fairly in their implementation of the laws of the land, and that those laws and constitutional and other arrangements are also, generally speaking, fair. This presupposes that governments and officials are accountable for their decisions and actions.

4. If a Peace Operation is deployed to a State either in which the rule of law has entirely broken down or in which there are significant shortcomings in the way in which important institutions, such as government, the police, the courts, the internal security services or other relevant institutions, are operating, establishing and/or securing peace and the establishment of a properly functioning State are likely to be achieved only if the rule of law institutions that are defective are first reformed to the extent that is necessary in order to ensure their proper future functioning. Indeed, all UN activities, including Peace Operations, must be committed to accepting and promoting full accountability to law. This includes a commitment to promote the establishment or re-establishment

---

adherence to the principles of supremacy of law, equality before the law, accountability to the law, fairness in the application of the law, separation of powers, participation in decision-making, legal certainty, avoidance of arbitrariness and procedural and legal transparency': Report of the Secretary-General, The Rule of Law and Transitional Justice in Conflict and Post-Conflict Societies, UN Doc. S/2004/616 (2004), para. 6.

[2] See the World Justice Project, www.worldjusticeproject.org/what-rule-law.

of the rule of law in a war-torn or failed State (see paragraph 6 of the Commentary to this Rule) and full compliance with legal obligations in their own operations (see Rule 17.2).

5. It is not possible in these paragraphs to produce a blueprint setting out a list of all of the circumstances that may result in the defective operation of the rule of law, nor to list all of the symptoms of such defects that may manifest themselves and the various tasks that the Peace Force may need to undertake in order to put matters right. Inevitably, much will depend on the particular circumstances applying in the State to which the Peace Force has been deployed. If a Peace Force has been specifically mandated to engage in promotion of rule of law activities, it will have to have clear and realistic goals set and co-ordinated with other actors. While the military and police components of a Peace Operation can play a role in training military and police personnel and helping to establish guidelines for how they should operate, their role in, for example, training the judiciary, reforming penal law and constructing prisons, will be limited or even inappropriate. In a civil society the military is not involved in such activities, and few contingents would be able to offer much with respect to those types of activity in most cases. So the emphasis here should be on providing the necessary security for civil actors inside and outside the Peace Operation to perform those types of task. It will be necessary at an early stage in the deployment for the Peace Force to assess which rule of law institutions require reconstruction, reform or support, to consider what specific action is needed and to list such actions in order of priority. The Peace Force will then need to give prompt attention to the shortcomings that, if left unaddressed even for a short period, risk prejudicing the success of the deployment as a whole. Such action may include recruiting and training of personnel for e.g. police or security services, recruiting and training members of the judiciary and corrections staff, reforming criminal and other legislation, constructing court houses, police stations, prisons and other facilities, and providing electoral assistance, activities that cannot be sufficiently performed by members of a Peace Operation alone and therefore require support by other players present in a war-torn territory.

6. It is frequently the case that the circumstances giving rise to the deployment of a Peace Operation are due to political systems and institutions that are not firmly anchored in the rule of law. Issues of legitimacy of institutions and a perception, either among the whole of the population of the relevant State or among a significant element of that population, of laws as being unjust or not meeting rule of law criteria

listed in paragraph 2 of the Commentary to this Rule are the main triggers for any Peace Operation. The mandate of the Peace Force will, in such circumstances, either explicitly or, at the least, implicitly, require the Peace Force to take positive action in order to establish, restore and thereafter to maintain respect for the rule of law. The Security Council has reiterated its determination to give clear, credible and achievable mandates to Peace Operations and special political missions towards this end.[3]

7. The mandate may determine the action that a Peace Force should take in this regard. The mandate may also address the prioritisation of such tasks. Equally, the need for action in support of the rule of law may arise on an unplanned basis and may therefore need to be undertaken without prior specific mandate-based authority or guidance. It will be up to the mandating organisation, the Troop (TCC) and Police Contributing Countries (PCC) and the mission leadership to ensure that there are sufficient resources, both human and material, to carry them out. The military component of a Peace Operation cannot be expected to do more than provide basic security in so far as possible to enable civilian actors to provide assistance to Host State authorities. Action taken to promote the rule of law should, as far as possible, take into account the cultural, political and legal traditions of the Host State.

8. The strengthening of police, justice and corrections institutions plays a key role in the restoration and consolidation of peace by facilitating the maintenance of law and order and fostering the peaceful resolution of disputes, while preventing impunity for crimes committed during, as well as after, a conflict. The demand for UN Peace Operations to provide assistance in the justice and corrections areas has been growing steadily. Since 1999, the Security Council has mandated all new Peace Operations led by the Department of Peacekeeping Operations (DPKO) to support Host State authorities in strengthening the rule of law, including through support to their justice and/or prison systems. As of June 2016 more than 240 justice personnel and over 400 corrections personnel were deployed to 12 UN Peace Operations. In 2016 more than 15,000 UN Police officers were authorised for deployment in UN peacekeeping operations and special political missions. Assistance provided by the justice and corrections components of field missions is based on international standards, which reflect applicable international human rights law (IHRL), international humanitarian law (IHL), international criminal

---

[3] Statement by the President of the Security Council, UN Doc. S/PRST/2014/5 (2014).

law and international refugee law. It is further based on the needs and priorities identified by national actors and consistent with the culture and legal traditions of the Host State. In all Host States, justice and corrections components seek to ensure national ownership of reform efforts and effective capacity building of national judicial, legal and corrections professionals and institutions. Justice and corrections components also strive to ensure a comprehensive and strategic approach to strengthening the rule of law by actively engaging partners across the UN system and the wider international community and donors to share resources, knowledge and experience.[4] It should, however, be considered that the primary focus of a Peace Force is the maintenance of order and security. It remains an exception that Peace Operations in Kosovo and East Timor have been mandated to perform executive functions in the rule of law area, with staff members serving as judges, prosecutors, defence counsel and ministry/department of justice officials including penal system managers.

9. The 2015 Report of the High-Level Independent Panel on Peace Operations[5] has placed new emphasis on the need for rule of law support in Peace Operations. It highlighted the need to make the security sector a particular focus due to its potential to disrupt peace in many countries, with efforts being directed towards the whole "justice chain"; indeed, the Report describes justice, the rule of law and human rights as 'mutually reinforcing elements' of UN Peace Operations.[6] Noting that rule of law activities are often reflected in the mandate and drawing attention to the role of rule of law experts, the Report links support for and development of the rule of law with promoting the protection of civilians.[7] The UN Secretary-General, in his first evaluation of this landmark assessment,[8] noted the role of many missions in supporting national authorities in carrying out their protection responsibilities, including through support to police, rule of law and security institutions, and directed that mission-wide strategies and coherent monitoring and reporting arrangements be put in place.[9]

---

[4] See Guidance Note of the Secretary-General: UN Approach to Rule of Law Assistance (2008).
[5] Report of the High-Level Independent Panel on Peace Operations, Uniting Our Strengths for Peace: Politics, Partnership and People, UN Doc. A/70/95-S/2015/446 (2015) (HIPPO Report).
[6] *Ibid.*, pp. 13, 53. The Panel specifically recommended that mission structures and co-ordination arrangements with United Nations country teams provide for an integrated approach to justice, the rule of law and human rights: *Ibid.*, p. 54.
[7] *Ibid.*, pp. 20, 38.
[8] Report of the Secretary-General, UN Doc. A/70/357-S/2015/683 (2015).
[9] *Ibid.*, p. 5. The capacity of the Global Focal Point for the Police, Justice and Corrections for joint program design and implementation should be strengthened, and the need to overcome current hurdles to the provision of rule of law support to special political missions is recognised: *Ibid.*, pp. 14, 16.

10. Peace Operations conducted by regional arrangements have similar priorities. Article 21 of the EU Treaty[10] reflects the rule of law as an EU external relations objective. The military tasks in NATO-led Peace Support Operations also include rule of law missions.[11] NATO supports the strengthening of the rule of law in its co-operative security initiatives, through training and advising missions and other partnership tools.[12]

17.2 All personnel engaged in Peace Operations, and the Peace Force itself, must demonstrate respect for the rule of law at all times.

1. While promoting the rule of law in the Host State and maintenance of discipline of the members of the Peace Operation are distinct requirements, it is clear that a Peace Force the members of which are not seen to demonstrate respect for the rule of law is likely to find it difficult to convince the population to show that respect. Accordingly, maintaining respect for the rule of law among the members of the Peace Force is effectively a precondition to the successful accomplishment of that – probably crucially important – part of the mission.

2. In addition, it is vital that discipline be maintained among peacekeepers, so that superior orders designed to further the needs of the mission are carried out speedily and efficiently, to ensure that the population of the Host State is treated with appropriate respect and to maintain the good names of the Peace Operation, of its sponsoring organisation and of the respective TCCs.

3. Peace Force commanders therefore have a special responsibility to foster discipline among their subordinates, to seek to monitor carefully

---

[10] Art. 21 Treaty on European Union, OJ 2016 No. C202, 7 June 2016, p. 13, describes the Union's action on the international scene as guided by principles 'which it seeks to advance in the wider world: democracy, the rule of law, the universality and indivisibility of human rights and fundamental freedoms, respect for human dignity, the principles of equality and solidarity, and respect for the principles of the United Nations Charter and international law'.

[11] See NATO, Peace Support Operations, AJP-3.4.1 (2001), pp. 6–7.

[12] NATO, Wales Summit Declaration (2014), para. 81, www.nato.int/cps/ic/natohq/official_texts_112964.htm, discloses the collective pledge to 'strengthen the political dialogue and practical cooperation with our partners who share our vision for cooperative security in an international order based on the rule of law'. In addition, NATO has run specific rule of law missions, such as the 2011 Rule of Law Field Support Mission (NROLFSM) in Afghanistan, which was tasked to support and enable Afghan officials and international actors in the accomplishment of their rule of law mandates.

action taken by units under command, to act in a timely way to prevent breaches of the law and to deal suitably with any that occur.[13] Particular care should be taken to ensure that vulnerable Host State citizens are not subjected to exploitation or abuse of any kind, including sexual exploitation and abuse (SEA), by members of the Peace Operation. Gender considerations, especially women's issues and women's representation, should be taken into account throughout all rule of law activities,[14] and the requisite expertise should be made available to all Peace Operations that are liable to be confronted with gender issues.

17.3   Strategies for rule of law reform must seek to ensure that affected populations, their recognised representatives and relevant institutions are appropriately involved in developing and implementing the required changes.

1. Local involvement in rule of law support and reform arrangements is likely to promote acceptance of the required changes. Broad co-operation with relevant Host State actors will enable local legal and social cultures and traditions to be taken into account in formulating new or reformed arrangements. The degree to which existing rule of law structures lack popular acceptance or fail to deliver generally accepted safeguards will tend to determine whether building on existing institutional arrangements, such as the existing civil police force, or starting from scratch and recruiting entirely new personnel, is required.

2. If the existing national rule of law arrangements are recognised as being below internationally acceptable standards, the international organisations concerned, the Host State and Sending States will need, in mutual consultations, to consider how to go about substituting alternative arrangements that combine respect for local preferences and social and cultural traditions with the achievement and maintenance of internationally accepted standards of justice, fairness and procedural propriety.[15]

---

[13] See Chapter 16.

[14] In UNSC Res. 2122 (2013), para. 3, the Security Council '[e]xpresses its intention to increase its attention to women, peace and security issues in all relevant thematic areas of work on its agenda, including in particular Protection of civilians in armed conflict, Post-conflict peacebuilding, *The promotion and strengthening of the rule of law* in the maintenance of international peace and security, Peace and Security in Africa, Threats to international peace and security caused by terrorist acts, and Maintenance of international peace and security' (emphasis added).

[15] See K. Simion, *Practitioner's Guide: Qualitative and Quantitative Approaches to Rule of Law Research* (INPROL, 2016).

17.4 Where rule of law issues require action by a Peace Force, the mandate should define clear, credible and achievable priorities for that action, and the necessary resources and strategies should be made available to the Peace Force.

1. The Security Council has emphasised that

> United Nations peacekeeping activities should be conducted in a manner so as to facilitate post-conflict peacebuilding, prevention of relapse of armed conflict and progress toward sustainable peace and development ...
>
> [M]ultidimensional peacekeeping missions may be mandated by the Security Council inter-alia to support the strengthening of rule of law institutions of the host country in a co-ordinated manner with other United Nations entities, within the scope of respective mandates in helping national authorities develop critical rule of law priorities and strategies to address the needs of police, judicial institutions, and corrections system and critical linkages thereof with a view to supporting the State's ability to provide critical functions in these fields, and as a vital contribution to building peace and ending impunity.[16]

This issue has a difficult history, especially in the process after the 2000 Brahimi Report.[17] While sustainable justice institutions are necessary for reaching the goal of lasting peace, post-conflict judicial reform is an essential requirement in this process.

2. With the political leverage of Security Council mandates, and the ability to deploy large numbers of specialised police, justice and corrections officers, the DPKO through its Justice and Corrections Service within the Office of Rule of Law and Security Institutions works to strengthen justice and corrections systems in post-conflict environments. Based on the overall objectives of peacekeeping – to advance political solutions, to improve security and to lay the foundations for institution-building – justice and corrections components have typically engaged in seven priority areas: (1) the basic functioning of the criminal justice system; (2) the investigation and prosecution of atrocity crimes and crimes that fuel conflict; (3) the resolution of disputes over land and other resources; (4) reductions in the level of prolonged and arbitrary detention; (5) the professionalisation of justice and corrections personnel; (6) the

---

[16] UNSC Res. 2086 (2013), paras. 2 and 8(c).

[17] Report of the Panel on United Nations Peace Operations, UN Doc. A/55/305-S/2000/809 (2000), paras. 80–82. For a critical assessment of implementation efforts and their failures, see T. Benner, S. Mergenthaler and Ph. Rotmann, *The New World of UN Peace Operations: Learning to Build Peace?* (Oxford University Press, 2011), pp. 109–145.

development and implementation of national justice and corrections reform strategies; and (7) the strengthening of the legislative and regulatory framework. Taking into account the political implications of such efforts, and of IHRL norms and standards, the Justice and Corrections Service works to reinforce national ownership of reform in the justice and corrections sectors. Peacekeeping missions have, for instance, used their convening authority to co-ordinate the development of criminal justice frameworks in Mali, helped re-open courts and prisons in "Islands of Stability" in the Democratic Republic of the Congo, supported military justice authorities to prosecute atrocity crimes committed by the national armed forces and rebel groups in the Democratic Republic of the Congo and have been assisting Central African Republic authorities in establishing a special criminal court. The mission in Afghanistan established dialogue on land conflict issues, while police components have supported national police institutions to maintain law and order, and through training at police academies have instilled respect for human rights, addressing gender and juvenile justice concerns.

3. The UN has been deploying police officers for service in Peace Operations since the 1960s. Traditionally, the mandate of police components in Peace Operations was limited to monitoring, observing and reporting. Beginning in the early 1990s, advisory, mentoring and training functions were integrated into the monitoring activities in order to offer Peace Operations the opportunity to act as a corrective mechanism with domestic police and other law enforcement agencies. UN Police are an important tool used by the Organisation to help promote peace and security. Frequently, UN Police personnel reinforce and re-establish security by patrolling, work closely with and advise domestic police services, help to ensure compliance with international human rights standards and assist in a wide range of activities to restore and promote public safety and the rule of law. The Global Focal Point for Police, Justice and Corrections Areas in Post-Conflict and other Crisis Situations, established in 2012, has proven to be an important platform for the DPKO, the UN Development Programme (UNDP), the Office of the UN High Commissioner for Human Rights (OHCHR), the UN Office on Drugs and Crime (UNODC), UN Women and other UN entities to jointly undertake responsibilities, including through co-location and integrated teams. Joint justice programmes have been developed or are in the process of being developed in the UN Multidimensional Stabilization Missions in the Central African Republic (MINUSCA), Mali (MINUSMA), Haiti (MINUSTAH), the Democratic Republic of

the Congo (MONUSCO) and the AU/UN Hybrid operation in Darfur, Sudan (UNAMID).

4. Where Peace Operations have an inherent task to establish or strengthen the rule of law, mission commanders should be supported by professional rule of law advisers in the performance of the mission. This does require additional staff, as rule of law tasks in UN Peace Operations are separate and distinct from those of the legal adviser.

Demining and Removal of Explosive Remnants

1. Peace Operations are often deployed to areas where anti-personnel landmines or explosive remnants of war are present. Such explosive ordnances represent a constant threat to the civilian population in the area. The ordnances also represent a threat to the Peace Force, both with regard to its security and with regard to its ability to achieve its mandate.[1] The present chapter discusses what responsibility a Peace Force has to remove explosive ordnances or otherwise to protect civilians against the danger they represent.

2. The issue must be considered in light of a number of international treaty provisions concerning removal and destruction of explosive ordnances: for anti-personnel mines, see article 5 of the Ottawa Convention;[2] for cluster munition remnants, see article 4 of the Cluster Munitions Convention (CMC);[3] for minefields, mined areas, booby-traps and other devices, see article 10 of the Amended Protocol II to the Conventional Weapons Convention on Prohibitions or Restrictions on the Use of Mines, Booby-Traps and Other Devices (CCW Amended

---

[1] See e.g. UN Doc. S/PRST/1996/37 (1996) (noting, at preambular para. 2, that 'the widespread and indiscriminate use of anti-personnel mines in areas of United Nations peace-keeping operations poses serious impediments to such operations and to the safety of United Nations and other international personnel'); UN Doc. S/PRST/2003/22 (2003); UNGA Res. 70/46 (2015); UNGA Res. 70/80 (2015). On mine action, see further *UNMAS Mine Action Programming Handbook* (UN Mine Action Service, 2012), http://reliefweb.int/sites/reliefweb.int/files/resources/Full_Report_3289.pdf; International Mine Action Standards, Battle Area Clearance (BAC), IMAS 09.11 (2007, Amendment 3, 2013), www.mineactionstandards.org/standards/international-mine-action-standards-imas; *The Role of the Military in Mine Action* (Geneva International Centre for Humanitarian Demining, 2003); *Handbook on United Nations Multidimensional Peacekeeping Operations* (DPKO, 2003), Chapter VI, pp. 71–82.

[2] Convention on the Prohibition of the Use, Stockpiling, Production and Transfer of Anti-Personnel Mines and on their Destruction (18 September 1997, in force 1 March 1999), 2056 UNTS 241 (Ottawa Convention).

[3] Convention on Cluster Munitions (30 May 2008, in force 1 August 2010), 2688 UNTS 39 (CMC).

Protocol II);[4] and, for other explosive remnants of war, see article 3 of Protocol V to the same Convention on Explosive Remnants of War (CCW Protocol V).[5]

18.1 The primary responsibility for demining and removal of explosive remnants of war lies with the Host State. Any responsibilities of a Peace Operation for demining and removal of explosive remnants of war must be stipulated in the mandate.

1. When Peace Forces are deployed to areas that are contaminated with anti-personnel mines or other explosive remnants of war, the primary responsibility for removal of such objects lies with the Host State. This is a fundamental Rule that is reflected in the relevant international legal instruments.

2. Peace Forces are frequently given mandates that include provisions relating to demining and removal of explosive remnants of war, but these provisions focus on providing assistance to other actors that perform the actual demining. In this respect, the President of the Security Council stated that the Council recognises 'the importance of ensuring that the provision of technical advice and support for mine action is reflected in the mandates and personnel planning for peacekeeping operations and expresses its intention to address mine action concerns in the mandate and personnel planning for peacekeeping operations whenever appropriate'.[6] By way of example, UN Security Council Resolution 1244 (1999) gave Kosovo Force (KFOR) the responsibility of 'supervising demining until the international civil presence can, as appropriate, take over responsibility for this task',[7] while Resolution 1990 (2011) mandated UN Interim Security Force for Abyei (UNISFA) to 'provide ... de-mining

---

[4] Protocol on Prohibitions or Restrictions on the Use of Mines, Booby-Traps and Other Devices as amended on 3 May 1996 (amended Protocol II) annexed to the Convention on Prohibitions or Restrictions on the Use of Certain Conventional Weapons which may be deemed to be Excessively Injurious or to have Indiscriminate Effects (3 May 1996, in force 3 December 1998), 2048 UNTS 93.

[5] Protocol on Explosive Remnants of War (Protocol V) annexed to the Convention on Prohibitions or Restrictions on the Use of Certain Conventional Weapons which may be deemed to be Excessively Injurious or to have Indiscriminate Effects (23 November 2003, in force 12 November 2006), 2399 UNTS 100 (CCW Protocol V).

[6] UN Doc. S/PRST/2003/22 (2003), para. 9.

[7] UNSC Res. 1244 (1999), para. 9(e).

assistance and technical advice'.[8] In the absence of a provision to this effect, Peace Forces have no responsibility to clear contaminated areas.[9]

3. International treaties specify that the prime responsibility to clear contaminated areas lies with the State that exercises jurisdiction or control over the area, even if this is a State other than the Host State. There is insufficient evidence to establish this as a rule under customary international law. Even if a Peace Force acquires "control" over such a territory, the unequivocal position of the UN is that the Peace Force does not have such a responsibility. Customary international law prescribes that protection against dangers to persons in a territory is an aspect of the sovereign responsibility of the territorial State. A further consequence of this sovereign responsibility is that the Host State has a duty to inform a Peace Operation of any contaminated area to enable the Peace Force to avoid landmines and unexploded ordnances that represent a danger to the operation.

4. The previous paragraphs have addressed obligations to undertake mine action. The absence of a legal obligation for a Peace Force to undertake demining, however, does not mean that a Peace Force cannot demine at all. A Peace Operation may also wish to undertake mine action out of operational or humanitarian needs on its own initiative. Here a distinction must be made between operational demining and humanitarian demining. The President of the Security Council has stated that operational demining (i.e. demining to ensure the movement and deployment of troops and other personnel, maintenance of supply lines to deployment sites and increased access to all parts of the mission area) should be considered as an integral part of peacekeeping mandates.[10] Humanitarian demining (e.g. for the purpose of reclaiming land for agriculture and the return of displaced persons), however, cannot be seen as an integral part

---

[8] UNSC Res. 1999 (2001), para. 2(c). All aspects linked to the mitigation of the threats from mines and explosive remnants of war are co-ordinated by the UN Mine Action Service (UNMAS), which is situated in the DPKO's Office of Rule of Law and Security Institutions. UNMAS collaborates with eleven UN departments, agencies and programmes, and provides direct support and assistance to eighteen countries/territories/missions including Afghanistan, the Central African Republic (MINUSCA), Colombia, Côte d'Ivoire (UNOCI), Cyprus (UNFICYP), the Democratic Republic of Congo (MONUSCO), Iraq, Lebanon (UNIFIL), Libya (UNSMIL), Mali (MINUSMA), Palestine, Somalia (UNSOA, UNSOM), Sudan, Abyei (UNISFA), Darfur (UNAMID), South Sudan (UNMISS), Syria, and Western Sahara (MINURSO).

[9] In 2015, the General Assembly adopted a resolution in which it recognised the importance 'of explicitly incorporating references to mine action, when appropriate, in ceasefire and peace agreements, as well as in the mandates of peacekeeping operations and special political missions': UNGA Res. 70/80 (2015), para. 13.

[10] UN Doc. S/PRST/1996/37 (1996), para. 3.

of peacekeeping mandates, and thus requires to be separately covered by a legal basis in the form of Host State consent or a Security Council resolution.

5. On 30 June 2017 the Security Council unanimously adopted its first stand-alone resolution on mine action. In Resolution 2365 (2017) the Council expresses grave concern over the threat that landmines and other explosive devices pose to civilians, refugees and peacekeepers. The resolution also stresses the importance of considering mine action during the earliest stages of planning and programming of Peace Operations, and of ensuring that Peace Operations are equipped, informed and trained to reduce the threat posed by these devices. The Security Council furthermore requests the UN Secretary-General to submit a report on the implementation of the resolution within a year.

18.2 A Peace Force should make feasible efforts to identify all areas under its control which are known or suspected to be contaminated by anti-personnel mines, cluster munition remnants or other explosive remnants of war.

1. This Rule is inspired by article 5(2) of the Ottawa Convention, which provides that '[e]ach State Party shall make every effort to identify all areas under its jurisdiction or control in which anti-personnel mines are known or suspected to be emplaced'. The CCW Protocol V and the CMC contain similar obligations to 'survey and assess the threat'.[11] This Rule satisfies two objectives during Peace Operations. It has benefits for the ability of Peace Forces to offer effective protection of civilians, but it is also important for the security of the forces.

2. The Ottawa Convention also stipulates that a State party 'shall ensure as soon as possible that all anti-personnel mines in mined areas under its jurisdiction or control are perimeter-marked, monitored and protected by fencing or other means, to ensure the effective exclusion of civilians, until all anti-personnel mines contained therein have been destroyed'.[12] Similar rules are provided by the CMC[13] and the CCW

---

[11] Art. 3(3)(a) CCW Protocol V (n. 5); art. 4(2)(a) CMC (n. 3).

[12] Art. 5(2) Ottawa Convention (n. 2).

[13] Art. 4(2) CMC (n. 3): 'Take all feasible steps to ensure that all cluster munition contaminated areas under its jurisdiction or control are perimeter-marked, monitored and protected by fencing or other means to ensure the effective exclusion of civilians.'

Protocol V.[14] The Group of Experts who prepared this Manual agree that current operational practice does not support a claim that legal obligations to this effect bind a Peace Operation.

3. The Rule is offered as a suggested best practice and is not intended to suggest a legal obligation to make such efforts (see Rule 18.1). States that are bound by the treaty obligations referred to earlier remain bound by these obligations to the extent that they apply to their participation in a Peace Operation.

4. In activities relating to demining and removal of explosive remnants, the approach of Peace Forces needs to adopt a clear gender perspective. UN Security Council Resolution 1325 (2000) calls for 'all parties to ensure that mine clearance and mine awareness programmes take into account the special needs of women and girls'. While demining is an objective that aims to protect all civilians, a gender perspective may increase the effectiveness of the efforts. For example, gender-segregated household tasks increase the likelihood that one of the two genders is more aware of the presence of explosive remnants in certain areas, for example around livestock fields or water points. These tasks are context- and culture-specific, but they can greatly inform the surveying process.

5. Attention should be paid to ensuring that all segments of the population are kept informed. In certain operational areas, women do not participate in information sessions either because they are represented by their male family members, or because there are other impediments to their presence at such meetings. Since the daily routines of women and girls often involve covering extensive territory in order to collect water or wood, women may be at greater risk of exposure to mines and other explosive remnants.

18.3 If this is required by a Peace Operation's mandate, a Peace Force shall make feasible efforts to clear, remove or destroy anti-personnel mines, cluster munition remnants and other explosive remnants of war in affected areas under its control. If a Troop Contributing Country is bound by applicable treaty obligations in this regard, it must comply with them.

1. This Rule is inspired by article 3(2) of the CCW Protocol V ('After the cessation of active hostilities and as soon as feasible, each High

---

[14] Art. 3(3) CCW Protocol V (n. 5): 'After the cessation of active hostilities and as soon as feasible, each High Contracting Party and party to an armed conflict shall take the following measures in affected territories under its control, to reduce the risks posed by explosive remnants of war.'

Contracting Party and party to an armed conflict shall mark and clear, remove or destroy explosive remnants of war in affected territories under its control'), article 5(1) of the Ottawa Convention ('Each State Party undertakes to destroy or ensure the destruction of all anti-personnel mines in mined areas under its jurisdiction or control'), and article 4(1) of the CMC ('Each State Party undertakes to clear and destroy, or ensure the clearance and destruction of, cluster munition remnants located in cluster munition contaminated areas under its jurisdiction or control').

2. International treaties establish this as a legal obligation incumbent on States parties. If the requirements for application of these treaty obligations are met during a State's involvement in a Peace Operation, the obligations must be observed by the State, even if such activities are not addressed in the mandate. The applicability of these treaties to Peace Operations is a contentious issue that has not been authoritatively resolved. This Manual takes the view that current operational practice does not support a claim that legal obligations to this effect exist during Peace Operations.

3. In the absence of a legally binding obligation to this effect, a Peace Force will have responsibilities to clear, remove or destroy anti-personnel mines, cluster munition remnants and other explosive remnants of war only to the extent that the mandate of the operation states this as a responsibility (see Rule 18.1).

4. If Peace Forces engage in such activities, they should engage with other actors in an inclusive consultation process when conducting impact surveys and establishing "priority areas" for clearance. Equal consultation of women may result in listing for priority clearance areas of greater significance to the whole community.

PART IV

Accountability and Responsibility

19

Accountability and Responsibility
in Peace Operations

1. Accountability is an expectation concerned with the legitimate exercise of power. It is based on the notion that those exercising power should be answerable for their actions.[1] As a normative concept, accountability reflects and promotes certain substantive values. These are commonly understood to include two broad sets of principles.[2] First is the rule of law, which stipulates that public power must be exercised in accordance with law and that no one, including those who occupy a position of authority, is above the law.[3] Second is the principle of good governance, which requires that decisions in public life should be adopted transparently, subject to institutional checks and balances, and in a manner which provides opportunities for participation in the decision-making process. Accountability sustains the rule of law and good governance, and vice versa.

2. Peace Operations invariably involve the exercise of public authority. As such, they engage the principle of accountability. This point is well established.[4] The standard of accountability that applies in a particular Peace Operation depends to a large extent on the nature and extent of the powers it exercises over third parties. Generally speaking, the broader the exercise of power and the more it affects others, the greater the demand for accountability. At one end of the spectrum lie Peace Operations carrying out governmental functions. Calls for accountability will be particularly intense in such cases, especially where they involve

---

[1] Accountability thus means answerability. See R. W. Grant and R. O. Keohane, 'Accountability and Abuses of Power in World Politics', 99 *American Political Science Review* (2005), pp. 29–30.

[2] I. F. Dekker, 'Accountability of International Organisations: An Evolving Legal Concept?', in J. Wouters, E. Brems, S. Smis and P. Schmitt (eds.), *Accountability for Human Rights Violations by International Organisations* (Intersentia, 2010), p. 24.

[3] On the rule of law in Peace Operations, see Chapter 17.

[4] E.g. A Comprehensive Strategy to Eliminate Future Sexual Exploitation and Abuse in United Nations Peacekeeping Operations, UN Doc. A/59/710 (2005), para. 38.

the administration of territory, as in the case of the UN administration of Kosovo.[5] At the other end of the spectrum are operations which perform only limited roles, such as the EU mission in support of security sector reform in the Republic of Guinea-Bissau.[6] Accountability is likely to be of a more limited concern in these cases. Demands for accountability will also be high in situations where Peace Operations directly affect the fundamental rights of individuals.

3. While it is desirable that Peace Operations should be subject to an appropriate degree of accountability, how such accountability is operationalised must take into account all relevant considerations, including their mission objectives and operational environment.[7] For this reason, it should be recognised that different degrees and forms of accountability may be appropriate for different Peace Operations or for the same operation at different points in time or space.[8] It is in the nature of the subject that the appropriate level of accountability for a particular operation cannot be determined in the abstract and with reference to legal standards alone, but depends on a broader range of factors and circumstances.

4. Accountability in Peace Operations may take different *forms*, including political, legal, administrative and financial accountability.[9] Legal rules and processes are a central feature of legal accountability. However, rules of international law also play a significant role in regulating and facilitating the discharge of other, non-legal forms of accountability. For example, specific treaty rules will normally govern the manner in which political and other disagreements between a Peace Operation and its Host State are to be resolved.[10]

---

[5] Cf. *Special Report No. 1 on the Compatibility with Recognized International Standards of UNMIK Regulation No. 2000/47 on the Status, Privileges and Immunities of KFOR and UNMIK and Their Personnel in Kosovo (18 August 2000)*, Ombudsperson Institution in Kosovo, Report of 26 April 2001, para. 24, www.ombudspersonkosovo.org/repository/docs/E4010426a_86354.pdf; European Commission for Democracy through Law (Venice Commission), *Human Rights in Kosovo: Possible Establishment of Review Mechanisms*, Opinion No. 280/2004, CDL-AD (2004)033, para. 68. See C. Stahn, *The Law and Practice of International Territorial Administration: Versailles to Iraq and Beyond* (Cambridge University Press, 2008), pp. 326–328.

[6] Council Joint Action 2008/112/CFSP of 12 February 2008 on the European Union Mission in Support of Security Sector Reform in the Republic of Guinea-Bissau (EU SSR GUINEA-BISSAU), OJ 2008 No. L40, 14 February 2008, p. 11 (as amended).

[7] Cf. *Behrami and Behrami v. France* and *Saramati v. France, Germany and Norway*, Application Nos. 71412/01 and 78166/01, Decision on Admissibility of 2 May 2007 [GC], para. 149.

[8] Venice Commission (n. 5), para. 95.

[9] International Law Association, 'Final Report on the Accountability of International Organizations', *Report of the Seventy-First Conference* (2004), p. 168.

[10] UN Model Status of Forces Agreement for Peacekeeping Operations, UN Doc. A/45/594 (1990) (UN Model SOFA).

5. It is useful to distinguish further between three different *components* of accountability.[11] The first component consists of the internal and external scrutiny of a Peace Operation's activities, regardless of whether this scrutiny engages the legal liability of the actors contributing to the operation. Examples include an operation's reporting requirements within its chain of command (internal scrutiny) or its exposure to the media (external scrutiny). The second component consists of tortious liability for injury or damage caused by an operation. Given that the mandates of Peace Operations often require them to engage in dangerous activities in the territory of the Host State, such injury or damage is quite common.[12] The third component involves international responsibility. This is a specifically legal form of accountability which is engaged when acts or omissions carried out by a Peace Operation amount to a breach of international law. These three components are examined in further detail in Rules 19.1 to 19.7.

6. Peace Operations typically involve a multitude of actors. As a consequence, accountability arises on at least three distinct levels. First, accountability attaches to the States and international organisations which establish, conduct or otherwise contribute to the conduct of a Peace Operation in the exercise of their respective powers. Second, accountability may also attach to the Peace Operation itself, to the extent that the operation has attained some corporate identity of its own, whether in law or in the public perception. Demands for accountability are thus often laid at the doorstep of Peace Operations as such, whether solely or in combination with the States and international organisations conducting them.[13] Third, accountability also arises at the level of the individuals participating in or contributing to an operation, for example under domestic and international criminal law. Individual accountability is the subject of another chapter[14] and will not be discussed in further detail in this chapter.

7. The different forms, components and levels of accountability are not mutually exclusive, but may be complementary. In the case of the Srebrenica massacre, shortfalls in obtaining political and legal

---

[11] This distinction is based on the one drawn in the ILA Final Report (n. 9), p. 169.

[12] See further Chapter 20.

[13] See *Georges* v. *United Nations*, US District Court of the Southern District of New York, Class Action Complaint, No. 13-cv-7146, Judgment of 9 October 2013, 84 F. Supp. 3d 246 (SDNY, 2015), a class action brought against the UN and the UN Stabilization Mission in Haiti (MINUSTAH) as a "subsidiary" of the UN in relation to the cholera outbreak in Haiti.

[14] See Chapter 21.

accountability at the international level fuelled calls for accountability at the domestic level in the Netherlands.[15] Dutch Prime Minister Wim Kok acknowledged this interrelationship in 2002 when his government accepted its share of the international community's political responsibility for not being able to prevent the events at Srebrenica and resigned.[16]

8. Because of its multi-faceted and multi-layered nature, it is often unclear how accountability should be allocated among the actors participating in a Peace Operation or where an appropriate balance between the different forms and components of accountability lies. The diffuse nature of accountability presents certain difficulties. Demands for accountability may not be addressed to the most appropriate actor. It may encourage tactical litigation by claimants and tempt States and international organisations to point the finger at each other in an effort to avoid their exposure to accountability.[17] No easy solution exists to address these difficulties. Tighter regulation may play a role. However, accountability is not an exclusively legal phenomenon and as such is not capable of exhaustive regulation through rules of law. Moreover, it would be overly optimistic to believe that some unified accountability regime could be devised which serves the diverging interests of all actors and potential claimants in an optimal manner. Consequently, it is difficult to imagine that holding Peace Operations to account could ever be anything other than an ongoing dialogue about what is appropriate and just in the specific circumstances.

9. Accountability in Peace Operations is therefore best understood and implemented as an iterative process. The actors participating in Peace Operations should adopt a proactive and holistic approach to render this process meaningful. This requires, first, that they accept accountability

---

[15] See A. Nollkaemper, 'Multi-Level Accountability: A Case Study of Accountability in the Aftermath of the Srebrenica Massacre', in T. Broude and Y. Shany (eds.), *The Shifting Allocation of Authority in International Law: Considering Sovereignty, Supremacy and Subsidiarity* (Hart, 2008), p. 363.

[16] In the words of the Prime Minister: 'Today's decision [of the Government to resign] acknowledges that the Netherlands shares political responsibility for bringing about a situation in which such an act was possible. The "international community" is faceless and cannot express its responsibility to the victims and survivors of Srebrenica. I can, and I do so now. Once again, as I have said before, I would like to emphasize that the soldiers of Dutchbat are not responsible for what happened there'; quoted in D. van den Berg, 'Rekindling a National Debate: How Public and Private Recognition Can Shift the Dutch Discourse on Srebrenica', in L. van Liere and K. Spronk (eds.), *Images of Enmity and Hope: Texts, Beliefs, Practices* (LIT, 2014), pp. 110–111.

[17] For an example of this in the context of international responsibility, see the pleadings in the *Use of Force* cases before the International Court of Justice: e.g. *Case concerning Legality of Use of Force (Serbia and Montenegro v. Portugal)*, Preliminary Objections of Portugal, 5 July 2000, paras. 135–136; *Case concerning Legality of Use of Force (Serbia and Montenegro v. France)*, Preliminary Objections of France, 5 July 2000, para. 24.

for their activities in a manner commensurate with the degree and nature of their powers. This duty applies at the level of the international organisation conducting the operation, just as much as it applies at the level of a Force Commander and his/her staff. Second, the actors engaged in Peace Operations should adopt whatever measures are necessary and appropriate, in the light of their powers and responsibilities, to discharge their duty of accountability. In this respect, it is important to bear in mind the interrelated nature of accountability. For example, an international organisation conducting a Peace Operation should make suitable legal and practical arrangements to ensure that Troop Contributing Countries (TCCs) conduct themselves in an accountable manner.[18] Since making such arrangements is reasonable and falls within the organisation's sphere of competences, a failure to do so could imply that the organisation is not fully discharging its duty of accountability. Similar considerations apply to subordinate levels of an operation. Force Commanders, for example, should exercise due diligence in reporting information that enables higher levels in the chain of command to discharge their responsibilities. Finally, in all of this, the actors concerned must proceed in a manner that respects basic standards of procedural and substantive justice, such as the principles of good faith and fairness.

19.1 Peace Operations, including their Troop and Police Contributing Countries and international organisations, must exercise their powers subject to appropriate forms of internal and external scrutiny. In particular, they should observe, in harmony with the requirements of the operation's mandate, the principles of good governance, good faith, oversight and due diligence.

1. The first component of accountability consists of the scrutiny of the conduct of Peace Operations through internal and external mechanisms. Internally, scrutiny may be exercised by certain elements of the operation over other elements, for instance by the Force Commander over his/her subordinates, and by the contributing States and international

---

[18] Agreements between the EU and third parties governing the latter's participation in EU crisis management operations typically contain provisions declaring that the third parties concerned shall be responsible for answering any claims linked to the participation of their personnel and for bringing any action, in particular legal or disciplinary, against such personnel, e.g. art. 3(4) Agreement between the European Union and the former Yugoslav Republic of Macedonia establishing a framework for the participation of the former Yugoslav Republic of Macedonia in European Union crisis management operations, OJ 2012 No. L338, 12 December 2012, p. 3.

organisations over the operation and its constituent parts,[19] for instance by TCCs over their national contingents. Externally, such scrutiny may be exercised by any party affected by a Peace Operation or by third parties, such as the media or non-governmental organisations, acting in the interests of those directly affected.[20] Although the range of parties seeking to exercise external scrutiny over a Peace Operation is potentially very broad, nothing requires an operation to subject itself to the same degree of external scrutiny as it does internally. On the contrary, operational considerations militate against this. For example, the sharing of classified information in the context of internal scrutiny procedures might be entirely appropriate, yet the disclosure of the same information to third parties might not be. To facilitate the exercise of scrutiny, Peace Operations must observe certain principles, discussed in the next paragraph.[21] The manner and degree to which they observe these principles therefore vary between the internal and external aspects of scrutiny.

2. The first principle that Peace Operations must observe in the present context is that of good governance. Good governance consists of a number of elements. Internally, Peace Operations should conduct themselves in a transparent manner, including by discharging internal reporting requirements, so as to allow the effective and responsible exercise of command and control by superior authorities. Their decisions must comply with their mandate and in doing so should adhere to the standards of efficiency, competence, integrity and sound financial management. Externally, Peace Operations should conduct themselves in a transparent manner to the extent permitted by their mandate and the operational environment. Second, Peace Operations must act in good faith, both internally and externally. Their conduct should conform to the standards of fairness and reasonableness at all times. Third, Peace Operations must subject themselves to the supervision and control of their parent States and organisations, in accordance with the chain of command applicable to them and their constituent units. Fourth, Peace Operations, including their contributing States and international organisations, must exercise

---

[19] In relation to the cholera outbreak in Haiti, see the joint letter by UN special rapporteurs concerning the allegation that the United Nations failed to take reasonable precautions to prevent the introduction of cholera in Haiti by the United Nations peacekeeping mission troops: JAL HTI 3/2014 (2014).

[20] For an example of external scrutiny relating to the Haiti cholera outbreak, see Amnesty International, 'Haiti: Five Years on, No Justice for the Victims of the Cholera Epidemic', Index AI: AMR 36/2652/2015 (2015).

[21] Cf. ILA Final Report (n. 9), pp. 172–185.

due diligence in ensuring the observance of these principles and to guarantee the lawfulness of their activities.[22] They should take necessary and appropriate measures to this end. A case in point is the UN's Human Rights Due Diligence Policy.[23]

19.2   Injury to persons or damage to property caused by Peace Operations may give rise to civil liability. Peace Operations, including their Troop and Police Contributing Countries and international organisations, should put in place arrangements to discharge that liability by providing appropriate remedies for the injury and damage caused by wrongful acts.

1. The second component of accountability in Peace Operations consists of tortious liability for personal injury or property damage. Such injury or damage may be caused by the operation to third parties or by one element of the operation to another element. Liability arises in both cases. In so far as liability towards third parties is concerned, providing appropriate remedies to acknowledge and mitigate the harm they have suffered often plays an important role in maintaining amicable relations with the local population and other stakeholders. Effective remedies therefore may make a significant contribution to mission success. However, the provision of such remedies may also constitute a legal requirement under the domestic law of TCCs, the internal law of the international organisation conducting the operation or the domestic law of the Host State. For example, Section 29 of the UN Privileges and Immunities Convention requires the UN to make provision for the appropriate mode of settlement of disputes of a private law character.[24] In addition, the expectation that Peace Operations will provide effective remedies to individuals who have suffered harm at their hands finds support in the form of more general rules of international law. The right of access to court, in particular, has been invoked to support this expectation and to cast a question mark over the scope of the immunities from jurisdiction traditionally enjoyed by Peace Operations and their

[22] International Law Association Study Group on Due Diligence in International Law, Second Report (2016), pp. 43–45, www.ila-hq.org/index.php/study-groups.

[23] Human Rights Due Diligence Policy on United Nations Support to non-United Nations Security Forces, UN Doc. A/67/775–S/2013/110 (2013), Annex.

[24] See also art. 340 Treaty on the Functioning of the European Union, OJ 2016 No. C202, 7 June 2016, p. 47, which directs the EU to 'make good any damage caused by its institutions or by its servants in the performance of their duties'.

members.[25] In so far as injury or damage caused by one element of a Peace Operation to another is concerned, it is common practice to regulate the settlement of such claims through mission-specific arrangements between the contributing parties.[26]

2. The claims procedures applicable in Peace Operations form the subject of another chapter[27] and will not be further discussed here.

19.3   Internationally wrongful acts committed in the context of Peace Operations give rise to international responsibility in accordance with international law. International responsibility is a legal form of accountability. There is an internationally wrongful act when conduct consisting of an action or omission is attributable to a State or international organisation under international law and constitutes a breach of an international obligation of that State or international organisation.

1. The third component of accountability in Peace Operations consists of international responsibility. It is a well-established principle that a breach of an international obligation by a State or by an international organisation engages its international responsibility. International responsibility is a form of legal accountability inherent in the concept of the rule of law at the international level.[28] The principle forms part of customary international law and has been codified by the International Law Commission in the Articles on State Responsibility (ARSIWA)[29] and the Articles on the Responsibility of International Organizations (ARIO).[30] Both instruments recognise that the international responsibility of a State or of an international organisation is engaged if two conditions

---

[25] In relation to the immunity of the UN under the Convention on the Privileges and Immunities of the United Nations (13 February 1946, in force 17 September 1946), 1 UNTS 15 and 90 UNTS 327 (Corr.), see *Georges* (n. 13). In relation to the immunity of members of military contingents participating in UN peacekeeping operations, see R. Burke, 'Status of Forces Deployed on UN Peacekeeping Operations: Jurisdictional Immunity', 16 *Journal of Conflict and Security Law* (2011), pp. 63–104.

[26] E.g. in the context of EU operations, see art. 3(5) Agreement between the European Union and New Zealand establishing a framework for the participation of New Zealand in European Union crisis management operations, OJ 2012 No. L160, 21 June 2012, p. 2.

[27] See Chapter 20.

[28] See J. Brunnée, 'International Legal Accountability Through the Lens of the Law of State Responsibility', 36 *Netherlands Yearbook of International Law* (2005), pp. 21–56.

[29] Articles on State Responsibility with Commentaries, in Report of the International Law Commission, Fifty-third Session, UN Doc. A/56/10 (2001), p. 59.

[30] Articles on the Responsibility of International Organizations with Commentaries, in Report of the International Law Commission, Sixty-third Session, UN Doc. A/66/10 (2011), p. 67.

are satisfied: conduct consisting of an action or omission is attributable to a State or international organisation and that conduct constitutes
a breach of an international obligation of that State or international
organisation.[31]

2. Legal personality is a precondition of legal responsibility.
International responsibility in Peace Operations therefore attaches only
to States and to those international organisations which are subjects
of international law. In principle, a Peace Operation itself may incur
responsibility directly under international law if it constitutes a subject of
international law. Although it is possible to endow Peace Operations with
separate international legal personality, this is not common in practice.
The Multinational Force and Observers (MFO), which was established
as an international organisation in its own right, offers one exception.[32]
Apart from such exceptional cases, Peace Operations are typically established either as part of the institutional structure of the international
organisation conducting the operation, and thus benefit from the legal
status and personality of the organisation itself,[33] or as self-standing
bodies enjoying whatever status is conferred upon them. There appears to
be no example in international practice, other than perhaps in relation to
the MFO, where a Peace Operation has incurred international responsibility directly. Rather, the acts and omissions of Peace Operations are normally attributed to the States or international organisations participating
in or conducting the operation.

3. Whether the activities undertaken by a Peace Operation are attributable to a State or an international organisation, and thus satisfy the
first element of an internationally wrongful act giving rise to international responsibility, is governed by the rules of attribution. Under
international law, States and international organisations are responsible
solely for their own conduct.[34] However, as legal entities they can act only

---

[31] Art. 2 ARSIWA (n. 29); art. 4 ARIO (n. 30).

[32] See arts. 2 and 3 Annex to the Protocol relating to the Establishment and Maintenance of a
Multinational Force and Observers (3 August 1981), 1335 UNTS 328; Israel–MFO Agreement
concerning the Authority of the Director-General of the MFO to enter into agreements with
States participating in the MFO (15 March 1982), 1336 UNTS 20. See R. C. R. Siekmann,
National Contingents in United Nations Peace-Keeping Forces (Martinus Nijhoff, 1991), p. 10;
M. Nash Leich, 'The Sinai Multinational Force and Observers', 76 *American Journal of
International Law* (1982), pp. 181–182.

[33] This has been the practice of the UN, starting with the UN Emergency Force (UNEF). See
Exchange of Letters constituting an Agreement concerning the Status of the United Nations
Emergency Force in Egypt (8 February 1957), 260 UNTS 62, para. 23.

[34] ARSIWA (n. 29), p. 80.

through natural or other legal persons.[35] The purpose of the rules of attribution is to determine what acts or omissions should be considered as conduct undertaken on behalf of a particular State or international organisation. In this respect, international practice recognises two basic paradigms.[36] The *institutional* paradigm holds that conduct performed in an official capacity by natural or legal persons possessing the status of officials or organs of a State or an international organisation under their internal law, and therefore forming part of their 'internal machinery',[37] should be attributed to that State or that international organisation.[38] By contrast, the *agency* paradigm states that the conduct of natural or legal persons not forming part of the institutional structure of a State or international organisation may nevertheless be attributed to the State or to the international organisation if the conduct in question was performed under its respective direction or control.[39] In addition to these paradigms, both ARSIWA and ARIO recognise certain other grounds for attributing conduct to a State or international organisation.[40] They also recognise that responsibility may arise in situations where States or international organisations are complicit in the wrongful conduct of others.[41]

4. Whether the activities of a Peace Operation constitute a breach of an international obligation owed by a State or by an international organisation, and thus satisfy the second element of an internationally wrongful act giving rise to international responsibility, depends on the content of the obligation in question. While the obligations of States do not raise any particular difficulties in this context, the obligations incumbent on international organisations do. It is widely accepted that, as subjects of international law, international organisations are bound by the applicable rules of customary international law, their founding instruments and any

---

[35] *German Settlers in Poland*, Advisory Opinion (1923), PCIJ Series B, No. 6, 22.

[36] *Application of the Convention on the Prevention and Punishment of the Crime of Genocide (Bosnia and Herzegovina v. Serbia and Montenegro)*, Judgment, ICJ Reports 2007, 15, para. 406. The language of paradigms is borrowed from T. Becker, *Terrorism and the State: Rethinking the Rules of State Responsibility* (Hart, 2006).

[37] Third Report on State Responsibility, by Mr Roberto Ago, Special Rapporteur, II(1) *Yearbook of the International Law Commission* (1971), p. 238.

[38] Art. 4 ARSIWA (n. 29); art. 6 ARIO (n. 30).

[39] Art. 8 ARSIWA (n. 29); art. 7 ARIO (n. 30).

[40] E.g. both instruments recognise that a State or international organisation could acknowledge or adopt the wrongful acts of third parties as their own: art. 11 ARSIWA (n. 29); art. 9 ARIO (n. 30).

[41] Arts. 14–17 and 58–62 ARIO (n. 30).

international agreements to which they are parties.[42] However, how and to what extent rules of conventional and customary international law originally developed by and for States apply to international organisations are often unclear.[43] While in some cases their founding instruments impose relatively detailed obligations on international organisations relevant to the conduct of Peace Operations, in other cases they do not.[44] Moreover, international organisations often are unable to become parties to key multi-lateral agreements, such as treaties on international humanitarian law (IHL),[45] which dramatically reduces the significance of these agreements as a source of treaty-based obligations for international organisations. Notwithstanding that such organisations remain subject to customary law-based obligations, these factors render the content and scope of the obligations that apply to international organisations in the conduct of Peace Operations uncertain in key respects. This contributes to an accountability deficit which should be mitigated by the international organisations concerned.[46] In some cases, international organisations have done so by declaring themselves bound by the relevant principles unilaterally.[47] However, even where the relevant standards are not formally applicable as a matter of law, they may still be invoked in support of other, non-legal forms of accountability. For example, in response to criticisms of the claims arrangements adopted for the United Nations Operation in the Congo (ONUC), the UN Secretary-General justified those arrangements with reference to 'the principles set forth in the international Conventions concerning the protection of the life and

---

[42] *Interpretation of the Agreement of 25 March 1951 between the WHO and Egypt*, Advisory Opinion, ICJ Reports 1980, 73, para. 37.

[43] With regard to international humanitarian law, see M. Zwanenburg, *Accountability in Peace Support Operations* (Martinus Nijhoff, 2005), pp. 131–208.

[44] Compare the relatively detailed provisions governing the conduct of EU crisis management operations under arts. 42–44 Treaty on European Union (EU Treaty), OJ 2016 No. C202, 7 June 2016, p. 13, with the well-known absence of any provisions expressly addressing the conduct of peace operations under the UN Charter.

[45] Accession to the four Geneva Conventions of 1949 (see Chapter 6, n. 4, for full details), for example, is reserved to 'Powers', that is States. However, occasionally special provision is made for the accession of international organisations. Art. 59(2) Convention for the Protection of Human Rights and Fundamental Freedoms (ECHR) (4 November 1950, in force 3 September 1953), ETS 5, as amended by Protocol No. 14 (in force 1 June 2010), permits the accession of the EU to the Convention.

[46] Compliance with international law contributes to the legitimacy of an international organisation's actions. See K. Daugirdas, 'Reputation and the Responsibility of International Organizations', 25 *European Journal of International Law* (2014), pp. 991–1018.

[47] E.g. UN, Secretary-General's Bulletin on the Observance by United Nations Forces of International Humanitarian Law, UN Doc. ST/SGB/1999/13 (1999).

property of civilian population during hostilities as well as by considerations of equity and humanity which the United Nations cannot ignore'.[48]

19.4   Conduct carried out in the context of Peace Operations may be attributed to more than one participating State or international organisation.

1. The fact that Peace Operations usually entail the participation of several States and one or more international organisation(s) raises the prospect that their acts and omissions may be attributed to more than one international legal person. The possibility of such multiple attribution arises for two main reasons. First, national contingents and officials placed at the disposal of an international organisation in the context of a Peace Operation do not lose their legal and institutional character as organs of their Sending State.[49] Were it otherwise, placing State organs and officials at the disposal of an international organisation would be tantamount to disbanding them or discharging them from national service. Second, because the organs and officials that are seconded to an international organisation retain their original legal and institutional status, Sending States continue to hold broad powers of control over them, even though they may undertake not to exercise some of these powers during the period of secondment.[50] Consequently, while Peace Operations and their constituent elements are linked to the international organisation conducting the operation through factual and, in some cases, institutional ties, those constituent elements will at the same time remain subject to certain institutional and factual bonds linking them to their Sending States. The possibility that the same conduct is attributable to more than one entity therefore cannot be discounted.

2. At present, the rules governing multiple attribution in Peace Operations are unsettled. In principle, it is admitted that the different rules of attribution are not mutually exclusive. The Commentary to ARIO thus acknowledges that 'dual or even multiple attribution of conduct cannot be excluded'.[51] Despite this admission, article 7 ARIO

---

[48] Letter dated 6 August 1965 from the Secretary-General addressed to the Acting Permanent Representative of the Union of Soviet Socialist Republics, UN Doc. S/6597 (1965).

[49] *Attorney-General v. Nissan*, House of Lords of the United Kingdom, Judgment of 11 February 1969, [1970] AC 179 (HL), 222.

[50] *Hasan Nuhanović v. the Netherlands*, Court of Appeal (Gerechtshof) of The Hague, the Netherlands, Judgment of 5 July 2011, ILDC 1742 (NL 2011), para. 5.10.

[51] ARIO (n. 30), p. 81.

expressly seeks to exclude or at least minimise the prospect of multiple attribution in the context of Peace Operations.[52] This provision stipulates that '[t]he conduct of an organ of a State or an organ or agent of an international organization that is placed at the disposal of another international organization shall be considered under international law an act of the latter organization if the organization exercises effective control over that conduct'. As the Commentary to ARIO explains, in the context of Peace Operations the role of the effective control test laid down in article 7 ARIO is to determine to which entity, the Sending State or the receiving organisation, the conduct of a national contingent or official should be attributed. The effect of article 7 ARIO is that it prioritises the effective control test in the context of Peace Operations.[53] This not only contradicts the notion of multiple attribution, since the declared purpose of article 7 ARIO is to allocate responsibility to only one of the implicated parties, but it also favours the agency paradigm of attribution over the institutional paradigm. Moreover, it overlooks the existence of State practice which seeks to attribute the conduct of Peace Operations on different grounds. For example, domestic courts sometimes have attributed the conduct of national contingents participating in Peace Operations to the organisation conducting the operation on the basis that the contingents were not acting in the name of their TCC, but were exercising the powers or competences of the organisation concerned.[54] Similar arguments have also been made by TCCs.[55] For these reasons it is doubtful whether ARIO's attempt to prescribe a single test of attribution applicable to all types of Peace Operation in the form of article 7 ARIO reflects the law as it currently stands. While the test of effective control is appropriate in some circumstances, in others priority should be given to the institutional paradigm of attribution, as detailed in Rules 19.5 and 19.6.

3. Since the application of the rules of attribution in Peace Operations remains unsettled, States and international organisations are well advised to make use of mission-specific agreements to define their respective roles in ensuring accountability in particular operations in express terms.

---

[52] *Ibid.*, pp. 84–85.
[53] See A. Sari, 'UN Peacekeeping Operations and Article 7 DARIO: The Missing Link', 9 *International Organizations Law Review* (2012), pp. 77–85.
[54] *N.K. v. Austria*, Superior Provincial Court (Oberlandesgericht) of Vienna, Austria, Judgment of 26 February 1979, 77 ILR (1979) 470, 472; *Anonymous v. German Federal Government (Kunduz Tankers Case)*, Administrative Court (Verwaltungsgericht) of Cologne, Germany, Judgment of 9 February 2012, ILDC 1858 (DE 2012), paras. 70–74.
[55] *Behrami* (n. 7), paras. 97–98 (Denmark), 104 (Germany) and 116 (United Kingdom).

For example, the model text used by the UN to negotiate participation agreements with TCCs specifies in some detail the respective duties of the UN and TCCs in upholding discipline among members of national contingents, the conduct of investigations into allegations of misconduct and the exercise of jurisdiction in such cases.[56] The model text also details their respective duties in settling claims by third parties.[57] Although agreements of this nature bind only the parties to them, they may be regarded as lex specialis arrangements which affect the general rules governing the allocation of responsibility between the UN and TCCs.[58] In any case, even if such agreements do not override the general rules of attribution, they are nevertheless likely to channel calls for accountability and thus affect its discharge in practice. As such, they provide a mechanism for States and international organisations to share responsibility even in the absence of authoritative rules and guidance on the concept of multiple attribution in general international law.

19.5   States and international organisations participating in Peace Operations are responsible for the conduct of their organs carried out on their behalf.

1. ARSIWA and ARIO recognise that States and international organisations are responsible for the conduct of their own organs in the performance of their official functions.[59] Whether or not an entity or person holds the status of an organ of a State or an international organisation must be determined with reference to the domestic law of the State and the internal law of the international organisation in question. The position that the organ holds within the institutional hierarchy of the State or organisation concerned is immaterial for the purposes of this Rule.

2. The present Rule applies to all organs acting on behalf of their parent State or international organisation during their participation in a Peace Operation. For example, the acts of officials of an international organisation deployed in the field are clearly attributable to the latter. In principle, the Rule also applies to organs made available by one State or international organisation to another State or international organisation

---

[56] Art. 7 Model Memorandum of Understanding between the United Nations and [participating State] contributing resources to [the United Nations Peacekeeping Operation], UNGA Res. 61/267 (2007); and UN Doc. A/C.5/69/18 (2014).
[57] *Ibid.*, art. 9.
[58] Art. 55 ARSIWA (n. 29); art. 64 ARIO (n. 30).
[59] Art. 4 ARSIWA (n. 29); art. 6 ARIO (n. 30).

in the context of a Peace Operation, given that such organs retain their formal legal and institutional status as organs of their parent State or international organisation during their secondment. However, matters are complicated in two respects. First, national contingents made available by a State to an international organisation are sometimes formally incorporated into the institutional structure of the organisation concerned, as in the practice of the UN.[60] As a result, they enjoy a dual institutional status as an organ of their parent State and as an organ of the beneficiary international organisation. In such cases, Rule 19.6 applies. Second, during its secondment, the seconded organ may act under the effective control or directions of the beneficiary State or international organisation. In this case, Rule 19.7 applies. However, even under these circumstances, the seconded organ will retain its legal and institutional links with its parent State or international organisation and will almost invariably act under its control at least in certain respects and for certain purposes.

19.6   International organisations are responsible for the internationally wrongful acts of Peace Operations which constitute organs of that organisation.

1. As noted earlier, international organisations conducting Peace Operations sometimes establish these operations as part of their institutional structure. Beginning with the United Nations Emergency Force (UNEF) created in 1956, "classic" UN peacekeeping operations have been established as subsidiary organs of the General Assembly and, more frequently, the Security Council. In the exchange of letters between the UN and Egypt concerning the legal status of UNEF in Egypt, the Secretary-General referred to UNEF 'as an organ of the General Assembly of the United Nations established in accordance with Article 22 of the Charter',[61] which entitles the General Assembly to 'establish such subsidiary organs as it deems necessary for the performance of its functions'. This precedent has been followed in subsequent UN Peace Operations, which too were established as subsidiary organs

---

[60] It should be emphasised that this practice is not universal. It is not shared, for example, by NATO.
[61] UNEF Exchange of Letters (n. 33). See also Regulations for the United Nations Emergency Force, UN Doc. ST/SGB/UNEF/1 (1957), reprinted as Annex II to Exchange of Letters (with Annexes) constituting an Agreement concerning the Service with the United Nations Emergency Force of National Contingent provided by the Government of Finland (27 June 1957), 271 UNTS 136.

of either the General Assembly or the Security Council.[62] Occasionally, this model has been adopted by other international organisations as well, such as the Arab League.[63] The formal integration of national contingents into the institutional structure of an international organisation, coupled with an effective transfer of authority by the TCCs to the organisation, creates a rebuttable presumption that the contingents in question act in an international capacity on behalf of the organisation and that their activities are therefore attributable to the latter. This presumption may be rebutted to the extent that national contingents act under the effective control of their parent State.

2. As organs of the international organisation establishing them, these Peace Operations benefit from the legal status of their parent organisation and share its international obligations. National contingents forming part of such Peace Operations become an integral part of the international organisation in question. Consequently, national contingents deployed in such operations enjoy a dual status: they retain their legal position as organs of their parent State, but they also assume the legal and institutional status of the international organisation. Article 7 ARIO attempts to resolve this dilemma by ignoring these legal and institutional links altogether in favour of applying the effective control test pursuant to the agency paradigm. For the reasons set out earlier, this does not reflect international law and practice as it currently stands. A more appropriate approach is to proceed on the basis that the integration of a national contingent into the institutional structure of an international organisation, coupled with the effective transfer of operational control over the contingent by the parent State to the organisation, triggers a presumption that

---

[62] This has been recognised in express terms in the applicable SOFAs, e.g. Exchange of Letters constituting an Agreement concerning the Status of the United Nations Peace-Keeping Force in Cyprus (31 March 1964), 492 UNTS 57, para. 23; art. IV(14) Agreement on the Status of the UN Protection Force in Bosnia and Herzegovina (15 May 1993), 1722 UNTS 77; art. IV(15) Agreement between the UN and the Government of the Central African Republic on the Status of the UN Mission in the Central African Republic (MINURCA) (8 May 1998), 2015 UNTS 734; art. 1(1) Memorandum of Understanding between the UN and the Government of the Republic of Uganda concerning the Activities of the UN Mission in the Democratic Republic of the Congo (8 August 2003), 2221 UNTS 298. See also the applicable force regulations, e.g. art. 6 Regulations for the UN Force in the Congo (ONUC), UN Doc. ST/SGB/UNOC/1 (1963); art. 6 Regulations for the United Nations Force in Cyprus (UNFICYP), UN Doc. ST/SGB/UNFICYP/1 (1964), reprinted as Annex II of Exchange of Letters (with Annexes) constituting an Agreement concerning the Services with the UN Peace-Keeping Force in Cyprus (UNFICYP) of the National Contingent provided by the Government of Canada (21 February 1966), 555 UNTS 119.

[63] Arab League Force Status of Forces Agreement, UN Doc. S/5007 (1961); also K. Schmalenbach, *Die Haftung internationaler Organisationen im Rahmen von Militäreinsätzen und Territorialverwaltungen* (Peter Lang, 2004), p. 517.

the contingent carries out its official functions on behalf of the beneficiary organisation during the period of the transfer of authority and therefore engages the organisation's responsibility. In the UN's practice, this presumption is reflected in the provisions of the 1990 UN Model SOFA, which describes the nature of UN peacekeeping operations and the duties of its members as being international in character.[64] The conduct of national contingents participating in UN Peace Operations is therefore caught by the general rule of attribution set out in article 6 ARIO, whereby the 'conduct of an organ or agent of an international organization in the performance of functions of that organ or agent shall be considered an act of that organization under international law'. Accordingly, the UN has consistently recognised that the wrongful conduct of members of its Peace Operations, including members of national contingents, is attributable to the Organisation and engages its international responsibility.[65] The presumption may be rebutted, however, if the parent State interferes with the Organisation's exercise of control.[66] In such cases, the acts of the national contingent must be attributed with reference to the effective control test pursuant to Rule 19.7.

3. Once a presumption has arisen that a national contingent is acting in an international capacity on behalf of an international organisation, responsibility for acts which are ultra vires the contingent's international mandate should, in principle, lie with the international organisation concerned, unless those acts were carried out under the control or direction of the Sending State. However, practice in this area is not consistent.[67]

4. Not all international organisations follow the approach of the UN, which establishes Peace Operations as part of its institutional structure. A case in point is the practice of the EU. While the EU benefits from an express capacity to use civilian and military assets 'on missions outside the Union for peace-keeping, conflict prevention and strengthening

---

[64] UN Model SOFA (n. 10), paras. 6–7.
[65] Financing of the United Nations Protection Force, the United Nations Confidence Restoration Operation in Croatia, the United Nations Preventive Deployment Force and the United Nations Peace Forces Headquarters: Report of the Secretary-General, UN Doc. A/51/389 (1996), para. 8.
[66] E.g. *Nuhanović* (n. 50), paras. 5.11–5.20. For a similar rebuttal in the context of EU and NATO operations, see *Anonymous* v. *German Federal Government (Arrest of Pirates Case)*, Administrative Court (Verwaltungsgericht) of Cologne, Germany, Judgment of 11 November 2011, ILDC 1808 (DE 2011), paras. 51–56, and *Serdar Mohammed* v. *Ministry of Defence*, High Court of Justice of England and Wales, Judgment of 2 May 2014, [2014] EWHC 1369 (QB), paras. 180–187, respectively.
[67] See Schmalenbach (n. 63), pp. 253–262.

international security in accordance with the principles of the United Nations Charter',[68] none of the legal acts launching such missions explicitly describes them as organs of the Council of the EU or otherwise formally incorporates them into the institutional structure of the EU.[69] In the absence of such formal incorporation, the activities of a Peace Operation may not be attributed to the international organisation conducting it pursuant to article 6 ARIO, unless the operation qualifies as a de facto organ of that organisation. The International Court of Justice has held that persons, groups of persons or entities not holding the status of a formal State organ may be equated with one of its organs for the purposes of international responsibility provided that they act in "complete dependence" on that State so that, ultimately, they are merely its instrument.[70] Applying this to international organisations, a Peace Operation, its members and constituent parts may be considered to be a de facto organ of an international organisation provided that they act in complete dependence on the latter. However, the threshold of dependence is high, as it requires proof of a particularly great degree of control.[71] It cannot be assumed to have been attained lightly.

5. In the case of Peace Operations which are not formally incorporated into the institutional structure of an international organisation, no presumption arises that their conduct is attributable to the organisation in question in line with the present Rule. On the contrary, because national contingents and officials made available by TCCs to an international organisation retain their legal and institutional status as organs of their parent State, the presumption must be that their conduct continues to engage the responsibility of their Sending State in accordance with article 4 ARSIWA. However, this presumption too is rebuttable should the national contingents or officials act pursuant to the control or direction of another participating State or international organisation. In such instances, attribution depends on the effective control test in line with Rule 19.7.

---

[68] Art. 42 EU Treaty (n. 44).

[69] See A. Sari and R. A. Wessel, 'International Responsibility for EU Military Operations: Finding the EU's Place in the Global Accountability Regime', in B. Van Vooren, S. Blockmans and J. Wouters (eds.), *The EU's Role in Global Governance: The Legal Dimension* (Oxford University Press, 2013), pp. 126–141.

[70] *Military and Paramilitary Activities in and against Nicaragua (Nicaragua v. United States of America)*, Merits, ICJ Reports 1986, 14, para. 109; *Genocide* (n. 36).

[71] *Genocide* (n. 36), para. 393.

19.7   States or international organisations are responsible for internationally wrongful acts committed by individuals or entities acting under their effective control or direction.

1. The present Rule reflects the agency paradigm of attribution. In Peace Operations, its application is triggered in a number of distinct circumstances. First, it applies to individuals or entities which act on behalf of a State or international organisation without necessarily being part of its institutional machinery. For example, the acts of private contractors or locally employed individuals may engage the responsibility of the State or international organisation which hired them, provided that the requisite level of control is met. Second, the Rule applies where an organ of one State or international organisation acts under the effective control or direction of another State or international organisation. For instance, State officials seconded or otherwise made available to an international organisation for the purposes of a Peace Operation without being formally integrated into its institutional structure may engage the responsibility of the beneficiary organisation, provided they act under its effective control or direction. Third, the Rule also applies in situations where national contingents formally incorporated into an international organisation nevertheless act under the effective control of their parent State and thus outside the international chain of command.[72] Under such circumstances, the presumption that their conduct should be attributed to the beneficiary organisation is rebutted, as detailed in the Commentary to Rule 19.6.

2. In recent years, certain disagreements have come to light regarding the degree of control necessary to trigger the application of this Rule. As is well known, in the *Nicaragua* case, the ICJ held that the acts of third parties are attributable to a State provided that the latter exercises 'effective control' over the commission of those acts.[73] This threshold of control was considered too high by the International Criminal Tribunal for the former Yugoslavia (ICTY), which in the *Tadić* case preferred the lower standard of 'overall control'.[74] In the *Behrami* case, the European Court of Human Rights too adopted a lower threshold in the form of the 'ultimate authority and control' test.[75] However, the ICJ re-affirmed

---

[72] *Nuhanović* (n. 50).
[73] *Nicaragua* (n. 70), para. 115.
[74] *The Prosecutor* v. *Tadić*, Judgment, IT-94-1-A, Appeals Chamber, 15 July 1999, para. 120.
[75] *Behrami* (n. 7), para. 133.

the effective control test as the governing standard in the *Genocide* case.[76] This is also the standard adopted in article 7 ARIO and the one favoured by the majority of commentators.[77] Although it never formally overruled *Behrami*, the ECtHR subsequently seemed to acknowledge this higher threshold in the case of *Al-Jedda*.[78] Accordingly, it is safe to regard the effective control test as the prevailing standard under the agency paradigm of attribution.

3. Nevertheless, the application of the effective control test in the context of Peace Operations raises certain difficulties, which so far remain unresolved. The first of these concerns the nature of the control required. In particular, it is unclear whether a relationship of effective control must be established with reference to factual criteria alone (actual control) or whether normative relations may also be taken into account (authority to control). In the *Nuhanović* case, the Dutch Court of Appeal adopted the latter position, holding that the Dutch government enjoyed the power to issue instructions to its armed forces to prevent the internationally wrongful act forming the subject matter of the proceedings.[79] This raises a second difficulty. Since States retain "full command" over their armed forces at all times, even in cases where they place them at the disposal of other States or international organisations, they retain at least a latent power of control over their troops. This raises the question whether full command should be considered as a sufficient link for the purposes of attributing the conduct of national contingents to their parent State. If the answer is yes, then the acts of national contingents in multi-national Peace Operations would always be attributable to the respective TCC. States would incur responsibility for the wrongful conduct of their forces even in circumstances where those troops in fact act under the effective control of another actor. This does not reflect existing international practice and would stretch accountability too far. Moreover, such a broad principle of attribution might encourage States to exercise constant control over their armed forces placed at the disposal of other States or international

---

[76] *Genocide* (n. 36), para. 406.

[77] E.g. P. Bodeau-Livinec, G. P. Buzzini and S. Villalpando, 'Behrami & Behrami v. France; Saramati v. France, Germany & Norway', 102 *American Journal of International Law* (2008), pp. 327–330; A. Sari, 'Jurisdiction and International Responsibility in Peace Support Operations: The Behrami and Saramati Cases', 8 *Human Rights Law Review* (2008), p. 164; M. Milanović and T. Papić, 'As Bad as It Gets: The European Court of Human Rights's Behrami and Saramati Decision and General International Law', 58 *International and Comparative Law Quarterly* (2009), pp. 281–289.

[78] *Al-Jedda* v. *the United Kingdom*, Application No. 27021/08, Judgment of 7 July 2011 [GC], para. 84.

[79] *Nuhanović* (n. 50), para. 5.18.

organisations in order to ensure that they do not engage in internationally wrongful conduct. While this might be welcome from the perspective of accountability, it would almost certainly undermine the ability of
the beneficiary State or international organisation to exercise meaningful
operational control over any foreign forces placed at its disposal. This
would thwart the creation of an effective international chain of command
and thus jeopardise the very notion of multi-national military operations.
This, in turn, exposes a third difficulty, which concerns the complexity of the command and control arrangements typically found in Peace
Operations (see Chapter 4.2). TCCs and international organisations
exercise control in different domains and do so in parallel. For example,
an international organisation may exercise operational control over troops
assigned to it, but disciplinary authority and criminal jurisdiction remain
with their respective TCC. This underlines the difficulty in attempt-
ing to disentangle, through the effective control test, what in reality is a
combined exercise of control.

20

Third Party Claims

20.1   Third parties who suffer personal injury or property damage due to any wrongful acts of Peace Forces are entitled to compensation. The right to a remedy is a recognised norm of customary international law. This right is, however, regulated by relevant treaties and may be further restricted by Status of Forces Agreements between the Host State and the States or international organisation deploying the Peace Forces.

1.   It is a general principle of law, whatever the community, that a legal entity is responsible for the proximate injuries its acts may cause.[1] The principle is fundamental in the regulation of private entities, and jurisprudence exhibits a clear trend towards the increasing subjection of governments to this same rule of law, resulting in a well-developed area of civil liability law of States in many countries.[2] The concept of international organisations incurring tort responsibility has been recognised by such organisations,[3] by judicial decisions and by past practice.

---

[1] See M. H. Arsanjani, 'Claims Against International Organizations: *Quis Custodiet Ipsos Custodes*', 7 *Yale Journal of World Public Order* (1981), p. 131; A. Tunc, 'Introduction to Torts', 11 *International Encyclopedia of Comparative Law* (1983), Chapter 1; S. C. Neff (ed.), *Hugo Grotius On the Law of War and Peace* (Cambridge University Press, 2012), Book 2, Chapter 17 (on damages caused through injury and the obligation arising therefrom); J. Hasanbasic, 'Liability in Peacekeeping Missions: A Civil Cause of Action for The Mothers of Srebrenica against the Dutch Government and the United Nations', 29 *Emory International Law Review* (2014), pp. 415–449. See also T. R. Phillips, 'The Constitutional Right to a Remedy', 78 *NYU Law Review* (2003), pp. 1321–1322.

[2] D. Shelton, *Remedies in International Human Rights Law*, 2nd edn (Oxford University Press, 2005), p. 22; e.g. The US Federal Tort Claims Act and the Foreign Claims Acts, 10 USC para. 2734 (1942); J. M. Prescott, 'Claims', in D. Fleck (ed.), *The Handbook of the Law of Visiting Forces* (Oxford University Press, 2001), p. 166; W. M. Reisman and R. D. Sloane, 'The Incident at Cavalese and Strategic Compensation', 94 *American Journal of International Law* (2000), p. 514.

[3] The constituent instruments of some international organisations recognise tort responsibility. See Section 29 Convention on the Privileges and Immunities of the United Nations (13 February 1946, in force 17 September 1946), 1 UNTS 15 and 90 UNTS 327 (Corr.). See also art. 340(2) Treaty on the Functioning of the European Union (TFEU), OJ 2016 No. C202, 7 June 2016, p. 47: 'in the

On account of the widespread compensation practice of international organisations in connection with military operations, it can be concluded that the principal obligation to compensate harmful acts attributable to the relevant organisation – provided that the facts of the case fulfil certain conditions (see Rules 20.3 and 20.4) – is a general principle of liability law of international organisations.[4]

2. When tortious liability is engaged, compensation should be paid with a view to redressing the situation, and restoring it, to the extent possible, to what it had been prior to the occurrence of the damage.[5] The right to a remedy is well established. It is even a norm of customary international law.[6] It includes both the procedural right of effective access and the substantive right to a remedy.[7] Remedies can be defined as means by which the violation is prevented, redressed or compensated,[8] and include judicial remedies, such as civil actions.[9] International organisations have

---

case of non-contractual liability, the Union shall, in accordance with the general principles common to the laws of the Member States, make good any damage caused by its institutions or by its servants in the performance of their duties'. The UN considers the financial and temporary limitations on its liability with regard to third parties as an exception to the general principle that when tortious liability is engaged compensation should be paid with a view to redressing the situation and restoring it to what it had been prior to the occurrence of the damage. See Administrative and Budgetary Aspects of the Financing of the UN Peacekeeping Operations: Report of the Secretary-General, UN Doc. A/51/389 (1996).

[4] K. Schmalenbach, 'Third Party Liability of International Organizations: A Study on Claim Settlement in the Course of Military Operations and International Administrations', 10 *International Peacekeeping: The Yearbook of International Peace Operations* (2006), pp. 33–51.

[5] This legal obligation to provide remedial mechanisms to States and non-State entities whose interests have been adversely affected applies to States and international organisations. See K. Wellens, *Remedies Against International Organizations* (Cambridge University Press, 2002), pp. 169–170.

[6] *Ibid.*, p. 17; Shelton (n. 2), p. 182. See *Case concerning the Factory at Chorzów (Claim for Indemnity) (Germany v. Poland)*, Judgment (1928), Merits, PCIJ Series A, No. 17, 47; *Military and Paramilitary Activities in and against Nicaragua (Nicaragua v. United States of America)*, Merits, ICJ Reports 1986, 14, 114; *Corfu Channel Case (the United Kingdom v. Albania)*, Judgment, ICJ Reports 1949, 4; *Reparation for Injuries Suffered in the Service of the United Nations*, Advisory Opinion, ICJ Reports 1949, 174, 184; *Interpretation of Peace Treaties with Bulgaria, Hungary and Romania (second phase)*, Advisory Opinion, ICJ Reports 1950, 221, 228. See also art. 1 Articles on State Responsibility with Commentaries, in Report of the International Law Commission, Fifty-third Session, UN Doc. A/56/10 (2001) (ARSIWA): 'Every internationally wrongful act of a State entails the international responsibility of that State.'

[7] Shelton (n. 2), pp. 14–15.

[8] *Black's Law Dictionary*, 9th edn (Thomson Reuters, 2009), pp. 1407–1408. The concept here is thus used in a broad sense and encompasses both procedural and substantive remedies, the former referring to the processes by which claims are heard and decided and the latter to the awarded relief or other outcome of the proceedings. See Shelton (n. 2), p. 7.

[9] See Srebrenica cases before Dutch courts, *The Netherlands v. Hasan Nuhanović*, Supreme Court (Hoge Raad) of the Netherlands, Judgment of 6 September 2013, 53 ILM (2014) 516; *Hasan Nuhanović v. the Netherlands*, Court of Appeal (Gerechtshof) of The Hague, the Netherlands, Judgment of 5 July 2011, ILDC 1742 (NL 2011). See also the cases and complaints concerning cholera in Haiti: *Georges v. United Nations*, US Court of Appeals for the Second Circuit, Class

become important players on the international scene, whose acts or omissions affect individuals, companies and States. The types of claim arising from Peace Operations are varied, including: breaches of contract, torts, claims regarding non-performance of treaty obligations, ultra vires acts[10] or labour relations. "Third party claims" in this chapter refers to tort claims of individuals with no contractual relationship to the international organisation or the Troop Contributing Countries (TCCs) and may include civil claims for compensation arising from acts of members of a Peace Force within a mission area.[11] Domestic nuances may be attached to the terminology describing such claims but tort claims are understood as synonymous with civil actions for damages arising from wrongful or negligent conduct.[12] Tort claims may engage either the liability or the responsibility of the international organisation or the TCC, with the former normally referring to damages caused by lawful activities and the latter to damages caused by unlawful conduct or breaches of obligations, whether domestic or international.[13]

3. In Peace Operations, the right to compensation is recognised and implemented in the form of specific claims procedures that are set out in the Status of Forces Agreement (SOFA) with the Host State and may be reflected in other applicable international agreements.[14] In principle, international organisations are responsible for damages caused by their wrongful acts. However, in administering its claim procedures, the international organisation can establish its own procedures within the limits of its obligations under international law.[15] It can transfer responsibility

---

Action Complaint, No. 15-455-cv, Judgment of 18 August 2016, 2015 WL 129657 (SDNY, 2015); *Laventure* v. *United Nations*, US District Court of the Eastern District of New York, Class Action Complaint, No. 14-CV-1611 (EDNY, filed 11 March 2014), www.phaionline.org/downloads/Laventure_Complaint.pdf. In the latter case, the US Government filed a Statement of Interests on 24 May 2017, which was followed by an opposing memorandum by the plaintiff on 23 June 2017. Both documents are available at http://opiniojuris.org/2017/06/29/un-faces-a-second-cholera-challenge-in-new-york-courts.

[10] An unauthorised act while on duty sometimes compensated ex gratia depending on the circumstances.

[11] Review of the Efficiency of the Administrative and Financial Functioning of the United Nations: Report of the Secretary-General, UN Doc. A/C.5/49/65 (1995), paras. 15–21.

[12] *Black's Law Dictionary* (n. 8), p. 1626.

[13] ARSIWA (n. 6), General Commentary, para. 4(c).

[14] In the case of the UN, this would include, principally, the UN Privileges and Immunities Convention (n. 3).

[15] For the UN, the modalities proposed for establishing these limitations in a legally binding manner are a General Assembly resolution, a liability clause in the SOFA and the terms of reference of the local claims review boards. They would, respectively, provide for a legislative authority for limiting the liability of the Organisation, a consensual basis for applying limited liability in the relationship between the Organisation and Host States, and a basis for the jurisdiction of the local claims

for settling claims to its Member States, to a judicial standing claims commission or to an arbitration court.[16]

4. The Host State normally agrees that the liability of the peacekeepers will be limited, that there are financial and temporal limitations in settling claims and that in some cases, such as damage attributable to operational necessity, no liability is assumed (see Rule 20.4). If a claimant has not received full reparation, he can turn to the Host State to recover the remaining compensation only to the extent the Host State is required under its laws to provide such additional compensation. If the claim was rejected by the international organisation or the relevant TCC, the only remaining recourses for the claimant are to persuade his State to take his claim to the diplomatic level,[17] to introduce his claim in national courts of the TCC or, if the factual circumstances support this, to turn to international human rights bodies. In the case of the EU, it may be possible to bring claims before the courts of EU Member States or before the EU Court of Justice (CJEU), depending on the circumstances.[18]

5. It should also be noted that claims settlement procedures and practices are specific to each organisation and, accordingly, they do not automatically form an independent source of legal obligation that is binding for all international organisations that undertake international military operations.[19]

---

review boards in claims submitted by individuals against the Organisation. See Administrative and Budgetary Report (n. 3).

[16] Schmalenbach (n. 4), p. 50. In some instances, States in whose territory international organisations are conducting operations will be responsible for claims lodged against the international organisation, e.g. art. VI, para. 1 of UNICEF's Model Agreement provides: 'The Government [in whose territory a plan is executed] shall assume, subject to the provisions of this Article, responsibility in respect of claims resulting from the execution of Plan of Operations within the territory'; UNICEF Field Manual (1961), vol. II, pt. IV-2, Appendix A, as summarized in Arsanjani (n. 1). A like transfer of responsibility seems unlikely in peacekeeping operations.

[17] Schmalenbach (n. 4), p. 43.

[18] The Court of Justice of the European Union (CJEU) is in principle not competent in relation to EU Peace Operations (see art. 24 Treaty on European Union, OJ 2016 No. C202, 7 June 2016, p. 13, and art. 275 TFEU (n. 3)) but the Court has nevertheless ruled that it is competent in relation to at least some aspects of civilian EU Peace Operations, in particular some staff and procurement matters. See Case C-439/13 P, *Elitaliana* v. *Eulex Kosovo*, Judgment of the Court (Fifth Chamber) of 12 November 2015, ECLI:EU:C:2015:753; Case C-455/14 P, *H* v. *Council and Commission*, Judgment of the Court (Grand Chamber) of 19 July 2016, ECLI:EU:C:2016:569. Furthermore, pursuant to art. 274 TFEU (n. 3), '[s]ave where jurisdiction is conferred on the Court of Justice of the European Union by the Treaties, disputes to which the Union is a party shall not on that ground be excluded from the jurisdiction of the courts or tribunals of the Member States'. Therefore, where the CJEU is not competent, the EU could not invoke immunity from jurisdiction before the courts of its Member States.

[19] Schmalenbach (n. 4), p. 51.

20.2   Harm caused by Peace Operations may arise from breaches of Host State law and/or international law. Breaches of international law may give rise to international responsibility, but generally this cannot be invoked by private parties directly against a foreign State. Breaches of Host State law may, in principle, be invoked by private parties. Jurisdictional immunities of international organisations and Sending States may preclude proceedings against them unless immunity is waived in a particular case. Therefore, alternative claims mechanisms may be required.

1. International responsibility concerns the consequences of breaches of international law owed to one or several States, to the international community as a whole, to international organisations or to an individual or group of individuals (see Chapter 19). The principles governing the responsibility of international organisations have been codified by the International Law Commission (ILC) in the Articles on the Responsibility of International Organizations (ARIO) but the rules of attribution are still evolving.[20] The impact of the ARIO rules on the case of a private claimant against an international organisation or Sending State is, however, limited.[21] First, the ILC explicitly outlined that the scope of obligations to pay full reparation does not cover the consequences of breaches committed by Peace Forces with regard to individuals. While it is true that a Sending State or international organisation may commit a breach of an international obligation owed to a private individual in the Host State (and thereby commit an internationally wrongful act), the enforceability of responsibility towards an individual is not regulated by ARIO.[22] That private individual is generally not able

---

[20] Articles on the Responsibility of International Organizations with Commentaries, in Report of the International Law Commission, Sixty-third Session, UN Doc. A/66/10 (2011), p. 54. See A. Sari and R. A. Wessel, 'International Responsibility for EU Military Operations: Finding the EU's Place in the Global Accountability Regime', in B. Van Vooren, S. Blockmans and J. Wouters (eds.), *The EU's Role in Global Governance: The Legal Dimension* (Oxford University Press, 2013), p. 140: 'We have suggested that the way in which the ILC purports to apply the rules on the allocation of responsibility to peace operations is too narrow. By focusing exclusively on factual control as a ground for attribution, the Commentary to [ARIO] deliberately disregards the institutional and legal ties which may exist between national contingents and international organizations.'

[21] See Schmalenbach (n. 4), p. 34; K. Lundahl, 'The United Nations and the Remedy Gap: The Haiti Cholera Dispute', 88 *Die Friedens-Warte* (2013), pp. 77–117.

[22] Part Two of ARIO (n. 20) (i.e. arts. 3–27, dealing with, inter alia, attribution and breach) applies irrespective of the nature of the entity or person to whom the obligation is owed. Parts Three (i.e. arts. 28–42, dealing with the content of responsibility) and Four (i.e. arts. 43–57 on

to invoke that breach directly as a matter of international law because, by and large, international responsibility may be invoked only by States or international organisations.[23] However, there may be cases where individuals can directly invoke a breach of international law, in particular where it concerns a breach of an obligation under a human rights treaty.[24] In other situations the Host State may take up the matter as a diplomatic claim or, if the rules on invoking responsibility permit, may invoke the Sending State's or international organisation's responsibility itself. In so far as a duty to provide effective remedies exists under international law, it cannot be excluded that a failure of a Sending State or international organisation to settle claims brought by individuals against it may engage its international responsibility for failing to offer an effective remedy. Second, the ARIO rules do not clarify how the specific rules governing, for instance, the responsibility for UN peacekeepers (including under the SOFA) ought to be interpreted. Third, the ILC said nothing about the primary rules to which international organisations are subject – nothing about whether, for instance, the United Nations needs to accord "effective remedies" or to respect either domestic private law or human rights.[25]

2. Peacekeeping activities are carried out with the consent of the Host State. The law of the Host State governs the military and civilian personnel for the duration of their stay. Wrongful acts primarily create a claim for the injured party under the Host State's national law of torts. Obligations arising therefrom can be owed by and towards any legal person recognised in the Host State's legal system.[26] However, some of the

---

implementation) of ARIO (n. 20), however, have a more limited scope, as they apply only to responsibility owed towards other organisations, States or the international community as a whole, but not towards individuals. See Commentary to art. 33 ARIO (n. 20), in particular paras. 4 and 5: '(4) While the scope of Part Three is limited … this does not mean that obligations entailed by an internationally wrongful act do not arise towards persons or entities other than States and international organizations … (5) With regard to the international responsibility of international organizations, one significant area in which rights accrue to persons other than States or organizations is that of breaches by international organizations of their obligations under international law concerning employment. Another area is that of breaches committed by peacekeeping forces and affecting individuals. The consequences of these breaches with regard to individuals … are not covered by the present draft articles.' See also Schmalenbach (n. 4), p. 34.

[23] M. Zwanenburg, *Accountability in Peace Support Operations* (Martinus Nijhoff, 2005), p. 257; Wellens (n. 5), p. 38; Schmalenbach (n. 4), pp. 34, 40.

[24] This may be before an international human rights body in those cases where the treaty concerned provides for an individual complaints mechanism or before domestic courts in case the provision at issue can be directly invoked by an individual under the domestic law of the State concerned.

[25] J. Alvarez, 'The United Nations in the Time of Cholera', 108 *AJIL Unbound* (2014), pp. 22–29.

[26] It is noted in this context that international organisations may enjoy both international legal personality and domestic legal personality. See J. Klabbers, *An Introduction to International Institutional Law*, 2nd edn (Cambridge University Press, 2009), pp. 38–52.

principles of international responsibility may become applicable under Host State law.[27] The immunities granted to States and their organs in connection with official acts prevent individual claimants from taking their claims to the courts of their Host State. To overcome this procedural bar, many privileges and immunities instruments contain express obligations for international organisations to make available 'appropriate modes of settlement of disputes arising out of contracts or other disputes of a private law character'.[28]

3. Although individuals lack standing to bring claims invoking international responsibility and do not directly derive rights from international agreements, it is not clear how this impacts the characterisation of the claim where breaches of obligations under both legal orders are invoked. The majority view appears to be that, in cases of tortious liability, national law including national public law applies unless its application is specifically excluded.[29] In implementing their obligation to provide for 'appropriate modes of settlement of disputes of a private law character', the UN local claims review boards have traditionally dealt with claims related to personal injuries or property damage caused by peacekeepers. Considering further that the UN recognises its liability in compensation for violations of international humanitarian law (IHL) committed by members of UN forces,[30] the characterisation of the applicable law as private or public, national or international, or a combination thereof does not appear to be decisive for determining the private law nature of the claim and by extension its receivability. There is no definition of private law claims in

---

[27] ARIO (n. 20), Commentary to art. 1, para. 3, p. 69: 'An international organization's responsibility may be asserted under different systems of law. Before a national court, a natural or legal person will probably invoke the organisation's responsibility or liability under some municipal law. The reference in paragraph 1 of article 1 and throughout the draft articles to international responsibility makes it clear that the draft articles only take the perspective of international law and consider whether an international organization is responsible under that law. Thus, issues of responsibility or liability under municipal law are not as such covered by the draft articles. This is without prejudice to the possible applicability of certain principles or rules of international law when the question of an organization's responsibility or liability arises under municipal law.'

[28] Art. VIII, Section 29 UN Privileges and Immunities Convention (n. 3); Section E, art. IX General Convention on the Privileges and Immunities of the Organization of African Unity (adopted and in force 25 October 1965), 1000 UNTS 395.

[29] H. G. Schermers and N. M. Blokker, *International Institutional Law: Unity Within Diversity*, 3rd edn (Martinus Nijhoff, 1995), p. 1000; M. N. Shaw, *International Law*, 5th edn (Cambridge University Press, 2003), p. 1198; A. Reinisch, 'Accountability of International Organizations According to National Law', 36 *Netherlands Yearbook of International Law* (2005), pp. 123–124, 147.

[30] Administrative and Budgetary Report (n. 3), para. 16. For local claims review boards, see 20.3 para. 4.

the UN Privileges and Immunities Convention. However, there is some practice that is relevant. For example, one category of cases considered to be public law are those that implicate the operational functioning of the UN, which go to the public heart of the Organisation.[31] A second category of public law claims is those that are 'based on political or policy-related grievances against the UN' such as those related to actions or decisions of the Security Council or General Assembly.[32] The political or policy-related distinction invoked by the UN regarding the receivability of third party claims has been criticised for lacking transparency (on the requirement of transparency, see Rule 20.5).[33]

4. As a matter of general international law, the question of attribution of responsibility is governed by the applicable rules of attribution of customary international law as reflected in the Articles on the Responsibility of States (ARSIWA)[34] and ARIO. However, TCCs and international organisations may agree on a different allocation of responsibility. For example, the relevant agreements may channel all claims into one particular settlement mechanism and towards one party, even though attribution may be possible to other parties as well under general international law. These agreements supersede customary rules of international liability and attribution without derogating from them.[35]

20.3 International law does not impose a uniform claims regime. International organisations active in Peace Operations may organise their civil liability towards third parties in different ways.

1. Constitutive and other treaty documents relevant to each international organisation define the scope of the organisation's obligations regarding the settlement of claims. In this connection, there may be a narrow definition of this obligation in order to share the burden of such claims between the organisation itself and its member States. Thus the international organisation may enter into special agreements, which may include the transfer of responsibility for settling claims to their member

[31] *Ibid.*, para. 13 (defining the term "operational necessity" as 'necessary actions taken by a peacekeeping force in the course of carrying out its operations in pursuance of its mandates').

[32] UNSG 1995 Report (n. 11), para. 23.

[33] K. E. Boon, 'The United Nations as Good Samaritan: Immunity and Responsibility', 16 *Chicago Journal of International Law* (2016), pp. 341–385.

[34] See n. 6.

[35] Schmalenbach (n. 4), p. 36.

States or to an arbitral mechanism. Special procedural rules usually apply to the bodies that settle the claims. In the absence of a generally applicable international law norm requiring all international organisations to settle claims arising from their military operations,[36] the claims settlement regimes have developed on the basis of each organisation's own law and practice.

2. *UN.* In the case of the UN, the organisation accepts international responsibility for the activities of its forces as an attribute of its international legal personality and its capacity to bear international rights and obligations.[37] The UN has, since the inception of Peace Operations, assumed its liability for damage caused by members of its forces in the performance of their duties.[38] This responsibility for damage by UN Peace Forces was confirmed in the ruling of the International Court of Justice (ICJ) in the *Reparation for Injuries* case.[39] When the ICJ

---

[36] 'There is no evidence of a presumption in law that the United Nations bears either an exclusive or a primary responsibility for the tortious acts of [its peacekeeping] forces, and the law remains undeveloped. In practice the United Nations has accepted responsibility for the acts of its agents': I. Brownlie, *Principles of Public International Law*, 6th edn (Oxford University Press, 2003), p. 655. As summarized elsewhere, 'The practice Professor Brownlie refers to concerns the wrongful acts of soldiers of the UN Force in the Congo. A Belgian claimed that his property had been burned and looted by the UN Force, and in 1962 he lodged a claim against the United Nations for compensation. M. v. Organisation des Nations Unies et l'État Belge, 45 Int'l L. Rep. 446 (1972). The United Nations initially disputed the facts of the claim, but, after intercession by the Belgian government, the UN declared it was prepared to "accept financial liability where the damage is the result of action taken by agents of the United Nations in violation of the laws of war and the rules of international law." The real reason for the paucity of international organization tort law cases appears to be that claimants accept the terms of a final settlement agreed upon before resolution of the matter through arbitral or judicial processes. In this case, the claimant refused to accept a settlement and brought an action against the United Nations and the Belgian government. The Civil Tribunal of Brussels dismissed the plaintiff's claim by stating, "one cannot see where the UN could be sued, nor how, nor on what legal basis ... so long as it shelters behind its immunity from jurisdiction"': E. Suzuki and S. Nanwani, 'Responsibility of International Organizations: The Accountability Mechanisms of Multilateral Development Banks', 27 *Michigan Journal of International Law* (2005), pp. 194–195, fn. 80 (references omitted).

[37] Administrative and Budgetary Report (n. 3).

[38] *Ibid.*, para. 7: 'In conformity with section 29 of the Convention on the Privileges and Immunities of the United Nations, it has undertaken in paragraph 51 of the Model Status-of-Forces Agreement (see A/45/594) to settle by means of a standing claims commission claims resulting from damage caused by members of the force in the performance of their official duties and which for reasons of immunity of the Organization and its Members could not have been submitted to local courts.'

[39] *Reparation for Injuries Suffered in the Service of the United Nations*, Advisory Opinion, ICJ Reports 1949, 174. In a ground-breaking decision, the ICJ opined that the UN does have the capacity to bring an international claim against another government, and even against non-Member States. The ICJ based its decision on the UN Charter, by which the Organisation has its own identity and personality, and is distinct from other Member States. Therefore, the UN was able to claim compensation from the Israeli government for the deaths of its personnel. The UN later received USD 100,000 from the Israeli government for the loss of its Swedish mediator and French translator.

established the rule in the *Reparation Case* that the UN had the capacity to bring lawsuits, it implied that it also had certain obligations under international law. In the *Immunity from Legal Process Case*, the ICJ also found that 'the United Nations may be required to bear responsibility for the damage arising from acts performed by the Organization or by its agents acting in their official capacity'.[40]

3. The legal basis of the UN claims procedures can be found in Section 29 of the UN Privileges and Immunities Convention, which provides that:

> The United Nations shall make provisions for appropriate modes of settlement of:
> (a) disputes arising out of contracts or other disputes of a private law character to which the United Nations is a party;
> (b) disputes involving any official of the United Nations who by reason of his official position enjoys immunity, if immunity has not been waived by the Secretary-General.

4. The 1990 UN Model SOFA provides for the establishment of a Standing Claims Commission,[41] which is an implementation of Section 29 of the UN Privileges and Immunities Convention. However, this Commission, which in accordance with the terms of the UN Model SOFA shall be composed of one UN representative, one representative of the Host State and one jointly appointed chairman, has never been established in practice. Instead, the claims brought in relation to UN Peace Operations have been settled through recourse to "local claims review boards".[42] Such boards are UN administrative panels that operate in each peacekeeping mission, and each board is authorised to examine claims based on facts established by the UN itself or local investigative authorities, where available. It may also consider recommendations from claims officers, who may have conducted discussions with claimants on possible settlement amounts. The board is authorised to recommend to the head of the administrative division of the operation settlement of those claims it finds to have merit, within the limits of the operation's delegated financial authority.[43] The maximum amount of compensation that may be paid for claims related to Peace Operations is USD 50,000, and no compensation

---

[40] *Difference Relating to Immunity from Legal Process of a Special Rapporteur of the Commission on Human Rights*, Advisory Opinion, ICJ Reports 1999, 62, 89.
[41] Art. 51 UN Model Status of Forces Agreement for Peacekeeping Operations, UN Doc. A/45/594 (1990).
[42] Schmalenbach (n. 4), p. 41.
[43] Administrative and Budgetary Report (n. 3).

for non-economic losses such as moral damages is allowed. Claims must also be introduced within six months of the accident or incident.[44]

5. The UN has established these financial limitations with the understanding that the Host State would ultimately be responsible for compensation, if any, beyond these limits. The UN has not set up a second judicial instance to settle disputes if a consensual agreement cannot be reached. However, arbitration, though not typically used for third party claims, may be resorted to by mutual agreement between the UN and the claimant, on a case-by-case basis. Claims related to contracts and, as a general rule, traffic accidents involving UN vehicles are not handled by the claims review boards. Contractual claims are addressed in accordance with dispute settlement provisions elaborated within the particular contract. The UN's General Conditions of contract also include a standard arbitration clause. For claims arising from traffic accidents, the UN has made insurance arrangements whereby the relevant insurance providers deal with such claims.

6. The UN regularly settles private law claims arising out of the activities of its Peace Operations. In settling large and complex claims, the Organisation has also sought, in addition to its usual procedures, to utilise political, diplomatic or other means. For instance, in the United Nations Operation in the Congo (ONUC),[45] the UN settled individual claims asserted by non-Congolese nationals by concluding global settlement agreements with the relevant States of nationality. Funds were then distributed among the injured persons by the State of nationality.[46] In the course of the operation, injured persons were to notify their claim with two ONUC claims review boards.[47] Their inquiries provided the basis for

---

[44] These provisions on liability are based on various legal sources, particularly on the general principles of national law of torts and on local provisions of the Host States. The former are mainly deduced from Anglo-American law of tort. The latter are limited to issues concerning the amount of compensation. See Schmalenbach (n. 4), p. 43.

[45] ONUC 1960–1964.

[46] Without prejudice to the privileges and immunities of the UN, the Secretary-General agreed to pay USD 1,500,500 to the government of Belgium; USD 150,000 to Greece; USD 15,000 to Luxembourg; and USD 150,000 to Italy plus 2,500,000 francs from the Democratic Republic of the Congo, in Schmalenbach (n. 4), p. 48. For the agreements between the UN and Belgium, Greece, Luxembourg and Italy, see respectively *United Nations Juridical Yearbook* (1965), pp. 39–42; *Ibid.* (1966), pp. 39–40 and 40–41; *Ibid.* (1967), pp. 77–78. The agreement reached between Belgium and the UN through an exchange of letters was approved by a Belgian law of 7 May 1965 (*Bulletin législatif* (1965), pp. 919–920).

[47] B. Vickers (Legal Officer), Draft Directive for the Guidance of the Proposed Claims Office in Leopoldville, 9 July 1962, UN Archives, NY File Stavropoulos, OLA, Congo-Claims, Box 26. See also UN document (internal) 'Terms of Reference of the Legal Claims Office at Elisabethville', UN Archives, NY File Stavropoulos, OLA, Congo-Claims, Box 26, in Schmalenbach (n. 4), p. 48.

the subsequent negotiations with the victim's State of nationality. Parallel to this, the claims not covered by the global settlement agreements were addressed by two ONUC claims review boards. The operation in the Congo is the only case in the history of the UN to date in which claims for compensation were settled through global settlement agreements.[48] The practice of the UN in utilising non-judicial modes of settlement is particularly important in preserving the immunity of the UN from legal process. Waiver of such immunity for the purpose of litigating claims is viewed as risking creating a practice that ultimately undermines the purpose for which immunity has been granted. The Memorandum of Understanding (MOU) concluded between the TCC and the UN also sets out the arrangement regarding claims arising out of the activities of national contingents and their personnel.[49] In case of gross negligence or wilful misconduct, the UN recovers the compensation paid from the contributing government. The UN accepts no liability for off-duty claims where the member of a peacekeeping mission was acting outside the scope of official duties at the time of the incident giving rise to the claim.

7. *NATO.* NATO favours the paradigm that "the costs lie where they fall",[50] for all conduct in Non-Article 5 Crisis Response Operations (NA5CROs), meaning that the participating States absorb any and all costs associated with their participation in such operations.[51] Consequently, the TCCs are liable for the damages caused by their respective contingents.

8. Within NATO there is no uniform NATO Claims Policy applicable to all operations. In 2004 NATO's Political Committee drafted a General Claims Policy for Designated Crisis Response Operations but this policy has not yet been approved by the North Atlantic Council (NAC).[52] This draft policy, however, may serve as a basic guidance for

---

[48] Schmalenbach (n. 4), p. 48. In his Administrative and Budgetary Report (n. 3), paras. 34–36, the UN Secretary-General considered lump sum agreements to be a system with many advantages.

[49] E.g. MOU between the UN and the Government of Belgium contributing Resources to the UN Interim Force in Lebanon (UNIFIL): 'Claims by Third parties: The United Nations will be responsible for dealing with any claims by third parties where the loss of or damage to their property, or death or personal injury, was caused by the personnel or equipment provided by the Government (i.e. Belgian) in the performance of services or any other activity or operation under this MOU. However, if the loss, damage, death or injury arose from gross negligence or wilful misconduct of the personnel provided by the Government, the Government will be liable for such claims.'

[50] See NATO, Revised Funding Policy for NATO-led NA5CRO Operations, PO(2005)0098.

[51] *Ibid.*, annex 1, para. 6.

[52] NATO, Claims Policy for Designated Crisis Response Operations, AC/119-N(2004)0058.

development of respective operational claims policies.[53] The TCCs are liable for the damages caused by their contingents. They apply their national laws and regulations in settling the claims, and it is the TCCs that decide whether or not they offer ex gratia payments. NATO will cover claims with common funding if they are not attributable to any contributing States or if a responsible State refuses to pay and such refusal would negatively affect the whole NATO mission. Claims arising from acts or omissions of NATO civilian employees, or of military personnel attached to NATO Operational Headquarters acting in a NATO capacity,[54] are settled by NATO. Claims between or among NATO/Partnership for Peace contributing States and/or NATO should be waived. Claims arising from combat, combat-related activity or operational necessity, or from the Host State for damage to property or death or injury of members of the armed forces while engaged in the performance of official duties, are generally considered as non-admissible. Contractual claims are addressed in accordance with dispute settlement provisions elaborated within the particular contract.

9. The agreements relevant for a specific operation are based on the claims procedures provided for in the NATO SOFA[55] and the Partnership for Peace SOFA,[56] the application of both of which is territorially limited to their Member States. There are differences in legal position as between NATO and partner States contributing to NATO operations with regard to ratification of the NATO SOFA or the Partnership for Peace SOFA arising from various reservations and from differing national legislation. Consequently, States have different practices for settling claims. There is little co-ordination, registration or control by NATO as an organisation.[57] In accordance with the aforementioned principle of "costs lie where they fall", NATO does not oversee the settlement of individual claims.

---

[53] E.g. ISAF Claims Policy, Claims against ISAF, Standard Operating Procedure 1151 (2009).

[54] Acting under operational or tactical control of the NATO operational headquarters.

[55] Agreement between the Parties to the North Atlantic Treaty regarding the Status of their Forces (19 June 1951, in force 23 August 1953), 199 UNTS 67.

[56] Agreement between NATO and other States participating in the Partnership for Peace regarding the Status of their Forces (19 June 1995, in force 30 January 1996), [2000] Cm 4701, and its Additional Protocol (19 June 1995), www.nato.int/cps/en/natohq/official_texts_24742.htm.

[57] Although the NATO ISAF Claims Office did have some co-ordination tasks and acted as the first contact for any claimant in helping to file a claim with the responsible TCC. See J. M. Prescott, 'EBAO and NATO Operational Claims', 10 The Three Swords (NATO Joint Warfare Centre) (2007), pp. 5–9.

10. The claims settlement mechanisms during NATO's Bosnia and Herzegovina missions[58] were not copied in later operations. For all disputes that were not settled between the injured party and the Member State whose contingent allegedly caused the injury, a Standing Claims Commission of four members – two members from the Member State and two from Bosnia and Herzegovina – was established with the right to appeal to an arbitral tribunal. The Standing Claims Commission was a forum more for political negotiations than for judicial decisions, given that the decision to award reparations required unanimity. However, the arbitral tribunal – comprising two members appointed by Bosnia and Herzegovina and IFOR/SFOR respectively, and a Chairperson appointed by a "neutral" third organisation – applied judicial methods.[59] When SFOR handed over to the EU mission European Force in Bosnia and Herzegovina (EUFOR Althea) in 2004, the claims settlement procedure remained, by and large, intact.

11. *EU*. Article 5 of the EU Model SOFA,[60] which serves as a basis for negotiating SOFAs for specific operations,[61] stipulates that claims 'shall be forwarded to EUFOR via the competent authorities of the Host State'. When no amicable settlement can be found, 'the claim shall be submitted to a claims commission composed on an equal basis of representatives of EUFOR and representatives of the Host State'. In case the dispute is not satisfactorily settled at this level, it shall be settled by diplomatic means 'between the Host State and EU representatives' or by an arbitration tribunal composed of arbitrators appointed by the Host State and the EU mission if the dispute exceeds a certain amount. The EU Model SOFA even foresees a role for the President of the European Court of Justice to appoint the third arbitrator when the two parties cannot agree on the appointment of this person. Under the Model SOFA, EU Headquarters has a significant co-ordinating role for all claims.

12. In financial terms, damage caused by EU Headquarters personnel is settled as a common cost from the common budget in accordance with

---

[58] IFOR/SFOR 1995–2005.

[59] K. Schmalenbach, 'Dispute Settlement', in J. Klabbers and A. Wallendahl (eds.), *Research Handbook on the Law of International Organizations* (Edward Elgar, 2011), pp. 251–284.

[60] For the EU Model SOFA, see EU Council Docs. 12616/07 (2007), 11894/07 (2007) and 11894/07 COR 1 (2007).

[61] For an example, see the Agreement between the EU and the Republic of Mali on the Status in the Republic of Mali of the EU military mission to contribute to the training of the Malian Armed Forces (EUTM Mali), OJ 2013 No. L106, 16 April 2013, p. 2.

the Athena mechanism.[62] Other damages are paid for by those who cause them, especially individual contingents, in line with the principle that, unless otherwise agreed, "the costs lie where they fall".

13. However, externally the legal and operational framework of EU operations is more ambiguous. Hence, while the SOFAs and Status of Mission Agreements (SOMAs) deal with claims procedures, the question of a division between EU and Member States' responsibilities is not regulated in any clear way, and internal funding rules and external claims procedures seem to identify different actors to some extent.[63] Once it enters into force, the EU Claims Agreement of 28 April 2004 will be the legal basis for the waiving of claims between EU Member States during their participation in EU crisis management operations.[64] The agreement stipulates that Member States will waive all claims for injury and death suffered by their military or civilian personnel,[65] or for damage to their property used in the EU operation.[66] If the damage was a result of wilful misconduct or gross negligence, the waiver does not apply. Furthermore, an Agreement exists between the Member States of the EU to regulate the status of their forces and personnel within each other's territory

---

[62] A number of costs have been defined as "common costs" for which there is common funding, managed by the 'Athena' mechanism. See Council Decision (CFSP) 2015/528 of 27 March 2015 establishing a mechanism to administer the financing of the common costs of European Union operations having military or defence implications (Athena), and repealing Decision 2011/871/CFSP, OJ 2015 No. L84, 28 March 2015, p. 39. On claims relating to headquarters, see art. 44(4) of this Decision. Athena operates on behalf of the twenty-seven EU Member States which contribute to the financing of EU military operations (Denmark has opted out of the Common Security and Defence Policy (CSDP) on military matters) and manages the financing of specified common costs for these operations as well as the nation-borne costs (that are charged to the States incurring them).

[63] For a more extensive analysis, see e.g. F. Naert, 'The International Responsibility of the Union in the Context of Its CSDP Operations', in P. Koutrakos and M. Evans (eds.), *The International Responsibility of the European Union* (Hart, 2013), pp. 313–338; F. Naert, 'European Union Common Security and Defence Policy Operations', in A. Nollkaemper and I. Plakokefalos (eds.), *The Practice of Shared Responsibility in International Law* (Cambridge University Press, 2017), pp. 669–700.

[64] Agreement between the Member States of the European Union concerning claims introduced by each Member State against any other Member State for damage to any property owned, used or operated by it or injury or death suffered by any military or civilian staff of its services, in the context of an EU crisis management operation, OJ 2004 No. C116, 30 April 2004, p. 1. Unfortunately not all Member States have ratified the EU Claims Agreement yet, so at the time of writing the Agreement has not entered into force. However, a declaration to this Agreement states that, as of signature, all Member States will endeavour to limit as far as possible their claims against each other for injury or death of their military or civilian personnel, or damage to any of their assets, except in cases of gross negligence or wilful misconduct.

[65] *Ibid.*, art. 3.

[66] *Ibid.*, art. 4.

(EU SOFA).[67] Pending its entry into force, other existing agreements are applied (e.g. the NATO SOFA)[68] and/or specific arrangements can be made (e.g. relating to EU Operational Headquarters).

14. *AU.* The AU is increasingly participating in regional Peace Operations under UN mandate. Its practice is quite recent but is partly grounded on previous operations by the Economic Community of West African States (ECOWAS). Operations within the framework of the AU are not always placed under the command of the organisation, and are frequently carried out under the leadership of one of the participating States.[69] Further, operations by the AU have occasionally involved the sequential deployment of a mission led by one State, subsequently subsumed by the AU.[70] Whether the UN claims system or the AU system applies depends on the nature of the mission.[71] The AU claims system is based on the UN system. There is an identical constitutional requirement to provide for appropriate modes of settlement for disputes arising out of contracts or other disputes of a private law character.[72] The same material and procedural limitations are applied, and damages due to operational necessity are excluded in the SOMAs. These Agreements provide for claims commissions but none has been established in practice.

---

[67] OJ 2003 No. C321, 31 December 2003, p. 6. See especially its art. 18 on claims. See A. Sari, 'The European Union Status of Forces Agreement (EU SOFA)', 13 *Journal of Conflict and Security Law* (2008), pp. 353–391.

[68] See n. 55.

[69] For instance, in the AU Mission in Sudan-Darfur (AMIS), the AU was clearly the entity vested with operational command and control over the forces in the field, whereas the African Union Mission in Somalia (AMISOM) was under the lead of Uganda. See B. Boutin, SHARES Expert Seminar Report 'Responsibility in Multinational Military Operations: A Review of Recent Practice' (2011), p. 16, www.sharesproject.nl.

[70] For instance, following the Arusha Peace and Reconciliation Agreement for Burundi (2000), South Africa was the only State 'willing and able' to respond to the call for troop contributions so it deployed the South African Protection Support Detachment (SAPSD), which later became the African Mission in Burundi (AMIB). See Boutin (n. 69), p. 16.

[71] Quite exceptionally, in the AU/UN Hybrid Operation in Darfur (UNAMID), the UN has agreed to pay for all damages caused by the mission despite the fact that troops are under the joint command of the UN and the AU. See Agreement between the UN and the AU and the Government of Sudan concerning the Status of the AU/UN Hybrid Operation in Darfur (9 February 2008, unpublished), para. 54: 'Third party claims for property loss or damage and for personal injury, illness or death arising from or directly attributed to UNAMID, except for those arising from operational necessity ... shall be settled by the United Nations ... Upon determination of liability as provided in this Agreement, the United Nations shall pay compensation.' See also Boutin (n. 69), p. 7.

[72] OAU Privileges and Immunities Convention (n. 28).

20.4 Although claims regimes vary, there are well-established exceptions to liability that are applied by all actors in Peace Operations. Damage arising from action in self-defence or from operational necessity, as well as combat-related damage, is exempt from liability but may be compensated through an ex gratia payment.

1. International organisations limit their liability for operational damages through an agreement with the Host State. Claims provisions may exempt the visiting forces from all damage claims but in practice broad exemptions have been softened by subsequent agreements[73] or by ex gratia payments.[74]

2. All agreements contain an exemption for damages due to "operational necessity". The concept of operational necessity has been developed in the practice of UN operations.[75] Damages due to operational necessity are: 'damages caused during ordinary operations by necessary actions taken by a peacekeeping force in the course of carrying out its operations in pursuance of its mandates'.[76] It is distinguishable from the concept of "military necessity". The principle of military necessity permits

---

[73] Under the Military Technical Agreement between KFOR and the Federal Republic of Yugoslavia and the Republic of Serbia (adopted and in force 9 June 1999), www.nato.int/kosovo/docu/a990609a.htm, KFOR forces were not liable 'for any damages to private or public property that they may cause in the course of duties related to the implementation of this Agreement' (appendix B, para. 3). This caused some political awkwardness, since the UN Interim Administration Mission in Kosovo (UNMIK) intended to pay claims. Eventually the problem was resolved by a UNMIK/KFOR joint declaration that included the commitment for both international entities to 'establish procedures in order to address any third party claims for property loss or damage and personal injury caused by them or any of their personnel.' (Prescott (n. 57), p. 7; Regulation No. 2000/47 on the Status, Privileges and Immunities of KFOR and UNMIK and their Personnel in Kosovo, UNMIK/REG/2000/47 (2000), www.unmikonline.org).

[74] Faced with an increase in the number of injured and killed Afghans and the amount of damaged civilian property, certain ISAF TCCs have created and contributed towards a Post-Operations Emergency Relief Fund (POERF). See NATO, 'NATO Nations Approve Civilian Casualty Guidelines', 6 August 2010, www.nato.int/cps/en/natohq/official_texts_65114.htm?selected Locale=en; J. M. Prescott, 'Operational Claims in Bosnia-Herzegovina and Croatia', 6 *Army Lawyer* (1998), pp. 1–8.

[75] Historically speaking, the operational necessity rule was developed by the UN legal department to justify the non-consensual use of private property and premises. Basically, the international mandate obliges the Host State to provide the UN with the required premises free of charge, taking possession of them if necessary. In view of respective provisions in several SOFAs, the UN now regards this obligation as being enshrined in customary law. However, Host States often do not fulfil their legal obligations. In these cases, the UN has regularly seized private land and premises itself, an action justified under the operational necessity rule. In each case, compensation was paid to the private owner and afterwards recovered from the Host State. See Schmalenbach (n. 4), p. 45.

[76] Administrative and Budgetary Report (n. 3), para. 6.

measures which are actually necessary to accomplish a legitimate military purpose and are not otherwise prohibited by IHL. The two concepts are, however, conceptually similar in that they serve as an exemption from liability, or a legitimisation of an act that would otherwise be considered unlawful. If the damage caused to private property is inevitable in pursuance of the Organisation's mandate, e.g. the destruction of a harvest within a security zone, the measure itself is lawful on the basis of the international mandate alone and thus has no consequences for the UN in terms of liability. The private owner is not entitled to claim compensation; his or her only recourse is to claim compensation from the Host State directly.[77]

3. Although the UN local claims review boards have denied operational necessity claims for years, they were excluded formally through a proposal by the UN Secretary-General to change the language of article 51 of the UN Model SOFA as part of the reform of the UN claims system in 1997.[78] The decision whether an action is necessary for the operation remains within the discretionary power of the Force Commander, who must attempt to strike a balance between the operational necessity of the force and respect for private property.[79]

4. The exemption of damages due to operational necessity has been criticised since the damages which result from ordinary operations are the most common.[80] In the view of the Secretary-General, however, the State receiving the UN Peace Force should bear part of the financial burden of the operation, since the Peace Operation is for its benefit and at its behest.[81] The decision on operational necessity has not always been correctly made. In the IFOR mission, damages caused by combat or combat-related activities have been referred to as damages due to "operational necessity". This demonstrates the confusion which can arise concerning the distinction between ordinary operations of a force and combat activities.[82]

5. Although the proposal of the Secretary-General is aimed only at damage to property, recent instruments concluded or adopted by the UN have extended the principle of operational necessity to cover also personal

---

[77] Schmalenbach (n. 4), p. 45.
[78] Report of the Secretary-General, UN Doc. A/51/389 (1997), p. 5. This view has been endorsed by the UN General Assembly in UNGA Res. 52/247 (1998).
[79] Administrative and Budgetary Report (n. 3), para. 14.
[80] Prescott (n. 2), p. 173.
[81] UNSG 1997 Report (n. 78), p. 5.
[82] Zwanenburg (n. 23), p. 291.

injury, illness or death arising from or directly attributed to the UN.[83] The disclaimer in the EU Model SOFA, on the other hand, is expressly limited to claims involving damage to or loss of property: 'EUFOR and their personnel shall not be liable for any damage to or loss of civilian or government property related to operational necessities or caused in connection with civil disturbances or the protection of EUFOR.'[84] Although the UN, Organization of American States (OAS), NATO[85] and EU have all rejected claims on the grounds of operational necessity,[86] there is some variation in international practice on the interpretation and application of the exemption.

20.5 International organisations and States should establish alternative means of dispute settlement where access to court is not possible because of immunities. Such claims procedures should be transparent and impartial, and should respect local laws. All international organisations should assume responsibility for the national contingents under their control in order to facilitate the settlement of third party claims.

1. There is room for improvement in the existing claim settlement procedures. International organisations often do pay compensation but prefer to do so outside formal mechanisms. Claims filed with UN local claims review boards have sometimes been dismissed because they are considered not to have a private law character,[87] creating legal uncertainty regarding the admissibility of third party claims. A claimant for such non-receivable claims has no recourse, other than through the diplomatic protection of his or her State of nationality.

2. In the outlining of a claims settlement procedure, inspiration can be found in 'The International Law Principles on Reparation for Victims of Armed Conflict', drafted by the International Law Association.[88]

---

[83] See art. VII(54) Agreement between Ethiopia and the UN concerning the Status of the UN Mission in Ethiopia and Eritrea (23 March 2001), 2141 UNTS 24; Section 7 UNMIK Regulation No. 2000/47 (n. 73).

[84] Art. 15(1) EU Model SOFA (n. 60).

[85] NATO's Claims Policy for Designated Crisis Response Operations (n. 52) defines as non-admissible claims: 'claims arising from combat, combat related activity or operational necessity'.

[86] For the OAS, see J. H. Rouse, Assistant Chief U.S. Army Claims Service, Paper presented to the Inter-American Bar Association, Meeting at San Jose, 9–15 April 1967, p. 10 (unpublished). For NATO, see Prescott (n. 74).

[87] See the Haiti cholera cases *Georges* and *Laventure* (n. 9).

[88] International Law Association, 74th Conference, Resolution No. 2/2010, 'Reparation for Victims of Armed Conflict'.

It provides a new model of claims settlement rules by prescribing that the reparation mechanism should have adequate rules for decision-making, including the valuation of claims and clear rules on legal recourse and exclusivity.[89] The possibility of an appeal should be taken into account.[90]

3. As a general rule, members of Peace Operations are under an obligation to respect the local laws of the Host State. Where the injured party is a third party individual, it would therefore be conceivable that standard rules of private international law would apply to determine the applicable law as lex loci delicti commissi or the law having the closest connection to the tort.[91] Today it is unclear which rules the UN,[92] EU or NATO Members apply in settling their private party claims, because the decisions are not made public.[93] The application of local law would be the most appropriate method from the victims' perspective, but a clear set of principles of tort law governing all Peace Operations of the international organisation would also be an acceptable approach, given the timeframe in which claims ought to be analysed and settled by the international organisation or the TCC[94] and the manpower requirement that this imposes.

4. Immunities accorded to Peace Operations and their members prevent the courts of the Host State from considering claims brought against them. Most international organisations have established permanent commissions or tribunals that deal with labour disputes of their staff.[95] Tort claims brought by third parties deserve equal treatment.

---

[89] Principles 6, 7 and 8 Draft Procedural Principles for Reparation Mechanisms, in International Law Association Report of the Seventy-Sixth Conference (2014), p. 780.

[90] However, this due process requirement needs to strike the difficult balance between providing an effective legal remedy to parties and the demands of efficiency so that all claims can be processed within an acceptable timeframe. See N. Wühler and H. Niebergall (eds.), *Property Restitution and Compensation: Practices and Experiences of Claims Programmes* (International Organization for Migration, 2008), p. 117.

[91] The former applies in civil jurisdictions, while the latter is used in common law. See Wellens (n. 5), p. 160; C. F. Amerasinghe, *Principles of the Institutional Law of International Organizations*, 2nd edn (Cambridge University Press, 2005), p. 389; Reinisch (n. 29), p. 136; P. Sands and P. Klein, *Bowett's Law of International Institutions*, 6th edn (Sweet and Maxwell, 2009), p. 470.

[92] See Lundahl (n. 21); Summary Study of the Experience Derived from the Establishment and Operation of the Force: Report of the Secretary-General, UN Doc. A/3943 (1958), para. 141; Schmalenbach (n. 4), p. 43; Wellens (n. 5), p. 160, stating that lex loci delicti commissi in fact applies to the merits of the tort claim.

[93] The UN opens archives after twenty years; NATO and EU do not keep databases on the claims practices of their contributing Member States.

[94] Principles 6, 7 and 8 Draft Procedural Principles for Reparation Mechanisms (n. 89).

[95] Labour disputes are not third party claims but arise out of the contract of employment between the international organisation and its staff. For contract claims of persons who are not staff, the UN also provides arbitration.

Although not all international organisations have made commitments to establish claims commissions like the UN has done under bilateral agreements,[96] recent human rights jurisprudence involving some regional organisations suggests that the provision of a dispute settlement mechanism open to individual claimants may be obligatory if individual rights to due process are to be realised. It would advance the human rights of potential third party claimants if the international organisation and the relevant Host State were to create an alternative dispute settlement mechanism where the relevant multi-lateral treaties and the bilateral agreements between the organisation and the Host State so provide.[97] These claims commissions should, in line with the SOFA provisions, involve a neutral third party.[98] The installation of standing claims commissions would provide claimants with a relevant alternative forum. As unilateral legislators of their claims procedures, international organisations should devise an illustrative list of legal criteria to be applied by the claims commissions in determining the admissibility of claims, allowing for specific and transparent determination of receivability.[99]

5. Domestic courts have refrained from carrying out a functional necessity analysis on the immunity of international organisations – which typically turns out in favour of the organisation – and have instead espoused a human rights approach.[100] Pursuant to this approach, a domestic court will inquire into whether the aggrieved individual can sufficiently exercise his/her right to a remedy; only if he/she has sufficient access to "alternative" dispute settlement mechanisms provided by the

---

[96] Section 29 UN Privileges and Immunities Convention (n. 3).

[97] *Interpretation of the Agreement of 25 March 1951 between the WHO and Egypt*, Advisory Opinion, ICJ Reports 1980, 73, para. 48.

[98] Administrative and Budgetary Report (n. 3), para. 10.

[99] F. Mégret, 'La responsabilité des Nations Unies aux temps du choléra', 47 *Revue belge de droit international* (2013), pp. 161–189; Lundahl (n. 21).

[100] Inspired by case law concerning the European Convention on Human Rights: *Waite and Kennedy* v. *Germany*, Application No. 26083/94, Judgment of 18 February 1999 [GC], para. 68 ('a material factor in determining whether granting [the European Space Agency] immunity from German jurisdiction is permissible under the Convention is whether the applicants had available to them reasonable alternative means to protect effectively their rights under the Convention'); *Beer and Regan* v. *Germany*, Application No. 28934/95, Judgment of 18 February 1999 [GC], para. 58. See further *Siedler* v. *Western European Union*, Court of Appeal (Cour d'appel) of Brussels, Belgium, Judgment of 17 September 2003, ILDC 53 (BE 2003); *L.M.* v. *Secretariat General of the ACP Group of States*, Court of Appeal (Cour d'appel) of Brussels, Belgium, Judgment of 4 March 2003, *Journal des Tribunaux* (2003), 684; *D.* v. *Decision of the EPO Disciplinary Board*, Federal Constitutional Court (Bundesverfassungsgericht) of Germany, Judgment of 28 November 2005, 2 BvR 1751/03. This is summarised by C. Ryngaert, 'The Immunity of International Organizations Before Domestic Courts: Recent Trends', 7 *International Organizations Law Review* (2010), pp. 121–148.

organisation will a court uphold the organisation's immunity. This case law involves disputes of a private/labour/contractual nature rather than on more politically sensitive disputes, e.g. in relation to international peacekeeping.[101] National jurisdictions should not be denied the power to verify whether an international organisation active in peacekeeping has established a dispute settlement mechanism permitting an individual to challenge its acts. This assessment is justified by the human rights principle of access to justice. However, national courts should compare the internal claims mechanisms established by international organisations to international administrative tribunals and not to national jurisdictions, given the specificities of international organs.[102]

6. In addition to the substantive and procedural weaknesses of the actual claims settlement systems, the approaches to attribution of harmful conduct differ depending on the international organisation that authorises military operations. UN operations are part of the UN's institutional structure and therefore the UN assumes responsibility for the acts of national contingents. This means that the UN adopts a single approach in each mission. The relationship between national contingents and the EU and NATO is different, meaning that Sending States are, at least to some extent, responsible for settling claims themselves. In the absence of binding standards shared by all contingents, this may lead to inconsistencies and the fragmentation of claims settlement practice along national lines, in particular in large operations. Consistency between different operations, and, to the extent possible, between different international organisations would also be welcome. However, lack of transparency in how claims are actually settled in practice is a major obstacle to this. A possible solution would be to attribute the conduct of national contingents

---

[101] C. H. Brower, 'International Immunities: Some Dissident Views on the Role of Municipal Courts', 41 *Virginia Journal of International Law* (2000), pp. 34 *et seq.* (arguing that the expansion of municipal court jurisdiction would impair the capacity of international organisations to discharge their obligations with respect to peace, security, human rights and other controversial issues). The immunity of the UN was confirmed by *Stichting Mothers of Srebrenica and Others* v. *the Netherlands*, Application No. 65542/12, Decision of 11 June 2013.

[102] *Siedler v. Western European Union* (n. 100). In this case concerning the Western European Union, the Court set aside immunity after noting that although an internal procedure was available to individuals it did not meet the guarantees inherent in the notion of a fair trial. The Court based itself upon characteristics of national jurisdictions (no publicity of debates, no enforcement measures, members appointed by the board of the Western European Union for two years and no disqualification possible) to assess the modalities of the internal appeals procedure of the organisation. This case law is overzealous and does not take into account the specificities of international organs. See J. Wouters and P. Schmitt, 'Challenging Acts of Other United Nations' Organs, Subsidiary Organs, and Officials', in A. Reinisch (ed.), *Challenging Acts of International Organizations Before National Courts* (Oxford University Press, 2010), pp. 77–110.

to NATO or the EU, under whose command structure these contingents operate in a Peace Operation.[103] The presumption of attribution to the EU or NATO would simplify the search for compensation by an individual claimant and would lead to the creation of a coherent claims system. Of course, this requires that the Sending States provide the EU and NATO with the financial and other resources to meet the liabilities of these organisations.[104]

[103] See Chapter 19.
[104] See Sari and Wessel (n. 20), p. 141.

Individual Criminal Responsibility and International Criminal Justice in Relation to Peace Operations

1. The purpose and scope of this chapter are to set out the law relating to individual criminal responsibility under international law in relation to Peace Operations. It takes the crimes listed under the Rome Statute of the International Criminal Court (ICC)[1] as a starting point for the examination of individual criminal responsibility under international law. It additionally will set out a number of legal considerations relating to the exercise of international criminal justice in relation to Peace Operations. Questions of criminal responsibility under national law, whether of Sending or Host States, the maintenance of discipline, and responsibility and accountability under general international law are examined elsewhere and will be given no attention here.

21.1 Recognised international crimes under conventional and customary international law which may arise in the context of Peace Operations include war crimes, crimes against humanity, genocide and torture.

1. The aforementioned crimes are recognised under both conventional and customary international law as crimes which entail individual criminal responsibility under international law. While it is highly unlikely that a Peace Operation would itself be directly responsible for acts constituting genocide or crimes against humanity, there is no reason to exclude these crimes from consideration in this chapter given the remote possibility that a Peace Operation or individuals connected with a Peace Operation might engage in acts which constitute or materially contribute to either of these crimes. War crimes can arise only in the context of

---

[1] Rome Statute of the International Criminal Court (17 July 1998, in force 1 July 2002), 2187 UNTS 90 (ICC Statute). As of 1 July 2017, the ICC Statute has 124 States parties.

an armed conflict of either an international (IAC) or non-international (NIAC) nature and, to the extent a Peace Operation has become party to an armed conflict, the possibility that personnel connected with the operation could be engaged in acts constituting a war crime cannot be ruled out. The crime of torture is not included in the ICC Statute but is nevertheless a recognised crime under both conventional and customary international law. In contrast to the previously mentioned crimes, torture is not dependent upon a widespread, systematic attack upon a civilian population, an intention to destroy in whole or in part a particular racial, religious, national or ethnic group, or participation as a party in an armed conflict. It is therefore of direct relevance to Peace Operations. By contrast, the crimes of piracy and engaging in the international slave trade, although also constituting international crimes, are by their nature not readily applicable to personnel forming part of a Peace Operation and will therefore not be considered here for the purposes of this Manual.

2. War crimes have their origin in the jus in bello and can be generically defined as serious violations of international humanitarian law (IHL). Traditionally, IHL distinguished between protection of vulnerable groups ("Geneva law") and the prohibition of certain means and methods of warfare ("Hague law"); however, this distinction is less relevant today as the two bodies have essentially merged. With respect to a specific category of "grave breaches" of the Geneva Conventions,[2] encompassing, inter alia, wilful killing, torture and forced conscription, States parties have an obligation to treat these crimes as criminal offences under their domestic law and have a duty to either prosecute or extradite the perpetrators (aut dedere, aut judicare). The "grave breaches" are identified as a separate category of war crimes in the Statute of the International Criminal Tribunal for the former Yugoslavia[3] (ICTY) and in the ICC Statute.[4] However, the applicability of the "grave breaches" regime is confined to IACs. Common article 3 of the four Geneva Conventions, which is applicable in NIACs, identifies a number of acts, committed against "protected persons", that are prohibited at all times

---

[2] Geneva Conventions (I–IV) on the (I) Wounded and Sick in Armed Forces in the Field, (II) Wounded, Sick and Shipwrecked Members of the Armed Forces at Sea, (III) Treatment of Prisoners of War and (IV) Protection of Civilian Persons in Time of War (12 August 1949, in force 21 October 1950), 75 UNTS 31, 85, 135, 287.

[3] Art. 2 Statute of the International Criminal Tribunal for the former Yugoslavia, annexed to UNSC Res. 827 (1993) (as amended) (ICTY Statute).

[4] Art. 8(2)(a) ICC Statute (n. 1).

and in all places.[5] In its landmark *Tadić* decision, the Appeals Chamber of the ICTY confirmed that violations of common article 3 entail individual criminal responsibility under customary international law.[6] The war crimes consisting of violations of common article 3 were considered to be implicitly included in the open-ended article 3 of the ICTY Statute ('Violations of the Laws and Customs of War'), but feature as an explicit category in the Rome Statute.[7] Article 4 of the Statute of the International Criminal Tribunal for Rwanda[8] (ICTR) includes as war crimes a number of serious violations of Additional Protocol II[9] that have acquired the status of customary international law.[10] That provision of the ICTR Statute has been copied verbatim in article 3 of the Statute for the Special Court of Sierra Leone[11] (SCSL). Article 3 of the ICTY Statute enumerates, again by way of example, a number of prohibited means and methods of warfare[12] which derive from the Hague Conventions

---

[5] These acts encompass:
   a) Violence to life and person, in particular murder of all kinds, mutilation, cruel treatment and torture;
   b) Taking of hostages;
   c) Outrages upon personal dignity, in particular humiliating and degrading treatment;
   d) The passing of sentences and the carrying out of executions without previous judgment pronounced by a regularly constituted court, affording all the judicial guarantees which are recognised as indispensable by civilised peoples.

[6] *The Prosecutor* v. *Tadić*, Decision on Defence Motion for Interlocutory Appeal on Jurisdiction, IT-94-1, Appeals Chamber, 2 October 1995, paras. 96–135.

[7] Art. 8(2)(c) ICC Statute (n. 1).

[8] Statute of the International Criminal Tribunal for Rwanda, annexed to UNSC Res. 955 (1994) (as amended) (ICTR Statute).

[9] Protocol (II) Additional to the Geneva Conventions of 12 August 1949, and relating to the Protection of Victims of Non-International Armed Conflicts (8 June 1977, in force 7 December 1978), 1125 UNTS 610.

[10] ICTR Statute (n. 8). The provision mentions (by way of example, as it emphasises that the enumeration is not exhaustive): collective punishments, acts of terrorism and pillage. In addition, art. 4 ICTR Statute adds rape, enforced prostitution and any form of indecent assault as examples of 'outrages upon human dignity' constituting war crimes.

[11] Agreement between the UN and the Government of Sierra Leone on the Establishment of a Special Court for Sierra Leone (with annexed Statute) (16 January 2002, in force 12 April 2002), 2178 UNTS 138 (SCSL Statute).

[12] The article mentions:
   a) Employment of poisonous weapons or other weapons calculated to cause unnecessary suffering;
   b) Wanton destruction of cities, towns or villages, or devastation not justified by military necessity;
   c) Attack, or bombardment, by whatever means, of undefended towns, villages, dwellings or buildings;
   d) Seizure of, destruction or wilful damage done to institutions dedicated to religion, charity and education, the arts and sciences, historic monuments and works of art and science;
   e) Plunder of public or private property.

of 1899[13] and 1907[14] and from Additional Protocol I.[15] Article 8 of the ICC Statute reflects Hague law and differentiates between prohibited means and methods in the context of IACs (article 8(2)(b)) and NIACs (article 8(2)(e)).

3. Crimes against humanity were introduced by the Nuremberg Tribunal in order to prosecute and try the atrocities that were committed by the Nazis against their own nationals or that were not directly related to battle. Although initially a connection with a crime against peace or a war crime was required, such a relation is no longer necessary, which implies that crimes against humanity can be committed outside the realm of armed conflict. While crimes against humanity have not yet been codified in a specific treaty, they are incontrovertibly crimes under customary international law, as has been authoritatively confirmed in Principle 6 of the Nuremberg Principles.[16]

4. Genocide, as a species of crimes against humanity, is the topic of a special treaty that defines the crime by reference to the perpetrator's specific intent to destroy a national, ethnical, racial or religious group in whole or in part.[17] The Genocide Convention enjoins States parties to enact the necessary legislation providing effective penalties for those guilty of genocide and anticipates the establishment of an international penal tribunal that may have jurisdiction over the crime (article VI). The Convention's definition has stood the test of time, as it has been copied verbatim in the statutes of the international criminal tribunals and courts.[18] The International Court of Justice has reiterated in the *Bosnian Genocide* case that 'the rights and obligations enshrined in the Convention are rights and obligations *erga omnes*'.[19] Together, crimes against humanity and genocide are often referred to as "systems crimes"

---

[13] Hague Convention (II) respecting the Laws and Customs of War on Land and its annex: Regulations concerning the Laws and Customs of War on Land (29 July 1899, in force 4 September 1900), 1 Bevans 247.

[14] Hague Convention (IV) respecting the Laws and Customs of War on Land and its annex: Regulations concerning the Laws and Customs of War on Land (18 October 1907, in force 26 January 1910), 1 Bevans 631.

[15] Protocol (I) Additional to the Geneva Conventions of 12 August 1949, and relating to the Protection of Victims of International Armed Conflicts (8 June 1977, in force 7 December 1978), 1125 UNTS 4.

[16] Nuremberg Principles, UNGAOR, 5th Session, Supp. No. 12, UN Doc. A/1316 (1950).

[17] Convention on the Prevention and Suppression of the Crime of Genocide (9 December 1948, in force 21 January 1951), 78 UNTS 227.

[18] See e.g. art. 6 ICC Statute (n. 1).

[19] *Application of the Convention on the Prevention and Punishment of the Crime of Genocide (Bosnia and Herzegovina v. Serbia and Montenegro)*, Preliminary Objections, Judgment, ICJ Reports 1996, 595, 616.

as they involve systematic acts of violence against a civilian population which require a degree of planning and organisation by the State or other organised entity which perpetrates them.

5. Torture will qualify as a war crime or crime against humanity whenever the "contextual elements" of those categories have been met (see Rule 21.2). Outside the context of system criminality, torture is the topic of a separate treaty.[20] According to the ICTY, the prohibition of torture has evolved into a peremptory norm or jus cogens, which entails that 'the principle cannot be derogated from by States through international treaties or local or special customs or even general customary rules not endowed with the same normative force'.[21]

6. While members of a Peace Force may be the *victims* of crimes against humanity, it is highly unlikely that they will be *perpetrators* of either genocide or crimes against humanity, because it would seem unlikely that they will possess the special intent to destroy a group, nor is it likely that they will engage in systematic and widespread attacks against the civilian population.[22] However, it is conceivable and even realistic to anticipate that members of a Peace Force could become involved in war crimes because the commission of those crimes is not reserved to the combatants of the warring factions. A case in point is the trial of a US sergeant, Frank Ronghi, who was convicted for raping and strangling Merita Shabiuan, an 11-year-old ethnic Albanian girl, while on peacekeeping service in Kosovo.[23] War crimes of a more structural nature were committed by members of the Canadian forces who were deployed to Somalia. Investigations of a Special Commission of Inquiry led to the prosecution of nine suspects for the torture and murder of a Somali boy and triggered recommendations for reform of the then poorly prepared Canadian forces.[24] Such crimes are usually offences of opportunity that meet the generic requirement of a nexus with an armed conflict (see Rule 21.2).

---

[20] Convention Against Torture and Other Cruel, Inhuman or Degrading Treatment or Punishment (10 December 1984, in force 26 June 1987), 1465 UNTS 85.
[21] *The Prosecutor* v. *Furundžija*, Judgment, IT-95-17/1-T, Trial Chamber, 10 December 1998, para. 153.
[22] M. O' Brien, 'Protectors on Trial? Prosecuting Peacekeepers for War Crimes and Crimes Against Humanity in the International Criminal Court', 40 *International Journal of Law, Crime and Justice* (2012), p. 225.
[23] *United States* v. *Ronghi*, US Court of Appeal for the Armed Forces, Judgment of 30 June 2004, 60 MJ 83 (2004).
[24] Dishonoured Legacy: The Lessons of the Somalia Affair, Report of the Commission of Inquiry into the Deployment of Canadian Forces to Somalia (1997), https://qspace.library.queensu.ca/handle/1974/6881. See also Rule 16.5, Commentary, para. 2.

21.2 Persons connected with a Peace Operation, in either a civilian or a military capacity, who engage in acts constituting any of the crimes referred to in Rule 21.1 or who materially contribute to or assist in the perpetration of any of these crimes incur individual criminal responsibility under international law.

1. Individual criminal responsibility under international law for participating in, assisting in the perpetration of or otherwise materially contributing to the perpetration of any of the crimes referred to in Rule 21.1 is well established and widely recognised under both conventional and customary international law and is non-controversial. Article III of the Genocide Convention acknowledged as early as 1948 that not only the physical perpetrator of genocide should incur criminal responsibility, but also those who conspire with or incite the perpetrator to commit genocide or who are complicit in the act. The ICC Statute has clarified the modes of individual criminal responsibility, distinguishing between principals (article 25(3)(a)) and accessories (article 25(3)(b)–(d)). The distinguishing feature between the two categories is the control over the crime that is exercised by the principal, which implies the essential nature of his or her contribution in the sense that the principal, including the perpetrator, the co-perpetrator and the perpetrator who commits a crime by means of another person, is able to frustrate the crime by abstention.[25] Accessorial liability connotes a more subsidiary involvement in the crime. Article 25(3)(b) clusters the accomplices that take the initiative by 'ordering, soliciting or inducing' the commission of international crimes. Ordering implies a position of authority, but does not – in contrast to "superior responsibility" (see Rule 21.3) – require a formal superior–subordinate relationship.[26] The "aider and abettor" (article 25(3)(c)) assists the principal by rendering a substantial contribution. He or she wishes to further the crime, but need not share the intent of the main perpetrator, as long as he or she has knowledge of this intent. Article 25(3)(d) addresses the criminal responsibility that emerges from contributing to a common purpose of a group. The provision resembles

---

[25] The "control theory" has been developed in the case law of the International Criminal Court, in particular in *The Prosecutor* v. *Thomas Lubanga Dyilo*, Judgment, ICC-01/04-01/06-2842, Trial Chamber, 14 March 2012, paras. 989–1006, with Dissenting Opinions of Judge Fulford and Judge Van den Wyngaert.

[26] *The Prosecutor* v. *Kordić and Čerkez*, Judgment, IT-95-14/2-A, Appeals Chamber, 17 December 2004, para. 28.

joint criminal enterprise responsibility which has gained a reputation in the case law of the ICTY, but it is arguably more restrictive, because it does not include responsibility for crimes that were not initially part of the common purpose.

2. The content of the three core crimes within the jurisdiction of the ICC can be derived from the Elements of Crimes which have been developed 'to assist the Court in the interpretation and application of articles 6, 7 and 8, consistent with the Statute'.[27] The Elements of Crimes indicate the conduct, consequences and circumstances of the crimes, address a particular mental element of the crime, when necessary, and conclude with the contextual elements (see paragraph 3 to this Rule). Torture as a separate international crime is defined in article 1 of the Torture Convention as

> any act by which severe pain or suffering, whether physical or mental, is intentionally inflicted on a person for such purposes as obtaining from him or a third person information or a confession, punishing him for an act he or a third person has committed or is suspected of having committed, or intimidating or coercing him or a third person, or for any reason based on discrimination of any kind, when such pain or suffering is inflicted by or at the instigation of or with the consent or acquiescence of a public official or other person acting in an official capacity. It does not include pain or suffering arising only from, inherent in, or incidental to lawful sanctions.[28]

3. As already briefly indicated, the international crimes under the jurisdiction of the ICC require the fulfilment of specific contextual elements. War crimes refer by definition to conduct that takes place in the context of and is associated with an armed conflict. In the seminal *Tadić* case, the ICTY has elaborated both on the essential concept of armed conflict and on the distinction between IACs and NIACs. The Appeals Chamber defined an armed conflict as a resort to armed force between States or protracted armed violence between governmental authorities and organised groups or between such groups within a State. The Chamber added that IHL would apply from the initiation of such conflict and would extend beyond the cessation of hostilities until a general conclusion of peace is reached. Moreover, it applied in the whole territory of the warring States, whether or not actual combat took place.[29]

---

[27] Report of the Preparatory Commission for the International Criminal Court, Addendum, Part II: Finalized Draft Text of the Elements of Crimes, UN Doc. PCNICC/2000/1/Add.2 (2000).

[28] See n. 20.

[29] *Tadić* (n. 6), para. 70. See further Chapter 6.

In order to distinguish between IACs and NIACs, the Appeals Chamber took the standard position of a conflict between two or more States as the point of reference and added that a NIAC 'may become international ... if (i) another State intervenes in that conflict through its troops, or alternatively if (ii) some of the participants in the armed conflict act on behalf of that other State'.[30] Acting on behalf of another State implied *overall control* by that State, 'going beyond the mere financing and equipping of such forces and involving also participation in the planning and supervision of military operations'.[31] While there must therefore be a spatial and temporal connection between the conduct and the armed conflict, there must also be some kind of functional correlation between the two, which is expressed by the requirement of a nexus. The ICTY has interpreted this element rather broadly in the *Kunarac* case: 'The requirement that the act be closely related to the armed conflict is satisfied if ... the crimes are committed in the aftermath of the fighting, and until the cessation of combat activities in a certain region, and are committed *in furtherance or take advantage of the situation created by the fighting*.'[32]

4. Crimes against humanity are very serious crimes, such as murder, enslavement, rape, torture etc., committed as part of a widespread or systematic attack directed against any civilian population. The perpetrator must have had knowledge of the attack. Article 7(2)(a) of the Rome Statute elucidates that an attack against any civilian population implies the multiple commission of acts 'pursuant to or in furtherance of a State or organisational policy'. The use of the disjunctive 'or' in itself indicates that a State need not necessarily be involved. However, the required features of an organisation, for the purpose of assessing which ones may qualify as perpetrators of crimes against humanity, is a matter of some controversy. In the Kenya decision, the majority suggested the 'capability to perform acts which infringe on basic human values' as an appropriate yardstick, while Judge Kaul advocated a more rigid standard, in the sense that the organisation should have the characteristics of a State.[33] Remarkably, the ICTY has denied that the existence of a plan

---

[30] *The Prosecutor* v. *Tadić*, Judgment, IT-94-1-A, Appeals Chamber, 15 July 1999, para. 84.

[31] *Ibid.*, para. 145.

[32] *The Prosecutor* v. *Kunarac et al.*, Judgment, IT-96-23-T and IT-96-23/1-T, Trial Chamber, 22 February 2001, para. 568 (emphasis added).

[33] *Situation in the Republic of Kenya*, Decision Pursuant to Article 15 of the Rome Statute on the Authorization of an Investigation into the Situation in the Republic of Kenya, ICC-01/09, Pre-Trial Chamber II, 31 March 2010, paras. 115–128, with Dissenting Opinion of Judge Hans-Peter Kaul.

or policy is a legal element of the crime. In the *Kunarac* case, the Appeals Chamber emphatically held that 'nothing in the Statute or in customary international law ... required proof of the existence of a plan or policy to commit these crimes'.[34] While different standards as to the policy element persist, there is at least general agreement that random acts of violence are excluded from the realm of crimes against humanity.[35]

5. In the case of a crime against humanity, the perpetrator must have knowledge of the attack against the civilian population, and in relation to genocide the perpetrator must have had the special intent to destroy a group. These are aspects of mens rea that pertain to the contextual elements. The general standard of mens rea that is required for criminal responsibility under the ICC Statute is clarified in article 30. It stipulates that a person shall, unless otherwise provided, be held responsible only if the material elements are committed with intent and knowledge. Intent is further defined in relation to conduct as 'meaning to engage in the conduct', while in relation to a consequence as 'meaning to cause that consequence or being aware that it will occur in the ordinary cause of events'. Knowledge means 'awareness that a circumstance exists or that a consequence will occur in the ordinary course of events'. The choice of words seems to exclude dolus eventualis and recklessness (merely taking the risk) as sufficient forms of mens rea, a conclusion that is corroborated by the Trial Chamber in the *Lubanga* judgment.[36] However, the findings of the *Lubanga* Chamber in this respect are controversial, and can be contrasted with the opinion of the ICTY Trial Chamber in the *Stakić* case which held that recklessness or dolus eventualis would suffice in case of murder as a war crime and for extermination as a crime against humanity.[37] The qualifier 'unless otherwise provided' suggests, however, that in respect of some crimes or modes of liability a less rigid mens rea standard would be acceptable. That is, however, not the case with regard to the notion of superior responsibility, which is dealt with in Rule 21.3.

---

[34] *The Prosecutor v. Kunarac et al.*, Judgment, IT-96-23 and IT-96-23/1-A, Appeals Chamber, 12 June 2002, para. 98.
[35] Compare R. Cryer, H. Friman, D. Robinson and E. Wilmshurst (eds.), *An Introduction to International Criminal Law and Procedure*, 3rd edn (Cambridge University Press, 2014), pp. 238–239.
[36] *Lubanga* (n. 25), para. 1011.
[37] *The Prosecutor v. Stakić*, Judgment, IT-97-24-T, Trial Chamber, 31 July 2003, paras. 587 and 642. On this topic, see also A. Cassese, P. Gaeta, L. Baig, M. Fan, C. Gosnell and A. Whiting, *Cassese's International Criminal Law*, 3rd edn (Oxford University Press, 2013), pp. 45–49.

21.3   Commanders and civilian superiors incur criminal responsibility when they knew or should have known under the circumstances that subordinate personnel under their command were committing the international crimes referred to in Rules 21.1 and 21.2 and failed to take adequate measures to prevent their commission, or to punish the perpetrators or to bring the matter to the attention of the designated authorities.

1. Commanders are required to exercise command and control over their subordinates 24 hours a day, 7 days a week, and military law and practice expect subordinates to obey the lawful commands of their superiors. The strict organisation of the military as a prerequisite to engage in warfare is reflected in the conditions that non-State actors have to fulfil in order to qualify as parties to an armed conflict. They must establish a command structure and conduct their operations in accordance with the laws and customs of war. The far-reaching superior responsibility is the direct result of the normative assumptions sustaining the jus in bello.

2. Explicitly elaborated for the first time in article 86 of Additional Protocol I, the concept of superior responsibility has been incorporated in the statutes of international courts and tribunals. In the landmark *Celebići* case, the Trial Chamber of the ICTY identified and elaborated on the three constituent elements of the doctrine.[38] The Trial Chamber held that, for the principle of superior responsibility to be applicable, the superior should have effective control, in the sense of having the material ability to prevent and punish the commission of offences committed by his/her subordinates. The Trial Chamber added that such authority could have a de facto as well as a de jure character and observed that civilian superiors could be held responsible under the doctrine only if they exercised a degree of control which was similar to that of military commanders.[39] Concerning the mental element of "knew or had reason to know" that was required under article 7(3) of the ICTY Statute, the Trial Chamber found that a superior could be held responsible only if some specific information was in fact available to him/her which would provide notice of offences committed by his/her subordinates. It would suffice that the superior was put on notice by the information, or that it indicated the need for additional investigation in order to ascertain whether offences were being

---

[38] *The Prosecutor* v. *Delalić et al.*, Judgment, IT-96-21-T, Trial Chamber, 16 November 1998.
[39] *Ibid.*, para. 387.

committed or about to be committed by his/her subordinates.[40] The failure to prevent or repress the commission of crimes ultimately constitutes
criminal responsibility. The superior need not always repress the crimes
him-/herself, but should at least inform the competent authorities and
submit the matter to them for further investigation.

3. Article 28(a) of the ICC Statute apparently extends the responsibility of the military commander – compared with the ICTY standard – by
holding the military commander criminally responsible if he/she knew
or, owing to the circumstances at the time, should have known that the
forces were committing or about to commit international crimes. For
civilian superiors, a more lenient mens rea standard applies, as they only
incur criminal responsibility if they knew or consciously disregarded
information which clearly indicated that the subordinates were committing or were about to commit such crimes.

4. Superior responsibility should not be confused with "ordering"
or other forms of direct participation. The superior is typically responsible for a crime of omission. He has failed to live up to the standards
that might be expected from a reasonable and responsible commander.
A superior does not intend the commission of crimes; he/she is often
even ignorant of them and he/she contributes to their commission only
by failing to exercise the necessary control. It has been observed in the
case law of the ICTY that the superior is not in fact responsible for the
crimes of his/her subordinates, but rather that his/her responsibility is
rooted in those crimes. Some Trial Chambers have explicitly advocated
the position that superior responsibility should be recognised as a separate offence of dereliction of duty, rather than a form of indirect participation in international crimes.[41]

21.4 Any member of a Peace Operation suspected of participation in, or of failure to take adequate measures to prevent or punish subordinates engaged in, any of the aforementioned international crimes is subject to prosecution by national and international courts within the scope of their respective jurisdictions.

1. Responsibility for international crimes triggers what is generally
referred to as "universal jurisdiction" under international law. Hence,

---

[40] *Ibid.*, para. 393.
[41] See for instance *The Prosecutor* v. *Hadzihasanović and Kubura*, Judgment, IT-01-47-T, Trial
Chamber, 15 March 2006, para. 2075.

members of Peace Operations who are suspected on compelling grounds of international criminal liability or negligence resulting from failure to act in relation to subordinate personnel under their command or authority are, in principle, subject to prosecution in the national courts of any State within the limitations posed under international and national law. While a Status of Forces Agreement (SOFA) conferring exclusive jurisdiction upon a Sending State may bar prosecution in the Host State which has concluded such an agreement, waiver of immunity should be given due consideration in any situation where the Sending State is unable or unwilling to act. In any case, any third State not party to such an agreement would not be barred from proceeding with an investigation and prosecution if the person in question was present on its territory in the absence of diplomatic or equivalent immunity under international law.

2. In addition, an international court or tribunal would have jurisdiction to investigate and prosecute without reference to any immunities, to the extent the court or tribunal had jurisdiction under either an international treaty, or if the UN Security Council had invested it with jurisdiction. The ICTY, the ICTR and the SCSL all had primacy over national courts, which entails that they could request national courts to defer to their competence at any stage of the procedure.[42] The ICC, on the other hand, is complementary to national jurisdictions, which implies that it is allowed to exercise jurisdiction only if national authorities appear to be "unable" or "unwilling" to genuinely carry out an investigation or prosecution. Article 17(2) and (3) of the Rome Statute respectively indicate what should be understood by unwillingness and by inability. The Court must assess ex officio whether a case is admissible in the light of the complementarity principle and the gravity of the case (the latter follows from article 17(1)(d)). Moreover, both the accused and the State which has jurisdiction over the case are entitled to challenge the admissibility of a case. It should be noted that issues of admissibility arise only if a State undertakes some action. In case of mere inactivity, the Court can proceed with investigations and prosecution, because otherwise a State would be able to paralyse the whole system.[43]

---

[42] Art. 9(2) ICTY Statute (n. 3); art. 8(2) ICTR Statute (n. 8). Art. 8(2) SCSL Statute (n. 11) stipulates that the Special Court shall have primacy over the national courts of Sierra Leone.

[43] *The Prosecutor* v. *Germain Katanga and Mathieu Ngudjolo Chui*, Judgment on the Appeal of Mr Germain Katanga against the Oral Decision of Trial Chamber II of 12 June 2009 on the Admissibility of the Case, ICC-01/04-01/07 OA 8, Appeals Chamber, 25 September 2009, para. 79.

3. The jurisdiction of the ICC is predicated on the territorial State, i.e. the State on the territory of which the conduct in question occurred, or the State whose national is accused of having committed the crime being party to the ICC Statute. The system of State consent as a basis for the ICC's jurisdiction does not apply in case of a referral of a situation to the Court by the Security Council acting under Chapter VII of the UN Charter.[44] The circumvention of State consent is particularly relevant for the demolition of immunities. While article 27 of the ICC Statute follows Principle 3 of the Nuremberg Principles by declaring that official capacity does not exempt a person from criminal responsibility under the Statute, that rule applies only in respect of States parties, in view of the pacta tertiis principle. The referral of the situation by the Security Council arguably puts the ICC on the same level as international criminal tribunals that have been established by resolution or by involvement of the Security Council.[45] By implication, the ICC Pre-Trial Chamber held in the *Bashir* case that the position of the accused person as Head of State of a non-party State 'has no effect on the Court's jurisdiction over the present case'.[46] More difficult is the assessment of the consequences for inter-State relations. A State party that is requested by the ICC to surrender a Head of State of a non-party State faces a conflict of obligations, because it is also bound to observe the personal immunities of the accused. In order to guard States against such predicaments, article 98(1) of the ICC Statute precludes the Court from proceeding with a request for surrender or assistance which would require the requested State to act inconsistently with its obligations under international law with respect to the State or diplomatic immunity of a person or property of a third State, unless the Court can first obtain the co-operation of that third State for the waiver of the immunity. There is no solid reason why a resolution of the Security Council would trump the inter-State obligations in the realm of personal immunities, unless it explicitly says so.[47]

---

[44] Art. 13(b) ICC Statute (n. 1).

[45] Cf. *The Prosecutor* v. *Charles Ghankay Taylor*, Decision on Immunity from Jurisdiction, SCSL-2003-01-I, Appeals Chamber, 31 May 2004, in which the Appeals Chamber qualified the Sierra Leone Court as an "international criminal court" before which neither functional nor personal immunities would prevail.

[46] *The Prosecutor* v. *Al Bashir*, Decision on the Prosecution's Application for a Warrant of Arrest against Omar Hassan Ahmad Al Bashir, ICC-02/05-01/09, Pre-Trial Chamber I, 4 March 2009, para. 41.

[47] In a similar vein, P. Gaeta, 'Does President Al Bashir Enjoy Immunity from Arrest?', 7 *Journal of International Criminal Justice* (2009), pp. 315–332. For a different point of view, see D. Akande, 'International Law Immunities and the International Criminal Court', 98 *American Journal of*

21.5　Making a member of a Peace Operation the object of an attack constitutes a war crime if the Peace Operation is not a party to an armed conflict and if the member of the Peace Operation retains the right to protection under international humanitarian law.

1. Under the 1994 UN Safety Convention,[48] the ICC Statute,[49] the statutes of certain hybrid international criminal tribunals[50] and the customary international law of armed conflict,[51] personnel forming part of a Peace Operation, including military personnel attached to it, possess protected status and may not be made the object of attack or of other acts of violence, so long as they are not taking a direct part in hostilities associated with an armed conflict and so long as the Peace Operation has not become party to an armed conflict. From the perspective of IHL, they are civilians and are not subject to attack. Acting in lawful self-defence does not constitute a hostile act or automatically result in becoming party to an armed conflict under IHL. Lawful self-defence includes protection of mission personnel and/or civilians from imminent physical danger and extends to proportionate action to counter attempts to disarm or otherwise incapacitate mission personnel or seize vital installations or equipment.[52] Such action must be exercised within the restrictions laid down in the mandate, in international human rights law (IHRL) and in the relevant national law of the personnel in question. So long as self-defence is conducted within these bounds, it does not constitute a hostile act, or result in loss of protected status. For IHL purposes all members of a Peace Operation, including military personnel, have such protected civilian status so long as the mission has not become party to an armed conflict. Such protection extends to the installations, vehicles or other materiel and equipment attached to a Peace Operation. Acts of violence against Peace Operations personnel might include co-ordinated attacks,

---

International Law (2004), pp. 407–433. See also UNSC Res. 1422 (2002) which requests the ICC to forgo, for a period of one year starting 1 July 2002, investigation or prosecution in cases 'involving current or former officials or personnel from a contributing State not a Party to the Rome Statute over acts or omissions relating to a United Nations established or authorized operation'. This request has been renewed once (see UNSC Res. 1487 (2003)).

[48] Optional Protocol to the Convention on the Safety of United Nations and Associated Personnel (8 December 2005, in force 19 August 2010), 2689 UNTS 59.

[49] Arts. 8(2)(b)(iii) and 8(2)(e)(iii) ICC Statute (n. 1).

[50] See e.g. art. 4(b) SCSL Statute (n. 11).

[51] See J.-M. Henckaerts and L. Doswald-Beck, *Customary International Humanitarian Law*, vol. I, *Rules* (Cambridge University Press, 2005), Rule 33, pp. 112–114.

[52] See Chapter 12.

sporadic acts of violence intended to kill or injure any member of a Peace Mission, kidnapping or unlawful detention of Peace Operation personnel and other related acts such as taking peacekeeping personnel hostage.

2. Attacks upon peacekeepers are increasingly frequent and in some missions are even a chronic occurrence. Members of a Peace Operation operating in an unstable and sometimes hostile environment will be confronted with repeated challenges to their safety and to their ability to carry out the mandate and may in some cases be confronted with frequent acts of violence or forcible attempts to frustrate the carrying out of the mandate. However, even if self-defence is resorted to on a regular basis as a response to such acts, it does not, in itself, result in the Peace Force losing protected status or becoming a party to an armed conflict. The threshold for applicability of IHL to a Peace Operation is dealt with elsewhere in this Manual,[53] but for the purposes of this chapter it is stressed that attacks upon protected peacekeeping personnel constitute an international criminal offence under both conventional and customary law. A number of decisions by international and internationalised criminal tribunals have given expression to this.[54]

21.6 Whenever and to the extent that they are so mandated, Peace Operations shall assist in the administration of international justice. In the absence of any such mandate, Peace Operations should, whenever possible, provide such assistance as is compatible with their mandate and within their capability to authorised international courts and tribunals in the administration of international justice. At a minimum, Peace Operations should bring the perpetration of international crimes by any actor within their area of operations to the attention of the UN Secretary-General and, where appropriate, the government of the Host State and the relevant Sending State.

1. Whenever so mandated a Peace Operation will clearly be under an obligation to provide such assistance as is required by the mandate and that it is able to provide. To date, there have been few if any mandates whereby a peacekeeping mission has been specifically tasked with providing assistance to an international criminal tribunal. Indeed, this might

---

[53] See Chapter 6.
[54] A. Gadler, 'The Protection of Peacekeepers and International Criminal Law: Legal Challenges and Broader Protection', 11 *German Law Journal* (2010), pp. 585–608.

conflict with one of the core principles of peacekeeping, namely the principle of impartiality in that assistance to a criminal tribunal could be seen as potentially compromising the impartial stance of the mission. Moreover, there are significant operational obstacles in some cases to providing such assistance due to a number of factors, such as lack of trained personnel to conduct criminal investigations, the need to maintain stable relations with the local population and others. However, there have been a number of missions which have provided various forms of assistance, albeit not always wholeheartedly, to international criminal tribunals, including most notably the UN-mandated NATO stabilisation missions in Bosnia and Herzegovina and in Kosovo, but this has not been without controversy and there have been significant problems in providing such assistance.[55]

2. In the absence of a mandate which explicitly or implicitly provides for a duty of assistance, there is no general duty under international law for a Peace Operation to provide direct assistance or to share intelligence with an international criminal tribunal. However, the relationship of international criminal justice to some peace missions (the occurrence of international crimes is why some missions are deployed in the first place) and the dependency of such tribunals upon peacekeeping forces for security and assistance in a number of areas have led to a practice of qualified co-operation in so far as this is not perceived as compromising the mission and is within the capabilities of the Peace Operation.[56] Such qualified co-operation has been provided by the UN to the ICC in a number of missions.

3. In any case, there are strong arguments for surmising that a Peace Operation should bring the occurrence of international crimes within its area of responsibility to the attention of the UN Secretary-General whenever there is clear evidence of such crimes or reasonable suspicion

---

[55] In its initial year of deployment in Bosnia and Herzegovina, NATO considered itself not bound to actively search for or apprehend persons under indictment by the ICTY. However, from 1997 this position altered due to a change in the operational circumstances and in the manner in which ICTY issued indictments, and SFOR provided very valuable assistance to the ICTY and rendered a significant number of suspects into custody. For a thorough discussion of the issues involved, see C. K. Lamont, *International Criminal Justice and the Politics of Compliance* (Ashgate, 2010), pp. 122–133. For an account of the different viewpoints among NATO members and between the ICTY and NATO in the providing of assistance by KFOR to the ICTY, see T. Brocades Zaalberg, *Soldiers and Civil Power: Supporting or Substituting Civil Authorities in Modern Peace Operations* (Amsterdam University Press, 2006), pp. 352 *et seq.*

[56] For an analysis of some of the issues involved, see P. Clark, 'The Challenges of International Criminal Law in Addressing Mass Atrocity', in B. A. Arrigo and H. Y. Bersot (eds.), *The Routledge Handbook of International Crime and Justice Studies* (Routledge, 2013), pp. 161–163.

that such crimes have occurred within the area of operations. This flows from the duty laid down in applicable treaties and under customary international law to take feasible measures to bring such crimes to justice and from the commitment of the UN and the international community at large to prevent and suppress international crimes. It is then up to the Secretary-General to bring such information to the attention of the Security Council under article 99 of the Charter.

Leuven Manual on the International Law Applicable to Peace Operations: List of Rules

Peace Operations

1.1 Peace Operations are based on three principles: consent of the parties, impartiality and limited use of force.

Mandate

3.1 Every Peace Operation requires a mandate to provide a legal basis for the operation and set out the objectives and legal and operational parameters which govern the operation. A mandate can be issued by a competent international organisation or by a Host State government inviting or consenting to a Peace Operation conducted by a competent international organisation on its territory, and in most cases will be a combination of both.

3.2 In addition to consent by the Host State, a mandate issued by the Security Council will complement and provide an additional legal basis alongside such consent for conducting a Peace Operation. If the mandate was adopted under Chapter VII of the UN Charter, it will prevail over any terms set by the Host State in consenting to the operation.

3.3 In the absence of consent by the Host State, a mandate issued by the Security Council under Chapter VII of the UN Charter is a strict legal requirement for the deployment of troops and other personnel onto a State's territory to conduct a Peace Operation. This applies irrespective of whether the operation is conducted by the UN directly, by a regional organisation or arrangement or by individual States operating independently of the UN or any other organisation, but with the authorisation of the Security Council.

3.4 Peace Operations are, in addition to the terms and conditions imposed by the mandate, always required to act in conformity with all relevant and applicable rules of international law and to respect Host State law in so far as it is compatible with international law and with the mandate. In addition, Troop Contributing Countries will require their forces to comply with relevant portions of their national law.

Organisation-Specific Legal Framework

4.1.1 Every Peace Operation conducted by an organisation or arrangement must have a legal basis in international law and in the internal law of the organisation.

4.1.2 The competent organ of an organisation or arrangement shall determine the mandate of a Peace Operation conducted by that organisation or arrangement.

4.1.3 The UN as well as regional organisations or arrangements shall set up and conduct their Peace Operations in accordance with the UN Charter, their internal rules and procedures, and other rules of international law applicable to them.

4.1.4 Regional organisations or arrangements within the meaning of Chapter VIII of the UN Charter shall report to the Security Council on their Peace Operations. All regional organisations or arrangements shall report to the Security Council on their Peace Operations if so required by the Security Council or by their own internal rules. Mandates issued by the Security Council for Peace Operations conducted by regional organisations or arrangements should contain clear reporting duties to the Security Council. In other cases they should report to the Security Council on their Peace Operations as appropriate.

4.1.5 Peace Operations conducted by regional organisations and arrangements remain distinct from the UN. When distinct Peace Operations conducted by a regional organisation or arrangement and the UN work alongside one another, co-operation arrangements should be put in place.

Command and Control

4.2.1 The command arrangements which are employed in a Peace Operation are provided for by the organisation which has undertaken to perform the Peace Operation. Peace Operations involve the partial transfer of authority and/or control from a Troop Contributing Country to the UN or to the regional organisation or arrangement which is undertaking the Peace Operation. Generally, operational command or operational control will be transferred, while full command (national command) and administrative control are retained by the Troop Contributing Country. The partial transfer of authority may include certain caveats or restrictions upon the use of the Troop Contributing Country's personnel or assets for the execution of particular tasks within the Peace Operation.

4.2.2 Personnel participating in Peace Operations shall observe the authority of the Force Commander and of the international or regional organisation or arrangement involved. While this authority is based on the internal law of the organisation or arrangement, it has to be assigned by Troop Contributing Countries. Command and control arrangements are set out in an agreement between the Troop Contributing Country and the international or regional organisation or arrangement, or in internal arrangements of the organisation involved.

African Union

4.3.1 Peace Operations deployed by the AU require a legal basis under international law and a decision pursuant to the Constitutive Act of the AU. Peace Operations by the AU shall be conducted in accordance with international law (including the UN Charter), and the internal laws and policies of the AU. Peace Operations deployed by the AU shall also comply with mission-specific agreements.

European Union

4.4.1 An EU Peace Operation requires a legal basis under international law. Its required legal basis under EU law is a Council decision adopted on the basis of the Treaty on European Union, following a proposal by a Member State or by the High Representative of the Union for Foreign Affairs and Security Policy. Such Council decisions set up and govern EU Peace Operations.

4.4.2 Additional legal acts which may be adopted in relation to EU Peace Operations include Council decisions launching an operation, Council decisions laying down funding arrangements, Status of Forces Agreements or Status of Mission Agreements, agreements on the participation of third States, and Political and Security Committee decisions accepting the participation of third States or appointing Force Commanders or Heads of Missions.

4.4.3   Peace Operations of the EU shall be conducted in accordance with applicable EU law and international law.

North Atlantic Treaty Organization

4.5.1   Each Peace Operation of NATO authorised by the UN Security Council requires a legal basis under international law and must be based on a decision by the North Atlantic Council. Peace Operations shall be conducted in accordance with international law, the Organization's applicable policies and doctrines, and the national laws of each Troop Contributing Country.

Sub-Regional Organisations

4.6.1   Peace Operations deployed by a sub-regional organisation require a legal basis under international law and a decision pursuant to the organisation's constituent instrument. Peace Operations shall be conducted in accordance with international law including the UN Charter, and the internal laws and policies of the particular sub-regional organisation. Peace Operations deployed by a sub-regional organisation shall also comply with mission-specific agreements.

International Human Rights Law

5.1   The human rights obligations that are applicable to a Peace Operation may be derived from the international obligations of the contributing States and/or from those of the international organisation undertaking the operation and may be based on treaty and/or customary law provisions.

5.2   The human rights law obligations of a State undertaking or participating in Peace Operations apply towards all persons who are within the jurisdiction of that State, as exercised in particular through its contingent or its personnel.

5.3 Each State contributing personnel to a Peace Operation shall ensure that contributed personnel comply with the international human rights law obligations that bind that State and are relevant to that operation.

5.4 In conducting Peace Operations, an international organisation shall comply with its international human rights law obligations.

5.5 In accordance with the obligation to respect Host State law, there is an obligation to respect international human rights law applicable to the Host State.

5.6 Interoperability issues may arise if the States contributing to a Peace Operation have divergent obligations under international human rights law. Applicable human rights obligations cannot be circumvented by reference to the fact that other actors in the same operation have different obligations.

5.7 If a Peace Force considers that it may be unable to comply fully with its international human rights law obligations while discharging its duties in accordance with the mandate, the State or international organisation, as the case may be, should consider seeking to derogate from the relevant human rights provisions where possible.

5.8 When applicable simultaneously, international humanitarian law and human rights law are complementary. In case of collision between a norm of international humanitarian law and a norm of human rights law, the more specific norm applies in principle.

5.9 In UN Peace Operations the UN Human Rights Due Diligence Policy and the UN Human Rights Screening Policy apply. Regional organisations and arrangements should consider applying similar policies.

International Humanitarian Law

6.1 International humanitarian law applies to a Peace Operation, in particular to its forces, when the conditions for the application of this body of law are met, irrespective of the nature of the operation.

6.2 The conditions for the applicability of international humanitarian law to Peace Operations are those set out in international humanitarian law itself and established by practice. They do not differ from the conditions that apply to forces other than Peace Operations. Peace Operations which are the subject of this Manual are operations deployed to situations of non-international conflicts; different conditions apply for determining the existence of international armed conflicts and non-international armed conflicts.

6.3   International humanitarian law does not regulate the conduct of a Peace Operation deployed in the context of an armed conflict to which it does not become a party but members of that force shall benefit from the protections afforded to civilians by international humanitarian law.

6.4   Members of the military component of a Peace Operation lose the protection from direct attack afforded to civilians if and for such time as the operation has become a party to the conflict. In cases where the Peace Operation has not become a party, individual members of a force lose such protection only to the extent that and for as long as they participate directly in hostilities.

6.5   If the requisite conditions are met, the Peace Operation may become a party to the conflict. Depending on the factual circumstances, individual Troop Contributing Countries may become parties to the conflict in their own right.

6.6   International humanitarian law will determine the geographical scope of an armed conflict to which a Peace Operation is a party.

6.7   If a Peace Operation participates in a pre-existing non-international armed conflict, or if there is no pre-existing armed conflict, the law of non-international armed conflict starts to apply when the hostilities involving the Peace Operation satisfy the requirements of a non-international armed conflict. International humanitarian law ceases to apply when the armed conflict comes to an end or when circumstances requiring the continued application of international humanitarian law (such as the continued detention of members of an armed group) cease to exist, whichever is later.

6.8   Where international humanitarian law applies, it determines which persons are protected.

Gender

7.1   Gender issues should be taken into account, in all mission aspects, including in Peace Operations. Participants in Peace Operations should consider gender issues in terms of both participation and substance.

7.2   Discrimination based on gender is prohibited. Gender-based violence and especially violence against women are a form of gender-based discrimination and constitute a violation of international human rights law.

7.3   A gender perspective should be taken into account throughout the
      life-cycle of a Peace Operation, from its inception and the develop-
      ment of its mandate to the performance of every task provided for
      in the mandate. Gender-specific indicators should also be included
      in the data collection and reporting requirements before, during
      and after a Peace Operation to provide a complete gender issues
      picture, to inform decision-making and to facilitate the learning of
      lessons.

7.4   Troop Contributing Countries should be aware of the gender
      considerations in the areas of primary national responsibility such
      as force generation, training and discipline, and should strive to
      ensure that the appropriate levels of capacity and competence are
      met prior to deploying Peace Operations.

Status of Forces and Mission

8.1   Rights and obligations of an organisation deploying military and
      civilian personnel in a Peace Operation, and those of such person-
      nel, should be specified in Status of Forces or Status of Mission
      Agreements. The immunity of personnel in the Host State and of
      Sending States' military personnel in any Transit State, which is
      based on customary international law and treaty law, is usually con-
      firmed in Status of Forces or Status of Mission Agreements relating
      to Peace Operations.

8.2   Although Sending States' military personnel enjoying immunity are
      exempt from criminal jurisdiction in the Host State and any Transit
      State, the Sending State has jurisdiction over such personnel.

8.3   For each Peace Operation, the responsibilities of the interna-
      tional organisation involved, the Troop Contributing Countries
      and the Host State should be clearly set out in appropriate form.
      Arrangements are usually concluded between the international
      organisation and the Sending States to facilitate the provision of
      national contingents.

8.4   Matters pertaining to entry and exit, freedom of movement,
      exemption from customs and taxes, the right to operate equip-
      ment and engage in communications, logistic support, and safety
      and security should be addressed in the Status of Forces or Status
      of Mission Agreements and in associated arrangements with the
      Host State.

Host State Law

9.1 Peace Operations and their members are subject to the Host State's laws while present or acting within its territory. In applying their national law to Peace Operations and their members, Host States must observe the relevant rules of international law governing the exercise of their jurisdictional competences, including any Status of Forces or Status of Mission Agreements, and any other applicable treaties or rules of customary law relating to immunities and privileges.

9.2 Peace Operations and their members must respect the law of the Host State.

Sending State Law

10.1 While the rights and duties of a Peace Operation in the Host State are primarily determined at the international level, Sending States retain certain powers and responsibilities.

10.2 In enforcing their jurisdiction in the territory of third States, Sending States must observe the relevant rules of international law governing the exercise of their jurisdictional competences, including any applicable treaties and rules of customary international law.

Memorandums of Understanding and Other Instruments

11.1 The international organisation or lead State undertaking a Peace Operation can conclude an arrangement with a Troop Contributing Country to set out the administrative, logistical and financial terms and conditions which govern the contribution of personnel, equipment and services provided by the Troop Contributing Country to the organisation. Generally, such an arrangement is called a Memorandum of Understanding. In accordance with the intention of the participants, the arrangement can be legally binding.

11.2 Support and services to the international organisation or lead State undertaking a Peace Operation and/or to the Troop Contributing Countries may be provided by the Host State authorities as well as by civilian international contractors. The administrative, logistical and financial terms and conditions regarding the provision of such support and services should be set forth in an arrangement and/or a contract.

11.3 Apart from mission-specific arrangements, non-mission-specific policies, guidelines and instruments providing operational and technical standards are employed by international organisations conducting Peace Operations to secure the interoperability of the contingents.

Use of Force

12.1 The use of force by members of a Peace Force may be permitted in accordance with the mandate or in self-defence.

12.2 The mandate may authorise the use of necessary and proportionate force for the achievement of tasks, purposes and objectives set out in the mandate when circumstances require the use of force.

12.3 Members of a Peace Force have the inherent right to use such force as is necessary and proportionate in personal self-defence or in defence of others.

12.4 Members of a Peace Force may have the right to use necessary and proportionate force in defence of mission-essential property or in the maintenance of their right to move freely.

12.5 Where international human rights law is applicable, that body of law will determine the circumstances and manner in which force may be employed.

12.6 A Peace Operation that becomes involved as a party to an armed conflict must comply with international humanitarian law when undertaking operations in connection with that conflict. In situations involving the conduct of hostilities against targets under the law of armed conflict, the rules of the law of armed conflict relating to the conduct of hostilities will apply. The use of force outside the context of hostilities will, in general, be governed by rules provided by other applicable bodies of law, in particular international human rights law.

12.7 A Peace Operation should be appropriately equipped to enable it to adjust the degree and nature of force that it employs to suit as closely as possible the requirements of foreseeable security situations.

12.8 Where the use of force is authorised beyond self-defence under Sending State law, Rules of Engagement should be issued by an authority superior to the Peace Force. The restrictions on the use of force referred to in this chapter should be reflected in such issued Rules of Engagement.

12.9 Planners of Peace Operations should put in place arrangements for post-incident investigations to be undertaken. Such investigations should be either administrative or disciplinary in nature, depending on what is known as to the circumstances.

Detention

13.1 Detention of persons during Peace Operations must not be arbitrary.

13.2 Detention may take place only on grounds recognised in applicable international law.

13.3 When circumstances justifying detention have ceased to exist, a detainee must be released.

13.4 Detention must be subject to procedural safeguards in accordance with applicable international law. These safeguards include in particular the possibility promptly to challenge the lawfulness of detention and the requirement that there shall be an appropriate periodic review at least every six months. Both the initial and the subsequent periodic reviews should in principle be undertaken by a court but shall in any event be undertaken by an impartial and independent authority.

13.5 Persons detained are to be promptly informed of the reasons for their detention in a language that they understand.

13.6 Persons detained are to be promptly informed of their rights and should have access to legal assistance where feasible.

13.7 Additional rights apply in relation to criminal proceedings including the principles of legality and fair trial.

13.8 Detained persons are to be promptly registered by the detaining authority, which must keep records while protecting personal data.

13.9 Access to detainees must be given to the International Committee of the Red Cross in accordance with international humanitarian law where applicable. Such access to the International Committee of the Red Cross should also be given in non-international armed conflicts and where warranted in other situations. Access to detainees must also be given to such competent human rights bodies as have a right of access and may be given to other relevant organisations where appropriate. The International Committee of the Red Cross and competent human rights bodies, as well as other relevant organisations where appropriate, should accordingly be notified of any detention.

13.10 Any right to consular and diplomatic protection of detainees which have a nationality other than that of the Host State shall be respected in accordance with the Vienna Conventions on Diplomatic and Consular Relations.

13.11 Detainees shall have a right to contact their families and the outside world as appropriate.

13.12 Detainees shall have the right to bring a complaint or to make a submission relating to any aspect of their detention.

13.13 Where applicable, detainees shall have the right to compensation in case of an unlawful arrest.

13.14 All persons detained will in all circumstances be treated humanely and with respect for their dignity without any adverse distinction founded on race, colour, religion or faith, political or other opinion, national or social origin, sex, birth, wealth or other similar status. Torture, and other cruel, inhuman or degrading treatment or punishment, is prohibited.

13.15 Detaining authorities are responsible for providing detainees with adequate conditions of detention including food and drinking water, accommodation, access to open air, safeguards to protect health and hygiene, and protection against the rigours of the climate and the dangers of military activities. Wounded and sick detainees are to receive the medical care and attention required by their condition.

13.16 A State or international organisation may transfer a detainee to another State or authority only in compliance with the transferring State's or international organisation's international law obligations. It must ensure that the detainee who is to be transferred is not subject to a real risk of treatment that would breach international law obligations concerning humane treatment and due process. This may require adequate ex ante assurances followed by ex post monitoring, as well as capacity building.

13.17 Detaining authorities should develop and implement standard operating procedures and other relevant guidance regarding the handling of detainees. Such guidance should reflect the different categories of detainees and the rules applicable to each of them.

General Protection of Civilians

14.1.1 In Peace Operations civilians are entitled to protection.

14.1.2 The protection of civilians is a Host State responsibility. Peace Operations have an important role to play in supporting governments to fulfil that responsibility. When the protection of civilians is prejudiced, a Peace Operation should use all means available to it to protect civilians who are under imminent threat.

14.1.3 Protection mandates must be sufficiently realistic and form part of a broader political strategy. The Security Council should be kept informed about what is needed to deal with threats to civilians, and Troop and Police Contributing Countries should provide the required resources and apply their leverage to respond to threats against civilians.

14.1.4 Whenever a Peace Operation is mandated to protect civilians, the protection task should be reflected in the operation's Rules of Engagement.

14.1.5 Whenever a Peace Operation is not expressly mandated to protect civilians, the operation's Rules of Engagement should allow for the possibility of carrying out tasks related to the protection of civilians.

14.1.6 Special protection and assistance must be given by the Peace Operation to particularly vulnerable groups of individuals requiring special attention.

Protection of Children

14.2.1 Children must be protected, at all times and without discrimination, from the direct and indirect impact of armed conflict. This protection stems from the rules and principles of all bodies of applicable law, generally, and from a set of specific measures for the protection of children in armed conflict.

14.2.2 Peace Forces should ensure that roles and responsibilities with respect to the protection of children in armed conflict are clear for all areas of the mandate and that planning, conducting and reporting on the mission reflect the children's specific needs for protection.

Protection Against Sexual Exploitation and Abuse

14.3.1 Sexual exploitation and abuse by military, police and civilian personnel of [UN] Peace Operations missions are prohibited.

14.3.2 Prevention should be part of the [UN's three-pronged] strategy to combat all forms of misconduct, including sexual exploitation and abuse. Prevention of sexual exploitation and abuse should take place through, inter alia, training, awareness-raising activities and practical preventive measures.

14.3.3 Enforcement of [UN] standards of conduct should be part of the [UN's three-pronged] strategy to combat all forms of misconduct, including sexual exploitation and abuse. Enforcement of the prohibition of sexual exploitation and abuse should take place through, inter alia, investigation and, where such exploitation or abuse is proved, administrative action and/or disciplinary measures.

14.3.4 Remedial action should be part of the [UN's three-pronged] strategy to combat sexual exploitation and abuse. Remedial action should take place through assistance and support and includes, inter alia, medical, legal, psycho-social and immediate material care as well as the facilitation of the pursuit of paternity and child support claims.

14.3.5 The [UN] prevention, enforcement and remedial action strategies to combat sexual exploitation and abuse should be continuously evaluated and where necessary further strengthened.

Protection of Refugees and Other Forcibly Displaced Persons

14.4.1 International refugee law is specialised human rights law. Unlike international human rights law, international refugee law does not allow for derogation in time of public emergency or conflict; it applies in full in time of peace and in time of war.

14.4.2 Refugees are persons who have been forced to flee their country of origin. They are entitled to international protection.

14.4.3 Recognition of refugee status is a declaratory and not a constitutive act. The right to international protection – including the protection that is prescribed by the Refugees Convention – is therefore not conditional on status determination.

14.4.4 A person who satisfies the criteria contained in the refugee definition of the Refugees Convention must be excluded from the benefits of this status when there are serious reasons for considering that (a) he/she has committed a crime against peace, a war crime or a crime against humanity, as defined in the international instruments drawn up to make provision in respect of such crimes; (b) he/she has committed a serious non-political crime outside the State of refuge prior to his/her admission to that country as a refugee; or (c) he/she has been guilty of acts contrary to the purposes and principles of the UN.

14.4.5   A person ceases to be a refugee when demonstrating no further need for international protection. This happens if (i) he/she voluntarily re-avails himself of the protection of his/her country of nationality; (ii) having lost his/her nationality, he/she voluntarily re-acquires it; (iii) he/she acquires a new nationality, and enjoys the protection of his/her new nationality; or (iv) he/she voluntarily re-establishes him-/herself in the country which he/she left or outside which he/she remained owing to fear of persecution. Alternatively, a person ceases to be a refugee when the circumstances in connection with which this status has been recognised have ceased to exist.

14.4.6   A refugee is protected against expulsion (*refoulement*) in any manner whatsoever to the frontiers of territories where his/her life or freedom would be threatened on account of his/her race, religion, nationality, membership of a particular social group or political opinion.

14.4.7   Refugees must not suffer adverse consequences on account of their formal nationality.

14.4.8   Refugees are entitled to the human rights listed in the Refugees Convention. These rights are geared to enabling refugees to become self-reliant in the Host State.

14.4.9   Persons who are displaced within their country of nationality or habitual residence are not refugees: they have not crossed an international border, and therefore do not qualify as refugees in any definition. They are internally displaced persons who remain subject to the jurisdiction of their country of nationality or habitual residence.

14.4.10   States are obliged to co-operate with the United Nations High Commissioner for Refugees in the exercise of his/her functions.

14.4.11   Refugee camps and settlements must be located away from the border.

14.4.12   The civilian and humanitarian character of refugee camps and settlements and sites with internally displaced persons must be secured.

14.4.13   Refugee camps and camps for internally displaced persons and their immediate surroundings must be protected.

14.4.14   Unhindered access of refugees and internally displaced persons to humanitarian assistance must be secured.

14.4.15   Refugees can return to their country of origin only on a voluntary basis. Both refugees and internally displaced persons have the right to return to their place of origin.

Aerial and Maritime Dimensions

15.1   All activities by Peace Operations in the maritime and aerial domains must be conducted in accordance with applicable international law.

15.2   Vessels and aircraft conducting, or operating in support of, Peace Operations enjoy the freedoms of navigation and overflight in and above the high seas and the exclusive economic zone. These freedoms must be exercised in accordance with international law.

15.3   Vessels engaged in, or in support of, Peace Operations enjoy the right of innocent passage in the territorial sea, archipelagic waters and certain international straits, the right of archipelagic sea lanes passage in archipelagic waters where applicable and the right of transit passage in certain international straits. These rights must be exercised in accordance with international law.

15.4   States exercise full sovereignty over their internal waters as well as the airspace above their land territory and territorial sea. A Peace Operation may operate in the internal waters or national airspace of a State only with its consent, unless provided otherwise in a Security Council resolution adopted pursuant to Chapter VII of the UN Charter.

15.5   The territorial sea is a maritime zone where the coastal State exercises sovereignty subject to the regime of innocent passage under customary international law as reflected in the UN Convention on the Law of the Sea. Vessels conducting, or in support of, a Peace Operation may operate in the territorial sea of a coastal State only in accordance with the regime pertaining to innocent passage or with the consent of the Host/coastal State if the right of innocent passage does not cover the envisaged activities, unless provided otherwise in a Security Council resolution adopted pursuant to Chapter VII of the UN Charter.

15.6   The coastal State possesses sovereign rights and jurisdiction but does not exercise sovereignty in its maritime zones beyond the territorial sea. A Peace Operation is not required to obtain the consent of the coastal State in order to operate in maritime zones beyond the territorial sea.

15.7   Flag States exercise exclusive jurisdiction over ships flying their flag on the high seas. Save in exceptional circumstances as regulated under international law, vessels conducting a Peace Operation may not board a ship without the consent of the flag State. A Security Council resolution adopted pursuant to Chapter VII of the UN Charter may provide an exception to this Rule.

15.8   In the conduct of Peace Operations, force may be applied only in conformity with the mandate and applicable international law. In carrying out maritime interdiction/interception measures force may be used only where the mandate has specifically authorised its use and as a last resort to enforce compliance. Boarding of vessels and detention of persons, in so far as authorised under the mandate, must be conducted in conformity with applicable international law. The use of force in the aerial dimension of Peace Operations must comply with the mandate and with applicable international law. The latter precludes, in most circumstances, the use of force against civil aircraft in flight. Any use of force must be strictly necessary and proportionate.

Monitoring Compliance

16.1   Setting the standards for conduct and discipline in UN Peace Operations is a shared responsibility of the UN, Troop Contributing Countries and Police Contributing Countries.

16.2   The UN, Troop Contributing Countries and Police Contributing Countries have a shared responsibility for pre-deployment training and "in-mission" training on conduct and discipline issues.

16.3   Monitoring compliance with standards of conduct and discipline is a responsibility of the UN and managers and commanders at all levels.

16.4   Managers and commanders are to ensure that personnel under their command or supervision are aware of the UN standards of conduct and are aware that they have an obligation to report misconduct by their subordinates.

16.5   Managers and commanders must be held accountable in terms of performance regarding the exercise of their conduct and discipline functions.

16.6   The UN and Member States have an important role to ensure compliance in the field of conduct and discipline. The UN has taken measures to strengthen the Organisation's role in the areas of prevention, enforcement and remedial action, in particular in cases of sexual exploitation and abuse.

16.7   Investigation and administrative action are responsibilities for the UN, Troop Contributing Countries and Police Contributing Countries.

16.8   As regards non-UN Peace Operations, the responsibility for setting the standards for conduct and discipline, for pre-deployment training and "in-mission" training on conduct and discipline issues and for monitoring and enforcing compliance with these standards, including through investigation and administrative action, is shared between the regional organisation or arrangement conducting the operation and the Troop Contributing Countries and Police Contributing Countries. Commanders and civilian hierarchy at all levels are to ensure that personnel under their command or supervision are aware of the applicable standards of conduct and reporting obligations and must monitor compliance with these standards at their level and within the scope of their responsibilities. They must be held accountable for their performance regarding the exercise of these conduct and discipline functions.

Rule of Law

17.1   Respect for the rule of law is fundamental to the proper functioning of all States and societies. Accordingly, where a Peace Operation is deployed to a country in which either the rule of law has broken down or respect for it is otherwise impaired, taking action to establish and thereafter maintain the proper functioning of the essential rule of law institutions and to foster respect for them and for the laws, procedures and proceedings associated with them is critical to the success of the Peace Operation.

17.2   All personnel engaged in Peace Operations, and the Peace Force itself, must demonstrate respect for the rule of law at all times.

17.3   Strategies for rule of law reform must seek to ensure that affected populations, their recognised representatives and relevant institutions are appropriately involved in developing and implementing the required changes.

17.4   Where rule of law issues require action by a Peace Force, the mandate should define clear, credible and achievable priorities for that action and the necessary resources and strategies should be made available to the Peace Force.

Demining

18.1   The primary responsibility for demining and removal of explosive
       remnants of war lies with the Host State. Any responsibilities
       of a Peace Operation for demining and removal of explosive
       remnants of war must be stipulated in the mandate.

18.2   A Peace Force should make feasible efforts to identify all areas
       under its control which are known or suspected to be contami-
       nated by anti-personnel mines, cluster munition remnants or
       other explosive remnants of war.

18.3   If this is required by a Peace Operation's mandate, a Peace Force
       shall make feasible efforts to clear, remove or destroy anti-
       personnel mines, cluster munition remnants and other explosive
       remnants of war in affected areas under its control. If a Troop
       Contributing Country is bound by applicable treaty obligations
       in this regard, it must comply with them.

Accountability and Responsibility

19.1   Peace Operations, including their Troop and Police Contributing
       Countries and international organisations, must exercise their
       powers subject to appropriate forms of internal and external
       scrutiny. In particular, they should observe, in harmony with the
       requirements of the operation's mandate, the principles of good
       governance, good faith, oversight and due diligence.

19.2   Injury to persons or damage to property caused by Peace
       Operations may give rise to civil liability. Peace Operations,
       including their Troop and Police Contributing Countries and
       international organisations, should put in place arrangements to
       discharge that liability by providing appropriate remedies for the
       injury and damage caused by wrongful acts.

19.3   Internationally wrongful acts committed in the context of Peace
       Operations give rise to international responsibility in accordance
       with international law. International responsibility is a legal form
       of accountability. There is an internationally wrongful act when
       conduct consisting of an action or omission is attributable to a
       State or international organisation under international law and
       constitutes a breach of an international obligation of that State or
       international organisation.

19.4   Conduct carried out in the context of Peace Operations may be
       attributed to more than one participating State or international
       organisation.

19.5   States and international organisations participating in Peace Operations are responsible for the conduct of their organs carried out on their behalf.

19.6   International organisations are responsible for the internationally wrongful acts of Peace Operations which constitute organs of that organisation.

19.7   States or international organisations are responsible for internationally wrongful acts committed by individuals or entities acting under their effective control or direction.

Third Party Claims

20.1   Third parties who suffer personal injury or property damage due to any wrongful acts of Peace Forces are entitled to compensation. The right to a remedy is a recognised norm of customary international law. This right is, however, regulated by relevant treaties and may be further restricted by Status of Forces Agreements between the Host State and the States or international organisation deploying the Peace Forces.

20.2   Harm caused by Peace Operations may arise from breaches of Host State law and/or international law. Breaches of international law may give rise to international responsibility, but generally this cannot be invoked by private parties directly against a foreign State. Breaches of Host State law may, in principle, be invoked by private parties. Jurisdictional immunities of international organisations and Sending States may preclude proceedings against them unless immunity is waived in a particular case. Therefore, alternative claims mechanisms may be required.

20.3   International law does not impose a uniform claims regime. International organisations active in Peace Operations may organise their civil liability towards third parties in different ways.

20.4   Although claims regimes vary, there are well-established exceptions to liability that are applied by all actors in Peace Operations. Damage arising from action in self-defence or from operational necessity, as well as combat-related damage, is exempt from liability but may be compensated through an ex gratia payment.

20.5   International organisations and States should establish alternative means of dispute settlement where access to court is not possible because of immunities. Such claims procedures should be transparent and impartial, and should respect local laws. All international organisations should assume responsibility for the national contingents under their control in order to facilitate the settlement of third party claims.

Individual Criminal Responsibility

21.1 Recognised international crimes under conventional and customary international law which may arise in the context of Peace Operations include war crimes, crimes against humanity, genocide and torture.

21.2 Persons connected with a Peace Operation, in either a civilian or a military capacity, who engage in acts constituting any of the crimes referred to in Rule 21.1 or who materially contribute to or assist in the perpetration of any of these crimes incur individual criminal responsibility under international law.

21.3 Commanders and civilian superiors incur criminal responsibility when they knew or should have known under the circumstances that subordinate personnel under their command were committing the international crimes referred to in Rules 21.1 and 21.2 and failed to take adequate measures to prevent their commission, or to punish the perpetrators or to bring the matter to the attention of the designated authorities.

21.4 Any member of a Peace Operation suspected of participation in, or of failure to take adequate measures to prevent or punish subordinates engaged in, any of the aforementioned international crimes is subject to prosecution by national and international courts within the scope of their respective jurisdictions.

21.5 Making a member of a Peace Operation the object of an attack constitutes a war crime if the Peace Operation is not a party to an armed conflict and if the member of the Peace Operation retains the right to protection under international humanitarian law.

21.6 Whenever and to the extent that they are so mandated, Peace Operations shall assist in the administration of international justice. In the absence of any such mandate, Peace Operations should, whenever possible, provide such assistance as is compatible with their mandate and within their capability to authorised international courts and tribunals in the administration of international justice. At a minimum, Peace Operations should bring the perpetration of international crimes by any actor within their area of operations to the attention of the UN Secretary-General and, where appropriate, the government of the Host State and the relevant Sending State.

Composition of the Managing Board of the International Society for Military Law and the Law of War

President: Brig. Gen. (ret.) Jan Peter Spijk (Netherlands)
Secretary-General: Ludwig Van Der Veken (Belgium)
Senior Vice-President: Lt Gen. Dimitrios Zafeiropoulos (Greece)
Vice-President: Maj. Gen. Blaise Cathcart (Canada)
Vice-President: Professor Wolff Heintschel von Heinegg (Germany)
Vice-President: Brig. Gen. Waldo Martínez Cáceres (Chile)
Treasurer (a.i.): Col Jacques Lefèvre (Belgium)

Composition of the Board of Directors
of the International Society for Military Law
and the Law of War

Col (ret.) Roy H. Abbot (Australia)
Professor Alison Duxbury (Australia)
Dr Rain Liivoja (Australia)
Marco Grill (Austria)
Dr Karl Satzinger (Austria)
Professor Andrei Kozik (Belarus)
Christian Gossiaux (Belgium)
Professor Stanislas Horvat (Belgium)
Col (ret.) Jacques Lefèvre (Belgium)
Ludwig Van Der Veken (Belgium)
Alfons Vanheusden (Belgium)
Justice Maria Elizabeth G. Rocha (Brazil)
Antoaneta Boeva (Bulgaria)
Col Josué Noël Bidoung (Cameroon)
Justice Pierre Boutet (Canada)
Maj. Gen. Blaise Cathcart (Canada)
Lt Col (ret.) Sylvain Fournier (Canada)
Lt Col Stephen Strickey (Canada)
Lt Col Tammy Tremblay (Canada)
Brig. Gen. Waldo Martinez Caceres (Chile)
Maj. Wen Tao (President of the Chinese Military Law Society, point of
    contact)
Professor Javier Gustavo Rincon Salcedo (Colombia)
Petra Ditrichová-Ochmannová (Czech Republic)
Lars Stevnsborg (Denmark)
Dr Frederik Naert (EU)
Gert-Jan Vanhegelsom (EU)
Jouko Lehti (Finland)
Thierry Chevalier (France)
Jean-Claude Schmitt (France)

Dr Dieter Fleck (Germany)
Ulrike Froissart (Germany)
Professor Wolff Heintschel von Heinegg (Germany)
Professor Stefan Oeter (Germany)
Dr Alexander Poretschkin (Germany)
Col Michael Scholze (Germany)
Stefan Sohm (Germany)
Athanassios Kossioris (Greece)
Lt Gen. Dimitrios Zafeiropoulos (Greece)
Maj. Gen. (ret.) Nilendra Kumar, AVSM, VSM (India)
Lt Col Richard Brennan (Ireland)
Col (ret.) William Nott (Ireland)
Col John Spierin (Ireland)
Cdr (Navy) Gianmatteo Breda (Italy)
Adm. (ret.) Fabio Caffio (Italy)
Capt. (Navy) Fabrizio Ratto-Vaquer (Italy)
Dr Fabrizio Scarici (Italy)
Brig. Gen. (ret.) Seok Ko (Republic of Korea)
Brig. Gen. Changsik Hong (Republic of Korea)
Ilona Drege (Latvia)
Steven Hill (NATO)
Brig. Gen. Paul A. L. Ducheine (Netherlands)
Marc Gazenbeek (Netherlands)
Professor Terry D. Gill (Netherlands)
Col Ben Klappe (Netherlands)
Brig. Gen. (ret.) Jan Peter Spijk (Netherlands)
Brig. Gen. (ret.) Onno van der Wind (Netherlands)
Col (ret.) Gerard van Vugt (Netherlands)
Dr Seerp B. Ybema (Netherlands)
Chris Griggs (New Zealand)
Arne W. Dahl (Norway)
Lars Bjørkholt (Norway)
Adm. Julio Pacheco (Peru)
Dumitru Toma (Romania)
Col Angel Serrano Barberan (Spain)
Maria Hedegård (Sweden)
Dr Roberta Arnold (Switzerland)
Col (ret.) Rolet Loretan (Switzerland)
Col Carl Marchand (Switzerland)
Dieter Weber (Switzerland)

Sr Col Ali Fatnassi (Tunisia)
Col Charles Barnett (United Kingdom)
Maj. Gen. (ret.) Michael David Conway (United Kingdom)
Col James Johnston (United Kingdom)
Brig. Gen. Darren Stewart, OBE (United Kingdom)
Dr David Turns (United Kingdom)
James Burger (United States)
Eugene R. Fidell (United States)
Col (ret.) Richard Jackson (United States)
Professor Michael Schmitt (United States)
Professor Roland Trope (United States)

Planning and Policy Aspects of the United Nations

Structure of a New Peace Operation, Planning and Deployment

1. At the request or with the consent of the Host State, the Security Council determines the deployment of a new UN Peace Operation. Prior to doing so, the Security Council often requests the UN Secretary-General to submit a proposal for the structure and mandate of the mission but the Secretary-General may also make such a proposal on his/her own initiative.

2. The Policy on Integrated Assessment and Planning (IAP) sets out the principles and requirements under which integrated assessments must be conducted. In order to formulate strategic options for the consideration of the Security Council, the UN conducts a strategic assessment with the participation of the Secretariat and relevant Agencies, Funds and Programmes (the AFPs). Ahead of mission start-up planning or during the life-cycle of established integrated presences, the Strategic Assessment provides a basis for the development of recommendations on the nature and configuration or reconfiguration of UN engagement for the consideration of the Secretary-General and, when required, subsequently the Security Council. Ultimately the purpose is to maximise individual and collective impact of peace consolidation interventions throughout the life-cycle of the integrated UN presence when and where an integrated UN presence is in place or is being considered. The AFPs that participate in such assessments, such as the World Food Programme (WFP), United Nations Development Programme (UNDP) and Population Fund (UNFPA), United Nations Children's Fund (UNICEF), the UN High Commissioner for Refugees (UNHCR) and others, normally also have independent programmes in the Host State and altogether constitute the United Nations Country Team (UNCT). The scope of participation in a Strategic Assessment will be context-specific but must include

those potentially affected (whether at the strategic or more limited level). Further guidance on this issue is provided in the *IAP Handbook*.[1] As part of the assessment, a conflict analysis is conducted to present a shared understanding of the conflict situation and inform the identification of strategic options, through consultation with relevant stakeholders, including parties to the conflict, civil society, Member States, and regional and international actors. Gender and human rights perspectives should also be included. Each option being submitted for consideration and decision must have withstood risk analyses and stress tests and therefore meet a certain degree of rigour.

3. The UN Secretariat may also deploy a technical assessment mission to the country or territory where the deployment of a UN Peace Operation is envisaged, which may focus on particular aspects related to the deployment of a Peace Operation. This entire strategic assessment process may feed into a report by the UN Secretary-General to the Security Council, presenting options that the Council may adopt, including the deployment of a Peace Operation.

4. Following the establishment of a peacekeeping operation by the Security Council, the Integrated Task Force (a forum bringing together the relevant UN actors in headquarters, chaired by the lead department, which is the Department of Peacekeeping Operations (DPKO) in the case of peacekeeping operations) develops a Secretary-General's Directive to the senior leadership on the ground, which sets out UN-wide strategic priorities. Once the Secretary-General's Directive is issued, the responsibility for planning shifts from headquarters to the field.

5. The Departments of Peacekeeping Operations and Field Support (DFS) plan, deploy, direct and manage peacekeeping and other operations on behalf of the Secretary-General under their responsibility to ensure the highest standards in the implementation of Security Council resolutions and other mandates.

6. The DPKO, which was established as a separate department of the UN Secretariat in New York in 1992, provides political and executive direction to UN peacekeeping operations around the world and maintains contact with the Security Council, troop and financial contributors, and parties to the conflict in the implementation of Security Council mandates. The DPKO works to integrate the efforts of UN, governmental and non-governmental entities in the context of peacekeeping

---

[1] *Integrated Assessment and Planning (IAP) Handbook* (UN, 2013).

operations. The DPKO works very closely with the Department of Political Affairs (DPA), which is the focal point in the UN system for conflict prevention, peacemaking and peacebuilding.

7. The DFS was established by the UN General Assembly in 2007 to strengthen the capacity of the Organisation to manage and sustain global Peace Operations. The DFS provides dedicated support to peacekeeping operations, special political missions and other field presences in the areas of budget and finance, logistics, human resources, general administration, information, and information and communication technology. In addition, the DFS is supporting specific AU Missions including the AU Mission in Somalia (AMISOM). The DFS provides logistical and other support by combining both civilian (in-house and commercially contracted) and military-provided services to support personnel and deliver mandates in the field. The DFS is headquartered in New York and has a Global Service Centre in Brindisi, Italy, a Support Base in Valencia, Spain, and a Regional Service Centre in Entebbe, Uganda.

8. In terms of the detailed mission planning, the DPKO has the lead and works in consultation and co-ordination with the DPA on the overall political dimensions, with the DFS on the logistical and other mission support aspects, as well as with other departments and offices of the UN Secretariat. Accordingly, the DPKO (or if there is already a Head of Mission (HOM) and sufficient capacity on the ground, the mission, in consultation with the DPKO) develops the Mission Concept, which is the document that contains the leadership's vision for the implementation of the mission's mandate, identifies phases, priorities and sequencing of mandated tasks, provides strategic guidance for component level planning (such as the military and police concepts of operations and the Mission Support Plan as well as component level plans) and informs resource allocation/budgets.

9. The strategic military Concept of Operations and the strategic police Concept of Operations are developed and issued by the Office of Military Affairs and the Police Division within the DPKO. For established missions these concepts are developed in close consultation with the mission's uniformed components which in turn issue Operational Orders to direct and task contingents and individually deployed uniformed personnel. In parallel with the development of the Concept of Operations for the uniformed components, the DFS in co-ordination with the support component of the mission develops the Mission Support Plan that secures support to the mission's deployment, employment and sustainment.

10. As part of the pre-deployment responsibilities, the UN Office of Legal Affairs (OLA) ensures that the foundation of a mission's legal framework is firmly in place by preparing and negotiating the Status of Forces Agreement (SOFA) or Status of Mission Agreement (SOMA) with the Host State. The Security Council usually calls upon the Secretary-General and the country concerned to conclude the mission-specific SOFA/SOMA within a specified period of time pending which the model SOFA applies.[2]

11. Deployment of an operation proceeds as quickly as possible, taking into account the security and political conditions on the ground. It often starts with an advance team to establish mission headquarters and leads to a gradual build-up to encompass all components and substantive entities, as required by the mandate. In some situations where the forces of a regional organisation or a Member State or group of Member States already operate on the ground, the Security Council may direct the DPKO and the DFS to plan the peacekeeping operation on the basis of parallel forces and/or of a re-hatting process.

Appointment of Senior Officials

12. The Secretary-General appoints a Head of Mission (HOM) (usually a Special Representative (SRSG)) to direct the peacekeeping operation and up to two deputies for a multi-dimensional UN peacekeeping operation. The overall command is vested in the Secretary-General; day-to-day management of peacekeeping operations is delegated to the Under-Secretary-General for Peacekeeping Operations (USG DPKO). The Secretary-General will provide regular reports to the Security Council on the implementation of the mission mandate. The Security Council reviews these reports and briefings, and renews and adjusts the mission mandate, as required, until the operation is completed or closed.

13. For a multi-dimensional UN Peace Operation, it is common for two deputies to be appointed, one of whom is responsible for political affairs while the other is the Resident Coordinator of the UN Country Team who also usually serves as the humanitarian co-ordinator and is thus responsible for co-ordinating humanitarian assistance by UN system

---

[2] UN Model Status of Forces Agreement for Peacekeeping Operations, UN Doc. A/45/594 (1990).

entities in the mission area. For operations with a primarily military mandate, the Force Commander is usually the HOM.

14. Although peacekeeping missions are not the UN's only presence in conflict zones, in multi-dimensional peacekeeping settings, the SRSG, through his/her deputy, who is also Resident and Humanitarian Coordinator, represents the UN system's efforts across the humanitarian, peacebuilding and development spectrum. The Resident and Humanitarian Coordinator (one person commonly holds both functions) brings together the UN country team, composed of field staff of UN Agencies, Funds and Programmes, among them UNHCR, UNICEF, UNDP, the WFP and the World Health Organization (WHO).

15. Although past military observer missions have also included non-military tasks, a growing number of UN peacekeeping operations have become multi-dimensional, composed of military, civilian police, political, civil affairs, rule of law, governance, security sector reform, human rights, humanitarian, reconstruction, public information and gender components among others. Increasingly, peacekeeping operations carry out their mandates alongside or after a regional national or multi-national peacekeeping force. In recent years, the protection of civilians has been included in the mandates of most such missions.

16. In addition, peacekeepers have been called upon to support the activities of non-governmental and other organisations engaged in providing humanitarian assistance to internally displaced persons and refugees as well as other victims of conflicts. In many mission areas, a SRSG provides, in addition to his or her other responsibilities, overall co-ordination for the humanitarian actors, Agencies, Funds and Programmes working in the mission area.

17. Member States transfer "operational authority" to the UN to use the operational capabilities of their national military contingents, units, formed police units and/or individually deployed military and police personnel to undertake mandated missions and tasks. Operational authority over such forces and personnel is vested in the Secretary-General, under the authority of the Security Council. "United Nations Operational Authority" involves the full authority to issue operational directives within the limits of (1) a specific mandate of the Security Council; (2) an agreed period of time, with the stipulation that an earlier withdrawal of a contingent would require the contributing country to provide adequate prior notification; and (3) a specific geographic area (the mission area as a whole).

18. The overall command is vested in the Secretary-General.[3] The Secretary-General delegates to the USG DPKO overall responsibility for the conduct of such peacekeeping operations. The SRSG reports to the Secretary-General through the USG DPKO on all matters related to the discharge of the mission's mandate. The HOM, normally the SRSG, provides political guidance for mandate implementation and sets mission-wide operational direction including decisions on resource allocation in case of competing priorities. The HOM delegates the operational and technical aspects of mandate implementation to the heads of all components of the mission. The HOM provides direction to those components through the component heads.

19. The Secretary-General also appoints a peacekeeping operation's Force Commander, Police Commissioner and senior civilian staff. The DPKO and the DFS are then responsible for staffing the civilian, military and police components of a peacekeeping operation with the Troop and Police Contributing Countries (TCCs/PCCs) as providers of military and police personnel to the mission.

Force Generation and Funding

20. The UN has no standing military or police force of its own, and Member States are asked to contribute military and police personnel as well as most of the equipment required for each operation. Member States deciding to participate in a peacekeeping operation become TCCs/PCCs with which a negotiated, formal agreement between the UN and the TCC/PCC either as a Memorandum of Understanding (MOU) and/or under a Letter of Assist will be concluded. These agreements establish the responsibility and standards for the provision of personnel, major equipment and self-sustainment support services for both the UN and the contributing country.

Arrangements with Troop Contributing Countries and in the Case of Non-UN Operations with Third States Contributing Troops

21. Chapter 5.2 of the UN Peacekeeping Operations Principles and Guidelines (the Capstone Doctrine)[4] refers to an Integrated Mission Planning Process (IMPP), now the Integrated Assessment Planning

---

[3] UN DPKO/DFS, Policy on Authority, Command and Control in United Nations Peacekeeping Operations, Ref. 2008.4.

[4] UN, United Nations Peacekeeping Operations: Principles and Guidelines (2008), www.un.org/en/peacekeeping/documents/capstone_eng.pdf (Capstone Doctrine).

Handbook, which is intended to facilitate a common understanding of strategic objectives in the Host State by engaging all relevant parts of the UN system.[5] Military planners should be aware of this wider spectrum of activities. Chapter 6.2 of the Capstone Doctrine describes the mission start-up process covering different levels of responsibility[6] and requiring effective leadership and conflict management skills. As stressed in that chapter, this can be a 'fast-paced and seemingly chaotic experience'. Efforts should be made in co-operation with competent authorities of the UN, the regional organisation involved and the Host State to regularise relevant tasks and develop best practice.

22. For deployment and mission start-up, multiple activities need to be considered and regulated. While planning efforts and arrangements, including stand-by arrangements, may facilitate a smooth conduct of operations, most pertinent activities will depend on ad hoc arrangements.

23. For the provision of mission components and the specifications of terms and conditions of their contribution, arrangements or agreements between the UN or regional organisation and the TCCs/PCCs will be required. To establish the responsibilities and standards for the provision of personnel, major equipment and support services for both the UN and the contributing Member States, a negotiated, formal agreement will be concluded as a Memorandum of Understanding or Letter of Assist.[7]

---

[5] The IMPP was formally endorsed through a decision of the Secretary–General's Policy Committee on 13 June 2006. It was replaced in 2014 by the *IAP Handbook* (n. 1), providing a comprehensive set of implementation guidelines developed in co-ordination with field missions and headquarters planners.

[6] Capstone Doctrine (n. 4), pp. 63–64:

Pre-deployment is largely a Headquarters responsibility and involves many tasks such as the United Nations budgetary process, pre-deployment visits to TCCs/PCCs to assess readiness, the negotiation of a Status of Mission/Status of Forces Agreement (SOMA/SOFA), the mobilization of Strategic Deployment Stocks (SDS), and the tendering of major supply and service contracts for the mission;

Rapid deployment involves the deployment of a small advance team to commence the establishment of mission premises and other prerequisite infrastructure and administrative systems, to allow for the reception of larger numbers of staff and contingents as start-up progresses;

Mission headquarters start-up is the period when the mission leadership team arrives, managerial and command and control systems are formed and increasing numbers of substantive and support personnel begin arriving in-mission to help achieve an IOC. It also involves the establishment of liaison offices and logistics hubs, if required;

Functional component and field office start-up occurs alongside the establishment of the central structures of mission headquarters and involves the coordinated establishment of the different substantive civilian, police and military command and managerial capacities. It also involves the start-up of sector headquarters and field offices of the mission.

[7] See Model Memorandum of Understanding between the United Nations and [participating State] contributing resources to [the United Nations Peacekeeping Operation], UNGA Res. 61/267 (2007) and UN Doc. A/C.5/69/18 (2014), Chapter 9.

Categories of Mission Personnel

24. Peacekeepers wear their national uniform and are identified as UN Peacekeepers by standard UN accoutrements (blue helmet or beret and a badge).

25. Civilian staffs of Peace Operations are international civil servants recruited by the UN Secretariat and national staff locally recruited and deployed by the mission. On the other hand, any civilian personnel provided by a TCC in agreement with the UN as part of a national military contingent and within the authorised personnel strength of that contingent are members of the mission whose status is set forth in the relevant SOMA. Unlike UN civilian employees, such contingent personnel are not international civil servants.

Planning and Policy Aspects of the African Union

Structure of a New Peace Operation, Planning and Deployment

1. The AU Commission is the main organ charged with co-ordinating between the various actors and bodies involved in AU Peace Operations, in particular the AU's Peace and Security Council (PSC AU) and the Regional Economic Communities (RECs) or regional mechanisms.[1] The AU Commission's Peace and Security Department (PSD), headed by the Peace and Security Commissioner, is composed of the PSC AU Secretariat, the Peace Support Operations Division (PSOD), the Conflict Prevention and Early Warning Division (CPEW), the Defense and Security Division and the Crisis Management and Post-Conflict Reconstruction Division.

2. The PSOD was set up pursuant to the 2002 Protocol Relating to the Establishment of the Peace and Security Council (PSC AU Protocol) and the 2004 Policy Framework on the Establishment of the African Standby Force and the Military Staff Committee. It is composed of four units: the Policy Development Unit, the Capability Development Unit, the Mission Support Unit and the Plans and Operations Unit.

3. The functions of the PSOD include developing legal and policy instruments relating to Peace Operations, co-ordinating with the RECs, regional mechanisms and AU Member States, and providing strategic oversight, monitoring, support and evaluation of Peace Operations (e.g. by drafting reports of the Chairperson of the AU Commission to the AU Peace and Security Council and other relevant AU components).

---

[1] A detailed overview of the AU's mandating and planning process for Peace Operations can be found in African Union Mandating Process – Aide Memoire: The African Union's Planning and Decision Making Process, Version 4 (2010), https://eeas.europa.eu/csdp/capabilities/eu-support-african-capabilities/documents/aide_memoire_en.pdf. See also African Union Peace Support Operations Doctrine, Final Draft (2013), Chapter 4 (Mission Planning), www.peaceau.org/uploads/au-pso-doctrine-chapter-4-edited.pdf.

4. The path from strategic direction to mandate development involves the following steps: Strategic Analysis, Strategic Assessment, AU Chairperson's Directive, AU Commissioner's Planning Guidance, Initial Draft Mission Plan, Technical Assessment Mission, Refined Draft Mission Plan and a final decision by the PSC AU.

5. As soon as a potential conflict is brought to the attention of the PSC AU, the CPEW will conduct a Strategic Analysis and presents this to the Chairperson of the AU Commission, who in turn informs the PSC AU. If the situation requires the deployment of a Peace Operation, the PSC AU will direct the Chairperson of the AU to constitute a Conflict Management Task Force (CMTF) whose core members represent the various departments of the AU Commission and representatives of the affected RECs/regional mechanisms. The CMTF undertakes a Strategic Assessment of the situation and develops scenarios and options that will outline the possible strategic objectives for an AU Peace Operation. After consideration of the strategic analysis and the Chairperson's recommendations, the PSC AU will decide on the option which provides the foundation for further planning efforts.

6. The Chairperson's Directive translates the PSC AU decision and additional guidance into strategic planning guidance for the development of the operational objectives. It states the broad, strategic objectives as well as the proposed form and scope of the Peace Operation. The Directive is issued to the PSD, to initiate detailed operational planning for the mission. Based on the Chairperson's Directive, the Peace and Security Commissioner formulates a Planning Guidance to the CMTF. Both documents assist the CMTF in formulating an Initial Draft Mission Plan, which translates the broad, strategic objective into operational objectives, expressed in the form of a planning matrix.

7. Following a Technical Assessment Mission (i.e. a short-term country level assessment) the PSOD will draw up a Refined Draft Mission Plan. This refined plan allows the Chairperson to draft a report with all necessary details, including an estimate of required resources and a draft mandate, in order for the PSC AU to make an informed decision. The final step is a decision or, in practice, a communiqué by the PSC AU approving or amending the proposed mandate. Once the mandate is given, the responsibility for the final planning is carried over from the CMTF to the Integrated Mission Planning Team consisting of the Head of the Mission (HOM), component commanders, senior mission staff and other relevant stakeholders.

8. The UN has developed a number of documents to identify logistical requirements of Peace Operations. These documents, if necessary adapted to fit AU parameters, are also used in the planning of AU Peace Operations. This will also assist in the smooth transition to UN Peace Operations, if necessary. The AU consults closely with the UN to gain access to the latest UN Peace Operations doctrine and training material and modifies this as necessary to suit African conditions. Rules of Engagement (ROE) for each mission are developed by PSOD in consultation with the AU Legal Counsel using the Draft AU Guidelines for the Development of Rules of Engagement for African Union Peacekeeping Operations.

Appointment of Senior Officials

9. Once the mission has been given a mandate, the Chairperson of the AU Commission appoints a Special Representative (SRCC), the Force Commander, the commissioner of police and the head of the civilian components. Their detailed roles and functions are spelt out in directives, in accordance with the Peace Support Standing Operating Procedures.

10. The SRCC shall report to the Chairperson of the AU Commission. The Force Commander shall report to the SRCC. Contingent Commanders shall report to the Force Commander, while the civilian components shall report to the SRCC.

Force Generation and Funding

11. Peace Operations under the auspices of the AU are carried out by the African Standby Force (ASF). Through the relevant RECs/regional mechanisms, Member States of the AU take steps to establish standby contingents of the ASF for participation in missions decided on by the PSC AU.[2] The strength and types of such contingents, their degree of readiness and general location shall be determined in accordance with established AU Peace Support Standard Operating Procedures. Troop Contributing Countries shall immediately, upon request by the Commission, following an authorisation by the PSC AU, release the standby contingents with the necessary equipment for the operations envisaged under the PSC AU

---

[2] On the African Standby Force and its relation to the AU and the RECs/regional mechanisms, see further Rule 4.3.1, Commentary, para. 8; Rule 4.6.1, Commentary, para. 4.

Protocol. The modalities of force generation are laid down in the Protocol, the Policy Framework on the Establishment of the African Standby Force and the Military Staff Committee, and a legally binding Memorandum of Understanding on Cooperation in the Area of Peace and Security between the AU and the RECs/regional mechanisms.

12. In order to provide the necessary financial resources for Peace Operations, the PSC AU Protocol established a special fund called the Peace Fund. It is made up of financial appropriations from the regular budget of the AU and voluntary contributions from Member States and from other sources within Africa, including the private sector, civil society and individuals, as well as through appropriate fund raising activities. The Chairperson of the Commission shall raise and accept voluntary contributions from sources outside Africa, in conformity with the objectives and principles of the AU. On average, only 6 per cent of the regular budget of the AU is allocated to the Peace Fund. The AU Special Summit in Tripoli (2009) decided to gradually increase the reserve to a total of 12 per cent by 2012, though this is yet to be realised as the Member States' contributions currently stand at 7 per cent.

13. Given the challenges the AU is facing with regard to the funding of Peace Operations, it relies heavily on donations by international organisations, agencies and donor States. A substantial share of external funding comes from the EU. The EU's African Peace Facility (APF) was established in 2004 in response to a request by African leaders. Financed through the European Development Fund, it constitutes the main source of funding to support the African Union's and African Regional Economic Communities' efforts in the area of peace and security with an overall amount of more than EUR 1.9 billion since 2004. The APF has its legal basis in the Cotonou Agreement and is funded through the European Development Fund (EDF). The direct beneficiaries of APF support are the AU and the RECs/regional mechanisms with a mandate in peace and security, and relevant institutions within or related to the African Peace and Security Architecture. According to the EDF regulations, APF funds can be used to finance costs incurred by African countries that are deploying their peacekeeping forces under the banner of the AU or a REC/regional mechanisms in another country. Following the relevant rules of eligibility of costs, the APF may, for example, cover allowances for the troops, salaries for civilians, logistical, transportation, medical and communication costs, but it must not fund military equipment, arms, ammunition or military training.

Arrangements with Troop Contributing Countries and in the Case of Non-UN Operations with Third States Contributing Troops.

14. See Force Generation and Funding.

Categories of Mission Personnel

15. The military component, designed to perform the full range of normal military tasks, includes the bulk of initial mission personnel. Their task will entail both military operations and humanitarian assistance. The military component invariably comprises land forces, complemented if necessary and appropriate by air forces and maritime forces. Particular tasks may be provided by e.g. special forces, engineers, military health services, military police and logistics units.

16. The role of the police component in a mission is to help establish and maintain law and order, and to ensure the long-term capacity of the local law and order forces through monitoring, advice and training. The activities of the police component tend to fall into three categories: (1) monitoring, mentoring and advising of local law and order forces, (2) reform and restructuring of local police infrastructure and (3) carrying out executive functions such as powers of arrest, search and seizure, detention, crowd control and investigation.

17. The civilian component of a mission consists of persons responsible for providing administrative support in, for example, human resources, finance and logistics management, but they also provide expertise in areas such as political affairs, public information, planning and co-ordination, human rights, humanitarian liaison and legal issues.

Planning and Policy Aspects of the European Union

Structure of a New Peace Operation, Planning and Deployment

1. EU Peace Operations are conducted under the EU's Common Security and Defence Policy (CSDP), which is part of the Union's Common Foreign and Security Policy (CFSP),[1] and are therefore subject to the rules applicable to these EU policy areas.

2. The formal right to propose an EU Peace Operation belongs to any EU Member State or the High Representative of the Union for Foreign Affairs and Security Policy (High Representative).[2] In practice, the first call to launch or consider the initiation of an EU Peace Operation is usually made in the Political and Security Committee (PSC EU), which is a preparatory body of the Council of the EU (referred to in this Appendix as 'the Council' to distinguish it from the European Council) that plays a key role in relation to CSDP missions and operations.[3] However, it may also be made first in the Council, or, even if this is rather exceptional, in the European Council.

3. When such a proposal is made, the PSC EU, or the Council or European Council, may formally agree that planning should commence pending further decision-making.[4] This will start an iterative process consisting of increasingly detailed planning documents, decision-making

---

[1] See Treaty on European Union (EU Treaty), OJ 2016 No. C202, 7 June 2016, p. 13, Title V (EU external action), Chapter 2 (CFSP), Section 2 (CSDP).

[2] See *Ibid.*, arts. 30(1) and 42(4). Even when the initiative comes from a Member State, it is usually the High Representative who will formally present proposals for legal acts relating to an EU Peace Operation, such as for the Council Decision setting up the operation.

[3] See art. 38 EU Treaty (n. 1), and Council Decision 2001/78/CFSP of 22 January 2001 setting up the Political and Security Committee, OJ 2001 No. L27, 30 January 2001, p. 1.

[4] Irrespective of whether the initiative comes from the High Representative or a Member State, more substantial work will be taken forward only when there is agreement between Member States to do so (the High Representative may initiate some early planning before that). That agreement will usually first be expressed at the level of the PSC EU but this can also be done directly at the level of the Council or European Council.

and the adoption of the necessary legal acts. This process is described in 'Crisis Management Procedures',[5] which, however, offer considerable flexibility including a fast track process in case of urgency. The planning and decision-making process goes back and forth between the planners, experts, politicians and diplomats, with key decisions being taken by the Council itself at the level of ministers. Planning is done in part by permanent EU structures, which continue to evolve, and in part by headquarters and commanders or Heads of Mission (HOMs) put at the disposal of and designated by the Union for a specific Peace Operation. The planning process results in the approval of an Operational Plan (OPLAN) or Mission Plan (MPLAN), including/and, where relevant, (military) Rules of Engagement or (civilian) Rules on the Use of Force.

4. In the initial stages, planning is done by permanent EU structures based in Brussels, notably by parts of the European External Action Service (EEAS), which assists the High Representative and works under his/her direction. Currently, the main EEAS departments involved in planning are the Crisis Management and Planning Directorate (CMPD), the EU Military Staff (EUMS), which will include a Military Planning and Conduct Capability (MPCC) for non-executive military missions, and the Civilian Planning and Conduct Capability (CPCC), and they draw on intelligence and analysis provided by the EU Intelligence Analysis Centre (INTCEN). The relevant geographical desks as well as EU Delegations in the Host State or the region also play a role. The initial planning normally includes a 'Political Framework for Crisis Approach' and a 'crisis management concept' and may include military or civilian strategic options.

5. For civilian EU Peace Operations, subsequent operational planning (typically a Concept of Operations (CONOPs) followed by an OPLAN, including Rules on the Use of Force where relevant) is also mainly done by the EEAS, especially the Civilian Planning and Conduct Capability, the head of which is normally designated as Civilian Operation Commander of all EU civilian crisis management operations,[6] albeit with the involvement of the HOM once designated.[7]

---

[5] Suggestions for crisis management procedures for CSDP crisis management operations, EU Council Doc. 7660/2/13 (2013). See also EU Concept for Military Planning at the Political Strategic level, EU Council Doc. 6432/15 (2015).

[6] For the command and control arrangements in civilian CSDP operations, see EU Council Doc. 9919/07 EXT 2 (2008) (this is a partially declassified version).

[7] The staff of the mission as well as the HOM, who leads the mission in theatre, are recruited specifically for each mission and are not staff of the EEAS.

6. For military EU Peace Operations, subsequent operational planning (typically a CONOPs followed by an OPLAN, as well as a statement of requirements[8] and a Rules of Engagement request) is done by Operation or Mission Commanders and their Operational or Mission Headquarters[9] which are designated for each operation. The reason for this is that the EU does not have a standing military headquarters which can plan and conduct EU military operations. However, the EU is setting up a Military Planning and Conduct Capability (MPCC) within the EUMS, which will be responsible at the strategic level for the operational planning and conduct of non-executive military missions. The Director General of the EUMS will be the Director of the MPCC and will assume in that capacity the functions of mission commander for the non-executive military missions.[10]

7. The planning process is also guided by a series of concepts on issues such as logistics, medical support, the use of force, command and control, etc.[11]

8. The planning process results in the approval of an OPLAN or MPLAN, which is the final planning document. The OPLAN or

[8] I.e. an identification of the required means, including personnel.

[9] For executive operations, an Operation Commander and Operational Headquarters (OHQ) in the EU are designated, as well as a Force Commander and Force Headquarters (FHQ) in theatre, whereas for non-executive (training and advisory) missions, a Mission Commander and Mission Headquarters (MHQ) in theatre are designated but the latter will change (see para. 6 of this Appendix). The OHQ may be made available to the EU (i) by a Member State or (ii) by NATO under the 'Berlin plus arrangements'; or (iii) may consist of the EU Operations Centre, which then has to be activated. FHQ and MHQ also have to be generated for each operation. See Chapter 4.2; EU Concept for Military Command and Control, EU Council Doc. 5008/15 (2015).

[10] See Chapter 4.2; Council conclusions on progress in implementing the EU Global Strategy in the area of Security and Defence, EU Council Doc. 6875/17 (2017), para. 5; Concept Note: Operational Planning and Conduct Capabilities for CSDP Missions and Operations, EU Council Doc. 6881/17 (2017). Some further steps are required before these new command and control arrangements will be applied.

[11] See e.g. EU Concept for Logistic Support for EU-led Military Operations, EU Council Doc. 15040/14 (2014) (not in the public domain); EU Concept for Contractor Support to EU-led Military Operations, EU Council Doc. 8628/14 (2014); Host Nation Support Concept for EU-led military operations, EU Council Doc. 7374/12 (2012); EU Concept for Strategic Movement and Transportation for EU-led Military Operations, EU Council Doc. 9798/12 (2012); EU Concept for Reception, Staging, Onward Movement and Integration (RSOI) for EU-led Military Operations, EU Council Doc. 9844/12 (2012); Comprehensive Health and Medical Concept for EU-led Crisis Management Operations, EU Council Doc. 10530/14 (2014) (this is one of the few Concepts covering both military and civilian missions); Concept for the Use of Force in EU-led Military Operations (not public; partially declassified in EU Council Doc. 17168/2/09 EXT 2 (2015)). See n. 10 for the command and control concept. For a good general overview, see the European Union Concept for EU-led Military Operations and Missions, EU Council Doc. 17107/14 (2014).

MPLAN contains the specifics of the operation and is often rather long, in part due to many annexes which normally address legal issues, the use of force and many other aspects. When the use of force may be required beyond self-defence, the OPLAN will be accompanied by Rules of Engagement for military operations or will include Rules on the Use of Force for civilian missions. The OPLAN and ROE are usually classified documents.

9. Key planning documents are approved by the Council. These documents include at least the crisis management concept, which is usually approved shortly before the Council adopts the Decision on the establishment of an EU Peace Operation,[12] and the (initial) OPLAN and ROE, which are adopted prior to or in the Council Decision to launch an operation.[13] The work of the Council in this regard is prepared by a series of Council preparatory bodies. These include especially the PSC EU,[14] the EU Military Committee (with its Working Group),[15] the Political-Military Group (PMG) and the Committee for Civilian Aspects of Crisis Management (CIVCOM).[16] The PSC provides advice and recommendations to the Council, whereas EUMC, PMG and CIVCOM provide advice and recommendations to the PSC. Some, less essential planning documents may be approved at the level of PSC or even EUMC.[17]

10. The OPLAN is supplemented and implemented by a series of further documents such as standard operating procedures, adopted within the operation.

11. Articles 42(5) and 44 EU Treaty provide for the possibility to entrust the execution of a task, within the Union framework, to a group of Member States which are willing and have the necessary capability for such a task. Those Member States, in association with the High Representative, shall agree among themselves on the management of the task but should the completion of the task entail major consequences or

---

[12] This is especially the case for military operations. For civilian operations there may be more time between the two.

[13] This is especially the case for military operations. For civilian operations, the Council does not usually adopt a second legal act to decide on the launching of a mission.

[14] See n. 3.

[15] See generally Council Decision 2001/79/CFSP of 22 January 2001 setting up the Military Committee of the European Union, OJ 2001 No. L27, 30 January 2001, p. 4.

[16] See generally Council Decision 2000/354/CFSP of 22 May 2000 setting up a Committee for Civilian Aspects of Crisis Management, OJ 2000 No. L127, 27 May 2000, p. 1.

[17] The latter is notably the case for the Initiating Military Directive, which translates the more political crisis management concept into military guidance for the Operational Commander to develop the CONOPs and OPLAN.

require amendment of the objective, scope and conditions determined for the task, the Council shall adopt the necessary decisions.[18] This mechanism has not yet been used.

12. In parallel with planning, several legal acts are prepared and adopted. As described in Chapter 4.4, these include a Council Decision establishing the EU Peace Operation, as well as the necessary decisions on funding. They may include a Council Decision launching the operation, as well as a PSC EU decision accepting the participation of third States and the conclusion or application of participation agreements with such third States. They also include obtaining appropriate status arrangements.

13. The difference between planning documents and legal acts is important. For the adoption of legal acts, the EU Treaties lay down clear rules. By contrast, for planning documents considerable flexibility exists as long as the prerogatives of the different EU actors are respected. Indeed, some planning documents can even be omitted (see para. 9 of this Appendix).

14. The Council Decision establishing an EU Peace Operation is an absolute necessity.

Appointment of Senior Officials

15. The different command levels in EU Peace Operations and their respective responsibilities are described in Chapter 4.2. The appointment of the main commanders/HOM is made by the Council (in particular when setting up a new operation) or the PSC EU (this is usually the case for subsequent appointments). Moreover, in principle for civilian missions the Director of the CPCC will be appointed as Civilian Operations Commander, and in future the Director of the MPCC will in principle be appointed as Military Missions Commander for non-executive military missions.

Force Generation and Funding

16. In parallel with planning and decision-making, a force generation process takes place to co-ordinate the allocation of the necessary personnel

---

[18] For a legal analysis, see e.g. Legal Service contribution on the conditions and modalities of recourse to Article 44 TEU – entrusting the implementation of a CSDP task to a group of Member States, EU Council Doc. 5225/15 (2015).

and assets by Member States, and as appropriate by other participating States. For EU military Peace Operations, this process is described in the EU Concept for Force Generation.[19] Problems with force generation may delay the actual launch of an operation. For civilian EU Peace Operations the manning process is based on "calls for contributions" and an associated selection/recruitment process which generally operates at the level of individuals, and only exceptionally on the basis of providing units. Staff are primarily seconded by Member States,[20] and, where relevant, third States participating in a mission, whereas recourse to (international or local) contracted staff is in principle limited.[21]

17. The relationship between the EU and participating Member States is governed by internal EU rules and arrangements. These rules and procedures include provisions in the EU Treaty,[22] provisions in Council Decisions on specific EU Peace Operations, other EU legal acts (e.g. on funding; see para. 18 and fn. 24 of this Appendix), various EU concepts (e.g. on force generation and command and control)[23] and the planning documents for specific EU Peace Operations.

18. The financial aspects of EU Peace Operations are described elsewhere in this Manual.[24]

Arrangements with Troop Contributing Countries and in the Case of Non-UN Operations with Third States Contributing Troops

19. When a third State participates in an EU Peace Operation (following a decision by the PSC EU accepting its participation), the necessary arrangements are concluded with the EU, in the form of a participation agreement. The third State may then participate in any Committee of Contributors meetings.

20. Participation agreements are nearly always legally binding international agreements.[25] They may be concluded on an ad hoc basis for a

---

[19] EU Council Doc. 14000/15 (2015).

[20] Art. 42(1) EU Treaty (n. 1), provides that the performance of EU peace operations 'shall be undertaken using capabilities provided by the Member States', and art. 42(3) adds that 'Member States shall make civilian and military capabilities available to the Union for the implementation of the common security and defence policy'.

[21] Secondment of staff from EU institutions is also possible but is rather exceptional in practice.

[22] E.g. arts. 24(3) and 26(3) EU Treaty (n. 1).

[23] See respectively n. 20 and n. 10.

[24] See Rule 4.4.2, Commentary, paras. 3–4.

[25] Concluded under art. 37 EU Treaty (n. 1), and art. 218 Treaty on the Functioning of the European Union, OJ 2016 No. C202, 7 June 2016, p. 47.

given operation or on the basis of a model agreement, or may take the form of framework agreements covering participation by a given third State in EU operations generally.[26] Framework participation agreements have been concluded with an increasing number of third countries, including Albania,[27] Australia,[28] Bosnia and Herzegovina,[29] Canada,[30] Chile,[31] Colombia,[32] Georgia,[33] Iceland,[34] the Republic of Korea,[35] Moldova,[36] Montenegro,[37] New Zealand,[38] Norway,[39] Serbia,[40] Turkey,[41] Ukraine[42] and the United States.[43]

21. In participation agreements the participating State normally associates itself with the Joint Action (now Council Decision) establishing an operation, commits itself to providing a contribution and bears the costs thereof. It may be exempted from a share in the common costs. Generally, such agreements also provide that the personnel of the third State participating in the operation are covered by any Status of Forces Agreement concluded by the EU. They also contain provisions on the transfer of command and control, jurisdiction and claims.[44] EU decision-making autonomy is safeguarded but usually all participating States have the same rights and obligations in terms of day-to-day management of the operation as participating EU Member States, and the EU will consult with participating States when ending the mission. A Committee of Contributors may be established to provide a forum for the exercise of these rights. Participation agreements also contain provisions on classified information.

---

[26] Such agreements do not create a right to participate in all EU Peace Operations but rather set out arrangements that will apply in those cases where it has been decided that this third State may participate in a given operation.

[27] OJ No. 2012 L169, 29 June 2012, p. 2, entered into force on 1 February 2013.

[28] OJ No. 2015 L149, 16 June 2015, p. 3, entered into force on 1 October 2015.

[29] OJ No. 2015 L288, 4 November 2015, p. 4, entered into force on 1 August 2016.

[30] OJ No. 2005 L315, 1 December 2005, p. 20, entered into force 1 December 2005.

[31] OJ No. 2014 L40, 11 February 2014, p. 2, entered into force on 1 October 2015.

[32] OJ No. 2014 L251, 23 August 2014, p. 8, not yet entered into force.

[33] OJ No. 2014 L14, 18 January 2014, p. 2, entered into force on 1 March 2014.

[34] OJ No. 2005 L67, 14 March 2005, p. 2, entered into force on 1 April 2005.

[35] OJ No. 2014 L166, 5 June 2014, p. 3, entered into force on 1 December 2016.

[36] OJ No. 2013 L8, 12 January 2013, p. 2, entered into force on 1 July 2013.

[37] OJ No. 2011 L57, 2 March 2011, p. 2, entered into force on 1 April 2011.

[38] OJ No. 2012 L160, 21 June 2012, p. 2, entered into force on 1 May 2012.

[39] OJ No. 2005 L67, 14 March 2005, p. 8, entered into force on 1 January 2005.

[40] OJ No. 2011 L163, 23 June 2011, p. 2, entered into force on 1 August 2012.

[41] OJ No. 2006 L189, 12 July 2006, p. 17, entered into force on 1 August 2007.

[42] OJ No. 2005 L182, 13 July 2005, p. 29, entered into force on 1 May 2008.

[43] OJ No. 2011 L143, 31 May 2011, p. 2, entered into force on 1 June 2011. In addition, there is also a distinct Acquisition and Cross-Servicing Agreement between the European Union and the United States of America (ACSA), OJ 2016 No. L350, 22 December 2016, p. 3, entered into force on 6 December 2016.

[44] As to claims, there is a broad but not full mutual waiver of claims.

Categories of Mission Personnel

22. In EU military Peace Operations, most personnel are military personnel made available by TCCs, usually in the form of national contingents and sometimes in the form of individual military personnel (one or a few), e.g. in an EU OHQ or in non-executive missions. There may also be (a small number of) international contract staff, e.g. in an EU OHQ, as well as local contract staff in theatre.

23. In EU civilian Peace Operations, most personnel are seconded by TCCs. Staff may also be seconded by EU institutions / bodies. When not all posts are filled by seconded staff, such operations may have recourse to international contract staff. They may also have recourse to local contract staff in theatre.

24. Both military and civilian EU Peace Operations may have recourse to support by contractors.[45]

---

[45] For military operations, see EU Concept for Contractor Support to EU-led Military Operations, EU Council Doc. 8628/14 (2014).

Planning and Policy Aspects of the North Atlantic Treaty Organization

Structure of a New Peace Operation, Planning and Deployment

1. NATO Member States[1] mainly express themselves through their permanent representatives sitting collectively in the North Atlantic Council (NAC). The NAC is the highest political body and therefore every decision made by Member States in NATO must be taken at this body. It is the only body explicitly mentioned in the NATO Treaty.[2] The NAC has the power to set up subsidiary bodies. Currently, in addition to the NAC, the principal NATO platforms for intensive consultations are the Military Committee, the Operations Policy Committee and the Civil Emergency Planning Committee.[3]

2. With respect to initiating and planning military operations NATO Member States have agreed on overarching policy 'Guidelines for NATO's Operations Planning'. That document describes how to initiate, develop, co-ordinate, approve, execute and review operations plans.[4] In practice the process mainly 'seeks to translate political-strategic guidance into military strategic direction for the operational commander'.[5] The responsibility for translating the NAC political decision issued in the form of an Initiating Directive into military concepts lies with the Supreme Allied Commander Europe (SACEUR). Based on the Initiative Directive, SACEUR will direct his/her staff to develop a strategic draft Concept of Operation.

---

[1] For consistency reasons this Manual uses the word "State" (except when it makes use of the concept of "Troop Contributing Country" or "Police Contributing Country"). Please note, however, that NATO uses the term "Nation" in its documents when referring to its Members.
[2] Art. 9 North Atlantic Treaty, also known as the Washington Treaty (4 April 1941, in force 24 August 1949), 34 UNTS 243.
[3] NATO: Crisis Management, www.nato.int/cps/en/natohq/topics_49192.htm.
[4] See NATO, Operations Planning, MC 133/4 (2011).
[5] NATO ACO, Comprehensive Operations Planning Directive, COPD Interim V2.0 (2013), pp. 1–6.

3. Once the Concept of Operations is approved by the NAC, SACEUR, in co-operation with subordinate commands, will prepare a mission operational plan (OPLAN).[6] The draft OPLAN contains detailed information on the mission objectives, i.e. what needs to be accomplished, and on how they should be reached, namely the conditions and limitations. NATO Member States have many opportunities to comment on the OPLAN draft. When the OPLAN is finalised, it is sent via the NATO Military Committee to the NAC for political approval. The same procedure and timeframe applies to approval of mission-specific NATO Rules of Engagement (ROE), as they usually form an annex to an OPLAN. After the NAC approves the OPLAN and ROE it issues an Execution Directive which serves for implementation and execution of an operation. The Execution Directive is then followed by Activation Order issued by SACEUR whereupon NATO's support to a UN mandated Peace Operation may actually commence.[7]

4. This process for the initiation of NATO operations through the development of an OPLAN displays the high degree of interconnectivity between NATO and its Member States. Decisions related to the conduct of operations are not taken by any NATO body or military headquarter independently. The NATO Member States sitting collectively in the NAC (plus any partner States participating in the NATO operation) and the NATO military command structure directed by SACEUR constantly interact. Each step in the decision-making process involves consideration by the NATO Member States, whether re-affirming their intent to execute an operation, or halting the planning process or changing the course of action at any stage.

Appointment of Senior Officials

5. The military structure within NATO consists of three tiers: strategic, operational and tactical (component) levels. In 2002 NATO undertook a complex reorganisation that resulted in a leaner, more flexible and more

---

[6] OPLAN means 'a plan for a single or series of connected operations to be carried out simultaneously or in succession. It is usually based upon stated assumptions and is the form of directive employed by higher authority to permit subordinate commanders to prepare supporting plans and orders. The designation "plan" is usually used instead of "order" in preparing for operations well in advance. An operation plan may be put into effect at a prescribed time, or on signal, and then becomes the operation order': NATO, Glossary of Terms and Definitions, AAP-06 (2016), p. 99.

[7] S. L. Bumgardner, Z. Hegedüs and D. Palmer-DeGreve (eds.), NATO Legal Deskbook, 2nd edn (NATO, 2010), p. 243.

efficient military command structure. As NATO continually adapts to the new security environment, this re-organisation in some form continues.

6. Because NATO is strictly based on the principle of full sovereignty of its Member States, all Member States contribute their forces or civilian components on a voluntary basis to NATO Headquarters, structures or other created military entities. Generally, appointment of senior officials is done through a call for submission of applications to fulfil vacant positions. This call is open to all NATO Member States. The appointments of the positions of NATO Secretary-General, Chairman of the Military Committee, SACEUR and Supreme Allied Commander Transformation (SACT) receive specific attention (for the case of SACEUR, see more details in para. 7 of this Appendix). Depending on the level of the position this person is either nominated and appointed by the NATO Member State or nominated by the Member State and approved/appointed by the Military Committee and/or the NAC. Very rarely does NATO appoint Senior Officials as happened in 2003 for Afghanistan (see para. 9 of this Appendix).

7. At the strategic level NATO now only has one command with an operational function – Allied Command Operations (ACO) based in Casteau (Mons, Belgium). This command is headed by SACEUR. SACEUR is responsible to NATO's highest military authority, the Military Committee (MC), for the conduct of all NATO military operations. SACEUR is traditionally dual-hatted, meaning that he/she is responsible for the overall command of NATO military operations, while also serving as Commander of the US European Command. For this reason the procedure of instalment is co-ordinated between NATO and the United States. The designation is approved by the North Atlantic Council (NAC), and the appointment is made by the President of the United States of America and confirmed by the Senate of the United States of America.

8. As a commander at the strategic level, SACEUR conducts analyses and identifies capability shortfalls. He conducts the military planning for all NATO operations that are authorised by the NAC. The heads of NATO operational commands, such as Joint Force Command Brunssum (the Netherlands) and Joint Force Command Naples (Italy) which concentrate on joint expertise at the operational level, work under his direction. The operational level consists of various commands (HQs) based on functional areas. For instance, HQ Aircom is in charge of all NATO air and space matters (based in Rammstein, Germany), HQ Landcom provides expertise in support of NATO's land forces (based in Izmir, Turkey) and HQ Marcom represents central command to all NATO maritime forces

(Northwood, UK). At the tactical level, NATO consists of a number of component commands which provide a specific service in areas of land, air or maritime expertise. These military entities which are within the NATO Command Structure are usually directed (on a rotation basis) by the senior military officials provided by the NATO Member States. In order to be more flexible and efficient, some of the NATO operational and tactical commands are deployable.

9. NATO does not have a tradition of appointing Senior Civilian Representatives for an operation or mission. This is done on an ad hoc basis as was the case with the current and only NATO Senior Civilian Representative for Afghanistan. In 2003 when NATO assumed the lead of the UN-authorised mission ISAF, it was apparent that there was a need for a Senior Civilian Representative who, in line with NATO's military presence, would represent NATO at the political level.

Force Generation and Funding

10. For the conduct of Peace Operations NATO does not have any of its own dedicated, standing forces. All military personnel acting in an operation undertaken by NATO are provided from NATO Member or partner States. Once NATO States have finalised their national procedures for their participation in a NATO operation, they will make their military personnel and assets available to the NATO Commander, i.e. the Commander charged with the given operation. This process is called the Force Generation process. After the NATO call for contributions for an operation, NATO States offer available land, air or maritime components and capabilities. The selected forces are then placed under the Operational Authority temporarily provided to the NATO Commander for effectuating either operational command (OPCOM) or operational control (OPCON) by means of a Transfer of Authority (TOA). In the TOA, NATO Member States usually declare if they hold any national caveats or restrictions on employment of the transferred military personnel and/or national assets. National restrictions usually refer to geographical limits of the provided troops or limits on use of force.

11. NATO States retain full sovereign rights and authority over the personnel that they contribute to an operation. This means that at any level of the decision-making process they may decide, state or change the course of action.

12. As regards funding, in line with the principle of Member States' sovereignty NATO is financially structured such that NATO Member States decide by consensus whether they support the costs of a given

operation or activity. Therefore, NATO Member States have ultimate control of NATO's expenditures. All NATO resources are overseen and managed by a Resource Policy and Planning Board that reports directly to the NAC. Within NATO various types of funding exist: (1) national funding; (2) multi-national funding; and (3) common funding.

13. National or indirect funding means that every NATO Member State allots funds for different purposes in its annual budget. The basic NATO principle is that "costs lie where they fall", and therefore this funding is used, for example, to cover salaries of the people working in national delegations, the costs of weapons systems and military forces provided to NATO etc.

14. Multi-national funding refers to a funding arrangement outside the NATO structures. It is based on bilateral and multi-lateral arrangements between concerned States.

15. The aim of common funding, also known as "direct funding" is to reinforce NATO cohesion. Such funding directly serves all NATO Member States. In order to be eligible for this type of funding, the requirement must have a priority and be eligible for it, e.g. command and control systems. In practice any common funded requirement must not exceed the Minimum Military Requirement. With respect to funding for Non-Article 5 Crisis Response Operations (NA5CRO), which in NATO terms would include a Peace Operation as defined in this Manual, the funding for such an operation would be as follows:

1. It is voluntary, meaning that it is the sovereign decision of the NATO Member State to contribute to a particular operation or not;
2. The funding follows the basic principle of "costs lie where they fall";
3. Contributions vary in form and scale, e.g. a contribution with a medical unit only or with thousands of troops and armoured vehicles.

Only those costs not attributable to a specific Member State and approved by the Resource Policy and Planning Board as eligible for common funding will be paid by NATO as an organisation.

Arrangements with Troop Contributing Countries and in the Case of Non-UN Operations with Third States Contributing Troops

16. Decisions to invite Partners and other non-NATO Troop Contributing Countries[8] (NNTCCs) to NATO-led Peace Operations are

---

[8] NATO, Glossary of Abbreviations used in NATO Documents and Publications, AAP-15 (2013), T-5.

also taken by the NAC, on a case-by-case basis, taking into consideration military authorities' advice.[9]

17. In principle, Troop Contributing Countries (TCCs) should be involved in the planning, preparation and decision-making in operations to which they contribute. For NNTCCs the process for their involvement is described in the Political-Military Framework for Partner Involvement in NATO-led Operations.[10] It sets out the governing principles, procedures, modalities and other guidance for partner involvement in both the political consultations and decision-making process throughout operational planning, command arrangements and mission execution. Specifically, the framework spells out the conditions for formal recognition as an operational partner, which include a formal statement of intent from the partner and a provisional recognition as a contributing partner. These trigger the execution of a series of arrangements, such as the proper security arrangements for sharing of operational classified information and the completion of a participation and financial agreement. Thereafter, in accordance with the Procedures for Acceptance of Troop Contributions to NATO-Led Operations from Non-NATO States[11] the signature of a technical Memorandum of Understanding (MOU) between the relevant Military Authorities of NATO and the operational partner may also take place if this is required.

18. As mentioned, NATO will enter into a Participation and Financial Agreement with NNTCCs. Like most practical arrangements, Participation and Financial Agreements are not binding under international law, but written arrangements setting forth the conditions under which the parties intend to co-operate in given areas and operational arrangements under a framework international agreement (in this case the Status of Forces Agreement (SOFA)). The Participation and Financial Agreement is also used for the regulation of technical or detailed matters.[12]

19. The purpose of Participation and Financial Agreements is in essence the same for all missions and operations, namely to ensure fairness in the conditions for both NATO and partner States operating together. They may therefore address the applicability of the OPLAN and

[9] NATO, Peace Support Operations, AJP-3.4.1 (2001), para. 0114.
[10] NATO, Political Military Framework for Partner Involvement in NATO-led Operations, PO(2011)0141, www.nato.int/nato_static/assets/pdf/pdf_2011_04/20110415_110415-PMF.pdf.
[11] NATO, MC 056/1 (2011), which implements the Political Military Framework for Partner Involvement in NATO-Led Operations (Ibid.).
[12] Bumgardner, Hegedüs and Palmer-DeGreve (n. 7), p. 127.

other relevant provisions such as the internal claims waiver, or the fact that TCCs absorb any and all costs associated with their participation in a NATO-led operation (also referred to as "costs lie where they fall").[13] Participation and Financial Agreements are somewhat generic in order to ensure equal treatment of participating operational partners. They list the specific national contributions, but also open up the possibility for relevant military authorities entering into lower level, more detailed agreements, as mentioned in para. 18 of this Appendix.

20. Furthermore, when a NA5CRO[14] mission is mandated, a SOFA is the first legal instrument to be envisaged before the mission physically deploys into a new theatre. In principle, NATO will negotiate such an agreement with the Host State where the Peace Operation is conducted, as well as with the countries that provide parts of their territory for use as Transit or Staging Areas.[15] A SOFA deals with the legal status of the NATO forces, both military and civilian, and that of NNTCCs. It contains provisions concerning immigration, claims and other matters such as tax exemption on the import and export of material, supplies and goods for operational purposes. It notably also regulates criminal jurisdiction and the immunities and privileges of foreign forces, which are 'rooted in the concept of State immunity'.[16] SOFAs may provide the possibility for potential NNTCC involvement, but they do not deal with the practical arrangements relating to the actual participation in operations that still have to be clarified between NATO and each TCC.

Categories of Mission Personnel

21. NATO does not possess its own standing forces. All forces present at a given operation are drawn from NATO Member States and operational partner States. For this reason the term "NATO Forces" is used to designate all military members, civilian components, military and civilian personnel attached to or employed by NATO, and civilian and military personnel provided by the operational partner States. In practice NATO also relies on the use of contractors and their employees in order to supply goods and services either to NATO or on its behalf to NATO Forces.

---

[13] NATO, Funding Policy for Contingency Operations, PO(2000)16, para. 3.
[14] NATO, Allied Joint Doctrine for Non-Article 5 Crisis Response Operations, AJP-3.4(A) (2010).
[15] NATO Peace Support Operations (n. 9), para. 4B1.
[16] M. Prassé Hartov, 'NATO Status Agreements', 34 *NATO Legal Gazette* (2014), p. 46.

22. The SOFA with the Host State defines who is entitled to bear arms and wear uniforms in the area of operation. Usually military members may wear uniforms and carry arms as required for performance of their duties and as authorised by their orders. Members of the civilian component normally wear civilian clothes; however, depending on the provisions of a given SOFA, they also may be authorised to carry arms, if required for the performance of their duties. In such a case they would be wearing military attire with an appropriate badge or logo (e.g. MOD CIV). NATO contractors and their employees are usually not permitted to wear military uniforms and may usually carry weapons only in accordance with the local Host State laws and regulations.

Glossary of Terms

For the purposes of the Manual, the following terms are defined as follows:

Civilian: Any person who is not member of the armed forces or of a (formed) police unit. For purposes of application of international humanitarian law (IHL) a civilian is anyone who is not a member of the armed forces of a State or a member of an organised armed group with a continuous combat function.

Command: The authority possessed by a State or an international organisation (or organ or sub-organ thereof) and vested in an individual member of the armed forces or police forces to exercise the direction, co-ordination and control of military or police forces. Command is usually exercised at various levels of operations (strategic, operational and tactical). Full command over a State's armed forces is normally an exclusive national prerogative. Other levels of command may be transferred to international organisations to perform a specific operation or mission in accordance with procedures agreed and set out by the relevant State(s) and organisation.

Consent: Authorisation by a Host State to conduct a Peace Operation on its territory in conformity with international law and the domestic law of the Host State. Consent is a requirement for any Peace Operation covered in this Manual. It may act as the sole legal basis for the operation, but more often will complement an authorisation by the UN Security Council and/or any competent regional organisation or arrangement to conduct a Peace Operation. Consent flows from the sovereign authority of a State over its territory and has been recognised by the International Law Commission (ILC) as a "circumstance precluding wrongfulness". The conditions for valid consent under international law are set out in Article 20 of the ILC Articles on State Responsibility and reflect customary international law. Alongside consent by the Host State, consent of other parties can be sought to assist in the deployment of a Peace Force and in the execution of the mandate. This is referred to where appropriate as "consent of the parties" to distinguish it from Host State consent. Consent by parties other than the State will enhance the operational performance of the mandate but is, in contrast to consent by the Host State, not a legal requirement.

Control: The authority exercised by a commander over part of the activities of subordinate organisations or units not normally under his/her command, which encompasses the responsibility for implementing orders or directives. All or part of this authority may be delegated. Operational control (OPCON) is the usual level of authority delegated to a commander of a multi-national Peace Force. It concerns the authority to direct forces assigned to that commander to accomplish specific missions or tasks, to deploy units to perform such missions or tasks and to retain or assign tactical control of those units. It does not include authority to assign separate employment of components of the units concerned, nor does it, in itself, include administrative authority or logistical control.

Formed police units: Units of approximately 140 police officers in Peace Operations conducted by the UN, trained to act as a cohesive unit under the command of a Police Commander exercising operational control over police units assigned to him/her. Formed police units have three core tasks in UN Peace Operations: public order management, protection of UN personnel and facilities and support to police activities that require a concerted response but do not address military threats. Other organisations conducting Peace Operations also employ formed police units, although their designation and tasks may differ in some respects from the terminology and tasks found in UN missions.

Gender: The state of being male or female. It focuses on the socially constructed, as opposed to biologically determined, sex identities of men and women in societies, and the roles and behaviours that are not only associated with them, but also expected from them.

Gender mainstreaming: The process of assessing the implications for women and men of any planned action, including legislation, policies or programmes, in all areas and at all levels. It is a strategy for making women's as well as men's concerns and experiences an integral dimension of the design, implementation, monitoring and evaluation of policies and programmes in all political, economic and societal spheres.

Host State: The State consenting to the deployment and conducting of a Peace Operation on its territory.

Internally displaced person: Persons who are displaced within their country of nationality or habitual residence and who have not crossed an international border. Internally displaced persons (IDPs) do not benefit from the protections afforded under international refugee law, but derive protection from international human rights law and where applicable from international humanitarian law similar to any citizen or habitual resident of the country concerned.

Legal basis: The authority under international law (and where relevant the internal law of the regional organisation or arrangement and domestic law) to conduct a specific activity. A legal basis determines whether and under which conditions a specific activity may be lawfully performed. For example, a mandate serves as the legal basis for a Peace Operation.

Legal regime: A body of international law (or where relevant domestic law) which governs how a specific activity must be performed. For example, international human rights law (IHRL) and international humanitarian law (IHL) will serve as legal regimes in the performance of a Peace Operation in accordance with their terms of application.

Mandate: The authority under international law to conduct a Peace Operation and the objectives of the operation. A mandate, as referred to in this Manual, will consist of consent given by the Host State, which is usually accompanied by authorisation by the UN Security Council, to conduct a Peace Operation on its territory. A mandate serves a dual purpose. First, it provides a legal basis under international law for the Peace Operation. Second, it sets out mission objectives and tasks and lays down any conditions, authorisations and restrictions which are applicable to the conduct of the mission. Internal rules of regional organisations and arrangements relating to the employment of forces assigned to them and domestic legal conditions relating to forces allocated for conducting a Peace Operation can also form a secondary or ancillary part of the mandate, but may not exceed the scope of authority to conduct the mission granted by the UN Security Council where this is relevant. The operative paragraphs of a relevant Security Council resolution authorising a Peace Operation will define this scope of authority.

Military members of the Peace Operation: The military component of a Peace Operation as the latter is defined in this Glossary. The military component consists of various contingents provided by Troop Contributing Countries (TCCs) placed at the disposal of the UN or a regional organisation or arrangement to conduct a Peace Operation under multi-national command acting under a mandate.

Peace Enforcement: Action undertaken under a Chapter VII mandate of the UN Security Council to restore international peace and security through the application of force. Peace Operations as defined in this Manual can be authorised to undertake one or more tasks involving peace enforcement. However, peace enforcement operations conducted by regional organisations and arrangements, or by individual States, are not addressed in detail in this Manual.

Peace Force: The military and, where relevant, the formed police component of a Peace Operation as the latter is defined in this Glossary. It normally consists of various contingents provided by Troop (TCCs) and Police Contributing Countries (PCCs) placed at the disposal of the UN or a regional organisation or arrangement to conduct a Peace Operation under multi-national command acting under a mandate.

Peace Operation (or Mission): A Peace Operation is defined as an operation undertaken with the consent of the Host State, usually alongside the authorisation of the UN Security Council for the purpose of maintaining and promoting international peace and security. It may comprise military, police and civilian personnel and may involve tasks relating to peacekeeping, peace enforcement, peacebuilding and peacemaking. It can be carried out by the UN, by a regional organisation or arrangement, or by an ad hoc coalition of States acting under a UN mandate and with the consent of the Host State. The following circumstances are not included within this definition and are not addressed in detail in this Manual, namely: enforcement and peace enforcement operations conducted by regional organisations, or by one or more States, with the purpose of restoring international peace and security through the use of coercive force; engaging in sustained hostilities against a State or organised armed group to restore governmental authority; and imposing the will of the international community.

Peace Support: A term used by and within NATO to refer to peacekeeping, peace enforcement, peacebuilding and peacemaking.

Peacebuilding: Activities undertaken within a Peace Operation directed towards addressing the root causes of a breakdown in peace and security and promoting long-term and sustainable peace. These can include activities aimed at conflict prevention, capacity building, promotion of the rule of law and post-conflict reconciliation. Peacebuilding can overlap with aspects of peacekeeping and peacemaking. It is part of an overall approach and is a civil/military activity which aims at laying the foundation for sustainable peace and development. The notion was first defined in the 1992 Agenda for Peace as '[a] range of measures targeted to reduce the risk of lapsing or relapsing into conflict by strengthening national capacities at all levels for conflict management, and to lay the foundation for sustainable peace and development'.

Peacekeeping: Activities conducted within a Peace Operation aimed, inter alia, at maintaining a ceasefire or cessation of hostilities, promoting a transition from a conflict situation to a peaceful and stable environment, implementing disarmament and demobilisation and promoting the rule of law. Peacekeeping in UN practice is governed by the bedrock principles of consent of the parties, impartiality and force limited to self-defence and defence against forcible attempts to frustrate the implementation of the mandate.

Peacemaking: Activities consisting primarily of preventive diplomacy which can be undertaken within a Peace Operation or independently, and which are aimed at conflict prevention, mediation and conflict resolution. In article 43(1) of the EU Treaty, 'peace-making' is used in the sense of peace enforcement.

Police Contributing Country: A Police Contributing Country (PCC) is a State contributing police units or individual police personnel to an international organisation to conduct a Peace Operation.

Protection of Civilians: The concept of protection of civilians (POC) includes both physical protection of civilians against the direct threat of violence and long-term efforts to build Host State capacity to ensure a stable environment and the rule of law. The physical protection of civilians is currently included in UN mandates authorising a Peace Force to protect civilians against imminent threat of violence within their area of deployment and mission capability. Protection of civilians is normally predicated on acting in partnership with the Host State authorities.

Refugee: A person who is outside his/her country of origin or nationality owing to well-founded fear of persecution and is unable or unwilling due to fear of persecution to avail him- or herself of the protection of his/her country of origin or nationality. Persons qualifying as refugees enjoy protection under international refugee law alongside any other rights or protection derived from other applicable bodies of international law in common with other persons.

Regional organisation or arrangement: An organisation or institutional arrangement acting in conformity with the UN Charter to perform tasks allocated to it by its Member States. Such organisations include but are not necessarily limited to intergovernmental organisations which are referred to in Chapter VIII of the UN Charter.

Self-defence: Within the context of a Peace Operation the right of the Peace Force and of individual members of the force to defend themselves and other members of the mission against unlawful attack. Different organisations use somewhat differing definitions and conditions for acting in self-defence. For example, in the case of UN Peace Operations, self-defence includes action in response to forcible attempts to prevent or frustrate the lawful execution of the mandate. This is not necessarily the case in operations conducted by other organisations or arrangements.

Sending State: A State providing military or police personnel to conduct a Peace Operation.

Stabilisation mission: A mission employing elements of peace enforcement. A mission mandated to perform stabilisation tasks will usually operate in an environment characterised by ongoing armed conflict and will provide for tasks in support of a Host State government to restore and maintain a stable environment. This will usually be done under a Chapter VII mandate issued by the UN Security Council providing authority to employ force beyond self-defence aimed at restoring governmental authority and may include authorisation to engage in offensive operations against one or more parties which attempt to undermine or supplant governmental authority in all or part of the Host State's territory.

Troop Contributing Country: A State providing military forces to an international organisation to conduct a Peace Operation. Troop Contributing Countries (TCCs) are referred to by some organisations as 'troop contributing nations'.

Index

Abbreviations can be found in the List of Abbreviations on page xxv.